U.S. Bank Deregulation in Historical Perspective

This book shows how and why deregulation is transforming the size, structure, and geographic range of U.S. banks, the scope of banking services, and the nature of bank–customer relationships. Over the last two decades, the characteristics that had made U.S. banks different from other banks throughout the world – a fragmented geographical structure of the industry, which restricted the scale of banks and their ability to compete with one another, and strict limits on the kinds of products and services commercial banks could offer – virtually have been eliminated. Understanding the origins and persistence of the unique banking regulations that defined U.S. banking for more than a century lends an important perspective to the economic and political causes and consequences of the current process of deregulation. History helps to define the political constituencies for and against deregulation, the political process through which bank regulations are determined, and the way deregulation likely will affect future bank performance and stability.

Professor Charles W. Calomiris is Paul M. Montrone Professor of Finance and Economics at the Graduate School of Business, and Professor in the Department of International and Public Affairs, School of International and Public Affairs, both at Columbia University. He also co-directs the Project on Financial Deregulation at the American Enterprise Institute and is a Research Associate of the National Bureau of Economic Research. Professor Calomiris previously taught at the University of Illinios-Urbana/Champaign, where he was Co-Director of the Office of Banking Research.

His most recent research, covering banking, corporate finance, financial history, and monetary economics, has appeared in the *American Economic Review*, *Journal of Banking and Finance*, *Journal of Money, Credit and Banking*, *The Cato Journal*, the AEI Press, and several edited collections of books. Professor Calomiris is also a member of the editorial boards of the *Journal of Banking and Finance*, *Journal of Financial Services Research*, *Journal of Financial Intermediation*, *Journal of Economic History*, *Journal of Economics and Business*, and *Explorations in Economic History*. He is the recipient of research grants or awards from the National Science Foundation, the World Bank, the government of Japan, the Herbert V. Prochnow Foundation, and the Garn Institute of Finance. He has served or serves as a consultant or visiting scholar for the Federal Reserve Banks of New York, Chicago, Cleveland, and St. Louis; the Federal Reserve Board; the World Bank; International Monetary Fund; and the governments of Mexico, Argentina, Japan, China, and El Salvador.

Professor Calomiris (with David Beim) designed and teaches an MBA course on emerging market financial transactions, which won the 1997–8 Chazen International Innovation Prize at Columbia Business School.

U.S. Bank Deregulation
in Historical Perspective

Charles W. Calomiris

Columbia University

CAMBRIDGE
UNIVERSITY PRESS

PUBLISHED BY THE PRESS SYNDICATE OF THE UNIVERSITY OF CAMBRIDGE
The Pitt Building, Trumpington Street, Cambridge, United Kingdom

CAMBRIDGE UNIVERSITY PRESS
The Edinburgh Building, Cambridge CB2 2RU, UK   http://www.cup.cam.ac.uk
40 West 20th Street, New York, NY 10011-4211, USA   http://www.cup.org
10 Stamford Road, Oakleigh, Melbourne 3166, Australia
Ruiz de Alarcón 13, 28014 Madrid, Spain

First published 2000

Printed in the United States of America

Typeface Times Roman 10/12 pt.   *System* QuarkXPress [BTS]

A catalog record for this book is available from the British Library.

Library of Congress Cataloging in Publication Data
Calomiris, Charles W.
U.S. bank deregulation in historical perspective / Charles W. Calomiris.
p. cm.
ISBN 0-521-58362-4 (hb)
1. Banks and banking – Deregulation – United States.   2. Banking law –
United States.   3. Financial institutions – United States.   I. Title.   II. Title:
United States bank deregulation in historical perspective.
HG2491.C348   2000
332.1'0973–dc21   99–40041   CIP

ISBN   0 521 58362 4   hardback

For William and Mary Calomiris, my parents

Contents

Acknowledgments

The primary debts incurred in the preparation of this volume are to my co-authors on three of the chapters – Gary Gorton, Dan Raff, and Eugene White – who generously agreed to have our joint work published here. I am also grateful to the original publishers of these papers for permitting them to be collected in this volume. All the chapters appear with the same titles as the original versions. Chapter 1 appeared in *Structural Change in Banking*, edited by Michael Klausner and Lawrence J. White (Business One-Irwin, 1993). Chapter 2 (co-authored with Gary Gorton) was published in *Financial Markets and Financial Crises*, edited by R. Glenn Hubbard (University of Chicago Press, 1991). Chapter 3 (co-authored with Eugene N. White) appeared in *The Regulated Economy: A Historical Approach to Political Economy*, edited by Claudia Goldin and Gary Libecap (University of Chicago Press, 1994). Chapter 4 was published in *The Coordination of Activity Within and Between Firms*, edited by Naomi Lamoreaux and Daniel Raff (University of Chicago Press, 1995). Chapter 5 (co-authored with Daniel Raff) appeared in *Anglo-American Financial Systems: Institutions and Markets in the Twentieth Century*, edited by Michael Bordo and Richard Sylla (Irwin Professional Publishing, 1995). Chapter 6 was published in the *Journal of Institutional and Theoretical Economics*, vol. 154 (1998). For the most part, the articles appear in their original form. I have made only minor modifications and have resisted the temptation to edit or revise the text in light of more recent research or regulatory changes, with the exception of some unavoidable correction.

Many colleagues commented on draft versions of Chapters 1 through 6, and their help is gratefully acknowledged at the beginnings of each of those chapters. Frank Edwards and Peter Wallison provided helpful criticisms of the Introduction. Scott Parris of Cambridge University Press offered encouragement and editorial guidance, and, along with Ernie Haim, shepherded the book through the production process. Shirley Kessel constructed the indices. My wife Nancy patiently and cheerfully assisted in editing the final manuscript.

Introduction

Charles W. Calomiris

The last two decades have witnessed dramatic bank deregulation in the United States. Of particular importance at the national level have been the relaxation of geographical and activity limitations on bank holding companies, achieved in the 1980s and early 1990s, respectively, by congressional action and new regulatory interpretations of existing law.[1] In the last several years, both the Federal Reserve Board and the Comptroller of the Currency further enhanced the flexibility of bank operations by reducing limits on bank activities, and in 1999 Congress passed landmark legislation to repeal outright the separation of commercial and investment banking imposed by the Banking Act of 1933, and to expand bank powers in other directions (notably into insurance products).

Although deregulation has been dramatic, it is worth noting that it has sparked little controversy, or even surprise, among scholars of banking or banking history. No prominent banking historians or economists have defended unit (single-office) banking or the historical restrictions on bank activities in underwriting or insurance (in contrast, disagreement arises over the extent to which, and the manner in which, noncommercial firms should be permitted to own banks, and vice versa).

The lack of controversy in the face of such dramatic changes reflects a remarkable degree of agreement among banking scholars – supported by an extensive body of research – that historic limitations on U.S. banks' locations and activities are inefficient. Furthermore, that literature not only argues that historical restrictions on banks are currently inefficient, but also that they were undesirable at the time of their passage.

Explanations for the origins of restrictive banking laws in the United States mainly are to be found in theories of political economy, not argu-

---

[1] See George Kaufman and Larry Mote, "Glass-Steagall: Repeal by Regulatory and Judicial Reinterpretation," *Banking Law Journal*, September–October 1990, pp. 388–421; Allen Berger, Anil Kashyap, and J. M. Scalise, "The Transformation of the U.S. Banking Industry: What a Long, Strange Trip It's Been," *Brookings Papers on Economic Activity* (1995: 2), pp. 55–218; and Chapter 6 of this volume.

ments about efficiency. Limits placed on banks – especially restrictions placed on bank consolidation from the mid-nineteenth century through the early 1990s, and the separation of commercial and investment banking beginning in 1933 – are artifacts of specific historical events and associated political battles in which facts and economic logic often took a back seat to special interest politics, and occasionally, to populist passions.[2]

Of course, political and regulatory history did not operate in a vacuum. Economic history shaped bank regulation through its effects on the sizes of gains and losses that potential regulatory changes posed for various interested parties, and through the way history altered the relative power those parties enjoyed. The parallel development of U.S. economic history and bank regulation did not follow a simple rule (as would be the case if efficiency alone guided policy). The ways that economic change was reflected in regulatory changes differed over time and depended not only on shifts in the *aggregate* costs and benefits of regulation (and thus efficiency), but rather on the ways those benefits and costs were distributed.

When considering the allocation of the costs and benefits of regula-

---

[2] For a critical discussion of the hearings leading to the passage of Glass-Steagall, see George Benston, *The Separation of Commercial and Investment Banking: The Glass-Steagall Act Revisited and Reconsidered*, Norwell: Kluwer Academic Press, 1989. For quantitative evidence against congressional claims that conflicts of interest between commercial and investment banking were problematic in the 1920s, see Randall S. Kroszner and Raghuram G. Rajan, "Is the Glass-Steagall Act Justified? A Study of the U.S. Experience with Universal Banking Before 1933," *American Economic Review*, Vol. 84 (September 1994), pp. 810–32; and Manju Puri, "The Long Term Default Performance of Bank Underwritten Securities Issues," *Journal of Banking and Finance*, Vol. 18, pp. 397–481, 1994. On the political economy of the passage of the 1933 Act more generally, see Chapter 3 of this volume. For a discussion of the historical costs to the United States of limiting banks' powers, see Eugene N. White, "Before the Glass-Steagall Act: An Analysis of the Investment Banking Activities of National Banks," *Explorations in Economic History*, Vol. 23 (January 1986), pp. 33–55; Charles W. Calomiris and Carlos Ramirez, "The Role of Financial Relationships in the History of American Corporate Finance," *Journal of Applied Corporate Finance*, Volume 9, Number 2 (Summer 1996), pp. 52–73; J. Bradford De Long, "Did J. P. Morgan's Men Add Value?," in *Inside the Business Enterprise: Historical Perspectives on the Use of Information*, pp. 205–36; edited by Peter Temin, Chicago: University of Chicago Press, 1991; Carlos D. Ramirez, "Did J. P. Morgan's Men Add Liquidity? Corporate Investment, Cash Flow, and Financial Structure at the Turn of the Twentieth Century," *Journal of Finance*, Vol. 50 (June 1995), pp. 661–78; Randall S. Kroszner, "The Evolution of Universal Banking and Its Regulation in Twentieth Century America," in *Universal Banking: Financial System Design Reconsidered*, pp. 70–99, edited by Anthony Saunders and Ingo Walter, Homewood, IL: Business One-Irwin, 1996; and Chapters 2 and 5 of this volume. For a review of the current policy debate, see Joao A. C. Santos, "Commercial Banks in the Securities Business: A Review," *Journal of Financial Services Research*, Volume 14; No. 1 (1998), pp. 35–60.

tion and deregulation, and the way that distribution of costs and benefits affected the history of bank regulation and deregulation, three factors have proven particularly important: (1) the degree of concentration of gains and losses among interest groups, (2) the implications of regulatory change for the power of existing regulatory agencies, and (3) the extent to which regulatory changes could be "framed" by political entrepreneurs to produce sufficient popular support to overcome the normal inertia of the political process. I discuss each of these three influences in turn.

The concentration of costs and benefits

A central principle of political economy is that concentrated minority interests can be more successful in extracting concessions from the political process than fragmented majorities. In a world where forming coalitions is physically costly, concentrated minorities face stronger incentives to lobby (and pay) for their desired outcomes.[3] That principle is reflected clearly in banking history. Ironically, it was sometimes the case that the more socially costly regulatory restrictions became for the majority, the more likely they were to succeed politically, because the benefits of those restrictions to vested interests were growing along with the costs to the majority. Such could be said of the movement to restrict bank consolidation in the late nineteenth century (see Chapter 2 of this volume), or the hallmarks of regulatory change during the Great Depression (discussed in Chapters 2, 4, and 6).

Sometimes, however, the pursuit of efficiency can be aligned with the goals of vested interests, as in the 1980s and 1990s, when the rising social cost of preexisting regulations was a key factor in deregulation (as discussed in Chapter 7). It is especially easy for efficiency to spur regulatory change if regulatory agencies take an entrepreneurial role in promoting efficient deregulation, as they have recently.

But why did efficiency gains favoring branching and expanded powers in the nineteenth and early twentieth centuries fail to win over regulators or politicians, whereas the efficiency gains from those same changes in the 1980s and 1990s were greeted by regulators and politicians with open arms? Part of the answer is that unlike earlier regulatory conflicts, in which small banks struggled with large banks over the economic rents of banking regulation, recent changes have taken place in the context of

[3] See Mancur Olson, *The Logic of Collective Action*. Cambridge, Massachusetts: Harvard University Press, 1965; and George J. Stigler, ed., *Chicago Studies in Political Economy*. Chicago: University of Chicago Press, 1988.

declines in the amount of potential regulatory rents available to all parties. This is an important difference. The decline in available rents reduces the amount of feasible regulation, and this in turn generates support for deregulation by financial regulators.

Market competition produces regulatory competition

The pressures of the 1980s that prompted efficient deregulation came largely from *outside* the American banking system, and mandated efficiency-enhancing changes that would permit banks to survive. Competitive pressure from abroad was reflected in the significant loss of U.S. banks' domestic and international market shares in the 1980s. The growth of securities markets, and increasing competition from mutual funds, pension funds, the commercial paper market, and nonbank intermediaries like finance companies and credit unions all added to the pressure to improve the efficiency of banks. More and more, U.S. bank regulators were faced with a choice between regulating less and having less to regulate. The dismal prospect of overseeing a shrinking banking sector galvanized the Fed to coax Congress into bank deregulation.[4]

Beginning in 1987, the Federal Reserve Board used its authority to relax restrictions on bank underwriting activities. The Fed also pressed for the relaxation of branching and consolidation limits, which culminated in the passage of a federal interstate branching law in 1994.

Initially, with respect to investment banking powers, the Fed proceeded with extreme caution. It allowed very limited underwriting of private debt, and later equity, but attached to those activities a host of "firewalls" intended to serve two different sets of purposes – (1) to prevent the transfer of loss from a (Section 20) underwriting affiliate to a chartered bank, and (2) to prevent "conflicts of interest" from arising from the mixture of commercial and investment banking. The first concern was largely that of economists who correctly worried about the abuse of deposit insurance and the discount window – the possibility of government subsidization of risk in new activities. The second concern was that banks might use their new powers to coerce client firms or cheat purchasers of securities (despite clear and strong economic incentives not to do so). That concern reflected the (then) unsubstantiated and

---

[4] See also Franklin R. Edwards and Frederic S. Mishkin, "The Decline of Traditional Banking: Implications for Financial Stability and Regulatory Policy," Federal Reserve Bank of New York *Economic Policy Review* (July 1995), pp. 27–45.

(now) discredited arguments that underlay the Pecora Hearings of 1932, which inspired the limitations imposed on the mixing of commercial and investment banking in 1933.[5]

In 1997, the Federal Reserve Board eliminated many of the remaining conflict-of-interest "firewalls" that had limited connections between banks and the nonbank affiliates of bank holding companies.[6] In arguing for these changes before Congress, the Fed noted that the experience of underwriting affiliates operating abroad (who were not required to comply with such firewalls) provided clear evidence of the lack of any need for such protections, and the disadvantages those limits imposed on domestic banks (by limiting the relationships between banks and clients).

In the meantime, the Fed has also permitted significant growth in other nontraditional banking activities, either within the bank itself (e.g., derivatives contracts) or through separate affiliates. Venture capital earnings – returns to bank investments in corporate equity – have been a particularly important profit center for a handful of large U.S. banks during the 1980s and 1990s. The recent merger of Citicorp and Travelers – which extended a bank holding company's reach into the full line of insurance products – was approved by the Fed, but under a provision of law that limited the approval to a maximum of five years. Some commentators have argued that the Fed intended to force Congress's hand in 1999 by creating a financial behemoth that Congress would have been unwilling to undo – that is, that Congress would not have wanted to force the divestiture of impermissible activities as a result of its failure to reach agreement.

Throughout the Fed's push for deregulation, a constant theme sounded by Chairman Alan Greenspan has been the need to preserve the competitive edge of U.S. banks. For example, in February 1999, Greenspan argued that "the global dominance of American finance" would be undermined unless Congress repealed the archaic restrictions under which U.S. banks continue to operate.[7]

Thus, an important influence on the deregulation movement has been

---

[5] For a discussion of why banks face a strong incentive to behave honestly, and how this leads to voluntary structural constraints (or "firewalls") within bank holding companies to ensure greater credibility, see Randall S. Kroszner and Raghuram G. Rajan, "Organization Structure and Credibility: Evidence from Commercial Bank Securities Activities Before the Glass-Steagall Act," *Journal of Monetary Economics*, Vol. 39, 1997, pp. 475–516.

[6] Federal Reserve Board, "Review of Restrictions in the Board's Section 20 Orders," January 9, 1997.

[7] Richard Wolffe, "Bank Laws 'Threaten Our World Dominance' ", *Financial Times*, February 24, 1999, p. 4.

regulatory competition. U.S. bank regulators lost their monopoly over the financial system as other intermediaries (domestic and foreign) began to compete for bank customers. The competition for clients among banks, nonbank intermediaries, and other financial market instruments encourages financial regulators to support the process of financial deregulation in order to preserve their regulatory base. Regulatory competition has been important outside the United States as well, and has been a common factor promoting banking deregulation in Europe, Japan, and many developing economies.

The increasing range of activities by the nonbank affiliates of bank holding companies has not only strengthened the position of U.S. banks, it has made the Fed an increasingly powerful regulator, and has created new conflicts over regulatory turf among financial regulatory agencies within the United States. The latter effect has also significantly furthered the process of deregulation. As U.S. bank regulatory agencies vie for control, they have tried to bolster their relative position by offering new powers to banks that choose them as the bank's primary regulator (through the bank's choice of charter and holding company structure).

The Fed is the primary bank regulator of bank holding companies, their state-chartered banks that are Fed members, and their nonbank affiliates. The primary regulator of national banks (irrespective of whether they are owned by a bank holding company) is the Office of the Comptroller of the Currency (OCC). As more bank activities have been placed in nonbank affiliates, the Fed's role as financial regulator has waxed relative to that of the OCC. Furthermore, since bank holding companies now perform a wide variety of over-the-counter (OTC) derivatives origination and trading functions, and securities underwriting and brokerage functions, the Fed has increasingly encroached into the realm of the Securities and Exchange Commission (SEC) and the Commodity Futures Trading Commission (CFTC), which regulate securities markets and futures, respectively.

The OCC is struggling for its share of regulatory authority over new banking transactions. The OCC has responded to the new Fed regulatory hegemony by inviting banks to channel their "non-banking" activities into national bank *subsidiaries* (as an alternative to bank affiliates that are bank holding company subsidiaries), which would thereby place the regulation and supervision of those activities under the authority of the OCC. Meanwhile, the Fed reaches for further power by declaring the need to transform itself into an overarching "umbrella" regulator to coordinate (within and outside the United

States) the financial regulation of increasingly diverse global financial intermediaries.

The SEC and CFTC are also challenging Fed authority over banking transactions in securities and derivative markets.[8] In addition to the conflict over whether bank regulators should have primary responsibility for regulating bank transactions in securities and derivatives markets, the CFTC and the SEC are battling over the definitions of the words "securities" and "futures," as the definitions of these terms also imply jurisdictional authority. There have been indications that the CFTC is trying to expand the definition of "futures" to include bank-originated swaps and forwards. The SEC has attempted to define various derivatives as "securities" so that it could have jurisdiction over them.

Political opportunism and the importance of path dependence

The "Chicago-school" view that the probability of success for a political initiative depends on the distribution of gains and costs from that initiative (to citizens or to regulators) has great appeal. But there is more to the success or failure of a regulatory initiative than that simple static calculus of gain and loss. Political "inertia" can prevent success even if the distribution of gains and losses favors it; and political "entrepreneurship" can achieve success even when the distribution of gains and losses makes it unlikely.

Inertia can be a powerful obstacle. Any particular action requires an expenditure of some advocate's effort to achieve it. Political entrepreneurship (by a politician or regulator) is the three-part process that overcomes inertia by (1) identifying a private benefit to the political entrepreneur from forming a successful coalition to push for an initiative, (2) overcoming the transactions and communications costs that might otherwise prevent vested interests from forming successful coalitions, and (3) framing the issue to enlist maximal support from uninformed parties. Knowing how to manipulate public opinion, and knowing how to convince the electorate and their representatives that support for a specific initiative entails support for a broader and uncontroversial principle, are the key attributes of a distinguished political entrepreneur. U.S. political history is rife with such figures.

Inertia creates barriers to successful coalition building, but it also magnifies the rewards of success, since laws and regulations are not so easily

---

[8] For example, see "Bank Regulators, SEC Jockey to Be the New Securities Czar," *Wall Street Journal*, February 24, 1999, pp. C1, C15.

undone. The history of U.S. banking regulation demonstrates repeatedly the importance of transient events (economic "shocks") for influencing long-run institutional history. That phenomenon – sometimes referred to as "path dependence" – leads one to take an historical view of the evolution of regulation, that is, one that recognizes that the *specific economic history* of a country matters. The long-run importance of shocks makes institutional change less predictable and less responsive to small changes in economic interests.

For example, it is hard to conceive of the passage of federal deposit insurance without the specific history of the Great Depression. As discussed in Chapter 4, federal deposit insurance had been advocated by special interests in Congress to no effect for fifty years prior to its passage in 1933.[9] Specific elements of the history of the 1930s – including political logrolling in Congress, and other transient influences – made a consistently losing piece of legislation finally pass. It now remains the primary regulatory legacy of the Banking Act of 1933, and it is difficult to imagine circumstances that will lead to its repeal.

As Alexander Hamilton noted, when commenting on the way political processes produce change, successful political entrepreneurs seize windows of opportunity to pass laws, and then rely on political transaction costs to prevent the laws from being repealed:

... why, it might be asked, if a disposition unfaithful to the public engagements, or unfriendly to public credit, should exist, would it not operate to produce a violation of a provision made, as well as to prevent the making of one? ... To undo ... requires more enterprise and vigor ... than not to do. ... This is particularly true where a number of wills is to concur. ... In collective bodies, *votes* are necessary to ACTION; absences may produce INACTION. It often happens that a majority of voices could not be had to a resolution to undo or reverse a thing once done, which there would not be a majority of voices to *do*. This reasoning acquires tenfold force when applied to a complex Government like ours ... acting through different organs ... the House of Representatives, the Senate, and the President.[10]

In the 1930s, Henry Steagall (the father of federal deposit insurance) was perhaps the most impressive political entrepreneur of his time. Today, Chairman Greenspan seems to be the one borrowing a page from Hamilton's book in the pursuit of expanding the geographical and product scope of America's banks.

---

[9] See also Nicholas Economides, R. Glenn Hubbard, and Darius Palia, "The Political Economy of Branching Restrictions and Deposit Insurance: A Model of Monopolistic Competition Among Small and Large Banks," *Journal of Law and Economics* 39 (October 1996), pp. 467–704.

[10] Alexander Hamilton, *Report of the Secretary of the Treasury*, 1795, p. 179.

Summary of individual chapters

This collection of essays shows how a combination of momentary political bargaining and long-run path dependence has produced the history of American banking regulation, and now, deregulation. Chapters 1 to 5 review the origins and consequences of the defining characteristics of U.S. banking regulation historically, and Chapters 6 examines the trends underlying recent changes.

Chapter 1 reviews the origins of branching restrictions, deposit insurance, and bank power restrictions, their costs and benefits, and the parallel and interrelated histories of the U.S. economy and banking regulation. Subsequent chapters explore the specific elements of American bank regulatory history in more detail.

Chapter 2 emphasizes the fundamental role of branching limitations in setting the stage for other regulatory battles, particularly over banking panics, deposit insurance, and banking powers. Court decisions, regulatory rulings, and the division of regulatory power between state and federal governments helped unit bankers and landowning farmers to effectively rebuff the bank consolidation movement of the late nineteenth century, despite the gains from consolidation that attended it.

A fragmented banking system was destined to be different in many ways. Bank diversification and coordination were impaired, thus making banks more vulnerable to individual bank failures (especially in relatively undiversified agriculture-producing areas) and to systemic banking panics (which are explored in detail in Chapters 1 and 2). These costs of branching restrictions were particularly harmful to the supply of credit in rural areas. Indeed, the relatively high cost of funds outside of U.S. financial centers was a unique feature of the U.S. financial system. Restricting the scale of banks also made industrial finance by banks more difficult, since the scale of potential industrial borrowers was large relative to the scale of banks. Nationwide branching also would have reduced the cost of commercial credit by facilitating the process of interregional transfer attendant to the flow of bills of exchange. The high cost of financing agriculture – also reflected in its form (which relied far less on bankers' acceptances than did banks outside America) – was an additional drag on financial market efficiency.

A central puzzle of bank regulatory history is the political support received for restricting bank branching. If branching restrictions were so inefficient, and if they especially increased bank failure risk, reduced the availability of banking services, and raised the costs of those services in rural areas, then why were branching restrictions a central element of the populist, agrarian platform in the nineteenth and twentieth centuries? Chapter 1 argues that restrictions on branching served the interests of wealthy farmers at the expense of poorer farmers and industrialists. Branching restrictions provided a commitment device that made banks more forgiving of declines in their loan customers' net worth, since it restricted banks' abilities to divert credit to borrowers located elsewhere in the wake of shocks to the net worth of their existing customers (such as agricultural price declines). Borrowers paid for that commitment in the form of higher interest rates – an insurance premium against declines in the supply of credit.[11]

Chapter 2 focuses on the peculiar U.S. propensity for banking panics during the national banking era (1863–1913), and shows that panics in the United States were not random phenomena. Panics occurred following sufficiently large observable aggregate shocks to the banking system (identifiable empirically as a *combination* of a sudden decline in asset prices and an increase in commercial failures). Unit banking facilitated panics because it reduced bank diversification and made coordination among banks to prevent panics more difficult. In the face of observable aggregate shocks with unknown consequences for individual undiversified banks, depositors faced strong incentives to withdraw funds as a precautionary measure until the incidence of the shock could be determined. Pooling of risks by coalitions of banks can remove the incentive for such panics, but that pooling of risk was limited in the U.S. unit banking system, where the number of banks and their geographical fragmentation made coordination, self-regulation, and interbank monitoring very difficult on a national basis.

Empirical work examining bank failures during the Great Depression has found that bank failures of the 1930s were largely a continuation of the wave of agricultural bank failures of the 1920s, and were quite distinct from the banking panics of the national banking era. For the most part, bank failures during at least the early years of the Depression (1929–mid-1932) reflected the observable insolvency of banks, and in most if not all cases depositors and supervisors seem to have been able to distinguish solvent from insolvent banks. Elmus Wicker argues that bank failures during the early 1930s were largely (though not entirely) a continuation of the process of agricultural decline that had produced a wave of agricultural bank failures during the 1920s. Eugene White shows that the determinants of bank failure during the 1920s are quite similar to the determinants of failure in 1930. In two recent studies I have co-authored – one studying Chicago banks during the early 1930s (with

---

[11] For additional empirical evidence in support of this argument, see Charles W. Calomiris and Carlos D. Ramirez, "Branch Banking Restrictions, Bank Profitability, and Credit Insurance in the 1920s," Working Paper, Columbia Business School, March 1999.

Joseph Mason), the other analyzing New York City banks during the entire interwar period (with Berry Wilson) – we find that deposit withdrawals varied greatly across banks. Banks that should have been judged as riskier *ex ante* suffered greater withdrawals of deposits. The study of Chicago banks uses failure prediction models to estimate *ex ante* failure risk, whereas the study of New York banks uses balance sheet and stock price information to estimate failure risk. In both cases, individual bank risk was a significant predictor of deposit withdrawal, which suggests that depositor withdrawal was a source of market discipline that penalized banks for observable weakness. In the case of New York, we also studied how banks responded to discipline. We found that when the risk of default rose and deposits fell banks tried to restore depositor confidence by contracting lending (to reduce asset risk) and by cutting dividends (to reduce leverage). The perspective that these various works share – that banks failed during the Great Depression because of observable losses, and that such failures stretched over many years – suggests a much smaller role for asymmetric information or bank panic in understanding bank failures during the 1930s.[12,13]

---

[12] Elmus Wicker, *The Banking Panics of the Great Depression*, New York: Cambridge University Press, 1996; Eugene N. White, "A Reinterpretation of the Banking Crisis of 1930," *Journal of Economic History* (March 1984), pp. 119–38; Charles W. Calomiris and Joseph R. Mason, "Contagion and Bank Failures During the Great Depression: The June 1932 Chicago Banking Panic," *American Economic Review* (December 1997), pp. 863–83; Charles W. Calomiris and Berry Wilson, "Bank Capital and Portfolio Management: The 1930s Capital Crunch and Scramble to Shed Risk," NBER Working Paper No. 6649 (July 1998).

[13] The June 1932 Chicago panic was the clearest and most famous case of an asymmetric-information banking panic during the Great Depression. The panic was confined to Chicago and clearly traceable to local shocks to the value of bank assets. Widespread withdrawals on city banks (from both *ex post* solvent and *ex post* insolvent banks) occurred for several days and several banks failed during the panic. We asked whether any healthy banks failed during the panic. We divided the sample of Chicago banks into three categories: those that survived through mid-1932, those that failed during the panic, and those that failed outside the panic window. We asked whether the banks that failed during the panic shared characteristics with those that failed at other times, and whether the characteristics of panic failures suggest that they were among the weakest banks. By all *ex ante* measures of default risk (including interest paid on deposits in the year prior to the panic, the decline in deposits in the year before the panic, estimated failure probability, and market valuation of bank assets), banks that failed during the panic were observably weaker banks (compared to panic survivors) months in advance of the panic. Furthermore, in all cases where we were able to find examiner records, examiners noted significant problems at these banks months in advance of the panic, including large loan losses and dishonest or imprudent banking practices. We conclude that despite the fact that many solvent banks experienced some withdrawal of deposits during the panic, bank failure was a selective process that targeted the weakest banks. The activities of the Chicago Clearing House, which acted to pool risk and protect solvent banks from the threat of bank runs, were an important element in the successful avoidance of solvent bank failures during the Chicago panic.

Advocates of government deposit insurance of banks have long noted that because deposit insurance removes the incentive of depositors to withdraw in response to bad economic news, deposit insurance can help avoid the unwarranted failure of solvent banks. But bank failures and withdrawals of deposits from banks during the Depression typically did not reflect uninformed panic, but rather fundamental bank weakness. Furthermore, when systemic panic did occur in early 1933, bank holidays, rather than closures of solvent banks, were the remedy. If the passage of federal deposit insurance in 1933 cannot be considered a reaction to an unprecedented set of costly panics, then what does explain it? That legislative struggle is the subject of Chapter 3.

Deposit insurance was the legacy of unit banking. It provided unit banks with subsidized protection against the instability produced by bank fragmentation. But that subsidy encouraged incompetent or imprudent behavior by banks, which was first apparent in state-level deposit insurance schemes of the antebellum era, and even more disastrously during the post–World War I collapses of several state-level deposit insurance systems (discussed in Chapter 1).

Despite the experience with these state-level disasters, federal deposit insurance passed in 1933, over the objections of President Roosevelt, Senator Glass, the Treasury, and the Fed. The successful passage of deposit insurance owed much to the clever politicking of Rep. Henry Steagall, who strongly and effectively advocated the interests of unit bankers, who were the law's prime beneficiaries.

Bank scale was restricted by unit banking laws, and this raised the cost of industrial finance, particularly beginning in the late nineteenth century, as the scale of industrial firms grew (Chapter 4). Small banks faced a size mismatch with industrial firms, which led them to move away from industrial finance (the financing of equipment and working capital needs of industrial firms) and toward commercial finance (the financing of national and international flows of commodities). Also, the economies of scope that would have encouraged large banks to enter securities underwriting in the nineteenth century (as did German banks) were scale-dependent, and thus not accessible to size-constrained U.S. banks. That constraint added unnecessarily to the cost of financing the second industrial revolution during the late nineteenth and early twentieth centuries.

Industrialization, the growth in securities markets, and the shocks buffeting agriculture (and agricultural banks) all served to promote the relaxation of branching laws during the 1920s and a merger wave in banking. Banks then became interested in underwriting and holding corporate debt and equity, beginning in the 1920s. The relaxation of branching laws during that period had created new opportunities for banks to become large. As they became large, they turned increasingly to industrial as opposed to only commercial finance, and they found it profitable to mix bank lending with underwriting. Doing so made it possible to better serve their corporate clients' funding needs, provide better access to investments for their trust customers, and reduce banks' costs of funds, since the new activities were highly diversifying.[14]

The gains from the scale and scope improvements in banking were temporary. The landmark 1933 banking act (discussed in Chapter 4) revived unit banks through the passage of federal deposit insurance, whereas the forced separation between investment and commercial banking brought economies of scope between lending and underwriting to an abrupt end.

Chapter 4 examines differences between Germany and the United States in corporate finance patterns and costs, as a way to gauge the consequences of the bank regulatory constraints on industrial finance. The mixing of lending and underwriting activities produced important synergies in German universal banking around the turn of the twentieth century (which were well understood in the United States by the 1920s), and made it easier for risky assets to be priced in public securities markets. German banks offered very rich portfolio opportunities to their trust customers, charged very little (even by late twentieth-century standards) for equity underwriting, and managed to promote large-scale industrialization in new industries in Germany at an unprecedented speed. Economies of scope in information gathering and use were made possible in Germany because banks operated nationwide branching networks that combined deposit taking, lending, underwriting, and asset management within the same bank. That allowed the reuse of information about borrowers, and the continuation of corporate control by banks (through share proxies) after bank lending had been replaced by securities flotations as the dominant means of corporate finance for a client.[15]

---

[14] Evidence on diversification advantages is presented in Eugene N. White, "Before the Glass-Steagall Act: An Analysis of the Investment Banking Activities of National Banks," *Explorations in Economic History*, Vol. 23 (January 1986), pp. 33–55. A review of the literature on efficiency gains in serving corporate clients is provided in Charles W. Calomiris and Carlos Ramirez, "The Role of Financial Relationships in the History of American Corporate Finance," *Journal of Applied Corporate Finance*, Volume 9, Number 2 (Summer 1996), pp. 52–73.

[15] Chapter 5 identifies benefits from combining activities within universal banks, but it is important to emphasize that those benefits depended on competition among banks for relationships. Recent work has argued that the current German banking system operates as a cartel, by virtue of the fact that the largest five banks own or control majority interests in each other. Although historical German banking seems to have been ineffi-

Chapter 6 reviews the history of underwriting costs in the United States from the 1920s to the 1970s. As noted in Chapter 5, underwriting costs (especially for equity) were extremely high in the United States initially, and only the most seasoned firms (those with low adverse-selection and corporate-governance costs) could afford to pay the price of accessing public markets. Those costs reflected the difficulty of convincing fragmented individual investors (who had little ability to observe or control issuing firms) to purchase equity.

In the early post-Depression years, the costs of public securities offerings for equity did not fall, and probably rose due to new regulatory costs imposed by the SEC. Private placements of debt became the primary vehicle for external finance. Equity offerings remained low throughout the 1940s and 1950s. The growth of institutional investors – pensions and mutual funds – as significant purchasers of equity in the 1960s forever changed the costs of access to public markets. Like the German universal banks, U.S. institutional investors were able to purchase and manage large blocks of shares, which significantly reduced the costs of marketing new issues. Those efficiency gains significantly contributed to the boom in equity offerings witnessed in the United States since the 1960s.

Chapter 6 examines some of the recent trends in bank performance, relates them to deregulation, and considers the new peculiarly U.S. form of universal banking. The synergies from mixing lending, equity holding, and underwriting in the United States in the 1920s and Germany in the pre–World War I era are present and visible in the United States today, even under the current limited incarnation of universal banking. Evidence from the current U.S. experience suggests that, in particular, underwriting affiliates increase average returns and reduce risk for their bank holding companies.[16] Venture capital finance is another area in which there are likely strong corporate finance synergies, with both

---

cient, and very useful as a low-cost mechanism for stock flotation, late twentieth-century German banks rarely underwrote stock offerings and were often criticized for inefficient operations, which may reflect the lack of competition among them (see Theodor Baums, "Universal Banks and Investment Companies in Germany," in *Universal Banking: Financial System Design Reconsidered*, pp. 124–60, edited by Anthony Saunders and Ingo Walter, Homewood, IL: Business One-Irwin, 1996).

[16] See Elijah Brewer, "Relationship Between Bank Holding Company Risk and Nonbank Activity," *Journal of Economics and Business*, Vol. 41 (November 1989), pp. 337–53; Myron Kwast, "The Impact of Underwriting and Dealing on Bank Return and Risks," *Journal of Banking and Finance*, Vol. 13 (1989), pp. 101–25; Vincent P. Apilado, John G. Gallo, and Larry J. Lockwood, "Expanded Securities Underwriting: Implications for Bank Risk and Return," *Journal of Economics and Business*, Vol. 45 (1993), pp. 143–58; Simon H. Kwan, "Securities Activities by Commercial Banking Firms' Section 20 Subsidiaries," Federal Reserve Bank of San Francisco, Working Paper, January 1997.

lending and underwriting, since venture capital finance precedes public stock offerings.

The primary synergies from universal banking derive from the reuse of information, the enhancement of corporate control, and the diversification of bank income.[17] The first two channels strengthen bank–client relationships, and thereby create valuable quasi-rents for banks. By lending and underwriting, banks are able to use knowledge about the performance and risk of their corporate borrowers to reduce the cost of underwriting and marketing securities. Furthermore, informed banks' involvement as holders of equity (mainly via trust account proxies) can enhance their control over firms and help them to protect their own interests or those of their trust customers. Finally, because lending, underwriting, and other activities tend to be imperfectly correlated risks, combining the activities can help banks to diversify their assets, which economizes on bank capital and reduces banks' costs of funds.

Historical perspectives on future bank regulation

With the passage of the 1999 banking reforms, Congress has reasserted its central position of control over changes in bank powers and structure. During the 1980s and early 1990s, the Fed, the OCC, the courts, and the state governments led the way to bank deregulation, consolidation, and expansion of powers; Congress implicitly approved of most changes by not challenging regulators' authority, or by codifying interstate branching at the federal level years after state laws made it a virtual fait accompli. But the Fed indicated in the early 1990s that further deregulation (a further expansion of the Section 20 powers of commercial bank holding companies) should await congressional action, and the Comptroller did not move aggressively to permit expansion of bank powers through national bank subsidiaries prior to congressional action, partly because of the negative reaction that idea received in Congress.

Critics of Congress had argued that the two congressional banking committees preferred not to pass legislation, since the perennial prospect of a bill works wonders in fund raising. But the 1999 banking bill demonstrated that this view was both too naive and too cynical – too naive because it discounted the intelligence of contributors, and too cynical because it discounted the public policy goals and entrepreneurship of influential legislators. Particularly now that Senator Phil Gramm has

---

[17] For a more detailed discussion, see Charles W. Calomiris, "Comments on Steinherr, Kroszner, and Benston Papers," in *Universal Banking: Financial System Design Reconsidered*, pp. 109–17 edited by Anthony Saunders and Ingo Walter, Homewood, IL: Business One-Irwin, 1996.

taken over the chair of the Senate committee, it would be a mistake to discount the role of either ideology or entrepreneurship in pushing some changes through the thorny legislative process.

Prior to the 1999 bill, three divisive issues made it hard to strike the compromise necessary to pass a sweeping reform of the U.S. banking system into law: (1) whether the Community Reinvestment Act (CRA) of 1977 should be expanded or curtailed, (2) the struggle between the Fed and the Comptroller over who will regulate and supervise the diversified universal banks of the future, and (3) the future of the Federal Home Loan Banks as competitors with banks and other government-sponsored mortgage intermediaries (i.e., Fannie Mae and Freddie Mac). A fourth controversy also arose during the 1999 debate, namely, whether it is desirable to limit banks' abilities to share private customer information with their subsidiaries and affiliates.

Critics of the CRA (which include Senator Gramm) argue that it penalizes banks for pursuing profit maximization, that it singles out banks to subsidize community programs in a competitive environment where other financial institutions face no such requirement, and that it empowers self-appointed "community groups" to extort resources from banks in exchange for political support. Supporters of CRA (including Senator Sarbanes, the ranking Senate Democrat on the banking committee) believe that banks have unfairly discriminated against minorities and the poor and see banks as a useful vehicle for accomplishing certain objectives.[18] The high profitability of U.S. banks in the 1990s has invited CRA supporters to try to lay claim to that free cash flow. Senator Gramm blocked passage of the banking bill of 1998 largely because of its failure to address his concerns about CRA laws. The initial Senate version of the 1999 banking bill would have reduced slightly the CRA regulatory burden, whereas the House version would have extended CRA oversight to all bank subsidiaries and affiliates, and would have substantially bolstered penalties for noncompliance. In the end, the bill adopted parts of both the House and the Senate CRA provisions. The debate over the future of CRA will continue.

---

[18] For a review of criticisms of and supporting arguments for CRA, see Lawrence J. White, "The Community Reinvestment Act: Good Intentions Headed in the Wrong Direction," *Fordham Urban Law Journal* (June), 1993, pp. 281–92; Charles W. Calomiris, Charles M. Kahn, and Stanley D. Longhofer, "Housing-Finance Intervention and Private Incentives: Helping Minorities and the Poor," *Journal of Money, Credit and Banking* 26 (August 1994), Part II, pp. 634–74; and Charles W. Calomiris, Charles M. Kahn, and George G. Pennacchi, eds., *Banking Under the Community Reinvestment Act*, Urbana–Champaign: University of Illinois, Office for Banking Research, September 1993. For an example of the affect of CRA conflict in blocking banking reform, see "Rubin Attacks Republican Lending Curbs," *Financial Times*, February 25, 1999, p. 8.

The power struggle between the Fed and the Comptroller (discussed earlier) also continues, although the 1999 bill resolved some of the controversy by allowing underwriting activities (but not insurance or merchant banking activities) to reside in bank subsidiaries as well as affiliates. Despite protestations to the contrary by both sides in this debate, there is no legitimate economic or legal argument that favors the placement of new bank powers in either national bank subsidiaries or affiliates of bank holding companies.[19] Turf remains the core issue. Here Congress has sided primarily with the Fed (owing to Chairman Greenspan's extraordinary ability to command respect from both sides of the aisle), but Secretaries Rubin and Summers guarded the regulatory and supervisory powers of the Comptroller vigorously, as their successors are likely to do as well. Once control of the Fed passes to a new chairman, and if the same political party comes to control both Congress and the White House, regulatory power could shift toward the Comptroller and away from the Fed.

The third contentious area of reform has been the future of the Federal Home Loan Banks (and, by implication, the other government-sponsored enterprises, GSEs). GSEs enjoy substantial taxpayer subsidies and implicit government protection, which permit them to compete with banks, especially in the mortgage market. Fannie Mae and Freddie Mac have earned extraordinarily large and unvarying profits relative to other financial service firms, owing to the duopoly status they enjoy in the secondary mortgage market. Large banks typically are in favor of reining in the GSEs, since the large banks would be the primary beneficiaries of creating an even playing field (i.e., non-subsidized market) in mortgage finance.

Small banks typically favor GSE expansion, especially the recent expansion into Mortgage Partnership Finance (MPF) by the Federal Home Loan Banks (FHLBs). MPF allows FHLBs to co-originate mortgage securitizations with member institutions, and offers more profit than institutions currently enjoy under Fannie Mae and Freddie Mac programs. Senator Hagel (a Republican banking committee member with a strong pro-FHLB constituency) offered an amendment to the 1998 banking bill that would have expanded FHLB powers into non-mortgage areas, which was strongly opposed by large banks. A modified version of that proposal survived in the 1999 bill, which provides new targeted subsidies for small banks. The likely growth in the economic and political power of the Federal Home Loan Banks will influence future regulation in ways that are difficult to forecast.

[19] See Gary Whalen, *Bank Organizational Form and the Risks of Expanded Activities*, Economics Working Paper 97-1, Office of the Comptroller of the Currency, January 1997.

The survival and expansion of the Federal Home Loan Banks exemplify how difficult it can be to eliminate existing institutions in an environment where political entrepreneurship offers high returns. The FHLBs were threatened with extinction in 1989, as the thrift industry suffered a collapse and the functions of thrifts became largely absorbed within the commercial banking sector. Federal Home Loan Banks pursued a two-pronged "regulatory arbitrage" strategy for survival aimed at attracting a new constituency of members to defend them in Congress – commercial banks. The two prongs of the strategy were (1) offering subsidized credit to mitigate the costs of CRA compliance by banks and (2) offering a new inexpensive general funding source (advances) to substitute for the curtailment of bank access to the discount window. That strategy boosted FHLB membership from less than 3,000 at year end 1990 to more than 7,000 in 1999.

The Federal Home Loan Bank's subsidized loans (advances) became particularly attractive to small, weak banks in the early 1990s. Those banks were finding it harder to access the Fed's discount window, owing to new restrictions on discount window lending passed in 1991 in the wake of congressional criticism of Fed lending to insolvent banks during the 1980s.[20]

What issues will arise in future bank regulatory debates? In addition to CRA reform, the Fed-OCC turf battle, and the future of the GSEs, three other issues seem likely to be important: (1) deposit insurance reform, (2) the possible removal of the barriers between commerce and banking, and (3) the access of non-bank affiliates of banks to financial and other information about bank customers – the so-called "privacy" issue.

The scaling back of deposit insurance is a likely bone of contention. Small banks are struggling to survive in a highly competitive environment that punishes their diseconomies of scale and their narrow range of services. For many of these banks, insured deposits are their primary source of funds (for some, their exclusive source of funds). Without government protection for deposits, those small banks would face much higher costs of funds, and many are afraid they might be unable to compete.

Interestingly, large banks – which enjoy "too-big-to-fail" protection as

---

[20] For a discussion of Fed lending policies to insolvent banks, see R. Alton Gilbert, "Determinants of Federal Reserve Lending to Failed Banks," *Journal of Economics and Business* 47, 1995, pp. 397–408; "Federal Reserve Lending to Banks that Failed: Implications for the Bank Insurance Fund," *Review* 76 (January/February 1994), pp. 3–18. For a discussion of Fed discount window policy changes, see these articles and Charles W. Calomiris, "Is the Discount Window Necessary? A Penn Central Perspective," *Review* 76 (May/June 1994), p. 35.

limited and codified under FDICIA in 1991 – seem willing to repeal that special protection provided that the removal of extended safety net protection is combined with a significant expansion of permissible bank powers as a quid pro quo. The Bankers' Roundtable – which represents the largest 150 banks in the country – has proposed several reforms to the safety net.[21] These include the elimination of the too-big-to-fail doctrine, the subordination of uninsured deposits to insured deposits, and a mandatory subordinated debt requirement to force banks with expanded powers to place themselves under market discipline.[22] Also, they have argued that banks wishing to remain with the current mix of limited powers and deposit insurance protection should be permitted to do so. That proposal for a two-tiered banking system reflects the desire to limit opposition by small banks to deposit insurance reform. Nevertheless, small banks are likely to oppose reforms that permit large banks to become more efficient.

Congress did not choose to allow an increased mixing of commerce and banking in its 1999 legislation. The debate continues over whether non-financial corporations should be permitted to own interests in full-service banks. To the extent that there are synergies from such linkages (e.g., one could imagine Microsoft making productive use of a banking franchise), international competition will likely place growing pressure on legislators to relax current limitations. But those pressures will have to overcome an almost religious opposition to mixing banking and commerce. Such opposition reflects concerns about the concentration of economic power. Those concerns may be warranted in small economies, where financial-industrial conglomerates often wield too much power, but in a country as large and competitive as the United States, the mixing of commerce and banking would likely spur rather than weaken competition by allowing new non-financial entrants to challenge traditional financial services firms.

By repealing the so-called "unitary thrift loophole" – which permitted non-financial companies to buy unitary thrifts (holding companies with only one thrift institution) – the 1999 law closed one door to the mixing of commerce and banking. But the law opened another door. The definition of a permissible "financial activity" for financial holding companies to pursue will be decided by the regulators – that is, by the Fed. It

---

[21] See Bankers' Roundtable, *Deposit Insurance Reform in the Public Interest*, Washington, D.C., May 1997; *Market-Incentive Regulation and Supervision: A Paradigm for the Future*, Washington, D.C., April 1998.

[22] See Charles W. Calomiris, *The Postmodern Bank Safety Net: Lessons from Developed and Developing Economies* (Washington, D.C.: American Enterprise Institute), 1997; and *Blueprints for a New Global Financial Architecture* (Washington, D.C.: American Enterprise Institute), 1998.

is likely that as pressures mount to combine communications firms and banks, the Fed will find that communications is a financial activity (indeed, there is already precedent for that finding in current Fed regulations), just as the Fed found that underwriting was permissible in the 1980s in response to competitive pressures. Thus the 1999 law likely will slow, but not preclude, the movement toward full deregulation of bank powers. In the meantime, the enormous discretion granted to the Fed by the law will further boost the power of the Fed relative to its competing regulators.

The newest regulatory debate – over bank privacy – pits potential efficiency gains from deregulation against the desires of opponents to protect consumers from invasions of privacy. From an efficiency standpoint, the gains universal banks offer often entail the reuse of information within the banking firm. Thus limits on information sharing across affiliates limits efficiency and reduces consumers' gains from deregulation. The 1999 law allows the sharing of information across related affiliates, but with few exceptions bars the sharing of customer information with outside firms without customer permission. The debate over the right balance between efficiency and privacy rights in the new era of high-tech information processing and universal banking is just beginning and is likely to be lively.

As we approach the uncertain future, what general lessons does history offer about how these regulatory struggles are likely to be resolved? Perhaps the most obvious lesson is that the political struggles over banking legislation today reflect to a large degree the political outcomes of past struggles. Past laws and regulations define the private and public institutions that battle for future changes.

The coexistence of small local banks alongside nationwide universal banks has divided the banking industry into two camps, and thus made it difficult for commercial banks as a group to lobby successfully for legislation. That division is an historical legacy of the century-long battle over branch banking. Similarly, the turf battle between the Comptroller and the Fed, the dominance of Fannie Mae and Freddie Mac in the mortgage markets, and the impressive growth by the Federal Home Loan Banks during the 1990s remind us of the irreversibilities that come from creating public financial institutions. These powerful public institutions are capable of mobilizing constituencies to suit their ends. All of these institutions use their powers and resources to influence the legislative process.

What does bank regulatory history tell us about the probability of enacting another major banking bill in the near term, or about the likely resolution of the most contentious issues in banking regulation today?

Will the banking legislation of the next several years continue to combine many thorny issues into one bill, or focus on specific issues one at a time (like the bills of 1989, 1991, and 1994)?

Arguments can be made in favor of either possibility. On the one hand, if there is a broad consensus on a narrowly defined set of issues, then it may be easier to proceed one issue at a time. The 1989 and 1991 banking laws reflected the broad consensus that capital standards and deposit insurance regulation had to be improved. The will to act in Congress was largely a byproduct of the crisis that had gripped thrifts and banks in the 1980s, and the desire in Congress to "deal with the crisis."

In 1994, the branch banking bill was similarly the product of a broad consensus in which congressional action recognized the inevitability of an initiative that had already been largely completed at the state and regional levels. There was little cost to small banks of opposing nationwide branching in 1994. The battle they cared about (to restrict entry) had been largely resolved by then. Indeed, many small banks may even have preferred a national branching law to state- or regional-level branching; given that entry barriers were already disappearing, nationwide branching increased the number of potential acquirers competing to bid for smaller institutions.

On the other hand, larger bills (like those of 1933 and 1999) may be more likely to succeed when such consensus is lacking. In the absence of consensus on a narrow range of issues, the success of banking legislation may require combining many disparate issues into one single piece of legislation, because doing so enhances logrolling. In 1933, the ambitious combination of Regulation Q, deposit insurance, and the separation of commercial and investment banking permitted a combination of interests (which individually could have successfully blocked any of these three initiatives) to agree to the overall package. That is one way to understand why a compromise on Glass-Steagall reform had been so elusive, and why so many amendments were added on to failed banking bills leading up to the 1999 bill.

Another interesting possibility is that technological change and global market competition will force the full deregulation of the banking industry, whether Congress acts to do so or not. The key to such a dramatic change could be the privatization of the payment system, made possible through the development of new wholesale and retail clearing arrangements via the internet. If financial institutions can develop networks to clear claims among their customers without the use of checking accounts and Fed-controlled payment networks, then there would be little need for them to maintain bank charters (which currently provide unique access to the payment system). Globally competing, unchartered financial service providers, accessing customers via the internet, would be very hard for any country's government to regulate.

Because the content and form of banking bills reflect hard-to-anticipate changes in technology, the political landscape, and existing financial institutions, history teaches us, above all, to be modest in our regulatory forecasts. Future history will be easier to understand than to predict.

Regulation, industrial structure, and instability in U.S. banking
An historical perspective

Charles W. Calomiris

1.1   Introduction

From the mid-1930s through the 1970s the fundamental institutional and regulatory features of the U.S. banking system were taken for granted as permanent and mainly beneficial by most policymakers and economists. Various aspects of the regulatory system (particularly reserve requirements and deposit interest rate ceilings) were blamed for inefficiencies in capital market allocation by banks and often were seen as an impetus for financial innovations in and outside of banking: for example, NOW accounts, and the growth of credit unions and money market mutual funds. But much of the regulatory structure was seen as benign or beneficial. Studies of economies of scale in banking seemed to indicate that unit banking restrictions had little economic impact on bank efficiency. The stability of the commercial banking system seemed to have been ensured by the regulatory "safety net," including federal and state deposit insurance program that removed depositors' incentives to run on their banks in response to adverse economic news, and by regulations on bank operations – notably, the separation of commercial and investment banking, justified in 1933 as a means to prevent dishonest or reckless practices by banks.

In retrospect, the faith in the post-Depression regulated system's ability to deliver bank stability is understandable given the unusual calm of the period from 1934 to 1980. Systemic banking panics or waves of bank failures had become a distant memory, easily attributable to a primitive state of affairs prior to the supposed rationalization of banking brought by the Depression-era reform. This view was shattered by the agriculture and oil busts of the early-to-mid-1980s, along with the economy-wide thrift debacle and Eastern real estate collapse of the late 1980s and early 1990s. While systemic banking panics were avoided

The author wishes to thank Michael Klausner, Geoffrey Miller, Eugene White, Lawrence White, and Gavin Wright for helpful comments.

through the safeguards of federal deposit insurance, recent loan losses have produced bank and thrift failure rates and bank asset declines of Depression-era proportion. Indeed, the losses per deposit dollar due to bank and thrift failures in the last decade dwarf the losses of failed banks in the 1930s (Baer and Mote, 1991).

Understandably, the upheaval of the past decade has led to an increased willingness to examine possible flaws in the industrial organization and regulation of the banking sector. Increasing numbers of economists and policymakers seem willing to fault bank regulation for the recent spate of costly failures. Restrictions on intrastate and interstate branching, obstacles to takeovers of inefficiently managed banks, limitations on bank activities, inadequate supervisory authorities, and the perverse incentives created by the federal safety net – which ironically was designed to reduce the threat of banking system collapse – have all been faulted for the poor performance of recent years. The Treasury Department, the Federal Reserve, and Congress have proposed altering the traditional post-Depression regulatory framework to correct the purported flaws in the regulatory system.

The recent openness to regulatory reform has spawned new interest in the history of financial institutions and regulation. Financial history has an important role in the current policy debate for at least two reasons. First, the history of bank regulation and instability can help provide a variety of regulatory "experiments" from which to identify more clearly desirable regulatory reforms. In particular, in the search for new alternatives to the existing system of federal deposit insurance (which Golembe and Warburton 1958, Golembe 1960, and E. N. White 1982, 1983, argue was motivated by the desire to avoid the disruption of bank panics) policymakers will want to ensure that any new institutional arrangement designed to reduce the costs of deposit insurance does not do so by increasing the propensity for panics. Second, the history and political economy of regulatory policymaking can help us understand how undesirable policy decisions have been made in the past and, possibly, how to avoid them in the future.

This chapter provides evidence from financial history, primarily of the United States, on the links between systemic instability of banking and the regulation of banks. The second section discusses the meaning of bank instability and provides a brief review of the literature on bank panics. The third section presents empirical evidence regarding the consequences of branching restrictions on bank instability. In the fourth section, I describe and attempt to explain the history of limitations on branching in the United States. In the fifth section, I review the history of bank liability insurance prior to the establishment of the FDIC in 1933 and its potential role as a stabilizing or destabilizing influence in banking. Finally, in the light of history I assess opportunities and pitfalls for regulatory reform.

1.2   Banking instability: Definitions and systemic differences

Banking instability – by which I will alternately mean a propensity for panic and a propensity for insolvency (to be distinguished below) – has differed widely across times and places. Despite the similarities across systems in the types of business undertaken and the contractual structure of banks (that is, illiquid loans as assets, and primarily liquid short-term or demandable deposits as liabilities), some banking systems have been more vulnerable than others. International comparisons of the incidence and costs of panics and bank failures, and comparisons across regulatory regimes within the United States, clearly document differences in banking instability associated with different regulatory regimes. The central lesson of these studies is that instability is associated with some historical examples of banking that had common institutional characteristics; it is not an intrinsic problem of banking per se. With respect to bank panics, models that abstract from institutional features of banking and focus only on the liquidity and maturity transformation common to virtually all historical banking systems cannot explain the varying incidence of panics across different times and places.

I will argue that the single most important factor in banking instability has been the organization of the banking industry. Systems based on large, geographically diversified banks that engage in a variety of activities have been the least susceptible to panic, have had a lower overall incidence of bank failure, and have suffered smaller losses when banks failed. Moreover, cross-sectionally within any particular banking system, relatively large, diversified banks have been least likely to fail. Finally, while branch banking systems have not been completely immune to extreme shocks, and some have experienced panics, they recovered more quickly than did unit banking systems under comparable circumstances.

Before reviewing the specific evidence along these lines it is useful to distinguish the propensity for panic from the propensity for failure. While bank liquidations or receiverships typically increased substantially during panic episodes, this was not always the case; and, conversely, there were episodes in which many banks became insolvent without causing a bank panic. Panics involved contractions of bank deposits and lending by all banks and often culminated in the general suspension of convertibility of bank liabilities. Nationwide panics in U.S. history include 1819,

1837, 1839, 1857, 1861, 1873, 1884, 1890, 1893, 1896, 1907, and the three successive waves of contraction from late 1931 to early 1933.

Calomiris and Gorton (1991) review and evaluate the recent theoretical literature on bank panics in light of new evidence from the National Banking Era (i.e., 1863–1913). Calomiris and Schweikart (1991) and Moen and Tallman (1992) provide complementary analysis of the Panics of 1857 and 1907, respectively. The salient facts about panics during this period are the following: Few banks actually failed during panics, while sometimes practically all banks in the country (with some notable exceptions) were forced to suspend convertibility for some period of time (one to three months), during which their claims (notes or cashier checks) circulated at discounts (typically between 0.5 and 4 percent for New York City cashier checks during the National Banking Era). Prior to the Great Depression, panics unrelated to wars occurred at both business cycle and seasonal peaks, during which times bank leverage was high and the variance of "news" about the state of the economy was greatest. Observable adverse shocks of sufficient magnitude prompted panics. During the National Banking Era, if and only if commercial failures (seasonally adjusted) increased by more than 50 percent and stock prices fell by more than 7.9 percent, during any three-month period, then a banking panic immediately followed.

The banking collapse of the 1930s differed sharply from these earlier episodes. The runs on banks did not occur at a cyclical peak. They were the result of deflationary policies that sharply reduced the net worth of banks (Fisher, 1933; Friedman and Schwartz, 1963; Bernanke, 1983; Bernanke and Hamilton, 1987; and James, 1991). In the 1930s banks did not suspend convertibility to halt disintermediation, possibly because self-regulation was pre-empted by the control of the Federal Reserve System. The Federal Reserve banks did not provide an adequate lender of last resort (Gendreau, 1990) or a coordinated response to the deflationary shocks. As a result, an unprecedented number of banks failed.

The banking collapse of the 1930s is explicable as a grand blunder of monetary and bank regulatory policy by the Federal Reserve. But the search for explanations of bank panics prior to the 1930s is more challenging. Theoretical models of these bank panics must explain why observable aggregate shocks with small eventual consequences for the banking system should cause widespread disintermediation and suspension of convertibility. Theory must also explain the optimality of the dependence on demandable debt to finance bank loan portfolios, since maturity-matched debt or equity would eliminate the first-come first-served rule for depositors that makes a panic possible.

Recent models have provided such explanations for the occurrence of panics and for the existence of demandable-debt banking. Beginning with Campbell and Kracaw (1980), Diamond (1984), and Boyd and Prescott (1986), economists have developed models of banks as repositories of scarce information capital about borrowers and their investment opportunities. Banks specialize in screening and monitoring borrowers and thus have better information about the value of their own loan portfolios than do outsiders.

Recent empirical evidence has lent strong support to this view of the function of banks. James (1987) and James and Wier (1989) find that the response of firm valuation in stock markets to announcements of bank loans is positive. This result is in sharp contrast to findings that stock or bond issue announcements reduce the value of a firm (Myers and Majluf, 1984; Asquith and Mullins, 1986; Korajczyk, Lucas, and McDonald, 1990). The positive news of a bank loan has been interpreted as evidence that banks provide information about firms to outsiders through their willingness to grant loans and that the same is not true of equity or debt placed outside the banking system. Another interpretation is that forming relationships with banks adds value to firms. Informed bank lenders may be better at disciplining management and may also be able to provide assistance more effectively to distressed firms, because of their superior information and control over borrowers. The special announcement effects of bank loans have been confirmed in numerous studies. James and Wier (1990) also find less underpricing of IPOs for firms with established borrowing relationships with banks. Other papers document the proposition that the costs of financial distress (renegotiation of debt) are reduced by close ties to banks (Sheard, 1989; Hoshi, Kashyap, and Scharfstein, 1990b; Gilson, John, and Lang, 1990; and Brown, James, and Mooradian, 1993). Finally, firms with close bank ties show less sensitivity of investment to current cash flow, an indicator of lower costs of external finance (Hoshi, Kashyap, and Scharfstein, 1990a, 1991).

This asymmetry of information inherent in bank lending makes bank loans illiquid, and it can lead to confusion about the incidence of shocks among banks, which can precipitate a bank panic. Gorton (1989) argues that because bank loans are not marked to market, depositors are unable to discover which banks are most likely to be observable by an observable adverse shock. Under these circumstances, even if depositors know that only a small subset of banks are likely to fail in response to an observable shock, they may find it advantageous to withdraw their funds temporarily until the uncertainty over the incidence of the shock is resolved. Event studies of the effects of one bank's difficulties on the returns of other banks indicate that the possibility for confusion regarding the incidence of shocks among banks may still be important in contemporary data (Aharony and Swary, 1983; Lamy and Thompson, 1986; Scary, 1986; Grammatikos and Saunders, 1990; Musumeci and Sinkey, 1988; R. Schweitzer, 1989; and Pozdena, 1991), although Wall and Petersen (1990) provide contrary evidence.

Given the possibility of confusion, why did not banks avoid costly panics by matching the maturity of their loans and liabilities? If bank liabilities matured at the same rate as loans, there would be no potential for confusion about shocks to cause runs on banks. Calomiris and Kahn (1991) and Calomiris, Kahn, and Krasa (1991) argue that despite the costs associated with demandable debt (that is, the potential for runs), this form of financing was optimal because of the discipline it placed on the banker during normal times, given the asymmetric information between depositors and their banker about the banker's behavior. It is also possible to argue that demandable debt provided benefits during banking panics. By prompting suspension of convertibility it provided an incentive for banks speedily to resolve uncertainty about the incidence of a particular shock (Gorton, 1989; Calomiris and Gorton, 1991).

The circumstances that give rise to bank failures can be very different from those that cause panics. Bank failures can occur during nationwide downturns (including panic episodes) but may also be confined to specific regions or types of banking activity. High rates of bank failure in the Midwest during the 1890s sometimes coincided with panics (especially in 1893 and 1896) and sometimes not. The devastating agricultural bank failures of the 1920s coincided with an era of expansion in much of the economy. The observable shocks of the 1920s did not lead to a general run on banks because in each case the adverse shock was isolated to certain locations and sectors (primarily producers of grains, livestock, and cotton) and their banks.

The industrial organization of banking affected the propensities for panics and for nonpanic waves of bank failures. Systems composed of a small number of diversified large banks were less likely to fail. This also meant that there was less opportunity for panic, since the potential confusion about the incidence of failure risk was reduced. Moreover, coordination among banks was enhanced by limiting the number of banks in any system and thereby promoting mutual assistance during crises. Gorton (1985, 1989), Gorton and Mullineaux (1987), Calomiris (1989, 1990, 1992), Calomiris and Gorton (1991) and Calomiris and Schweikart (1991), emphasize that panics could be averted, or their costs reduced, if banks could form a coalition to coinsure credibly against an observable shock to the system. If banks as a group agreed to bear the risk of any individual bank's default, then so long as depositors were confident of the solvency of the group, they would have no incentive to withdraw their funds. The mutual benefit of such coinsurance is the avoidance of the panic and the consequent disruption of commercial payments and credit.

The feasibility of such coordination depended crucially on the ability of banks to form successful coalitions, which depended in turn on the number and locations of banks. Coalitions had to be able credibly to guarantee support and to prevent free riding from individual banks on the support of the group. This required self-regulation and the enforcement of regulations by voluntary mutual monitoring among members. City clearing houses, like that of New York (which was organized in 1853), and systems with a small number of geographically coincident branching banks were quite successful at forming coalitions, establishing rules for participation in the coalition, and enforcing compliance. But systems of many geographically isolated unit banks could not do so. The costs of monitoring were higher, and the benefits to any member bank from monitoring a neighbor's actions were too diffuse given the large number of coinsurers. This explains why the United States, with its prohibitions on intrastate and interstate branch banking, has never developed a nationwide coalition of coinsuring banks, unlike many other countries.

I divide the evidence on the importance of bank market structure in the next section into evidence on the incidence of panics and evidence on the risk, incidence, and cost of bank failures.

1.3   Branch banking and bank panics in the United States

With the exception of the first and second Banks of the United States, which operated from 1791 to 1811 and 1816 to 1836, respectively, there has been no interstate branch banking historically in the United States. Except for these two banks, prior to the establishment of national banks during the Civil War all banks were incorporated according to the laws of individual states and operated within the confines of those states. Banks were not free to establish any form of corporate entity they pleased, and the location and activity of a bank was defined by its charter. The earliest banks chartered in the North were unit banks, while those in the South as a rule either were chartered with the intent of establishing branches or soon were granted branching authority upon request. By the 1830s there were several states in the South (Virginia, North Carolina, Louisiana, Kentucky, South Carolina, Georgia, and Tennessee) operating substantial branch networks. The reasons for this initial difference and its persistence are examined below.

During the Panics of 1837 and 1839 branch banking enabled Southern banks to weather the storm of the credit crunch in international trade (which, according to Temin, 1969, produced the panics) remarkably well compared to their counterparts in the North. Evidence of cooperation among Southern banks within and across state lines is provided in Govan's (1936, pp. 15–19) analysis of the banks' response to the Panic of 1837. He finds that Southern banks suspended as a group in response to the exhortations of merchants who feared a drastic contraction of credit. The banks acted collectively to set the timing of suspension, the intended date of resumption, the rules governing the clearing of interbank transactions during the suspension, and rules limiting individual bank liabilities during the suspension. Similar coordination seems to have characterized the Panic of 1839 and seems to have helped to limit the incidence of bank failure during that panic. In the North during the Panic of 1839 suspension was less common and not coordinated among banks, and failure rates were higher than in the branching states of the South (Calomiris and Gorton, 1991, pp. 117–18).

Banks in states dominated by centralized urban control (Delaware, Rhode Island, Louisiana, and the District of Columbia) also coordinated suspension and avoided widespread failure during the Panic of 1839. Similarly, banks in the mutual-guaranty system of Indiana suspended together in 1837 and 1839 and avoided any failures during the panics. Like the branch banking South, city-dominated systems in the North were able to coordinate better because they involved a small number of geographically coincident banks. The Indiana system, though composed of unit banks spread throughout the state, was uniquely suited to coordination. The number of members was limited, the banks regulated one another through a collective board of directors, and they guaranteed each other's liabilities without limit. The board of directors had broad authority (including the right to close banks, regulate capital ratios, and restrict dividends) and had strong incentives to monitor and penalize violations. During its entire history, from 1834 to 1865, no member bank failed. Indeed, the stability of the system was so great that during panics after 1839 it was even able to avoid suspension of convertibility (Golembe and Warburton, 1958; Calomiris, 1989).

During the Panic of 1857, once again Southern banks and the mutual guaranty banks of Indiana and Ohio (which imitated Indiana's system in 1845) coordinated effectively, recovered their pre-panic asset levels relatively quickly and saw relatively few bank failures (Calomiris and Schweikart, 1991). As before, branching banks acted together to coordinate their own and other banks' behavior, establish interbank markets for clearing notes and checks, transfer funds, and enforce agreed upon rules during the panic. For example, within one week of the onset of the panic, banks in Charleston agreed to receive each other's notes and the notes of other South Carolina banks and Augusta and Savannah banks at par. In his discussion of the Panic of 1857, Hammond (1957, p. 712), along with many other observers, notes that the successful coordination of the Southern banks was not possible in states like New York, where many geographically isolated unit banks in the periphery were forced to act independently. Markets for bank notes reflected these differences in coordination through lower discounts on the notes of Indiana, Ohio, and Southern banks before and during the crisis (Calomiris and Schweikart, 1988; Gorton, 1990).

The Panic of 1857 also saw the origin of crisis management among members of the New York City clearing house (Cannon, 1910; Gorton, 1985). Member banks pooled funds and issued joint liabilities, coordinated plans for maintaining credit to brokers and merchants, eventually suspended jointly, established the date of joint resumption, and after the panic organized the orderly flow of country bank notes (which had accumulated in New York City banks prior to the crisis) to enable the country banks to resume convertibility in a timely fashion. The successes of the New York City clearing house led to imitation in 1858 when Baltimore and Philadelphia banks established their own clearing houses.

Interestingly, formal clearing houses never developed in the branching South during the antebellum period. Understandably, the small number of branching banks had a lesser need to coordinate clearings and were able to respond to panics effectively without the formal rules and enforcement mechanisms of the clearing house. Similarly, clearing houses did not develop in Canada's branch banking system until 1887. As Breckenridge (1910, pp. 162–3) writes:

The volume of transactions for settlement, of course, had always been smaller than what would be expected of a system of an equal number of banking offices, each under independent control. The settlement between two or between all the branches of the same bank, of course, would be effected in the books of that bank, and is so still, independently of the clearing house.

The large financing needs and the ultimate defeat of the South in the Civil War led to the insolvency of its banking system, which was called upon to bear much of the burden for the South's war finance. At the same time, the mutual-guaranty systems operating in Indiana, Ohio, and (beginning in 1858) Iowa ceased to operate, as many of their members converted to national bank charters (after 1863) in order to avoid the 10 percent federal tax on state bank notes. With the demise of Southern branch banks and Midwestern mutual-guaranty banks, and the decision by the Comptroller of the Currency to restrict branching by national banks, the only form of interbank cooperation that remained in place during the immediate postbellum era was the clearing house, which had spread to the major cities of virtually every state by the end of the nineteenth century. As Johnson (1910, p. 10) writes in describing the Canadian branch banking system to an American audience:

> ... to the student of the history of banking in the United States there is little that is radically new in the Canadian system. He finds in it many of the practices and expedients that were found excellent in the United States in the first half of the nineteenth century, and is almost persuaded that but for the civil war what is now known as the Canadian banking system would everywhere be called the American system.

While useful in coordinating the actions of local banks in large U.S. cities, clearing houses were unable to establish a national organization to coordinate clearings or the banking system's response to panics. Given its unusual position as the reserve center for the nation's interbank deposits, New York City banks and their clearing house came to play an increasing role as the main originator of policy during the panics of the National Banking Era. The clearing house continued to pool assets and issue joint liabilities (clearing house loan certificates) during panics, which at first were used only for interbank clearings but by 1893 were being used as a cash substitute by the public.

The ability of the New York clearing house to act as a lender of last resort for the economy as a whole was limited by the amount of high-quality assets that its members could contribute to the pool as backing for its loan certificates and by its ability to distinguish good from bad risks in interbank lending outside its own organization. While the use of loan certificates may have been helpful in forestalling suspension in 1884 and 1890, larger disturbances (1873, 1893, and 1907) resulted in widespread disintermediation followed by suspension of convertibility. The uncertainty regarding the incidence of shocks, which gave rise to panics, could not be entirely resolved by coinsurance of risk within the banking system (as it was in many other countries, notably England's resolution of the Baring Crisis in 1890). Thus the resolution of panics in the United States required prolonged delays in the convertibility of deposits on demand.

1.3.1 *International evidence on branch banking and bank panics*

International comparisons provide similar evidence on the role of branch banking, with its advantages of diversification and coordination, in reducing the incidence of panics. Bordo's (1985) useful survey of banking and securities-market panics in six countries from 1870 to 1933 concludes that "the United States experienced banking panics in a period when they were a historical curiosity in other countries." (p. 73) Bordo, like many others, notes the likely association between the unique unit banking system in the United States and its unique propensity for panics. But because the regulatory environment of any country differs from others along dimensions other than unit versus branch banking, it is difficult to attribute the relative stability of other countries to branching per se. To facilitate comparison, I will limit my discussion of other countries' banking systems to the English speaking world, which shared a legal tradition and many common institutional features. A more inclusive survey (including France and Germany) would corroborate the evidence presented here; Kindleberger (1984) provides an introduction to these literatures.

Scotland: Scotland's early banking system is usually held up as an example of a virtually unregulated system of branching banks, and its panic-free history is often attributed to its large number of branches. Banks in Scotland were free to branch as they pleased. By 1845 19 banks of issue operated 363 branches (L. H. White, 1984, p. 37). The Scottish Bank Act of 1845 restricted Scottish bank note issues to those outstanding at that date plus any additional issues backed 100 percent by specie reserves. This was less restrictive than the Peel Act of 1844, which was designed to shrink the note issues of English banks (see Hughes, 1960; Capie and Webber, 1985, p. 211). Both acts helped to consolidate the power of the Bank of England. After 1845, branch banking continued to flourish in Scotland, but Scotland ceased to be independent of the English system. Commenting on Scotland's panic-free history of branch banking, L. H. White (1984, p. 143) quotes two observers (from 1845 and 1832, respectively) as claiming that "runs are the last things that would ever enter into the mind of any man who is acquainted with the history of banking in this country," and that "A run upon a bank, such as happens in England sometimes, or a panic, are terms the meaning of which is hardly understood in Scotland."

The difficulty in attributing the stability of the Scottish system to branch banking per se is due to other unique features of the early Scottish system. Scottish banks generally were unlimited liability banks (with the exception of three limited-liability banks); thus depositors and noteholders of banks enjoyed greater protection than that afforded by the capital of a limited-liability bank. Furthermore, Scottish banks could be formed by as large a partnership and capital base as they chose, unlike banks in England where restrictions limited the number of partners and the amount of bank capital (L. H. White, 1984, pp. 41–2). Finally, Scottish banks before 1845, unlike banks in the United States and elsewhere, faced no limitations on their note issues. In fact, within the British Isles Scottish bank notes often were brought into England and constituted a permanent component of the money stock, particularly in the Northern regions.

The right to issue bank notes was deemed especially important for allowing the branching network to expand. Withers et al. (1910, pp. 43–4) argue that the costs of holding "till money" in the form of specie or equivalently the notes of other banks was an important restriction to branching in other countries, but in Scotland banks were able to avoid this cost. Scottish banks (around 1910) held reserves (specie plus other banks notes) of less than 10 percent of their total liabilities (Withers et al., 1910, p. 46), which Withers et al. show is low by comparison to England and other countries. Munn (1981, p. 141) shows that from 1811 until the restriction imposed by the Scottish Bank Act, the ratio of specie to demand liabilities for each bank ranged between 0.5 and 1.6 percent. This confirms the view that, particularly in the early period of branch expansion, Scottish banks had a distinct advantage in the form of low till costs.

These features of the Scottish system raise a caveat for the purposes of comparison with the U.S. system. Before using the observed stability of early nineteenth-century Scottish banks to answer the counterfactual question "How different would the history of panics have been during the National Banking Era in the United States if national banks had been allowed to branch?," one should control for differences in the regulation of note issues, which may have influenced the potential for expansion and therefore diversification of the branching system (see the extended discussion of Canada below) and also control for differences in extended liability. Both of these features enhanced the Scottish system's stability.

England: Unlike that of Scotland, England's banking system experienced panics in the eighteenth and early nineteenth centuries, but saw none after 1866. It is hard to know whether to attribute the end of panics to the transformation of the English banking system from one of mainly unit banks to one of mainly branching banks, or to changes in the Bank of England's approach to dealing with crises. Private unit banks operated in England prior to the creation of joint stock banks in 1826. Initial restrictions on joint stock bank operations in London (to benefit the Bank of England) were relaxed somewhat in 1833. By 1836, the 61 registered joint stock banks operated 472 banking facilities, and the trend toward branching continued in the ensuing decades. By 1870, 111 joint stock banks operated 1,127 banking facilities. For Britain as a whole in 1870, there were 378 banks operating 2,738 banking facilities (Capie and Webber, 1985, p. 576).

At the same time, changes were occurring in the Bank of England's role in managing crises, and it is hard to separate this effect on the propensity for panic from that due to expanded branching. The monopolization of new English note issues in the hands of the Bank of England after 1844 and the restrictions on the note-issuing powers of the Bank of England (a 100 percent specie reserve requirement) limited the banking system's ability to protect itself from panics and made the system's fortunes heavily dependent on the discretionary policies of the Bank of England and the government during crises. The government had to provide the Bank with a special letter during the panics of 1847, 1857, and 1866 allowing it to violate its 100 percent reserve requirement on notes in order to create liquidity. By the 1870s (especially with the publication of Walter Bagehot's *Lombard Street* in 1873) such a relaxation of the rules during crisis was expected, and the mature view of the Bank of England's role as a lender of last resort had been articulated, perhaps most eloquently by Bagehot:

... whatever bank or banks keep the ultimate banking reserve of the country must lend that reserve most freely in time of apprehension, for that is one of the characteristic uses of the bank reserve, and the mode in which it attains one of the main ends for which it is kept. Whether rightly or wrongly, at present and in fact the Bank of England keeps our ultimate bank reserve, and therefore it must use it in this manner.

And though the Bank of England certainly do make great advances in time of panic, yet as they do not do so on any distinct principle, they naturally do it hesitatingly, reluctantly, and with misgiving. In 1847, even in 1866 – the latest panic, and the one in which on the whole the Bank acted the best – there was nevertheless an instant when it was believed the Bank would not advance on Consols, or at least hesitated to advance on them. The moment this was reported in the City and telegraphed to the country, it made the panic indefinitely worse. What is wanted and what is necessary to stop a panic is to diffuse the impression, that though money be dear, still money is to be had ... (p. 64).

Interestingly, Bagehot lamented England's peculiar reliance on one bank to manage lending during crises and preferred the Scottish multicentric approach:

I shall have failed in my purpose if I have not proved that the system of entrusting all our reserve to a single board, like that of the Bank directors, is very anomalous (p. 66).

... the natural system – that which would have sprung up if Government had let banking alone – is that of many banks of equal or not altogether unequal size (p. 67).

After 1866, the Bank managed to preserve liquidity without deviating again from the provisions of the 1844 Act, perhaps, paradoxically, because of its known willingness to do so (Dornbusch and Frenkel, 1984; Dutton, 1984; Hughes, 1984; Pippenger, 1984). In one of the more interesting examples of interbank coordination, during the Baring Crisis of 1890, the commercial banks of London bailed out the Baring investment banking house by agreeing jointly to insure against losses to its creditors (with the Bank of England backing up the private bank co insurers). In so doing, the banks succeeded in dispelling uncertainty about the incidence of losses among their number from the Baring collapse, thus avoiding the threat of a bank panic. According to Eichengreen (1992), the Bank of England's increasing success in preventing panics during the late nineteenth and early twentieth centuries, and even in quelling disturbances outside its borders, was due in part to successful coordination across national boundaries with central bankers on the continent – something that set the mature classical gold standard of the late nineteenth century apart from previous and subsequent arrangements among central banks.

Canada: The comparison between the incidence of panics in the United States and Canada possibly provides the most convincing evidence of the efficacy of branching for reducing the risk of panic, since the two nations and their banking regulations were otherwise quite similar. Both countries are vast geographically. Neither country had a central bank in operation in the nineteeth century. The Bank of Canada began operation in 1935, although the government had a limited role as a lender of last resort beginning in 1907, which was expanded in 1914 and 1923, as is discussed in Bordo and Redish (1987). The trade and activities of the two nations were similar and interlinked. Johnson (1910, pp. 9–10) writes:

Financially Canada is part of the United States. Fully half the gold reserve upon which its credit system is based is lodged in the vaults of the New York Clearing House. In any emergency requiring additional capital Montreal, Toronto, and Winnipeg call on New York for funds just as do St. Paul, Kansas City, and New Orleans. New York exchange is current and universal medium in Canada and is in constant demand among the banks. A Canadian wishing to invest in securities that may be quickly marketed commonly turns to the New York market for stocks and bonds. Yet the American banker visiting in Canada ... finds himself in a land of financial novelties, for Canada has a banking system unlike any in operation in the United States at the present time. Twenty-nine banks, known as the "chartered banks," transact all the banking business of the Dominion. They have 2,200 branches, and each may establish new branches without increase of its capital stock. They issue notes without depositing security with the government and in such abundance that no other form of currency in denominations of $5 and above is in circulation. Notwithstanding the fact that the notes are "unsecured," their "goodness" is unquestioned among the Canadian people.

Indeed, given the close connections among the two financial systems it is remarkable that the Canadian system did not suffer panics when they occurred in the United States.

One difference between the U.S. and Canadian systems worth commenting upon was the elastic supply of bank currency in Canada. As in Scotland, Canadian banks were permitted to issue their own currency. Until 1908, national banks wishing to issue currency in the United States had to deposit government bonds in the Treasury and await delivery of their notes from the government. Canadian banks were allowed to issue their own notes, during normal times, up to the amount of unimpaired paid-in capital. After July 1908, they were also allowed to issue an additional amount equal to 15 percent of capital and surplus during the crop-moving season (October 1 to January 1). As with the 1908 Aldrich-Vreeland Act authorizing emergency currency issues in the United States, emergency currency issues in Canada could be taxed. Unlike American banks in both the antebellum and postbellum periods, Canadian banks faced no reserve requirements on their note issues. Furthermore, the ceiling implied by paid-in capital was never a binding constraint on Canadian note issues (Johnson, 1910, Chart IV, after p. 66). The difference in the flexibility of the Canadian and United States currency stocks was widely noted historically (see, for example, Gage, 1906). Gage (1906) shows that the Canadian pattern was typical of other elastic-note-supply, branch-banking countries.

This differing flexibility in the supply of currency was noted by many contemporaries. As in Scotland and many other countries, banks' ability to issue notes in Canada likely reduced the specie reserves held by the banking system and facilitated branching. Conceivably, this could have reduced the propensity for panics to the extent that adding loans from especially thinly populated rural areas helped to diversify bank portfolios.

The option to issue notes also likely reduced the cost of providing credit in the form of an exchange medium for seasonal currency payments to agricultural workers (particularly in August and September). By accommodating credit needs in a liquid form, banks limited the seasonal fluctuations in interest rates in the periphery (see Breckenridge,

1899a, pp. 51–2; Gage, 1906; Eichengreen, 1984a; Miron, 1986). It is difficult to separate the effects of branching and note issuing on credit cost seasonality. Branch banks – by virtue of greater diversification and greater potential for interregional and interbank coordination – should have had flatter loan-supply functions than unit banks in the United States irrespective of note issuing authority. That is, banks should have been able to bear seasonal increases in the loan-to-reserve ratio without charging as high a cost to borrowers because the risk to the bank of doing so would have been less in Canada than in the United States. The marginal contribution of note issuing authority on the effective supply of credit depends on how large was the substitutability between notes and deposits as exchange media on the margin. To the extent the only exchange medium acceable to peripheral borrowers in August and September was currency, and currency was costly to import seasonally for this purpose, the supply of loans would effectively have been more inelastic seasonally (borrowers would have to pay a seasonal currency premium).

Regardless of its effects on seasonal credit cost or access of branches to remote areas, the ability to issue notes in and of itself seems not to have been an important determinant of panics in the United States or, conversely, a protection against panics in Canada (although one can strain to make such a connection, in theory, as a recent model by Champ, Smith, and Williamson, 1991, illustrates). During the antebellum period in the United States and in Canada, note issues were highly elastic but this did not prevent panics from occurring in both countries in 1837 and 1839 and in the United States in 1857.

Data on the cyclical elasticity of note supply under New England's Suffolk System show cyclical variation comparable to that shown for Canada in the nineteenth century. (For discussions of and data for Suffolk System note issues, see Root, 1901, p. 211; Mullineaux, 1987, p. 889; *Hunt's Merchants' Magazine*, 1840, vol. 2, pp. 137–42; Calomiris and Kahn, 1996.) *Hunt's Merchants' Magazine* (1851, vol. 25, p. 467) provides data on note redemptions under the Suffolk System. From month to month, note redemptions often varied as much as 10 percent. Calomiris and Schweikart (1988) find similar cyclical elasticity for bank notes in the South. For example, in Virginia, outstanding currency fell from $14.3 million to $10.8 million from January 1854 to January 1855. By the following January, outstanding currency was $13.0 million. Under New York's free-banking system note supply also showed elasticity. For example, from September 1855 to September 1856, total outstanding currency of New York banks increased from $31.3 million to $34.0 million. Weekly returns of New York City, Boston, Pittsburgh, and St. Louis banks in 1858 as reported in *Hunt's Merchants' Magazine* (1859, vol. 40, p. 215) show large seasonal changes in note circulation. For example, in New York City, circulation increased nearly 12 percent from March 27 to May 8 and fell more than 6 percent from May 8 to May 29. In Indiana's mutual-guaranty banking system, outstanding note issues changed by more than 10 percent (from the beginning to the end of the year) 16 times in 27 years between 1835 and 1862, with 12 increases and 4 decreases (Golembe and Warburton, 1958, p. IV–11). Monthly changes also could be large for these banks, as shown in Harding (1898, pp. 279–81). From January to August, 1842, circulation fell 40 percent; from July to December, 1844, notes outstanding rose 14 percent. From 1845 to 1862, Ohio's insured banks varied their outstanding currency annually by more than 10 percent in 9 out of 17 years, with 7 increases and 2 decreases (Golembe and Warburton, 1958, p. VI–17).

The fact that elasticity of note issues was a common feature of many different regulatory regimes in the United States during the antebellum period did not prevent panics in the United States. This contradicts the view that panics were caused by inelastic supply of currency and large random currency-demand shocks, as Chari (1989) and Champ, Smith, and Williamson (1991) argue. Calomiris and Gorton (1991) and Calomiris and Schweikart (1991) show that panics were caused not by the scarcity of a particular form of medium of exchange, but by adverse economic disturbances that created confusion regarding the potential insolvency risk of commercial banks.

In summary, despite the advantages attributable to note issuing authority, it seems reasonable to attribute differences in the vulnerability of the U.S. and Canadian banking systems to panics primarily to the branching laws of the two countries, rather than to the elasticity of currency supply, or perhaps to the combination of branching and the elasticity of currency.

Canada's system allowed nationwide branching from its beginnings in the early nineteenth century. Ironically, at that time, it was following the banking doctrines of Alexander Hamilton to the letter (Breckenridge, 1910, pp. 7–8) and the precedent established in the United States by the Bank of the United States. Banks relied on coordination among a small number of banks (roughly 40 in the nineteenth century, falling to 10 by 1929) to resolve threats to the system. The Canadian Bankers' Association, formed in 1891, marked the formalization of cooperative arrangements that served to regulate failures of individual banks and mitigate their consequences for the banking system as a whole. The Bank of Montreal – the depository of most government funds, and the largest of the Canadian banks, with 20 percent of the banking system's assets in

1910 – sometimes acted as a private lender of last resort, stepping in to assist troubled banks (Breckenridge, 1910; Johnson, 1910; Vreeland et al., 1910).

Canada experienced no banking panics after the 1830s. During their history, Canadian banks suspended convertibility only twice, from May 1837 to June 1838 and from November 1838 to June 1939. Breckenridge (1910) describes these suspensions as of questionable necessity and mainly motivated as a defensive action to prevent large outflows of specie to the United States (which was the origin of the problem). The Canadian banks did not suspend during the Panic of 1857 and saw a reduction in their activities (presumably reflecting the large outflows of specie abroad). Still, no bank failed in Canada during or immediately after the panic.

During subsequent panics in the United States, Canada followed a similar path to that of 1857, acting as a shock absorber for the difficulties originating in the United States. Inflows of Canadian bank notes, as well as specie, helped to offset contractions in the U.S. money supply attendant to panics. These contractions had little effect on Canadian banks. For example, in the Panic of 1907, banks reduced their lending temporarily and rapidly rebounded. Johnson (1910, p. 96) describes 1908 as . . .

. . . a breathing spell in Canadian industry and finance, but the bank returns show that there was no lack of confidence in the banks and that the floating capital of the country had not been seriously impaired.

Schembri and Hawkins (1988) argue that Canadian branches in the United States benefited from the relative stability of Canada's banks during panics in the United States. U.S. depositors transferred funds to these banks in times of trouble, viewing them as a safe haven.

Coordination among banks within Canada is nicely illustrated by the events of the Panic of 1907. The Sovereign Bank of Canada failed during the crisis, but without loss to its liability holders because of the intervention of other Canadian banks (led by the Bank of Montreal) who guaranteed its liabilities against loss. As the English banks had done during the Baring Crisis of 1890, the Canadian banks sought to eliminate any confusion regarding the incidence of loss among banks by standing together as a group, whose collective solvency was beyond question. The Canadian banks had done the same for the Bank of Ontario in 1906.

On the evening of October 12 [1906] the bankers in Toronto and Montreal heard with surprise that the Bank of Ontario had got beyond its depth and would not open its doors the next morning. Its capital was $1,500,000 and its deposits $12,000,000. The leading bankers in the dominion dreaded the effect which the failure of such a bank might have. The Bank of Montreal agreed to take over the assets and pay all the liabilities, provided a number of other banks would agree to share with it any losses. Its offer was accepted and a representative of the Bank of Montreal took the night train for Toronto . . . the bank opened for business the next day with the following notice over its door: "This is the Bank of Montreal." (Johnson, 1910, pp. 124–5).

The Bank of Montreal did not always bail out failing banks. When smaller banks failed (never with any losses to noteholders, and usually with small or zero losses to depositors), the bank did not intervene (Vreeland et al., 1910, p. 219; Johnson, 1910, p. 127).

Over time, beginning in 1907, the government provided additional protection to the Canadian banking system, through authorization of loans of currency (Dominion notes) against collateral of worthy securities. Johnson (1910, p. 121) argues that the intervention was unnecessary in 1907 and did not occur at the request of the banks, who opposed it. Bordo and Redish (1987) conclude that the rise of the Bank of Canada as a Depression measure in 1935 was not the result of economic necessity, but of political expediency due to domestic and international political pressures.

There is some disagreement about the role of Canada's branching system in preventing the collapse of the system during the Great Depression. Haubrich (1990) argues that Canada's resistance to panics during the Great Depression prevented Canada's financial system from propagating the severe external shocks that buffeted it, in contrast to the U.S. banking collapse, which Bernanke (1983) argues was so instrumental in prolonging the Depression in the United States. Both countries saw a large decline in GNP from 1929 to 1933 (42 percent in Canada and 46 percent in the United States). Kryzanowski and Roberts (1989) recently have questioned whether the success of the Canadian banking system in surviving the Depression was due to branch banking and coordination, or alternatively as they suggest, to an implicit guarantee by the government that depositors would be protected from loss. While they provide some interesting evidence in favor of the likelihood that some attempt might have been made to protect Canadian banks in the absence of successful private intervention, there is room for doubt regarding their conclusions. It seems unlikely that Canadian depositors would have resisted running on their banks because of the possibility of government backing, the existence of which remains controversial even today.

Australia: The single exceptional case of a mature, relatively laissez-faire, nationwide branch-banking system that experienced a panic involving widespread bank suspension was the Australian banking collapse of 1893. But even here, the particulars of the experience hardly constitute an indictment of the potential efficacy of diversification and coordination through branching.

In the latter half of the nineteenth century Australia grew rapidly, with GDP rising at a rate of 5 percent per annum from 1860 to 1890. In the fifteen years prior to the crisis Australian banks' real assets tripled, as the banks moved away from traditional commercial lending to participate in the financing of the speculative land and construction boom (Pope, 1989). Throughout the period the banking sector was highly concentrated, with roughly half of the banking system's deposits residing in four of the 26 banks in existence. Despite this concentration (and despite the operation of a clearing house in Melbourne since 1867), the crisis caused half the banks in the country, operating nearly 1,000 branches, to suspend convertibility.

Coordination among banks did occur to some extent. The clearing house issued loan certificates during the crisis and thereby managed to reduce the specie needed for interbank clearings from 20 percent in 1892 to 5 percent during the crisis (Pope, 1989). But apart from this, there was no explicit interbank risk sharing to promote public confidence in the banking system, as there had been in Canada and Britain during financial crises.

Pope (1989) argues that part of the explanation for the lack of coordination among banks during the crisis was that some of the largest banks in the system did not perceive a great benefit to themselves from providing the necessary assistance to the failing banks. The logic of voluntary *ex post* mutual assistance requires that the assisting banks see a large negative externality from not providing such help. Pope (1989) claims that two of the larger banks in the country (the Australasia and the Union) entered the crisis in a relatively strong position and thus were unwilling to participate in a proposed mutual-assistance plan. Both had high reserve ratios, had not participated as much as other banks in financing the land boom, saw little threat to their own position from the run on other banks, and may have viewed the collapse of their competitors as an opportunity to expand their market share. The opposition of these two banks was sufficient to undermine the initial promises of mutual assistance among banks.

This interpretation suggests that the Australian case may not have been a "classic" panic (one involving substantial confusion about the incidence of the disturbance among banks). Indeed, Pope (1989) shows that available measures of balance sheet liquidity positions and risk exposure provide reasonably good predictions of which banks were forced to suspend during the crisis. This supports his view that banks could be distinguished vis-à-vis their exposure to the shock. Moreover, the lack of interest in collective action suggests that the long-run social costs of the panic, in terms of disruption to the potential provision of credit by the banking system as a whole, were likely to be small. The existence of a few large nationwide branching banks of unquestioned health eventually would have provided a substitute source of commercial credit supply for failing banks.

All 12 of the banks that suspended in April and May of 1893 were able to reopen within three months. The Federal Bank, which alone had failed in January and had been denied assistance by all the banks at that time, was the only bank unable to resume business. The banks that were able to resume did so with the help of their depositors, who cooperated in providing capital infusions to their banks and converting their demandable obligations into shares or long-term debt. The fact that the failing banks were able to come up with a plan and have the plan successfully adopted at a national scale so quickly suggests that there may have been substantial ex post "coordination benefits" from bank concentration after all.

In summary, the Australian banking collapse involved an unusual set of circumstances (a very large shock to fundamentals with different consequences for different banks), and this explains the large suspension rate and lack of coordination among Australian banks. Furthermore, the social cost of the Australian banking collapse was probably small compared, for example, with the numerous bank failures during the similar land bust of the 1890s in the United States (see Calomiris and Gorton, 1991). In the United States, there was systemic suspension of convertibility (suggesting more ex ante confusion about the incidence of the disturbance among banks), failing banks were not able to reorganize through a coordinated recapitalization financed by depositors, and failed unit banks were not easily replaced (due to the prohibition on entry that branch banking restrictions entailed – see Calomiris, 1990, 1992, for related evidence on the role of branching in providing for replacement of failed banking facilities in the 1920s). Finally, the 1893 crisis was an isolated incident in the history of Australian banking. As one observer wrote in 1933,

Perhaps the most remarkable feature of Australian banking since the crisis of 1893 is the almost complete absence of bank failures. No commercial bank, except the Federal Deposit Bank, which was a small bank in Queensland, has failed since the troublesome days of 1893. . . . As Australia is essentially an agricultural and pastoral country that suffers from prolonged drought, the almost complete absence of commercial bank failures since 1893 is truly remarkable (Jauncey, 1933, p. 30, cited in Chapman and Westerfield, 1942, p. 256).

The stability of the post-1893 banking system coincided with increased concentration of banking and expansion of access through an enormous increase in bank facilities. In 1912, there were 23 banks operating 2,064 facilities. By 1929 there were 16 banks operating 3,262 facilities.

1.3.2 Branch banking and diversification

As discussed above, diversification of individual bank assets is one of the key elements linking branch banking and a reduced propensity for bank panics. The benefits of greater asset diversification under branching appear in a variety of other indicators as well. For example, as noted above, seasonal smoothing of interest rates is enhanced (the loan-supply function is flatter) under branching; equivalently, increases in bank leverage and reserve ratios can be accommodated with smaller increases in interest rates charged borrowers when banks are well diversified. Another piece of evidence is the lower market discount rates on the bank notes of branching banks during the antebellum period (Calomiris and Schweikart, 1988; Gorton, 1990). As noted above, both of these pieces of evidence can be interpreted in other ways. The elasticity of currency under the branch banking systems of Canada, Scotland, and other countries may have facilitated the smoothing of interest rates, in addition to the effects of asset diversification due to branching. The coordination benefits during panics from branching, rather than within-bank diversification per se, may have been important in lowering discount rates on notes.

In what follows I consider several other indicators of lower asset risk of branching banks, which I will argue are clearer indicators of asset risk differences. These include: the propensity for bank failure (during and outside of panic episodes) across different types of systems; the propensity for failure of different types of banks within the same system; the recovery of banking (number of locations and asset levels) in response to shocks across different types of systems; the role of banks in equalizing rates of return across different locations; the greater expansion of branch-banking systems into thinly populated areas; and the reserve holdings of banks in branching and nonbranching systems.

Bank Failures: Prior to the 1980s four national waves of bank failures occurred in the United States: the disastrous episodes of 1837–1841, 1890–1896, 1921–1930, and 1931–1933. Especially in the first three of these episodes, bank failures were closely linked to the type of enterprises banks financed. Banks with close links to international trade (Temin, 1969, pp. 142–5) or to infrastructure investment (Schweikart,

1988a) were hardest hit by the collapse of 1837–1841. In the 1890s banks that had financed the rapid land expansion "on the middle border" in Kansas and Nebraska suffered the highest risk of failure (Bogue, 1955; Calomiris and Gorton, 1991, pp. 156–9). In the 1920s, the agricultural bust of the post-World War I period caused widespread bank failures in some states (those with many grain, cotton, and livestock producers, in particular), while leaving others unaffected (Calomiris, 1992).

The activities of banks and the shocks that buffeted them were important factors in predicting failure propensity during these disastrous episodes, but regulatory factors were important as well. In particular, systems that permitted branching saw lower failure rates and losses than systems that did not. During the 1837–1841 period, Virginia and South Carolina (two Southern states with advanced private branch banking systems) saw no bank failures (Klebaner, 1990, p. 51).

Regrettably, this same pattern persists to the present day. Comparisons across states, using evidence from the agricultural crisis of the early 1980s, confirm that branch banking systems have suffered lower failure rates than others, controlling for other factors. Calomiris, Hubbard, and Stock (1986, p. 469) found that California had an exceptionally high rate of troubled agricultural loans during the early 1980s. As of 1984, 8.4 percent of California's agricultural loans were in nonaccrual status, compared to an average of 4.7 percent for the rest of the country. The agricultural loan delinquency rate for California was 13.1 percent, compared to a national average of 8.9 percent. Net charge-offs as a percentage of agricultural loans were 6.1 percent in California and 1.8 percent in other states. Despite these difficulties, California accounted for only 1 of 68 agricultural bank failures in 1985. The reason they weathered the storm so well is that most agricultural lending in the state comes from large well-diversified banks, which hold only 3 percent of their portfolios in agricultural production loans.

Laderman, Schmidt, and Zimmerman (1991) show that bank diversification is inhibited by unit banking. After controlling for a variety of other factors, they find that rural banks devote a significantly larger proportion of their loan portfolios to agricultural loans than do urban banks. When statewide branching is allowed, rural and urban banks' portfolios are much more diversified. Smith (1987) shows that branching restrictions increase failure risk for agricultural and nonagricultural banks by limiting the potential for diversification.

... banks in restricted-branching states are generally at greater risk of closure because of less diversified loan portfolios than are banks in statewide-branching states ... in restricted-branching states, the probability of closure of banks seems equally influenced by the share of loans in the commercial and industrial category and the share in the agricultural category ... several of the financial ratio coefficients are statistically different between restricted-branching and statewide-branching states. (p. 35)

Historical comparisons across countries provide similar evidence of the benefits of diversification through branching. L. H. White (1984, pp. 44–9) emphasizes the low failure rates of Scottish banks compared to their counterparts in England during the early nineteenth century. Chapman and Westerfield (1942, p. 257) write:

The last two bank failures in Scotland were the Western Bank of Scotland in 1857 and the City of Glasgow Bank in 1878. . . . The shareholders suffered seriously, but the depositors and noteholders were paid in full.

Johnson (1910, p. 127) makes a similar point about the mature Canadian system:

Since 1889 six small banks have failed, but note holders have lost nothing and depositors very little. They were local institutions with few branches and their failures possess little significance in a study of the banking system as a whole.

Thirteen Canadian banks failed from 1868 to 1889. The available data indicate that the costs of these failures for noteholders were quite low (zero in the 11 cases where data are available); and in at least 8 of the 13 cases, depositors' losses were essentially zero as well (Vreeland et al., 1910, p. 219). During the period 1870–1909, when the failure rate for national banks in the United States was 0.36, the failure rate of Canadian banking facilities (banks and their branches) was less than 0.10 (Schembri and Hawkins, 1988). Comparing average losses to depositors over many years, Williamson (1989) finds an annual average loss rate in the United States of 0.11 percent, and in Canada, 0.07 percent. Perhaps even more telling, during periods when both economies were buffeted by substantial regional or economy-wide shocks (the agricultural bust of the 1920s and the drastic decline in GNP during the Great Depression), Canada's banks performed exceptionally well. E. N. White (1984a, p. 132) finds:

In Canada, from 1920 to 1929, only one bank failed. The contraction of the banking industry was carried out by the remaining banks reducing the number of their offices by 13.2 percent. This was very near the 9.8 percent decline in the United States. . . . In spite of the many similarities with the United States, there were no bank failures in Canada during the dark years of 1929–1933. The number of bank offices fell by another 10.4 percent, reflecting the shocked state of the economy; yet this was far fewer than the 34.5 percent of all bank offices permanently closed in the United States.

Chapman and Westerfield (1942, p. 258) show that losses to depositors in Canada were typically confined to small banks, which "could not by any reasonable test be regarded as branch banks . . ."

Within the United States, failure rates were lower for large banks, particularly those that branched. This pattern is evident beginning with the first and second Banks of the United States. During the Panic of 1857, Southern branch banks all survived, while a handful of small Southern unit banks failed (Calomiris and Schweikart, 1991).

Of the 5,714 bank suspensions in the United States from 1921 to 1929, only 459 had capital in excess of $100,000. Large banks accounted for only 8 percent of all suspensions, though they comprised roughly 25 percent of the number of banks in operation (American Bankers Association, 1935, pp. 33–6). States that allowed branching in the United States saw lower failure rates in the 1920s (measured either in bank numbers or bank deposits) than other states. In the six states with the most firmly established branch-banking systems by 1925 (California, Louisiana, Massachusetts, Michigan, New York, and Ohio), only 13 banks failed. The failed banks held only 0.03 percent of the total deposits of these states (E. N. White, 1983, pp. 218–19).

The vulnerability of small banks to failure in the 1920s and 1930s has been documented by a number of other researchers, including Bremer (1935), E. N. White (1983, 1984a), and Calomiris (1992). Prior to the general economic decline of the Great Depression, failures by large branching banks were virtually nonexistent. From 1921 to 1929, only 37 branching banks operating 75 branches were liquidated. More than two-thirds of these banks operated a single branch, and only 6 of them operated three or more branches (U.S. House of Representatives, 1930, vol. 1, p. 462). The failure rate for branch banks was roughly 4 percent for the entire period 1921–1929. The bank failure rate for this same period for the country as a whole was upwards of 20 percent.

The states with long-standing branching systems were not particularity hard hit by the agricultural decline of the 1920s, which might explain their superior performance; but more detailed evidence on the incidence of failure confirms a link between unit banking and bank vulnerability. Regional comparisons confirm the view that the period prior to 1930 saw exceptional stability of branching banks even in the hard-hit "agricultural-crisis" areas of the country. Calomiris (1992) identifies 32 states that were most affected by the agricultural bust of the 1920s. In 1924, the 32 agricultural-crisis states contained 1,312 of the 3,007 branching facilities in the country. State-by-state decompositions of failures by type of bank are not readily available, but even if all branching failures had been concentrated in these states during the 1920s, the annual rate of branch-bank facility failure would be only 0.85 percent. Overall failure rates for these states typically were several times as large (Calomiris, 1992, p. 42 and Table 20).

In some cases, specific within-state comparisons of branch and unit banks are possible. In the states that prohibited new branching from 1924 to 1928 but allowed banks to continue to operate existing branches (Alabama, Arkansas, Indiana, Minnesota, Nebraska, Washington, and Wisconsin), the annual failure (disappearance) rate of branch banks was a remarkably low 0.02 percent. Using *The Bankers Encyclopedia* one can trace the presence or absence or banks from 1920 to 1929. In all cases, a careful review of entries revealed whether disappearances were due to acquisitions or to closings. Calomiris (1992) traces the entries for the branching banks of three states, chosen because they experienced high rates of overall bank failure and had a small number of branching banks (making data collection easier) and because branching banks in these states were allowed to operate branches outside their home city. In Mississippi, all 24 branches in operation in 1920 were located outside their home banks' cities. The same was true of Arizona's 20 branches in operation in 1920. In South Carolina, 13 out of 15 branches operated outside the home city. These states, therefore, provide a useful measure of the potential advantages of statewide branching during a crisis.

Arizona permitted statewide branching throughout the period. In Arizona in 1920, 8 banks operated 20 branches. By 1929, 2 of these (each operating one branch) had been acquired by larger branching banks. One of the branching banks (operating one branch) failed. In the interim, three new branching banks had entered. The average annual failure rate for total branching facilities was 1.6 percent for 1921–1929, compared to 4.3 percent for Arizona's state-chartered banks as a whole.

Mississippi had allowed branching outside home cities, but later prohibited branching, except for the establishment of limited agency facilities within home cities. Nevertheless, the existing statewide branches were permitted to continue operating. During the 1920s none of the 10 branching banks operating 24 branches failed, while the average annual failure rate for state-chartered banks as a whole was 1.4 percent.

In South Carolina from 1920 to 1929, 4 out of 8 branching banks in operation in 1920 closed, but all of these were banks that operated a single branch, and 2 of the 4 operated branches within their home city. Thus of the 23 towns or cities in which branch-banking facilities were located, 19 retained their branch-banking facilities. This is important because the lack of available banking facilities in thinly populated areas (where virtually all branches were located in Arizona, Mississippi, and South Carolina) increases transactions costs in those locations and can inhibit the flow of capital to worthy enterprises located there. The overall failure rate of existing branching facilities in South Carolina was 2.9

percent, compared to a rate of 4.9 percent for all state-chartered banks. Entry into branching was especially strong in South Carolina in the 1920s, and entrants apparently learned the importance of establishing multiple branches. Two new banks – The Peoples Bank of South Carolina and the South Carolina Savings Bank – entered during the 1920s and established 18 and 9 branches, respectively, operating outside the banks' home cities.

The lessons of the high survival rates of branching banks during the 1920s agricultural crisis were not lost on bankers and policymakers. As Calomiris (1992, Table 17) shows, in states where branching was allowed, it flourished and increasingly took the form of multibranch banks, where possible. Four of the eight states that had deliberately enacted deposit insurance plans as an alternative to allowing branch banking prior to the 1920s passed laws allowing branching by the end of the 1930s. By 1939, for the United States as a whole, 19 states permitted full branching and 17 allowed limited branching, compared to 12 statewide and 6 limited-branching systems in operation in 1924 (Chapman and Westerfield, 1942, pp. 126–30). Of the 18 states that permitted branches to exist early on, only 3 saw a reduction in the number of total facilities from 1924 to 1928. These reductions all occurred in states that prohibited the establishment of new branches, but allowed existing branches to be maintained (Georgia, Minnesota, and Washington). In all three cases, the reductions consisted of the departure (failure or closure) of a single bank. In all the other states that allowed branching to continue, but prohibited the establishment of new branches, the number of branches remained the same. In states that allowed new branching, branches uniformly increased at a rapid rate, often as the total number of banks declined, and branching thus came to constitute a much larger fraction of total banking facilities (Calomiris, 1992).

Moreover, the recovery of total bank asset levels was higher for state banking systems that permitted growth in branch banking. Arizona, Kentucky, Louisiana, Michigan, North Carolina, Ohio, Tennessee, and Virginia all saw relatively high rates of asset recovery in the late 1920s relative to other states experiencing agricultural distress. These were also the states that experienced the largest increases in the average size of banks. South Carolina was the only exception to the rule, with negative asset growth over the 1920s. But despite its overall banking contraction, South Carolina witnessed a more than doubling of its branch banking facilities from 1924 to 1929.

More formally, Calomiris (1992) regresses bank asset growth from 1920 to 1926, and 1920 to 1930, for a sample of 32 agricultural-crisis states, on a variety of control variables and branching dummies for limited and statewide branching. While the few degrees of freedom warrant a cautious interpretation, the branching indicator variables are both economically large and statistically significant, and they grow in importance with the longer time horizon. States that allowed branching enjoyed 40 percent higher growth in assets from 1920 to 1930, controlling for other differences.

In summary, evidence on the mortality rates and losses of failed banks indicate substantial advantages from branching. Branching also enhanced the banking system's ability to absorb weak institutions and to recover quickly from adverse shocks. It is worth noting that the examples of successful branching within the United States are all intrastate branching systems. A full nationwide system of banks would have done much better, as the example of Canada during the Depression illustrates. Indeed, at least two large branching banks (notably in the undiversified cotton-dependent economies of Georgia and South Carolina) did fail during the Depression.

1.3.3   Financial integration and diversification

In most countries, interregional capital flows are an important means of equalizing rates of return and providing diversification for capital providers. One way to examine whether nationwide branch banking facilitates diversification of banks' risk across regions is to ask whether branch banking systems do a superior job of equalizing interregional interest rates on loans.

There is a large literature on the question of capital market integration in the postbellum United States (Davis, 1965; Sylla, 1969, 1975; James, 1976a, 1976b, 1978; Eichengreen, 1984b; Snowden, 1987; Sushka and Barrett, 1984; Binder and Brown, 1991). This literature seeks to explain the rate of convergence of rates of return across regions of the United States during the late nineteenth century. While there has been some disagreement about which factors contributed most to the convergence in rates of return over time, all authors agree that the disparities in regional rates of return were the result of branching restrictions combined with the increasing geographical dispersion of economic opportunities. Bodenhorn (1990) shows that similarly large interregional differences in bank lending rates did not characterize the antebellum period. The antebellum environment differed both in terms of superior bank organization (branch banks operated in the South and coordinated groups of mutual-guaranty banks operated in Indiana, Ohio, and Iowa) and in less geographical dispersion of economic activity. These factors may explain the greater integration of capital markets prior to the Civil War.

Interregional interest rate differences continued to be important in the United States throughout the late nineteenth and early twentieth centuries. Table 1.1 provides data on interest rates for first-class two-name commercial paper in various cities during the 1890s, collected and published by *Bradstreet's* and quoted in Breckenridge (1899b). The accuracy of these data has been questioned by James (1978, pp. 252–62). James (1978, pp. 16–19) provides alternative measures of interregional interest rate differentials, using estimated average bank loan interest rates, which show a greater degree of convergence by 1900 (the maximum interregional interest rate differential falls from roughly 4 percent in the mid-1890s to 3 percent by 1900) than do those reported in *Bradstreet's*. In defence of the accuracy of the *Bradstreet's* data one can point to the appearance of reproductions of Table 1.1 in many contemporary academic and trade journals and books. These data were often used by proponents of branch banking to show the extent of segmentation of U.S. capital markets. If the data were grossly inaccurate, one would expect that their validity would have been questioned at the time. Regardless of whether one prefers the James or the *Bradstreet's* data, however, both indicate large, persistent interest differentials across regions in the postbellum period.

The commercial paper instruments priced in *Bradstreet's* were nearly default-free money-market instruments. Greef (1938, p. 56, footnote 65) shows that during the 1880s and 1890s, when many other debts were in default, commercial paper default rates were trivial (0.2 percent from 1886 to 1892 in New York according to one estimate; 0.05 percent from 1891 to 1895 in New York according to another estimate; 0.001 percent from 1897 to 1902 in Chicago according to a third estimate). Commercial paper was uniquely liquid during banking panics (Greef, 1938, p. 57). During the Great Depression default rates on commercial paper remained extraordinarily low (0.03 percent in 1931 and 0.02 percent in 1932, according to Greef, 1938, p. 309).

Clearly, the commercial paper market neither provided a means for interregional diversification (risky loans simply were not admitted to the market) nor a means for completely integrating the national capital market for riskless instruments (otherwise riskless rates of return would have been identical across regions). The large interregional differences in essentially riskless returns show that the elasticity of capital flows across regions in the United States was low. Commercial paper was purchased mainly by bankers, and commercial paper houses received their bridge financing from local banks. The reliance on local banks for funding

Table 1.1. *Average rate of discount on first-class two-name commercial paper in 43 cities of the United States, for the years 1893–1897, as reported weekly in* Bradstreet's

	Lower rates – percent					Higher rates – percent				
Place	1893	1894	1895	1896	1897	1893	1894	1895	1896	1897
Boston	5.27	2.76	3.19	4.92	2.99	6.60	3.77	4.84	6.29	4.03
New York	6.73	2.90	3.55	5.40	3.46	8.72	3.65	4.24	6.17	4.00
Baltimore	6.11	4.62	4.00	4.00	4.09	6.63	5.23	4.82	4.50	4.64
Hartford	6.09	3.43	4.06	5.72	3.70	7.16	4.32	4.61	6.67	4.27
Philadelphia	6.15	3.46	4.31	5.57	3.69	7.01	5.31	5.56	6.27	8.88
Providence	6.12	3.81	4.65	6.07	4.24	6.80	4.83	5.25	6.82	4.96
Cincinnati	5.88	4.60	4.83	5.61	4.12	6.96	5.44	5.61	6.17	5.17
Chicago	6.49	5.24	5.33	6.54	5.08	7.19	6.25	6.24	6.92	6.07
Pittsburgh	5.94	5.28	5.96	6.00	6.00	6.46	6.00	6.01	7.00	7.00
New Orleans	7.01	4.98	4.76	6.50	6.00	7.61	6.34	6.65	7.78	6.88
St. Louis	6.65	5.38	5.25	6.23	6.00	7.74	7.01	6.98	7.44	7.00
Portland, ME	6.00	6.00	6.00	6.00	6.00	6.00	6.00	6.00	6.00	6.00
Richmond	6.00	6.00	6.00	6.00	6.00	7.00	7.00	6.00	6.00	6.00
Buffalo	6.11	6.00	6.00	6.00	5.92	7.78	7.65	7.00	7.94	7.92
Memphis	7.48	5.98	5.38	6.25	5.42	8.03	7.96	7.86	8.00	7.42
San Francisco	7.11	5.80	5.94	6.00	—	8.48	6.78	6.32	6.00	—
Milwaukee	6.98	6.11	6.00	6.28	6.00	7.00	6.98	7.00	7.15	7.00
Indianapolis	7.15	6.69	6.00	6.00	6.00	8.00	8.00	8.00	8.00	8.00
Cleveland	7.00	6.88	6.00	6.00	6.00	7.00	7.00	7.00	7.00	7.00
Detroit	7.00	6.23	6.00	6.84	6.00	7.19	7.23	6.09	6.84	6.00
St. Paul	7.61	7.69	6.00	6.34	5.38	8.00	7.69	6.32	7.69	7.38
Nashville	8.00	7.65	5.96	6.00	5.75	8.00	8.00	8.00	8.00	6.53
Louisville	7.03	6.40	6.78	6.94	6.96	7.07	7.23	7.00	6.96	7.00
Minneapolis	7.57	6.98	6.50	7.21	6.25	8.00	7.82	7.84	7.96	7.40
Kansas City	6.90	6.26	6.53	8.00	6.84	8.00	8.00	7.86	9.57	8.48
St. Joseph	6.84	7.00	7.00	7.00	7.00	7.84	8.00	8.00	8.00	8.00
Charleston	7.13	7.00	7.00	7.00	7.00	7.84	8.00	8.00	8.00	8.00
Los Angeles	7.28	7.00	7.00	7.00	7.00	9.28	9.00	9.00	9.00	9.00
Duluth	7.96	7.01	7.00	7.38	6.90	9.00	7.88	8.00	8.26	8.00
Galveston	7.01	7.00	7.00	7.53	8.00	8.00	8.00	8.00	8.00	8.00
Mobile	7.78	8.00	8.00	8.00	8.00	8.00	8.00	8.00	8.00	8.00
Omaha	8.00	8.00	8.00	8.00	7.90	8.65	10.00	10.00	10.00	9.80
Savannah	8.00	8.00	8.00	8.00	7.96	8.80	10.00	10.00	10.00	9.96
Atlanta	8.00	8.00	8.00	8.00	8.00	8.03	8.00	8.00	8.00	8.00
Birmingham	8.00	8.00	8.00	8.00	8.00	9.46	10.00	10.00	10.00	9.88
Houston	8.00	8.00	8.00	8.00	8.00	8.00	8.00	8.00	8.00	8.00
Portland, OR	8.00	8.00	8.00	8.00	8.00	10.00	10.00	10.00	10.00	10.00
Salt Lake City	8.00	8.00	8.00	8.00	8.00	10.00	10.00	10.00	10.00	10.00
Little Rock	8.07	8.00	8.00	8.00	8.00	9.88	9.84	10.00	10.00	8.73
Dallas	8.78	7.57	8.42	8.92	8.00	10.38	9.15	10.00	10.00	10.00
Tacoma	10.00	9.36	9.00	9.00	9.00	11.69	11.00	11.00	11.00	11.00
Seattle	10.00	10.00	10.00	10.00	9.84	12.00	12.00	12.00	12.00	11.84
Denver	10.00	10.00	10.00	10.00	10.00	10.38	12.00	12.00	12.00	12.00

Source: Breckenridge (1899b, p. 7).

limited the ability of the banking industry in the nation as a whole to channel funds elastically through the commercial paper market to their best use. The immobility of capital even in the riskless market likely reflected problems of delegated monitoring (Diamond, 1984; Calomiris and Kahn, 1991; Calomiris, Kahn, and Krasa, 1991). Local commercial paper houses were funded by local banks because banks made sure that they performed their duties as "delegated monitors" properly. The financing of commercial paper dealers was limited to local banks and was therefore constrained by local bank capital, because of problems of enforcing appropriate screening and monitoring of potential borrowers. Local bank capital was, in turn, limited by the capital of the local economy. A study of national banks by the Comptroller of the Currency in 1897 showed that out-of-state holdings of bank stock were limited. The largest out-of-state holdings were for the Western and Pacific regions, which had outsiders' holdings of less than 12 percent. Citing this evidence, Breckenridge (1899b, p. 10) concludes that "there is nothing which takes the place of branch banks. The local borrower is at the mercy of the local lender."

The exclusivity of the commercial paper market, combined with limitations on interregional financing of commercial paper, kept the commercial paper market small compared to total bank loans and discounts. For banks in the nineteenth century, the ratio of commercial bills to total loans and discounts never exceeded 3 percent and averaged 1.3 percent for 1892–1897 (Breckenridge, 1899b, p. 9). As late as the 1920s, the number of firms issuing single-name (open-market) paper in the United States and Canada never exceeded 2,754. In 1930, 1,674 firms issued open-market paper, of which only 292 originated in cities west of the Mississippi (Minneapolis, Dallas, Kansas City, and San Francisco), and only 9 originated in Canada. Firms in the textiles, foodstuffs, and metals industries accounted for 1,101 of the 1,674 firms. At the trough of the Great Depression, in 1933, only 548 firms issued open-market paper (Greef, 1938, pp. 246–8). Default rates remained low on commercial paper during the Depression because the quantity of short-term paper could fall quickly as default risk rose.

Data on interest rates for bank loans during the early twentieth century provide additional evidence of financial market segmentation. Riefler (1930, p. 79) reports data on prime commercial loans, interbank loans, and loans secured by stock or warehouse receipts for major cities in the United States at the end of 1926. The ranges reported in Table 1.2 are *not* the highest and lowest rates charged, but rather "the rates at which the bulk of the loans of each class are made by reporting banks." Thus some of the rates charged in these locations might have been higher

Table 1.2. *Money rates in federal reserve bank and branch cities: prevailing rates charged customers during the week ending December 15, 1926*

	Prime commercial loans	Interbank loans	Loans secured by prime stock exchange collateral		Loans secured by warehouse receipts	Cattle loans	Range
			Demand	Time			
Boston	4¾	4½	5	5	—	—	4½–5
New York	4½–4¾	4½–5	5	4¾–5	—	4½–5	4½–5
Buffalo	5–6	4¾–5	5–6	5–6	6	—	4¾–6
Philadelphia	4½–4¾	5	5	4¾–5	5–5½	—	4½–5½
Cleveland	6	5	6	6	—	5–6	5–6
Cincinnati	5½–6	5½–6	5½–6	6	6–7	—	5½–7
Pittsburgh	5–6	5–6	5–6	6	6	—	5–6
Richmond	5½–6	4¾–5½	4¾–5¼	5½–6	5½–6	—	4¾–6
Baltimore	5–5¾	5–5½	5–6	5½–5¾	5½–6	—	5–6
Atlanta	5–6	5–6	5–6	5–6	5–6	—	5–6
Birmingham	5–6	5–6	6	6	6	—	5–6
Jacksonville	4½–6	6	5–6	6	5–6	—	4½–6
Nashville	6	5½–6	5–6	6	5½–6	—	5–6
New Orleans	5½–6	5–6	5½–6	5½–6	5½–6	—	5–6
Chicago	4¾–5	5	5	5–5½	4¾–5½	5–5½	4¾–5½
Detroit	4½–6	5–6	5–6	5–6	5–6	—	4½–6
St. Louis	4¾–5½	5–5½	5–5½	5–5½	4¾–6	5½–6	4¾–6
Little Rock	5½–6	6	6	6–7	6–8	8	5½–8
Louisville	5½–6	5	6	5½–6	6	—	5½–6
Minneapolis	4½–5½	5–6	4¾–5½	4⅞–6	4¾–6	—	4½–6
Helena	8	6–8	8	8	6–8	6–8	6–8
Kansas City	5–5½	6	5	5–6	5–6	6–7	5–7
Denver	6	6	5½–6	5½–6	5½–8	6–8	5½–8
Oklahoma City	5–6	6	6	6–7	6	7–8	5–8
Omaha	4¾–7	6	5½	5½–6	5–7	7	4¾–7
Dallas	4½–6	5	6–7	5–7	6–7	6–7	4½–7
El Paso	8	6–7	8	8	7–8	6–10	6–10
Houston	5–6	5	5–6	5–6	5–7	6–8	5–8
San Francisco	5–5½	5–5½	5–6	5–6	6	—	5–6
Los Angeles	6	6	6–7	6–7	7	6	6–7
Portland	6	6	6–7	6	6	6	6–7
Salt Lake City	6	6	6	6	7	7–8	6–8
Seattle	6–7	6–6½	6–7	6–7	6–7	—	6–7
Spokane	6	6	—	6	7	6–8	6–8
Range	4½–6	4½–8	4¾–8	4¾–8	4¾–8	4½–10	—

Source: Riefler (1930, p. 79).

Table 1.3. *Cities having highest and lowest annual average interest rates on six major types of loans, by years, 1919–1925*

Year	Highest average rate for six types of loans		Lowest average rate for six types of loans		Difference between lowest and highest
	City	Rate (%)	City	Rate (%)	
1919	El Paso	7.82	New York	5.45	2.37
1920	El Paso	7.99	New York	6.22	1.77
1921	El Paso	7.92	New York	6.31	1.61
1922	El Paso	7.97	Boston	5.05	2.92
1923	Helena	8.00	New York	5.18	2.82
1924	El Paso	7.74	Boston	4.59	3.15
1925	El Paso	7.36	Boston	4.48	2.28

Source: Riefler (1930, p. 95).

or lower than indicated by the ranges reported here. Even at this late date, there were substantial differences in loan interest rates for these low-risk commercial loans. In all categories, the range of differences across cities within the United States was equal to or in excess of 3.25 percent. Even within cities, differences in rates were often between 1 and 2 percent. New York and Boston showed the lowest range of rates and among the smallest within-city range of rates, while El Paso, Helena, Spokane, Little Rock, Omaha, and Denver showed the highest maximum rates and wider ranges of rates within their respective locations. Riefler (1930, p. 95) also reports average rates charged on bank loans in selected cities for 1919–1925, which are reproduced in Table 1.3. Of course, all of these are *city* loans, so the comparable rates on loans in peripheral areas outside the high-interest-rate cities likely were even higher.

Riefler (1930, p. 80) argues that the rate differentials were not attributable to differences in risk:

Fairly consistent differences are reported between the rates charged customers in different cities, but they apply to loans where the risk is constant as well as to those where differentials in risk can be inferred. Banks in the city of Chicago, for example, consistently reported higher rates for loans secured by Liberty bonds than did banks in the city of New York, yet Liberty bonds are just as secure for loans in Chicago as in New York.

Summarizing these and other related data, Riefler (1930, p. 82) writes:

So far as rates customarily charged on the bulk of customers' loans are concerned, therefore, differentials between cities and between different types of collateral security appear as frequently and consistently in those cases where there is no difference in risk involved as in those cases where differentials in risk can be inferred to exist.

Riefler (1930, p. 94) explains within-bank differences in interest rates as having at least as much to do with market power as with risk:

... good "risks" are not distinguished so much by the type of collateral upon which they borrow as by their importance to the bank, the size of their balances, the amount of business which they bring to it, and their ability to establish banking connections elsewhere. These are the qualities which induce rate concessions, and distinguish those borrowers who pay the highest and lowest rates at the same bank on the same type of loan.

The establishment of the Federal Reserve System, with its intent to unify the national market, was not successful because it had little effect on the industrial organization of banking. Peripheral regions continued to be isolated from the main sources of capital in the East, and local bankers continued to enjoy substantial monopoly rents in the lending market. In part, the failure of the Fed to integrate the national money market resulted from the costs of Fed membership (which kept small peripheral banks from joining the system) and the resistance to branch banking, which would have increased membership in the Fed and promoted interregional capital flows and local competition in peripheral areas (E. N. White, 1983, pp. 149–87).

The interest rate differentials reported in Tables 1.1, 1.2, and 1.3 are large in comparison to similar interest rate differentials within and across countries. Using data on interest rates, exchange rates, and bill of exchange prices, Calomiris and Hubbard (1996) show that the comparable real interest differential between London and New York from the 1890s on was bounded by 3 percent and averaged roughly 2 percent. Breckenridge (1899b, p. 6) also discusses international interest rate differences:

... as compared with an international system which hurries capital across frontiers and over seas, for the sake of differences of often less than one percent, it might better be said that the United States has nothing in the way of arbitrage apparatus for domestic purposes, in any worthy sense of the name.

By the criterion of tolerance for riskless interest rate divergence, one could argue that the Eastern United States was less integrated with the Western United States than it was with the rest of the world.

Studies of interest rate variation within other countries show similarly small differences in interest rates. Comparing the United States to the branch banking systems of Europe, Breckenridge (1899b, p. 5) writes:

... there is not one of the leading States of Western Europe in which this process of equalization between domestic discount markets is not already far advanced.

Take whichever of these one may, it will be found that the price of capital in provincial cities varies in close and usual correspondence to the rates prevailing in the principal financial centers. In Germany, for example, there are no less than 260 towns where paper of a standard quality is discounted at precisely the same rate paid upon like securities in Berlin. In France there are more than 200 communities in which borrowers in good standing and credit can obtain loans on terms as favorable as those accorded in Paris. Similar conditions exist in Italy, Belgium, and Holland. In England again the country bank rate is seldom more than five or less than four percent an any part of the Kingdom, while in Scotland the banks of issue have agreed to charge, and do charge, identical rates at each of their thousand banking offices.

Gillett (1900, pp. 185–6) provides some additional information on interest rate divergence within other countries. Over the last 15 years of the nineteenth century, interest rates across regions in Denmark typically differed by less than 0.5 percent, while the level of interest rates varied within the range of 2.5 to 6 percent. In 260 peripheral towns in Germany and 200 towns in France interest rates were identical to those charged in Berlin and Paris, respectively. H. White (1902, pp. 53–4) claims that "the rate of interest in the smaller towns of the West [in Canada] is only 1 or 2 per cent. higher than in the large cities of the East on the same kind of loans." H. White may have been referring to the findings of a study in 1898 that found "the difference in interest paid by high-class borrowers of Montreal and Toronto and the ordinary merchants of the Northwest was not more than 1 or 2 per cent." (Chapman and Westerfield, 1942, p. 194). A similar study of Canadian interest rate differentials (cited by Willit, 1930, p. 185) also concludes that "so perfectly is this distribution of capital made, that as between the highest class of borrower in Montreal or Toronto, and the ordinary merchant in the Northwest, the difference in interest paid is not more than one or two percent." Johnson (1910, p. 92) writes that the "transference of funds from sluggish to active communities is the inevitable result of a system of branch banking and is the cause of the tendency of the rate of interest toward uniformity in all parts of Canada." Breckenridge (1899a, p. 55) concludes:

If a substantial uniformity in the rate of interest, extending to hundreds of widely separated markets, has been established in each of these countries [Canada, England, Scotland, Germany, and France] by means of branch banking, the "theory" that like results will follow the sanction of this device by the United States is entitled to some respect.

The fact that comparisons of low-risk interest rate differentials in other countries are typically for bank loans rather than for commercial paper illustrates another peculiar consequence of the American unit banking system – the reliance on commercial paper. In particular, an exceptional characteristic of U.S. financial markets was the use of commercial paper rather than bank trade acceptances to finance inter-regional movements of goods. Only in the United States, two-name commercial paper, and later single-name paper, dominated the scene (Myers, 1931, pp. 47–52). As in many other areas of financial innovation in U.S. capital markets during the late nineteenth century (including innovations in life insurance, futures markets, mortgage securitization, and investment banking), the exceptional growth of the commercial paper market was an outgrowth, in part, of the failure of the U.S. banking system to provide an integrated national market for commercial credit.

Trade acceptances were defined by R. H. Treman (1919) as follows:

A trade acceptance is a time draft drawn by the seller of merchandise on the buyer for the purchase price of the goods and accepted by the buyer, payable on a certain date, at a certain place designated on its face. (Quoted in Steiner, 1922, p. 113)

In essence, a trade acceptance is "an acknowledgment of the receipt of goods and a promise to pay for the same at a fixed date and place" (Steiner, 1922, p. 114). Bankers' acceptances financing trade were secured by goods in transit.

The advantage of trade acceptances from the standpoint of the seller of goods is the reduction in the need for credit during the interim period between the time goods are produced and the time payment is received from the buyer. The legal liability of sellers for delivery of goods as promised (the "doctrine of implied warranties") encouraged sellers (or their agents) to maintain ownership of the goods while in transit and to obtain credit to finance the costs of shipment. The commonly used alternative to the acceptance to finance trade within the United States during the nineteenth century was the "open account" system, in which sellers transfer goods to buyers, grant temporary trade credit to buyers (often for more than a month), and finance the float with bank credit or commercial paper.

The absence of bankers acceptances in the nineteenth-century United States is especially strange given the high costs of credit in the periphery, especially during the crop moving seasons. If bank credit was relatively costly in the region of production (as Table 1.1 shows, it often must have been), then a trade acceptance would be a useful means for the seller to obtain cheaper credit. The seller could trade his acceptance (say, on New York) for deposits in his home bank. The acceptance would also be a superior credit instrument to the extent that creditworthiness could be ascertained better by a local bank lending officer than by a distant merchant (Steiner, 1922, pp. 161–4).

Why then were trade acceptances so rare? One answer revolves around unit banking. The difficulty of a seller's obtaining credit from a distant unit bank could explain the disuse of acceptances. A local office of a nationwide branching bank, however, could provide the needed monitoring of the seller's goods and general creditworthiness, but provide delivery of the acceptance at another location. Interestingly, trade acceptances were used to a relatively large degree during the existence of the second Bank of the United States, but not as much before or afterward in the pre-World War I era. (After World War I, acceptances became more common, under the sponsorship of the Federal Reserve System, which saw them as the means to fulfill the dictates of the "real bills doctrine.") From 1823 to 1834, trade acceptances on the books of the Bank of the United States increased from $1.9 million to $16.3 million, while commercial paper increased from $22.5 million to $33.7 million (Myers, 1931, p. 50). Myers (1931, pp. 49–50) quotes Biddle's testimony describing the connection between the second BUS and acceptances:

The crop of Tennessee is purchased by merchants who ship it to New Orleans, giving their bills founded on it to the branch at Nashville, which furnishes them with notes. These notes are in time brought to New York for purchasing supplies for Tennessee. They are paid in New York and the Nashville bank becomes the debtor of the branch at New York. The Nashville branch repays them by drafts given to the branch at New York on the branch at New Orleans, where its bills have been sent, and the branch in New York brings home the amount by selling its drafts on the branch at New Orleans; or the New Orleans branch remits.

Bodenhorn (1990, p. 37) finds that antebellum banks in the Southern branch-banking states of Tennessee and Kentucky, and in the mutual-insurance system of Indiana (a closely intertwined system of unit banks), had much higher holdings of trade acceptances than country (unit) banks in Pennsylvania. Comparable detailed data on bank asset holdings are not available for other states.

Similarly, in Canada's branch-banking system trade acceptances provided credit for transfer of goods from the point of production, freeing the seller from having to borrow on his personal credit to finance the transfer of goods to the buyer:

Throughout the entire transaction, from the purchase from the farmer to the final sale to the eastern customer, the bank practically has title to all agricultural products which are being moved by means of its funds (Johnson, 1910, p. 48).

Clearly, unit banks would be unable to manage such transactions across regions.

1.3.4   Access to remote areas

One way in which branch banking facilitated bank diversification was by allowing banks access to thinly populated areas. Because of the relatively low overhead costs of establishing a branch office, branches could operate in locations where unit banks could not. This allowed expansion into new areas and activities and led to diversification of bank portfolios.

Calomiris and Schweikart (1988) show that in Georgia and Virginia during the antebellum period the locations of new branches closely followed the economic opportunities of the time. In Virginia, the opportunities included the rich grain-producing area of the Shenandoah Valley during the boom in the wheat market of the 1850s. In Georgia new offices followed the expansion of cotton production westward. Both movements involved diversification of loans by reducing the coincidence of risks among bank borrowers (from weather, factor prices, and product prices).

Evanoff (1988) provides a detailed empirical comparison of entry into remote areas by branch and unit banking systems within the United States. He measures access by the number of banking offices per square mile at the county level in 1980 and controls for other factors, including population and income. The results are striking. Branching increases the number of banking offices per square mile by 65 percent in remote areas.

Root (1897, p. 10) makes the same argument less formally for the Canadian branching system. He provides a plot of banking facilities in Canada in 1897 and notes a substantial presence of branch banking offices in remote and thinly populated locations. Chapman and Westerfield (1942, pp. 342–3) point out that the number of persons per banking office in Canada in 1940 was 3,410, compared to 7,325 in the United States. They also show that even in the most sparsely populated provinces the number of persons per banking office was in all cases less than 4,230. The comparable number for rural unit-banking states was sometimes much larger. For example, if one uses census data on population in 1940 (from US. Department of Commerce, 1975, Part 1, pp. 24–37) and Federal Reserve data on the number of banks in 1941 (commercial banks plus mutual savings banks, as reported in Board of Governors of the Federal Reserve System, 1976, pp. 24–32), the comparable ratios are: Illinois, 9,500; Texas, 7,700; and West Virginia, 10,500.

1.3.5   Reserve and capital ratios

Temin (1969, pp. 73–7) was among the first to relate cross-sectional evidence on bank reserve holdings across regions in the United States to the riskiness of banks. He finds that in the 1830s banks in the Northwest held substantially higher ratios of reserves to liabilities than banks in other parts of the country. The largest difference was between the New England banks (with a reserve ratio of 0.06 in 1834), and the Northwest banks (with a reserve ratio of 0.46 in 1834). Temin argues that the reserve ratios in the Northwest had to be high to inspire confidence in the banks. In part, this reflected the perceived riskiness of banks' assets, as well as the absence of coordination among Western banks, which was present to a greater degree in the East, for example under New England's Suffolk System (see Calomiris and Kahn, 1996).

To the extent that branch banking reduced the riskiness of banks by allowing diversification in loans across locations it should have reduced banks' demand for reserves. In addition to reductions in bank-specific asset risk through diversification, interbank coordination (motivated by advantages of diversification across banks) could have reduced depositors' risk. As Calomiris and Kahn (1991) and Calomiris, Kahn, and Krasa (1991) argue, reserves may serve as "bonding" to reward monitoring by some depositors with a first-come first-served preference. To the extent branching reduces the costs of monitoring by other banks (through the creation of lower-cost monitoring and insurance arrangements among banks, as argued above), then branching could reduce the riskiness of deposits and the demand for reserves, independent of bank-specific diversification of assets.

Inferences about risk from comparisons of reserve ratios across banks are complicated by the need to adjust for other differences. For example, if one bank has a higher capital-to-asset ratio than another and a lower reserve-to-asset ratio, the riskiness of its deposits could be the same for a given riskiness of its assets. Thus, variation in asset risk due to location and variation in capital ratios (a substitute risk buffer for depositors) complicate drawing inferences about bank risk from reserve ratios. Nevertheless, there are a few relatively well-controlled "experiments" useful for isolating the effect of branching on bank asset risk through the window of reserve demand.

Large branching banks in Georgia in the 1850s had lower ratios of reserves to assets and lower capital-to-asset ratios than unit banks in Georgia. For example, in 1856 the four large branching banks had a capital ratio of 0.27 and a reserve ratio of 0.09, while all reporting banks averaged a capital ratio of 0.46 and a reserve ratio of 0.20 (Calomiris and Schweikert, 1988).

Comparisons across locations do not control for all relevant differences in regulations or economic environment. Nevertheless, such comparisons do provide some support for the proposition that branch-banking systems entail lower risk than do unit-banking systems. Gillett (1900, pp. 203–4) compares reserve ratios of national banks in the United States to those of British joint stock banks in the late nineteenth century. He finds reserve ratios of U.S. national banks were more than double their British counterparts.

The comparison between the United States and Canada is more revealing. Table 1.4 compares loan-to-asset and capital-to-asset ratios of Canadian banks and U.S. national banks in the various states for 1904, a relatively calm year before any substantial presence of branching within (postbellum) state-chartered U.S. banking. Using the loan-to-asset ratio (rather than the reserve-to-asset ratio) to control for the ratio of risky assets biases the results against finding lower asset risk for Canadian banks, since relatively unrestricted Canadian loans, and the complement of loans and reserves in Canada, were probably riskier. Securities other than national government bonds accounted for roughly equal shares of bank assets in the two economies (8 percent in Canada, and 9 percent for national banks), but Canadian banks held fewer government bonds and more of other investments. The comparison of national banks across states allows one to maintain constancy of the regulatory regime to identify state-specific environmental factors. Data are from Johnson (1910, Appendix C) and Board of Governors of the Federal Reserve System (1959, passim).

Table 1.4 shows that the capital ratios for American and Canadian banks were roughly comparable, but the American banks had much lower loan ratios. This is consistent with greater portfolio risk for American banks. That is, banks had to hold more "reserves" (broadly defined) to reduce depositors' risk in the American system for any given ratio of deposits to assets.

The introduction of branch banking in California was associated with a reduction in capital ratios and an increase in loan ratios for state-chartered and national banks, as shown in Table 1.5. Branching began in 1909. By June 1928, 63 California banks were operating 826 branches (Board of Governors of the Federal Reserve System, 1929, p. 102). Fourteen of these were national banks (operating 478 branches), and 39 were state banks (operating 348 branches). National banks in California maintained the same loan ratio in 1928 as they had in 1904, but substantially reduced their capital ratio from 0.22 to 0.12. Over this same period, other banks in the United States maintained roughly the same ratios of loans-to-assets and capital-to-assets as in 1904. Data for the ratios of all member banks of the Federal Reserve System for 1928, which include national banks and state member banks, are identical to the ratios of the

Table 1.4. *Loans-to-asset and capital-to-asset ratios, U.S. national banks and Canadian banks, June 1904*

	Loans / Assets	Capital + Surplus/Assets
Canada	0.73	0.19
United States	0.55	0.20
Alabama	0.53	0.24
Arizona	0.44	0.17
Arkansas	0.60	0.24
California	0.51	0.22
Colorado	0.38	0.12
Connecticut	0.52	0.35
Delaware	0.53	0.32
Florida	0.53	0.20
Georgia	0.64	0.27
Idaho	0.53	0.19
Illinois	0.57	0.16
Indiana	0.50	0.19
Iowa	0.61	0.20
Kansas	0.54	0.19
Kentucky	0.53	0.24
Louisiana	0.59	0.21
Maine	0.58	0.31
Maryland	0.53	0.23
Massachusetts	0.58	0.23
Michigan	0.61	0.18
Minnesota	0.61	0.20
Mississippi	0.61	0.26
Missouri	0.52	0.16
Montana	0.62	0.20
Nebraska	0.53	0.17
Nevada	0.64	0.21
New Hampshire	0.45	0.27
New Jersey	0.54	0.26
New Mexico	0.55	0.21
New York	0.53	0.17
North Carolina	0.64	0.25
North Dakota	0.67	0.21
Ohio	0.57	0.21
Oklahoma	0.57	0.30
Oregon	0.45	0.16
Pennsylvania	0.53	0.23
Rhode Island	0.57	0.38
South Carolina	0.60	0.26
South Dakota	0.59	0.21
Tennessee	0.55	0.19
Texas	0.57	0.29
Utah	0.48	0.20
Vermont	0.46	0.34
Virginia	0.58	0.21
Washington	0.56	0.14
West Virginia	0.57	0.23
Wisconsin	0.61	0.17
Wyoming	0.61	0.21

Sources: Board of Governors of the Federal Reserve System (1959, passim); Johnson (1910, Appendix C).

Table 1.5. *Loan-to-asset and capital-to-asset ratios of California state and national banks, June 1928*

	State banks	National banks	All U.S. Banks belonging to Federal Reserve System
Loans/Assets	0.60	0.55	0.54
Capital + Surplus/Assets	0.10	0.12	0.19

Sources: Board of Governors of the Federal Reserve System (1959, pp. 152–9) and Board of Governors of the Federal Reserve System (1976, pp. 72–3).

national banks reported in Table 1.4 (Board of Governors of the Federal Reserve System, 1976, p. 72).

Under the provisions of the McFadden-Pepper Act of 1927, national bank branch locations were more restricted than those of state banks. Thus one might expect California's state banks to have achieved better diversification and therefore to have been able to maintain lower capital ratios and higher loan ratios than its national banks. Table 1.5 confirms that prediction. In 1928 state banks had capital ratios of 0.10 and loan ratios of 0.60, which represented a substantial improvement over their 1904 ratios of 0.19 and 0.57, respectively.

1.3.6   Summary

In summary, bank balance sheets provide ex ante evidence that branching banks were perceived as less risky, which complements the ex ante evidence on bank note discount rates of branching banks, the ex post evidence on bank failures, and the other indicators of diversification discussed above. Taken together the evidence shows that unit banks were less diversified, more vulnerable to failure, less able to grow in the aftermath of adverse shocks, less efficient in their use of scarce bank capital and reserves, less able to provide credit at low cost during times of peak demand, less able to provide services in remote areas, less competitive in local markets, less able to transfer capital across regions, and less able to finance interregional commodities trade. It is no wonder that the unit banking system was so uncommon in the international history of banking. The main puzzle is why it persisted so long, despite its disadvantages, in the American banking system.

1.4   The persistence of branching restrictions in U.S. banking

One can divide the question of why branch banking has been so limited in the U.S. experience into two parts: First, why did the U.S. system start with a system based primarily on unit banks (with the notable exception of the South); and, second, why did limitations on branch banking persist in many states, despite the obvious advantages (enumerated above) of liberalizing branching laws? Once one poses the question this way, the puzzling predominance of unit banking in the American experience can be analyzed *historically*. Rather than offering a disembodied "model" of the choice for unit banking, I will offer a model embedded in a "story" – a story in which the economic, legal, and political contexts in which banks originally were chartered and regulated combined with subsequent historical events to produce a particular (in retrospect, possibly a very inefficient) set of regulations. Before one can answer the difficult questions about governments' choices of industrial organization for banks, one must understand the context in which the controversies over branching arose.

1.4.1   A brief history of bank chartering

The story of unit banking in the United States begins with the historical motivations that underlay the chartering of banks. In the beginning, of course, there were no banks in America. Colonial "commercial banking" was carried on as a part of general merchant enterprises, along with importing and exporting, insurance, and transport. While some colonials called for the formal establishment of banks to promote greater liquidity, land development, and commerce (notably, Franklin, 1729), there was substantial resistance to the chartering of banks in the colonies and in England. The corporate form based upon limited liability was viewed with great suspicion – sometimes it was seen as a means for avoiding responsibility for debts incurred – and the granting of such a corporate form was seen as a privilege of government to be used selectively, until the mid-nineteenth century. Moreover, money-issuing authority for banks was sometimes viewed as a means to government-sponsored inflation, which was feared by creditors. (For a review of the debates over the inflationary effects of early currency creation by governments and banks see Bullock, 1895, 1900; Davis, 1900, 1911; Nettles, 1934; Lester, 1939; Ernst, 1973; Hurst, 1973; Brock, 1975; McCusker, 1978; Smith, 1985a, 1985b; Wicker, 1985; Michener, 1987, 1988; Calomiris, 1988a, 1988b; M. Schweitzer, 1989).

The first commercial bank in the United States, the Bank of North

America, was chartered in 1781 by the Confederacy to help finance the Revolution, was opposed by some from its inception, and was forced to abandon its controversial national charter to take up business as a state-chartered bank, first in Delaware, and later (in 1787) in Pennsylvania (Hurst, 1973, p. 7). The history of the Bank of North America illustrates two important elements of the political and legal context of early bank chartering in the United States. First, the constitutional basis for chartering banks by the federal government was unclear and highly controversial. Second, bank charters granting the right to issue money and allowing limited liability for stockholders were not freely available to all who wanted them, but were seen as a privilege and as a tool of the state (and, possibly, federal) governments to be used to achieve specific, appropriate objectives.

Americans were free to sign contracts of indentured servitude, but they were not free to establish limited-liability corporations, in banking or in other areas. As Hughes (1976, 1991), Hartz (1948), Handlin and Handlin (1947), and many others emphasize, the legal system of the United States grew out of the mercantilistic colonial system, in which the guiding principle was the exchange of monopoly privileges (including charters, land grants, exclusions of competition, and licensing) for advantages to the government (including new sources of government revenue, and strategic military advances). This was a system for promoting expansion, but in a heavily controlled atmosphere, in which society's interests (as interpreted by the government) took precedence over individual gain and the freedom to contract in particular ways. In banking, in particular, government would decide which activities and places warranted the establishment of banks and would tax, regulate, and own substantial shares of the banks that were created.

Early state chartering of commercial banks differed greatly across states with respect to the scope of bank activities and assets permitted and required, bank capital requirements, collateralization of note issues, extended liability of directors and stockholders, and a host of other regulations, including those pertaining to branching (Sumner, 1896; Knox, 1900; Dewey, 1910; Redlich, 1951; Hammond, 1957; Fenstermaker, 1965; Rockoff, 1972; Schweikart, 1988a; Calomiris and Schweikart, 1988; and Bodenhorn, 1990). Prior to 1838 charters were typically granted by state legislatures upon special request. Even banks within the same state often faced very different regulations on their lending and financing.

The Panic of 1837 was a watershed in the history of bank chartering in the United States. The destruction of banks brought an increase in the demand for new banks and offered an opportunity to change the form of chartering throughout the country. In the North, the "free-banking" movement emerged as a means to allow entry into banking for anyone willing to abide by the terms of a common set of regulations. Following New York's example in 1838, some systems (primarily in the North) permitted free entry into banking. Banks under the free-banking laws of a particular state faced many regulations, including a 100 percent reserve requirement against note issues in the form of government bonds (see Rockoff, 1972, for the details of the different state laws). Despite the spread of free banking in the 1840s and 1850s, many banking systems (notably in the South) continued to rely on special chartering, requiring that applicants demonstrate a public need for new banks before granting a new charter.

As states established new charters for banks, they typically allowed older chartering forms to continue. For example, in Ohio in the 1850s there were four different types of banking institutions in existence: old individually chartered banks, and three newer types of bank charters, including free banks and insured banks. In New York, there were three chartered forms: insured banks (dating from 1829), limited-liability free banks, and banks with unlimited liability. Some bank charters were perpetual, some were limited in duration. In some cases, banks were chartered to promote specific projects, including canals, bridges, roads, and railroads (for example, the Manhattan Company of New York was chartered to provide water to New York City), while others had no specific mandate.

All chartering systems helped to finance their respective state governments. In some cases, states taxed banks; in others (notably Pennsylvania and South Carolina) governments owned substantial shares in the banks; and in still others (free banks) governments forced banks to hold their bonds as security for notes. Sylla, Legler, and Wallis (1987) report data on the share of state revenues from banks in the antebellum period. They show that in some states, banks were the main source of revenue. For example, from 1811 to 1860 the bank share of state revenue in Massachusetts varied between 37 and 82 percent, with a median of 66 percent. The trend over time was to rely increasingly on taxation and bond reserve requirements, rather than direct ownership or control, as the method of rent extraction for the government. As Schweikart (1988a) shows, in the South, the period from 1837 to 1841 was something of a watershed in this respect. The high failure rates and large losses of banks organized and owned by the state governments (which often were involved in specific – typically unprofitable – public works projects) encouraged a movement away from direct government control and ownership. Similar lessons from the panic and depression years of 1837 to 1841 motivated the free-banking movement in the North.

With respect to the national government, chartering was sporadic. Despite constitutional and political controversies surrounding the federal chartering of a nationwide bank, the Bank of the United States (BUS) was chartered in 1791. This bank was founded by Alexander Hamilton with specific purposes in mind: to facilitate the marketing of government debt, to facilitate the collection of government revenues, and to make loans to the government in times of need at subsidized interest rates. In addition to performing these services for the government (Calomiris, 1991a, pp. 70–1), the government also owned a substantial stake in the bank and profited greatly from it. The Treasury Department estimated that the earnings for the government from dividends and sale of stock (in 1796) from its interest in the BUS amounted to $573,580, representing a return on capital of 28 percent (U.S. Treasury, 1897, cited in Love, 1931, p. 31). The bank's 20-year charter was not renewed in 1811, and its absence was sorely felt by the government during the War of 1812. This led to the bank's rechartering in 1816. Subsequent controversy over whether the bank constituted a national monopoly, and disagreement between Biddle and Jackson over the details of the renewed charter, led to a confrontation and a Presidential veto of the rechartering of the bank, which was not overridden by Congress (contrary to Biddle's expectations). From 1836 until 1863 there was thus no federal government presence in the chartering of banks.

Initially, limitations on branching seem not to have been an important constraint on what bankers who received charters wanted to do. From the beginning, banks in the South operated branches (Schweikart, 1988a, pp. 52–7, 62, 76, 98–9, 102, 120, 125–7, 174, 179, 202–3, 262), and banks in the North did not (Redlich, 1951, p. 193), but there was little clamor in the North to allow or prohibit branching. It seems not to have been an important bone of contention (Chapman and Westerfield, 1942, pp. 59–60). Opposition to the second BUS has sometimes been identified with an early opposition to branching, per se, but this seems incorrect. As Martin (1974) and Schweikart (1988b) show, Jacksonian opposition to the Bank mainly was fueled by a desire to reduce the connection between bank lending and bank currency issuing and to curtail the Bank's monopoly power, not by an opposition to federal chartering or branching, per se (see also Duncombe, 1841). Indeed, the branching South was a Jacksonian stronghold.

1.4.2   *Branching and consolidation controversy in the 1890s*

After the virtual disappearance of branch banks in the South in the 1860s (due to Southern banks' financing the Civil War), branching was restricted in many Southern states relative to its status before the War. Interestingly, Southern state governments, which had generally favored branching in the antebellum period, showed less interest in it in the immediate postbellum period, although Southern branching grew in importance in the early twentieth century. Although it is often difficult to describe the extent to which branching was prohibited, since it often was prohibited by the discretionary actions of regulators rather than by legal rules, the presence of branches is a fairly good indicator of the freedom to branch. In 1900, for the United States as a whole, there were 87 branching banks operating 119 branches. Forty-eight of these banks were in the South (which I define to include the obvious candidates, as well as Kentucky, Tennessee, Oklahoma, and Texas), and each of them operated only one branch located in the city of its head office (Board of Governors of the Federal Reserve System, 1976, pp. 298–9).

In the North, there was no significant movement in favor of branching until the bank-consolidation/branching movement of the 1890s. Only then did major struggles ensue over whether state-chartered or national banks could operate branches. This was the era that saw the mobilization of special lobbying groups to oppose bank consolidation and branching in particular (notably, the American Bankers Association).

National banks from the beginning were prohibited from opening new branches (but allowed to operate existing ones upon change of charter from a state system). The first Comptrollers of the Currency gave the National Banking Act a very narrow interpretation, arguing that it prohibited the establishment of branches. With minor and brief exceptions, this remained the policy of the Comptroller's office until the enactment of the McFadden Pepper Act of 1927.

The consolidation/branching movement of the 1890s in the North had two important sources. One was the high rate of bank failures during the 1890s, which prompted consideration of the advantages of large, nationwide, diversified banks (Chapman and Westerfield, 1942, pp. 62–74). Bank stress would also play a dominant role in the dramatic merger wave in banking during the 1920s (Willit, 1930, pp. 125–30, 159–247; Cartinhour, 1931; Chapman, 1934; Chapman and Westerfield, 1942, pp. 109–15; E. N. White, 1985). As before, unit bankers would react to the demand for consolidation and branching by lobbying to oppose it (and, in 1930, by establishing the Independent Bankers Association, to spearhead the opposition).

The second source of demand for bank branching and consolidation was the secular changes occurring elsewhere in the economy in the production, distribution, and management systems of corporations, which affected their borrowing needs. In the United States, particularly with the expansion of transcontinental railroads after the Civil War and the coming of the "second industrial revolution" of the latter quarter of the nineteenth century, the scale of firms and their financial requirements increased dramatically. Aside from the growth of firm size for technological reasons (for example, in the chemical and steel industries) the spread of the railroad and the associated extension of a firm's relevant "market" led to the emergence of the large-scale enterprise, with a managerial hierarchy and a complex nationwide distribution network for coordinating movements of factors and output (Chandler, 1977). These dramatic changes in the scale of corporate financing needs first appeared in the financing of railroads, which were the harbinger of the new wave of large-scale national industrial and commercial enterprises.

The demand for large-scale corporate finance affected the propensity for bank consolidation and branching in at least four important ways. First, there was the direct effect of the increase in demand by the bank's customers for large-scale loans. Limitations on the amount any bank was willing to loan (or legally could loan) to an individual customer favored the establishment of large banks. To some extent, the American banking system had participated in the financing of the railroads of the 1840s and 1850s, but these financings were on a smaller scale than those of the transcontinental railroads of the postbellum era, and they were not accompanied by the enormous increase in corporate scale and scope witnessed in the last quarter of the nineteenth century (Fishlow, 1965).

Second, because the fragmented unit banking system in the United States was ill-suited to finance the new corporate giants, and because of existing limitations on branching and mergers, competing methods of corporate finance arose that began to erode bank profitability, thus compounding bank distress and encouraging consolidation. The new markets for commercial paper and corporate stocks and bonds helped to motivate efforts by bankers to consolidate. Corporate finance prior to the 1890s was a local endeavor. As the demand for capital by large-scale firms grew, however, the credit system adapted, and competition on a national scale (for the business of a limited class of firms) became important. Part of that adaptation was visible within the banking system. Prior to the 1890s banks did not have formal credit departments with systematic procedures for evaluating creditworthiness (Lamoreaux, 1991a). Rather, they relied on informal knowledge of local borrowers in determining access to, and the cost of, credit. As banks turned outward in the 1890s, that began to change.

Financial innovations outside of banking were at least as important, and these allowed competitors of banks to gain a foothold in the credit market. As early as 1857, *Bradstreet's* printed the first rating book – a volume of 110 pages, listing 17,000 firms located in nine cities (Schultz, 1947, p. 57). The coverage of the various rating agencies increased over the latter half of the nineteenth century, and the data reported became more detailed and systematic, as the national and international markets for commercial paper and inter-firm trade credit grew. Growth in the commercial paper market was especially large from 1873 until the mid-1880s (Greef, 1938, p. 54), and the ability of commercial paper to remain safe and liquid during the panics of the 1890s led to its increasing use. The Mercantile Agency (the predecessor of Dun and Bradstreet's) opened 90 offices in the United States between 1871 and 1890. From 1891 to 1916, 115 new offices were opened, including 83 outside the borders of the United States (Foulke, 1941, pp. 294–5). As noted above, the United States was unique in its reliance on commercial paper for commercial and industrial finance of high-quality borrowers.

Another peculiarity of U.S. financial history that was an outgrowth of changes in corporate scale and branching restrictions was the development of securities markets and investment banking syndicates in the nineteenth century. In other countries, commercial banks financed firms, often owning equity as well as debt and often involving themselves in corporate decision making, as well as finance. Markets for corporate stocks, bonds, and commercial paper were virtually nonexistent. The Japanese keiretsu (Hoshi, Kashyap, and Scharfstein, 1990a, 1990b, 1991) and the similar German system dating from the nineteenth century (Riesser, 1911) provide examples of large-scale corporate finance within the banking system. In the United States in the 1890s, for the first time, investment banking houses (which previously had dealt almost exclusively in railroad securities issues and the financing of corporate reorganizations) began to market the common stock of other corporations on a national scale (Carosso, 1970, pp. 29–50). During this period New York became the preeminent center for investment banking, as investment banks relied increasingly on commercial banks as a source of funding, financed through the pyramiding of reserves in New York (due to New York's dominance as a commercial center). Ironically, the fragmented banking system would help to finance its own decline by fueling its main sources of competition in credit markets. The pioneering efforts in common stock flotations for relatively small firms were by Lehman Brothers and Goldman-Sachs, beginning in 1906 with the United Cigar Manufacturers and Sears, Roebuck flotations (Carosso, 1970, pp. 82–3).

Significant changes in corporate law helped to usher in the increasing reliance on large-scale enterprise and the growing attractiveness of corporate bonds and stocks, by clarifying and extending the protection afforded corporations in the law. Changes in attitudes toward incorporation, which had evolved over the previous century (Horwitz, 1971, 1977, 1985; Hurst, 1970), accelerated in the 1880s and 1890s, giving rise to what Sklar (1988) terms the "corporate reconstruction of American capitalism." In a series of cases beginning in 1886, for example, changes in the law of property and views of contractual liberty gave corporations rights similar to those of individuals, which served to protect large-scale corporations from arbitrary government disappropriation:

... the [Supreme] Court established a legal doctrine of substantive and procedural due process, which further elaborated the reformulation of liberty attached to corporate property. In effect, with the limited liability of the stockholder it combined the limited liability of the corporation in the face of the legislative and executive powers of government. ... It defined property to include the pursuit, and therefore the legal protection, of intangible value, or earning power ... (Sklar, 1988, p. 49)

... the resort to the corporate form of enterprise based upon negotiable securities and limited liability as a mode of property ownership became increasingly more compelling in the United States than in Britain and continental Europe, and its extension to intercorporate combination a familiar routine. Protected in part by law and otherwise by executive policy, the property form matched inducement and need with effective and available market instrumentalities. (p. 166)

Banks in the United States were forced as never before to compete with new forms of finance.

A third connection between the increased scale of corporate finance and the consolidation/branching movement also came from the growth of the securities market. Commercial banks played a crucial role as conduits of information and outlets for the marketing of securities flotations by investment-banking syndicates. This role dates back to Cooke's government bond syndication campaign of the 1860s, in which the initial links between Eastern investment bankers and commercial banks throughout the country were forged (Carosso, 1970, pp. 51–3). Benveniste and Spindt (1989) argue that a crucial feature of investment banking syndicates is that they collect information necessary to price new issues from the same parties who ultimately purchase the new issues. By combining the two, Benveniste and Spindt show, syndicates can minimize information costs by creating appropriate incentives for the collection and sharing of information within the coalition. This model seems well suited to understand the role of commercial bankers in early stock and bond flotations. They may have had special insights about individual firms' credit histories and about the types of securities their local customers were most interested in purchasing. The involvement of commercial bankers in underwriting and trust activities was a two-edged sword from the standpoint of the banking industry. It allowed them to share in the profits from the new financial innovations, but it also made them unwitting accomplices in the decline of banks as a source of direct finance. Banks that saw the possibility of participating more directly in underwriting of securities (at a higher level in the syndicate pyramid) and that saw potential economies of scale in trust activities and securities marketing (E. N. White, 1985) yearned to increase their size and their geographical range, which would enhance their role in the syndicate.

Fourth, and finally, the changes in the scale of corporate finance, and the consequent growth of investment banking, reduced the costs of arranging bank mergers, which encouraged banks to consolidate and branch. In addition to planning new securities issues and coordinating the marketing and pricing of the issues and the distribution of fees within the syndicate, investment bankers assisted in reorganizing the banking industry. By the turn of the century, bank consolidation in New England began, and investment banks played an important role in the process:

At the urging of an organization of Massachusetts savings associations, which collectively owned more than 40 percent of Boston's bank stock, a syndicate of private bankers under the leadership of Kidder, Peabody & Company liquidated nine of [Boston's] national banks and consolidated their operations into an enlarged and reorganized National Shawmut Bank. A year later, the Industrial Trust Company, under the aggressive leadership of Samuel P. Colt, acquired two banks in Providence and seven others elsewhere in the state. Each of these consolidations triggered a number of smaller mergers in their respective locales. As a result, by 1910 the number of banks in Boston had fallen to 23, little more than a third of the 60 banks operating in the city in 1895. . . . Over the same period, the number of national banks in Providence fell from 25 to 9. . . . (Lamoreaux, 1991b, p. 549)

Lamoreaux (1991b, pp. 549–50) finds that the profits of the new merged banks were substantially raised by the mergers. In explaining the timing of the mergers in New England, Lamoreaux (1991b, p. 551) emphasizes the importance of the demand for credit by large-scale industrial enterprises, which

may explain why private banking houses like Kidder, Peabody showed a sudden interest in merging national banks. The heightened level of activity in the securities markets may thus explain much about the timing of the merger movement in banking.

The concentrated holdings of stock in the national banks, and the adept management of Kidder, Peabody allowed stockholders to merge the banks, despite the frequent opposition of "entrenched" bank managers (especially in Massachusetts).

Despite all these motivations for consolidation and branching, major changes in industrial organization of banking from 1900 to 1909 were confined to a few states and banks, as Table 1.6 shows (Chapman, 1934, pp. 52–3; Board of Governors of the Federal Reserve System, 1976, pp. 298–9). National banks, as already noted, were prohibited from opening new branches, and prior to 1918 bank consolidation was only allowed after banks went through the costly process of asset liquidation (Chapman, 1934, p. 43). State banking laws also acted as a continuing impediment to consolidation or branching. In addition to requiring very large supernumerary majority votes by stockholders as a condition for merger, regulators in all states reserved for themselves the right to deny consolidations (Chapman, 1934, p. 46).

One way around restrictions on new branching or merging, which offered an alternative means to expand in size and geographical scope, was to form "chains" (more than one bank owned primarily by the same shareholders) or "groups" (banks owned directly by a bank holding company). While the degree of control and organization of chains and groups was not as great as that of branching banks, it certainly encouraged some joint decision making in lending, cooperation in marketing and trust activities, and interbank lending within the group on favorable terms. Chain banking developed considerably after 1890, and became displaced in importance by group banking by the 1910s. As Cartinhour (1931) and Calomiris (1992) show, some of the states with the largest chain and group presence were unit banking states. The rise of chain and group banking in Minnesota was particularly dramatic. By 1930, chain and group banks controlled 30 percent of the banks and 66 percent of bank assets in the state (Cartinhour, 1931, p. 110). By 1929, for the United States as a whole, 10 percent of the banks, and 21 percent of bank assets, were in groups or chains (Cartinhour, 1931, p. 101). Roughly half of these entities were controlled by holding companies (Cartinhour, 1931, p. 103). Beginning in the 1930s, the number and assets of groups and chains began to decline, in part due to failures of individual members and to the replacement of these entities with branching banks (Chapman and Westerfield, 1942, pp. 328–9). Perhaps most importantly, regulation at the state and federal level began to be restrictive. The Banking Act of 1933 prevented the shares of any member bank of the Federal Reserve System from being voted by a group without a permit from the Board of Governors (Chapman and Westerfield, 1942, p. 334).

Clearly, Sklar's (1988) spirit of "corporate reconstruction" that dominated the legal and institutional changes of corporate capitalism did not extend to banks. Government remained opposed to consolidation (through mergers or holding companies) and branching, with few excep-

Table 1.6. *Bank mergers and consolidations, by state, and branching, 1900–1910*

State Banks	Consolidations and Mergers[a]										
	1900	1901	1902	1903	1904	1905	1906	1907	1908	1909	Total
Arizona	—	—	—	—	—	—	—	—	—	1	1
Connecticut	—	—	—	—	—	1	—	1	—	—	2
Florida	—	—	—	—	—	1	—	—	1	—	2
Georgia	—	—	—	—	—	—	—	—	13	10	23
Idaho	—	—	—	—	—	—	1	1	4	—	6
Illinois	—	6	—	4	1	6	7	4	4	2	34
Indiana	—	—	1	—	1	—	1	1	1	1	6
Kansas	1	1	1	—	—	—	—	—	—	—	3
Louisiana	—	—	1	1	2	5	4	2	—	—	15
Michigan	—	—	—	—	6	—	2	4	7	4	23
Minnesota	—	1	1	—	1	—	3	2	5	9	22
Missouri	—	3	3	3	5	7	6	7	5	11	50
Nebraska	1	5	5	2	1	4	2	—	4	2	26
North Carolina	—	—	2	1	—	—	2	3	5	2	15
Ohio	—	—	—	—	1	3	—	—	—	—	4
Oklahoma	—	—	—	—	—	—	—	—	2	8	10
Oregon	—	—	—	—	—	—	—	—	4	—	4
Pennsylvania	—	1	2	4	3	4	1	1	1	1	18
Rhode Island	1	2	1	—	2	1	1	—	—	1	9
South Carolina	—	—	—	—	—	—	—	—	4	2	6
South Dakota	—	—	6	—	1	1	—	—	—	—	8
Texas	—	—	—	—	—	—	1	—	—	1	2
Utah	—	—	—	—	—	1	—	—	—	—	1
Washington	—	—	—	—	—	—	—	—	7	—	7
West Virginia	1	—	2	—	—	—	2	1	—	—	6
Wisconsin	—	—	—	2	5	2	1	—	—	—	10
Wyoming	—	—	—	—	2	—	—	—	—	—	2
Total											
All State Banks	4	19	25	17	31	36	34	27	67	55	316
All National Banks	16	22	25	20	32	33	22	27	30	25	252
Grand Total	20	41	50	37	63	69	56	54	97	80	568

	Branching		
	1900	1905	1910
State banks with branches	82	191	283
Number of branches	114	345	536
National banks with branches	5	5	9
Number of branches	5	5	12
All banks with branches	87	196	292
Number of branches	119	350	548

[a] Data are incomplete. See Chapman (1934, pp. 52–3) for a discussion.
Sources: Chapman (1934); Board of Governors of the Federal Reserve System (1976, p. 297).

tions. The state and federal governments' responses to increased demand for banking in rural areas and to the bank failures in the 1890s were to decrease capital requirements and thereby promote bank expansion through small, unit banks. For national banks, minimum capital requirements were reduced in 1900. Details of state policies are provided in James (1978, p. 230).

The limits on banks' participation in large-scale corporate finance due to restrictions on branching imposed large costs on the economy. We have already noted that local firms in peripheral locations faced high costs of external finance due to the scarcity of bank capital. The instability of unit banks and the lack of competition in rural areas also increased costs to these borrowers periodically when their local banks failed (Calomiris, Hubbard, and Stock, 1986). And all bank-dependent borrowers suffered from general contractions of credit at cyclical and seasonal frequencies (Miron, 1986; Calomiris and Hubbard, 1989).

By impeding the integration of the national market for capital, branching restrictions also imposed costs on large-scale firms, which had to rely on investment banking syndicates to finance their large fixed-capital investments. SEC data on the fees paid to investment bankers in the late 1930s (Butters and Lintner, 1945) and estimates of external finance costs derived from firms' responses to the taxation of retained earnings in 1936–1937 (Calomiris and Hubbard, 1995) both indicate that for publicly traded firms excess costs of external finance through securities issuances often averaged in excess of 20 percent of the value of the issue. The SEC data are a lower bound on excess financing cost since these fees do not include other costs, like losses to shareholders due to the undervaluation of stock issues, as discussed in Myers and Majluf, 1984; Asquith and Mullins, 1986; and Korajczyk, Lucas, and McDonald, 1990. Calomiris and Hubbard (1995) find that more than 20 percent of the firms in the economy in 1936 likely faced excess financing costs in excess of 25 percent. Similarly high investment banking fees seem to have characterized earlier years, although data on these earlier transactions are scarce. Brandeis (1914, p. 95) cites scattered evidence on the fees for common and preferred stock and for bonds that are quite similar to those reported for the 1930s. Brandeis views such high fees as prima facie evidence of monopoly power by the "money trust." While it is difficult to distinguish the extent to which the high costs borne by some U.S. borrowers resulted from information production or monopoly rents (for the former view, see Chapter 5 of this volume), in either case U.S. costs were unusually high compared to the "main bank" system of financing large corporate investment, like that employed in Germany to finance the second industrial revolution (Riesser, 1911; Tilly, 1966; Neuberger and Stokes, 1974; Kindleberger, 1984, pp. 122–9; Chapter 4 of this volume).

The contrast with the German system is striking. German joint stock banks, which came into existence after 1848, combined investment and commercial banking activities and exercised enormous control over the enterprises they financed. Enterprises typically borrowed from only one bank, and the degree of integration and information exchange between bank and firm management was unprecedented. As Neuberger and Stokes (1974, p. 713) write:

Contemporaries who analyzed the role of the *Kreditbanken* were most fascinated by the intimate relations with the major German industrial firms. The origins of this intimacy are not at all mysterious. Such close relations were a natural outgrowth of the scheme according to which the banks arranged industrial financing. The policy of granting large credits for fixed capital against security of uncertain value was unusually risky so that measures to reduce risk must have been a matter of special concern. One simple expedient was the requirement that the borrower conduct all business through one bank (or in cases where a loan was made by a consortium, through the leading bank). If this rule was followed, a bank was guaranteed adequate knowledge of a firm's condition. A second measure was the requirement that bank officials be appointed to the supervisory boards of the firms to which credit was granted.

The directorships ensured the banks a voice in policy making in the industries they financed.

While Morgan's men in the United States performed a similar function in monitoring firm activities (De Long, 1991), German banks were able to internalize the costs and benefits of monitoring within a single entity and to avoid the complications and costs of marketing securities and coordinating information flows among thousands of syndicate participants. Unbelievably (by American standards) this internalization of costs and benefits in the German main bank system allowed large-scale industrial firms in Germany to borrow and finance large amounts of fixed capital on the same terms as merchants financing import and export trade. The form of finance was very short term, which further facilitated the discipline of banks over firms, since it gave banks a useful threat (the withdrawal of funding) if firms deviated from the straight and narrow (Neuberger and Stokes, 1974, pp. 713–5). (For a theoretical discussion of the use of short-term debt as a disciplinary device, see Calomiris and Kahn, 1991; Calomiris, Kahn, and Krasa, 1991.)

Despite the costs of regulatory limitations in the United States, it took the disaster of the 1920s to prompt meaningful regulatory reform in branching. Even then, local special interests that opposed liberalization were protected, in part, by the continuing dominance of state law over federal in matters of industrial organization. Under the stress of the

1920s many states in all regions of the country, especially agricultural states that previously had resisted branching reform, liberalized their branching laws. (For a useful and compact description of state and federal regulatory changes on branching from 1910 to 1990, see Mengle, 1990.) Branching restrictions for national banks were also liberalized to conform more to the regulations prevailing in the various states. The National Banking System followed, rather than led, the procession to branch banking. The 1920s saw a reversal in the position of the Comptroller of the Currency, who now pressured Congress to relax branching regulation (Chapman and Westerfield, 1942, pp. 95–7), due to concern over the loss of membership to the state chartering authorities, with their more liberal branching laws. But the initiatives of the Comptroller in the early 1920s were limited by the initially strong opposition of unit bankers (many of whom had disappeared by the end of the 1920s, or possibly lost the financial capability to influence their elected officials), and by a Supreme Court ruling in 1924 that gave state governments the right to restrict branching by national banks, if their banks were similarly limited and if Congress did not specifically legislate otherwise. In other industries, state laws that restricted trade were unconstitutional (through the "commerce clause"); in banking, however, commerce-clause protection was found not to apply, and state law ruled supreme.

Interestingly, the first attempt at meaningful reform for national banks occurred only after the Comptroller had received the assent of the American Bankers Association, as a result of its 1921 convention held in Los Angeles, which was apparently dominated by California banks.

> The ... Comptroller ... was encouraged to take a more aggressive attitude for branch banking by the fact that the National Bank Division of the American Bankers Association had at its Los Angeles convention, after extensive debate, resolved to request the Congress ... to permit national banks to maintain and operate branches within a prescribed radius from the head office of such a national bank in states in which state banks were authorized to have branches ... (Chapman and Westerfield, 1942, pp. 95–6)

The approach advocated by Comptroller Crissinger in 1921 would eventually become codified in the McFadden-Pepper Act of 1927, but in 1922 Congress was not so disposed. Neither was the American Bankers Association, which reversed the position advocated at the Los Angeles convention and adopted a strong antibranching platform at its 1922 convention (Chapman and Westerfield, 1942, p. 97). When the Comptroller decided to push through the changes on his own authority, Congress rebelled, and the political heat that was generated was sufficient to drive him from office. The weakening of the opponents of

Table 1.7. *Consolidation and branching, 1910–1931*

Year	Chapman series		White Series		Branching banks	Branches	Loans and investments of branching banks ($ millions)
	Number of mergers	Banks absorbed	Banks absorbed	Total Assets ($millions)			
1910	127	128	—	—	292	548	1,272
1911	119	119	—	—	—	—	—
1912	128	128	—	—	—	—	—
1913	118	118	—	—	—	—	—
1914	142	143	—	—	—	—	—
1915	154	154	—	—	397	785	2,187
1916	134	134	—	—	—	—	—
1917	123	123	—	—	—	—	—
1918	119	125	—	—	—	—	—
1919	178	178	172	650	—	—	—
1920	181	183	184	874	530	1,281	6,897
1921	281	292	250	710	547	1,455	8,354
1922	337	340	311	750	610	1,801	9,110
1923	325	325	299	1,052	671	2,054	10,922
1924	350	352	341	662	706	2,297	12,480
1925	352	356	280	702	720	2,525	14,763
1926	429	429	348	1,595	744	2,703	16,511
1927	543	544	477	1,555	740	2,914	17,591
1928	501	507	455	2,093	775	3,138	20,068
1929	571	575	529	5,614	764	3,353	21,420
1930	699	698	627	2,903	751	3,522	22,491
1931	706	719	635	2,757	723	3,467	20,681

Sources: Chapman (1934, p. 56); E. N. White (1985, p. 286); Board of Governors of the Federal Reserve System (1976, p. 297).

branching and the demonstrated benefits of branch banking during the 1920s hastened the passage of the McFadden-Pepper Act in 1927 and led to further liberalization of national bank branch locations in the Banking Act of 1933.

After 1920, states also allowed greater consolidation through acquisition and merger (Table 1.7). The large number of unit bank failures and the relative success of branch-banking systems during the crisis years weakened opposition to branching and consolidation (Chapman, 1934; Chapman and Westerfield, 1942; E. N. White, 1985). From 1920 to 1930 the number of banks operating branches (and branches) increased from 530 (1,281 branches) to 751 (3,522 branches). The annual number of banks absorbed by mergers from 1910 to 1920 averaged 139. From 1921 to 1931, mergers increased steadily, averaging 467 per year and reaching a peak of 719 in 1931 (Chapman, 1934, p. 56).

1.4.3   Modeling the political economy of branching restrictions

From the standpoint of optimal-contracting models of banking, which assume frictionless bargaining (no transactions costs), freedom of contracting, and freedom to choose asset and liability composition optimally (as in, for example, the very simple visions of banking in Fama, 1980, or Diamond, 1984), the absence of large, multibranch banks is puzzling. Opportunities for the diversification of risk, coordination in response to shocks, and a superior allocation of capital across regions should have been irresistible to a competitive banking system, which would be governed by the principles of cost minimization of banks and utility maximization of depositors. From this perspective opposition to branching seems inexplicable on economic grounds and instead appears to be the result of irrational populist distrust of large, big-city bankers.

From the standpoint of the historical context in which banks were chartered in the United States, however, restrictions on branching and bank consolidation are less puzzling and can be understood as a rational economic strategy of some segments of the population. In a world where banks are a tool of the state, where their activities are deemed a proper subject for public debate and government control, where it is presumed that their supply should be limited and their income should be shared with the state in compensation for the granting of the privilege of limited liability, it is little wonder that the maximization of depositors' utility was not achieved.

Bank regulations, and branching laws in particular, clearly were determined in large part by the lobbying of special interest groups. Indeed, the mercantilist partnership between banks and government often gave the interests of existing banks special weight. For example, in Rhode Island and Massachusetts in the antebellum period bank supervisors explicitly stated that their opposition to branching was based on the concern that existing banks (sometimes in the country, sometimes in the city) might be damaged by allowing competition in their lending markets (Dewey, 1910, pp. 141–2). While in some states the demands of the 1890s prompted a move toward branching (for example, in New York in 1898, see Klebaner, 1990, p. 71), in other states the lobbying by unit bankers and farm interests successfully blocked branching. Indeed, the number of states specifically authorizing branching fell from 20 to 12 over the years 1896 to 1910 (Klebaner, 1990, p. 71), although several other states allowed branching without specific legislation.

Given the transactions costs of lobbying the government, only those with special interests (i.e., with a lot to gain or lose) will pay the price to express their opinion and influence policymakers. This explains why bank regulation seldom maximizes depositors' welfare and why borrowers heavily dependent on banks, and bankers, would be the dominant players in the political regulatory game. This perspective also helps to explain why once a banking system begins as a unit banking system (giving location-specific rents to particular unit banks), unit bankers would resist change and often were able to do so successfully. And this explains why the destruction of unit bankers or the reduction in their wealth (and hence, influence) in the 1920s (and again, in the 1980s and early 1990s) coincided with the relaxation of branching and consolidation restrictions. Indeed, these are common themes in the political history of branching (Cartinhour, 1931; Chapman and Westerfield, 1942; E. N. White, 1982, 1983).

Understanding the differences in regulatory structure across states and over time, however, is far more challenging than stating the truism that change was governed by dominant special interest groups. In what follows, I address what I think are the three most puzzling features of the regulatory differences across states and eras, relying on economic theory to construct conjectures of what might have governed particular groups' interests and on some empirical evidence to buttress these conjectures. The three puzzles are: (1) Why was branching initially a feature of Southern, but not Northern banking? (2) Why did some agrarian areas in the South embrace branching in the antebellum period and not in the early postbellum era? (3) Why was California a major exception to this rule – that is, why was consolidation and branching into agricultural areas in California not successfully opposed?

The answer to the question of why antebellum Northern bankers and bank-dependent borrowers did not push for branching, while Southerners did, seems to come down to the specific differences in the goals of the states and to the common mercantilist principle that connected bank chartering to these goals. As discussed above, bank charters were initially established to promote particular activities. In the North, the main growth opportunities, and the activities promoted by the government, were primarily financing commerce and industry in cities; in the South they were primarily financing the crop cycle and moving the crops to market. The differing nature of the activities affected the desirability of branching. The special advantages of branch banking in the rural South were well understood in contemporary discussions of banking (Schweikart, 1988a; Calomiris and Schweikart, 1988). These included enhanced intrastate and intraregional capital mobility, access to thinly populated areas, and the ability to move agricultural goods long distances easily through the use of trade acceptances.

Similarly, three agriculture-dependent states in the North – Indiana, Ohio, and Iowa – established successful mutual-guaranty systems, which as noted above approximated some features of branching systems (coordination of clearings and acceptance transactions, diversification of risk *ex ante*, and coordination in the face of disturbances, *ex post*). The main difference between these Northern states and their counterparts in the South was that, like the free-banking systems of the antebellum Midwest, entry was sharply limited in the Northern mutual guaranty systems, while it was not so limited in the South. In the three Northern systems, banks were not permitted to branch into each other's local markets, which Southern banks often did.

In the Northeast, the commercial and industrial lending by banks typically had a different purpose from that of bank lending in the South, and the absence of branches was not an important obstacle to the satisfaction of those goals. In her studies of New England's banks, Lamoreaux (1991a, 1991b) argues that early nineteenth-century banking was nicely adapted to the needs of local industry:

At that time, scarcity of information and the modest scale of enterprise had combined to keep credit markets localized and financial institutions small . . . (1991b, p. 539).

According to Lamoreaux, New England bank managers, particularly in Boston and Providence, often ran banks as credit cooperatives to finance their own firms' needs for working capital. They would have had less interest in diversifying risk, since they were most interested in lending money to themselves.

Maryland provides an interesting case of a banking system that allowed, but did not take advantage of, branching. Maryland's banking system was modeled on the Scottish system. Like the Scottish system, it allowed free branching. Bryan (1899, p. 15) writes:

This principle was introduced into Maryland in 1804, but it has received comparatively little development. No bank in Maryland has had more than two branches performing a regular banking business, and but a limited number have had branches at all; these were organized early. . . . Perhaps on this account outlying agricultural districts were developed more slowly than they might have been under a system of branch banking.

Furthermore, attempts to charter a state branching bank on the Southern model specifically to channel resources to the countryside were debated in great detail and defeated several times from 1829 to 1837 (Bryan, 1899, pp. 83–5). Why was there so little private branching or support for a public initiative to organize an agricultural branch bank?

Like other Mid-Atlantic coastal cities, Baltimore was a hotbed of commerce and industry, and its banks concentrated on financing these activities, rather than searching out opportunities in rural Maryland. For these purposes, from the standpoint of bankers, Baltimore entrepreneurs, and politicians, branches were not particularly necessary.

These conditions changed in the last third of the nineteenth century. Lamoreaux (1991a) shows that in New England as local industrial and commercial opportunities waned and the potential for profits in other regions increased (notably the Midwest and the low-wage South, as discussed in Gates, 1951; Johnson and Supple, 1967; Wright, 1981), New England banks (and some industrialists) became more outward-looking and began channeling funds to borrowers in other regions. Banks evaluated creditworthiness with newly developed formal methods implemented by newly created credit departments. Now the profitable opportunities for Northeastern banks involved outward-looking participation in the financing of large-scale enterprise in the national capital market. These changes were also related to changes in the sources of banks' external finance (their increasing reliance on deposits), and a change in the relationship between banks' management and shareholders (Lamoreaux, 1991b; Calomiris, 1991b). Changes in the incentives of bankers – whose opinions were instrumental in shaping regulatory policy – which encouraged them to pursue opportunities in the burgeoning national capital market help to explain the timing of the relatively successful branching and consolidation movements in the postbellum North.

In addition to its advantages in helping move crops, branch banking provided other benefits to wealthy antebellum Southerners, who could gain from capital mobility in the South in ways that wealthy Northerners could not. Wright (1986) argues that the profit-maximizing strategy of Northerners was to increase the value of land and local capital and that this encouraged large expenditures on public works and local "boosterism." Wright argues that Southerners with large slave holdings, who were the dominant political force, had little incentive to invest in local public works; instead, they wished to augment the value of their main capital asset, which was slaves. Territorial expansion, and the ability to move slave labor to its highest use were the hallmarks of this strategy. One can see the promotion of branch banking in the South as an example of the pursuit of this interest. Branching promised greater mobility of capital and greater access to new, remote areas, as needed.

From this perspective, one can also understand why the Northwest opted for its mutual-guaranty and free-banking systems, rather than free-entry branching. Entry restrictions helped to create location-specific bank capital and thereby limited potential capital losses on local property values. Location-specific bank capital ensured that banks would not move on to marginally "greener pasture" at the expense of local businesses and farms. One can view this arrangement as a form of insurance of wealth (where the "insurance premium" is the inefficiency, potential for bank failure, and high costs of borrowing in the unit banking system). In the absence of Arrow-Debreu markets, or nationwide mutual funds that offered opportunities to diversify all systematic risk, as imagined in the frictionless capital asset pricing model, landowners saw location-specific bank capital as a way to tie banks' fortunes to their own. If their city or town received an adverse shock associated with a long-term negative revision in expectations regarding the profitability of investment there (say, an expected long-term decline in the terms of trade), local farmers and businessmen could be confident that their bankers would continue to lend to them, even on reduced collateral. The unit bankers had little choice. Branches of banks, facing those same choices, might simply close or at least sharply curtail their lending in that community.

Similarly, the motivation farmers would have had for creating location-specific bank rents was a desire for "loan insurance." In addition to limitations on diversification of wealth holdings, to the extent that borrowers faced external finance constraints, their creditworthiness may have depended importantly on their level of wealth (Leland and Pyle, 1977; Stiglitz and Weiss, 1981; Myers and Majluf, 1984; Gale and Hellwig, 1985; Williamson, 1986; Bemanke and Gertler, 1990; Calomiris and Hubbard, 1990). Given that wealth – particularly in undiversified land – was highly volatile in value, middle-class landowning borrowers had an additional motive to "purchase" loan insurance by supporting unit banking. The desire to tie banks to local lending markets is also visible in more recent regulation, notably the Community Reinvestment Act of 1977. Out-of-state banks that acquire local banks must commit to continue making local loans and not merely use the acquired banks as sources of deposits.

These explanations do not imply that branching restrictions or the earmarking of loans to specific regions are "optimal," or even "second-best," for society as a whole. One can argue that branching restrictions were a way for early settlers to benefit at the expense of later settlement elsewhere in the state – a "beggar-thy-neighbor" regulatory policy supported by the agrarian middle class. In any case, welfare comparisons, which are relatively easy in a frictionless world, are much more difficult in a setting where the standard assumptions of welfare economics (including no costs of information or bargaining) do not hold. These costs, as already noted, are precisely what give rise to "incompleteness" in capital markets, which motivates the taste for unit banking.

In summary, the antebellum South favored branching because the dominant economic interests (wealthy slaveholders) benefited from it. High costs of financing the movement of crops over long distances through peripheral unit banks explains this in part. Additionally, in the South the dominant form of collateral in the antebellum period was slaves rather than land (Kilbourne, 1992); thus there was little advantage from "bonding" the banker to a particular locale. In the Northeast, branching restrictions were not an important constraint on the dominant economic class, composed of merchants and industrialists. Indeed, they benefited by the creation of charter rents to the extent they could use their control of banks to improve their own costs of credit. In the Northwest, the middle-class farmer (later the "populist') would carry the day. In the mutual-guaranty systems of Indiana, Ohio, and Iowa farmers received many of the benefits of branching, while retaining the advantages of location-specific bank capital. Other banking systems of the Northwest opted simply for unit free banks. None authorized free entry in the form of branch banks.

The Civil War brought an end to slavery in the South. The declining price of cotton, as well as the reorganization of labor and land allocation after the War, made the South much poorer than it had been (Ransom and Sutch, 1977; Wright, 1986). There was no longer a plantation elite with an interest in establishing branch banks to promote the efficient movement of capital or commodities. Indeed, one could argue that the wealthy landlords benefited by the lack of competition in finance, which facilitated the "debt peonage" of tenants (Ransom and Sutch, 1977, 148–70). Despite its own antebellum successes with branch banking, there was no powerful political constituency to push for branching in the immediate postbellum period.

1.4.4   Empirical support

There is a great deal of qualitative evidence to support the generalization that "rural interests" have opposed the branching movement from 1890 to the present. But that opposition has not been uniform. For example, Illinois has had a long history of opposition to branching. In a 1924 statewide referendum, the public voted against permitting branching, two to one (E. N. White, 1982, p. 38, citing Bradford, 1940, p. 17). Similar opposition was present in many states prior to the 1920s, but some relaxed their regulations after the destructive 1920s and 1930s, while others did not. Other states with a large agricultural sector – perhaps most notably, California – favored branching long before the 1920s.

One way to verify the "insurance model" of the rural support for unit banking after 1890 is to see whether cross-sectional variation in the "taste" for branching is correlated with variables that should matter from the standpoint of the "insurance model." The greater the demand for land and loan insurance, the greater the support should have been for unit banking laws. A formal econometric study of this type is beyond the scope of this paper, but there are some facts that appear consistent with it.

Table 1.8 reports data on rural per-capita wealth in 1900 for various agriculture-dependent states. I divide these states into two categories: those that made progress toward relaxing branching restrictions by 1910, and those that did not. Interestingly, with the exception of California, with its very high rural wealth per capita, branching states tended to have much poorer farmers than states that prohibited (new) branching. This is true even controlling for the presence of the Southern states in each group (which were dominated by tenant farming and sharecropping). The median index of relative rural wealth for the branching states was 0.5 (1.2 for non-Southern states), while the states that prohibited branching had a median index of 1.4 (1.8 for non-Southern states). In the latter states, landowning farmers would have been able to lobby politicians more effectively and may have been more interested in protecting their accumulated wealth through the "land and loan insurance" provided by unit banking. Much more empirical work needs to be done, however, before one can interpret this tentative finding conclusively.

E. N. White's (1984b) study of the 1924 Illinois referendum on branching provides evidence consistent with the insurance model. He finds that the presence of banks increases the probability of opposition to branching at the county level and interprets this as evidence that the public was influenced by local unit banks' propaganda. That may be true, but another interpretation of this finding is that the existence of a bank is a proxy for wealth insurance by banks. According to this interpretation, relatively well-off agrarian communities in Illinois were more prone to have banks and to support unit banking. Future empirical work can distinguish between these two interpretations by close examination of county level data.

The case of California is somewhat anomalous from the standpoint of the model and the patterns shown in Table 1.8. California, however, was an unusual state in other ways. For example, the long distances within the state that commodities had to travel and the consequent benefits of coordination of finance through a branching system may have appealed

Table 1.8. *Rural wealth and branching restrictions*

	Rural per capita wealth index, 1900[a]	Number of banks with branches, 1910	Number of branches 1910	Ratio of branch-banking facilities to total banking facilities 1910
	States allowing some branching, 1910			
Alabama	0.3	6	17	0.07
Arizona	0.7	7	15	0.34
California	2.5	34	45	0.12
Florida	0.3	5	7	0.07
Georgia	0.3	15	17	0.05
Louisiana	0.5	3	3	0.03
Michigan	1.1	23	55	0.10
Mississippi	0.4	15	30	0.12
North Carolina	0.3	8	13	0.05
Ohio	1.3	22	39	0.05
Oregon	1.4	5	6	0.05
South Carolina	0.3	2	7	0.03
Tennessee	0.5	3	4	0.02
Virginia	0.5	18	37	0.13
Washington	1.2	8	12	0.06
Mean	0.8	—	—	—
Median	0.5	—	—	—
Mean (non-South)	1.4	—	—	—
Median (non-South)	1.2	—	—	—
	States not allowing further branching, 1910			
Arkansas	0.4	3	3	0.02
Colorado	1.3	0	0	0.00
Idaho	1.0	0	0	0.00
Illinois	2.1	0	0	0.00
Indiana	1.4	0	0	0.00
Iowa	2.6	0	0	0.00
Kansas	1.8	0	0	0.00
Minnesota	1.6	0	0	0.00
Missouri	1.2	0	0	0.00
Montana	1.9	0	0	0.00
Nebraska	2.2	1	1	0.00
Nevada	1.9	0	0	0.00
New Mexico	0.6	0	0	0.00
North Dakota	2.1	0	0	0.00
Oklahoma	0.9	0	0	0.00
Pennsylvania	0.9	8	8	0.01
South Dakota	1.8	0	0	0.00
Texas	0.9	0	0	0.00
Utah	0.9	0	0	0.00
Vermont	0.9	1	1	0.03
West Virginia	0.6	0	0	0.00
Wisconsin	1.4	7	9	0.03
Wyoming	3.0	0	0	0.00
Mean	1.5	—	—	—
Median	1.4	—	—	—
Mean (non-South)	1.7	—	—	—
Median (non-South)	1.8	—	—	—

[a] The per-capita rural wealth index is the ratio of a state's share of national rural wealth, as calculated in Lee et al. (1957, pp. 730–811), divided by a state's share of national rural population, as reported in U.S. Department of Commerce (1975, Part 1, pp. 24–37).
Sources: Lee et al. (1957); U.S. Department of Commerce (1975); Board of Governors of the Federal Reserve System (1976, p. 298).

to wealthy farmers in the California interior, much as it had to antebellum Southern plantation owners. Moreover, the details of the history of California branching seem to provide some support for the model. Specifically, branching was permitted only after the acquiescence of powerful agricultural interests to entry by city banks, and this entry seems to have been the result initially of local distress and eventually of the benefits to this powerful group from allowing branching. Branching was subject to the approval of the State Superintendent of Banks, whose approval was subject to the influence of special interests.

The first branch of the Bank of Italy that A. P. Giannini opened (with the requisite permission of state regulators) was in San Jose. The Superintendent of Banks found that San Jose "needed" the bank's help in the face of the collapse of the local bank. In fact, the failing local banker, himself a large landowner whose family had relied on his bank for large land-backed loans for the past 30 years, visited San Francisco to suggest the acquisition of his bank by Giannini. This was a crucial ingredient in the Superintendent's willingness to have the branch open. Large landowners stood to benefit from the preservation of the bank's stock value and the preservation of the local economy, which depended on the bank. The small landowners, many of whom were Italians who knew Giannini from his childhood days in San Jose, also saw the entry by the Bank of Italy as a favorable change, since previously they had not been granted equal access to the bank, which was being run first and foremost in the interests of large local landowners (James and James, 1954, pp. 48–51). Giannini realized that further expansion of branching required the support of the powerful land interests:

Giannini realized that, unless his branches could do more for the California ranchers than existing unit banks were doing, there would be little excuse for the branches (James and James, 1954, p. 52).

Giannini's next acquisition was in Los Angeles in 1910, where, again. the "reason for the speed of this acquisition was the fact that the Park Bank [of Los Angeles] was not in good shape" (James and James, 1954, pp. 58–9). Other attempts at takeovers in Los Angeles by the Bank of Italy met with failure. "These deals fell through in a manner that suggests intervention by the larger banking interests of Los Angeles" (James and James, 1954, p. 59). Giannini acquired another Los Angeles bank in 1913, again only after a fight with local bankers.

Giannini's statewide branching campaign did not begin in earnest until 1916, as the Bank of Italy expanded into the Santa Clara, San Joaquin, and Napa Valleys. The wartime increase in demand, his previous successes and growing popularity, and the scarcity of sound institutions willing and able to finance the expansion all helped Giannini to win over farmers, regulators, and politicians who otherwise might have been opponents to branching. Just as important was Giannini's adept handling of the financing of large movements of goods over long distances, a natural comparative advantage of branching:

Valley farming is pretty big business. Many of the crops were perishable or semi-perishable; their movement had to be rapid; their handling and packing, skillful; and their flow to the distant consumer, flexible and constantly under control. Moreover, the principal markets lay as far east as Chicago and New York. Much of the barley harvest was sold on the London market; valley orchardists had long supplied Europe with a good part of her prunes; delta rice was shipped to Japan; and Cuba and Puerto Rico were regular customers for California beans. (James and James, 1954, pp. 88–9)

Giannini also was able to enlist the strong support of the Italian community and of small farmers involved in farm co-ops, which the Bank of Italy strongly supported.

In summary, several factors combined to make Giannini the right man in the right place at the right time. Initially, he fought an uphill battle against other banks and entrenched landowners who did not welcome his competition. At first, it was bank distress that would allow acquisitions. But gradually, he was able to convince the powerful, and the not so powerful alike, that on balance they stood to benefit from branch banking. In another state, or even in California at another time, he may never have been able to overcome the obstacles to branching.

Giannini's experience and the data in Table 1.8 run contrary to the view that the populist agrarian support for unit banks came from poor farmers. Instead, it was established farmers with significant land holdings (and often interests in unit banks) who opposed competition from outside. Indeed, agricultural impoverishment (like the destruction of agricultural banks in the 1920s and 1980s) has been good news for branching. Fifteen states allowed expanded branching from 1920 to 1939. During the expansionary years from 1939 to 1979 only 4 states relaxed their branching laws. In the face of the agricultural crisis of the 1980s once again 15 states loosened restrictions on branching (Mengle, 1990; Calomiris, 1992).

1.4.5   Explaining the uniqueness of U.S. unit banking

Other countries have agricultural middle classes (notably Canada), yet the successful U.S. support for unit banking is unique. Why was the United States so different? The answer lies in the institutional and historical peculiarities of the American political experience: the protection of local interests ensured by federalism, the distinctly American method for allocating power among national legislators (which also gives disproportionate weight to regionally concentrated minorities), and the legal precedents established by the Supreme Court, which gave states great latitude in the chartering of banks.

By not extending constitutional protection to banking as an activity involving interstate commerce the Supreme Court opened the way to state regulatory prohibitions on bank activities across and within states. Throughout the nineteenth and twentieth centuries state banking authority was limited only by the increasing incursions of the federal government in chartering and regulating banks, which were justified constitutionally by appeal to the federal government's special role in regulating the money supply, and therefore banks, and not by appeal to any constitutional protection on banking activities under the commerce clause. In 1924 the Supreme Court further insulated state government control over banking by ruling that state banks could enforce branching restrictions against state and national banks alike within their borders (in the absence of specific contrary action by Congress). Through these rulings the Supreme Court ensured that the struggle over branching would be fought locally rather than nationally, unless Congress decided to intervene. This approach was codified by Congress in 1927.

The Court's and Congress's willingness to allow state governments to limit the activities of state and national banks within and beyond their boundaries gave locally concentrated special-interest groups a better forum for lobbying than the national arena where they would have been up against all the opposing interest groups in the national economy. Thus federalism's decentralization of legislative power, supported by some crucial Supreme Court rulings and the absence of action by Congress, helps to explain the unique success of unit bankers and their allies in the United States.

The American method for electing national legislators and the means of allocating power within Congress also have helped to constrain opposition to unit banking and to enhance the power of geographically concentrated minorities that opposed branch banking. In contrast to many countries' parliamentary systems in which the national performance of the party can determine which individual representatives hold office, the support of local constituents is a sufficient condition for election to Congress. This tends to enhance the power of geographically concentrated interest groups on politicians. Moreover, congressional committees control the agenda of Congress, and these committees are often dominated by representatives whose constituents tend to agree and feel strongly about the set of issues under the aegis of that committee. Thus representatives from pro-unit banking agricultural states have tended to dominate the congressional committees that control banking regulation. Other states' representatives "trade" influence over these committees for committee appointments in areas of greater concern to their constituents. Congressional "horse-trading" over committee appointments and votes have thus tended to stifle the advocacy of branch banking by the "silent majority" and have favored the power of regionally concentrated enclaves of support for unit banking.

1.5   The origins and effects of pre-FDIC bank liability insurance

Studies of the political history of deposit insurance legislation show that it was the desire to preserve unit banking and the political influence of unit bankers and their supporters that gave rise to the perceived need for deposit insurance, both in the antebellum period and in the twentieth century (Golembe, 1960). It was understood early on (through observing the successful operation of branch banks in the South and in other countries) that branching – with its benefits both of greater diversification and coordination – provided an alternative stabilizer to liability insurance. But unit banks and their supporters successfully directed the movement for banking reform toward creating government insurance funds. All six antebellum states that enacted liability insurance were unit-banking states. In the antebellum branch-banking South neither government insurance nor urban clearing houses developed. Similarly, the eight state insurance systems created from 1908 to 1917 were all in unit-banking states.

In evaluating the performance of the various government-created liability-insurance schemes, Calomiris (1989, 1990, 1992) analyses which experiments failed or succeeded, and why. Deposit insurance in many cases destabilized historical banking systems, as recent theoretical and empirical analyses of banks and savings and loans suggest it has today. The failures of insurance systems seem mainly attributable to flaws in their design, rather than to insurmountable exogenous shocks.

1.5.1   Antebellum successes and failures

Detailed analysis of each of the antebellum bank insurance programs is provided in Golembe and Warburton (1958). New York's Safety Fund was the first, established in 1829, funded by limited annual contributions of members and regulated by the state government. Losses severely depleted the accumulated resources of the fund from 1837 to 1841 until, in 1842, it ceased to be able to repay losses of failed banks and thus ceased to provide protection to the payments system.

New York in 1838 created an alternative to the insured system through its free-banking statute and allowed Safety-Fund banks to switch to that system. The depletion in membership of the insured system kept its losses small during subsequent panics. After 1840 Safety-Fund banks comprised a small and continually shrinking proportion of total banks or total bank assets. Losses were also limited by the 1842 restriction on coverage of member banks' liabilities to bank notes, thus excluding the growing liability base in deposits.

Ultimately, the small number of banks that chose to remain in the system and make continuing annual contributions to its fund did manage to repay in 1866 the obligations incurred some thirty years earlier, but this "success" was not anticipated in the intervening years (as shown by the high discount rates attached to failed member-banks' notes during the 1850s), and the fund did not protect current bank liabilities or the payments system *ex ante*, as it was intended to do.

Not only did the system fail to provide protection to the payments system, but it also suffered unusually large losses due to fraud or unsound banking practices. While a supervisory authority was established to prevent fraud and excessive risk taking, supervision was ineffectual, and fraud or unsafe practices were common. Ten of sixteen member-bank failures prior to 1842 (the period when insurance was still perceived as effective) were traceable to fraud or unsafe practices. Moreover, such problems were not detected until after they had imposed large losses on the fund.

The failure of the Safety Fund was not the fault of external shocks, severe as they were. In aggregate, banking capital was large relative to losses, and thus coinsurance among all New York banks would have been feasible. Rather it was the design of the insurance system that made it weak. Upper bounds on annual premia prevented adequate *ex ante* insurance during panics, and ineffectual supervision allowed large risk takers to free ride on other banks. Finally, adverse selection caused a retreat from the system through charter-switching to the alternative free-banking system, once solvent banks realized the extent of the losses.

Vermont and Michigan followed New York's example and suffered its problems. In Vermont banks were even allowed to join and depart at will. It took only two bank failures to cause the dissolution of that system; one failure was due to fraud, and the other was that of a bank that joined the system after that bank's prospects had deteriorated. Again, an incentive-compatible, broadly based system could have provided coinsurance among banks, but adverse selection and poor supervision prevented this.

Michigan's system, created in 1836, collapsed because it (like the other two systems) depended for its resources on accumulated contributions to the collective fund, which would be used to support banks during a crisis. The Michigan system had no time to accumulate a sufficient fund prior to the Panics of 1837 and 1839 and thus was unable to provide protection.

Not all antebellum experiments ended so disastrously as these three. Indiana enacted a different sort of liability insurance plan in 1834, one based on the principles of self-regulation and unlimited mutual liability that would later be imitated by private clearing houses. The Indiana system did not suffer the supervisory laxity or membership retreat of New York and Vermont, nor the illiquidity of Michigan and New York. Coverage was broad-based, and there was no problem in attracting and keeping members. During its thirty-year history no insured bank failed. There was a suspension of convertibility in 1837 and again in 1839, but this was the last time banks were even forced to suspend. During the regional panic of 1854–1855 and the national Panic of 1857, all insured banks maintained operations and convertibility. During those same panics 69 of 126 nonmember, uncoordinated free banks failed in Indiana.

The Indiana system relied on bankers themselves to make and enforce laws and regulations through a board of directors and, importantly, gave it authority to decide when to close a bank. Unlimited mutual liability provided bankers the incentive to regulate and enforce properly. The Indiana system was imitated in Ohio and Iowa, with similarly successful results. Ohio's law granted its Board of Control even greater author- ity than Indiana's Board, allowing it virtually unlimited discretionary powers during a banking crisis, including the right to force banks to make loans to one another. Interbank loans were successfully used during the Panic of 1857 to avoid suspension of convertibility. The insured banks, it seems, even came to the assistance of nonmember banks during the Panic, as indicated by flows of interbank loans. Only one Ohio bank failed during the crisis, and it was not a member of the insured system. Iowa's system was in place for a shorter and more stable period, but its operation was similarly successful.

Like clearing houses, these three successful insurance schemes aligned the incentive and authority to regulate and made insurance protection credible through unlimited mutual liability among banks. Like Southern branch banks in the Panics of 1837 and 1857 these systems were able to minimize systemic disruption through a coordinated, incentive- compatible response. They were brought to an end not by insolvency, but by federal taxation of bank notes designed to promote the National Banking System.

1.5.2   The second, postbellum wave of state insurance

The eight deposit-insurance fund systems of the early twentieth century failed to learn the lessons of the antebellum experience; they repeated and compounded the earlier errors of New York, Vermont, and Michigan. Supervisory authority was placed in government, not member bank, hands, and often its use or disuse was politically motivated (Robb, 1921). Furthermore, the numbers of banks insured were many more than in the antebellum systems (often several hundred), and this further reduced the incentive for a bank to monitor and report the misbehavior of its neighbor banks, since the payoff from detection was shared with so many and the cost of monitoring was private.

During the halcyon days for agriculture, from 1914 to 1920, deposit insurance prompted unusually high growth, particularly of small rural banks on thin capital. The insured states' banks grew faster, were smaller, and had lower capital ratios than their state-chartered counterparts in fast-growing, or neighboring states. Table 1.9 reports regression results that confirm the unusually high growth of state-chartered insured banks (controlling for other variables) relative to other agricultural states. A decomposition among voluntary- and compulsory-insurance laws reveals that the incentives to grow were especially pronounced in the compulsory-insurance systems (where the potential for cross-subsidization, or free riding through excessive risk taking, was highest).

When agricultural prices fell, insured banking systems suffered the highest rates of decline and failure among state-chartered banks in agricultural states (although the statistical significance of failure rate comparisons is sensitive to choice of data and controls for interstate comparisons – see Thies and Gerlowski, 1989; Calomiris, 1992; Alston et al., 1994). All the insurance fund systems collapsed during the 1920s (American Bankers Association, 1933; Federal Deposit Insurance Corporation, 1956). Insured systems also saw greater delays in closing and liquidating insolvent banks, reminiscent of politically motivated delays that have occurred during the recent thrift crisis (Calomiris, 1992).

Comparisons of losses by failed banks, however, leave little doubt that the presence of insurance was associated with greater bank stress. North Dakota, South Dakota, and Nebraska – the three states that had long-lived, free-entry, compulsory deposit insurance, which provided the worst and most prolonged incentives for risk taking – experienced the most drastic losses by far among the state- and national-chartered systems. While several state-chartered systems experienced shocks comparable to those suffered by these three, in no other cases were the asset shortfalls of insolvent banks nearly large enough to threaten the capital

Table 1.9. *Regression results: Asset growth of state-chartered banks*[a]

Independent variables	Coefficient	Standard error	Significance level
Dependent Variable: Growth in total assets of state-chartered banks, 1914–1920			
Intercept	0.101	0.465	0.829
National bank growth	0.681	0.147	0.000
(Reserve center) × (National bank growth)[b]	−0.132	0.060	0.038
Growth in land values, 1914–1920	0.555	0.333	0.107
Ratio of farm to nonfarm population	−0.283	0.654	0.669
Presence of voluntary or compulsory insurance	0.518	0.165	0.004
$R^2 = 0.670$			
$\bar{R}^2 = 0.607$			
Dependent Variable: Growth in total assets of state-chartered banks, 1914–1920			
Intercept	0.156	0.468	0.741
National bank growth	0.682	0.147	0.000
(Reserve center) × (National bank growth)[b]	−0.115	0.063	0.080
Growth in land values, 1914–1920	0.526	0.334	0.127
Ratio of farm to nonfarm population	−0.328	0.655	0.621
Presence of voluntary insurance	0.327	0.251	0.205
presence of compulsory insurance	0.609	0.189	0.004
$R^2 = 0.683$			
$\bar{R}^2 = 0.607$			

[a] Asset growth is defined as the log difference of total assets. All variables are defined at the state level for a sample of 32 agricultural states.
[b] National bank growth in each state is used as a control for state-chartered bank growth. In reserve-center states, national bank growth may be larger, as it reflects growth of correspondent banks outside the state as well. To control for this difference, I interact national banking growth with an indicator variable for states with reserve centers.
Source: Calomiris, 1992.

of the banking system as a whole (Table 1.10). In contrast, banks in these states showed shortfalls of between 1.5 and 5 times the remaining bank equity of state banks. In light of the differences in the failure experiences of insured and branch banking in the 1920s, it is little wonder that four of the eight states that previously had opted for deposit insurance were among those liberalizing their branching restrictions during this period.

Table 1.10. *Estimated asset shortfalls of failed banks relative to remaining bank equity in "severe-failure" states*

	National banks						State chartered banks					All banks	
	Deposits of suspended banks ($000) 1921–30[a]	Number of liquidations relative to suspensions[b]	Size ratio[c]	Rate of asset shortfall[d]	Estimated shortfall[e]	Total bank equity ($000) June 1930	Deposits of suspended banks ($000) 1921–30[a]	Number of liquidations relative to suspensions[b]	Size ratio[c]	Rate of asset shortfall[d]	Estimated shortfall[e]	Total bank equity ($000) June 1930	Ratio of shortfall to equity
Arizona	1,256	0.67	0.83	0.50	349	3,815	15,056	0.80	0.06	0.09	65	8,496	0.03
Colorado	11,003	0.94	0.45	0.40	1,862	13,776	12,187	0.95	0.95	0.32	3,520	10,273	0.22
Georgia	16,538	0.84	0.09	0.49	613	39,064	46,318	0.75	0.70	0.56	13,618	39,805	0.18
Idaho	10,601	0.81	0.65	0.53	2,958	4,612	9,185	0.85	0.63	0.51	2,509	4,983	0.57
Iowa	55,984	0.79	0.50	0.31	6,855	35,750	138,995	0.75	0.66	0.46	31,649	74,935	0.35
Minnesota	28,338	0.97	0.59	0.42	6,812	69,387	80,634	0.77	0.47	0.52	15,174	38,417	0.20
Montana	16,287	0.87	0.44	0.66	4,115	9,999	31,361	0.89	0.47	0.48	6,297	9,947	0.52
Nebraska	13,695	0.80	0.94	0.56	5,767	26,083	78,093	0.85	1.04	0.65	44,872	27,760	0.94
North Dakota	17,438	0.84	0.80	0.55	6,445	9,210	45,199	0.92	1.05	0.83	36,240	9,695	2.26
Oklahoma	27,364	0.72	0.70	0.57	7,861	41,251	38,986	0.79	0.28	0.44	3,794	11,493	0.22
South Carolina	12,153	0.92	0.57	0.49	3,123	11,665	50,970	0.91	0.58	0.34	9,147	17,069	0.43
South Dakota	21,109	0.93	0.60	0.49	5,772	9,477	91,619	0.77	1.00	0.76	53,615	10,848	3.07
Wyoming	9,154	0.91	0.45	0.30	1,125	4,819	7,536	0.80	0.48	0.46	1,331	3,844	0.28

[a] Deposits are defined at the time of bank suspension.

[b] The number of bank liquidations relative to suspensions measures the proportion of suspended banks that were liquidated.

[c] The average size of liquidated banks is divided by the average size of suspended banks to produce this ratio.

[d] The rate of asset shortfall equals 1 minus the ratio of the value of liquidated assets to deposit liabilities.

[e] The estimated shortfall is the product of the preceding four columns.

[f] The all-bank ratio of shortfall to equity divides estimated asset shortfall for state and national banks by the equity of surviving banks of both types.

Source: Calomiris, 1992.

The evidence of moral–hazard and adverse–selection problems in these antebellum and postbellum liability insurance plans provide a fortiori evidence of similar dangers in current federal deposit insurance. The state insurance systems of the 1920s limited interest paid on deposits, typically required ratios of capital to deposits in excess of 10 percent, and were funded by the accumulated contributions of members. By contrast, today's federal insurance does not restrict interest payments to depositors, requires a smaller proportion of capital to deposits, and is supported by the full faith and credit of the federal government. Thus today's financial intermediaries can maintain higher leverage and attract depositors more easily by offering higher rates of return with virtually no risk of default. From this perspective, the unprecedented losses of Texas banks and thrifts in the 1980s should come as no surprise (Horvitz, 1991).

1.6 From history to informed policy

Notwithstanding political-economic explanations, which I have argued can help to explain bank regulation, the regulatory mistakes of American banking history are remarkable and unique. Is there any hope for undoing the mistakes of the past, which have produced a fragmented, unstable, and inefficient banking system? Can we learn usefully from history?

In principle, the lessons are straightforward: The United States should move to an uninsured, interstate branching system with broad powers for banks (for historical perspectives on the advantages of broad powers for banks prior to Glass-Steagall see Osterweis, 1932; Peach, 1941, E. N. White, 1986; and Kaufman and Mote, 1989, 1990). In practice there are many obstacles. Change is often less comprehensive than we would wish, and introducing "lessons from history" is more risky than one might expect. The problem in the openness to "learn" from history is the possibility one will learn incorrectly or too selectively. In the history of banking regulation in the United States policymakers have been perhaps too willing to learn from immediate history. Banking regulation has traditionally been forged in the crucible of crisis. Consider the following examples: the rechartering of the Bank of the United States in the aftermath of the War of 1812; the introduction of entirely new chartering forms (including free banking) as a means of rapidly increasing the number of banks in the 1840s; the creation of the National Banking System as a Civil War measure; the enactment of state deposit insurance plans and the Federal Reserve Act on the heels of the Panic of 1907; branching and consolidation reforms during the agricultural distress of the 1920s; and the creation of the FDIC and the separation of investment and commercial banking during the trough of the Great Depression. In each case, policy-makers in the United States have seemed incapable or unwilling to look farther back than the last crisis, farther ahead than the next election, or beyond the borders of their own nation or state. In some extreme cases, like the Glass-Steagall Act, one can find little rational basis for Congressional action (E. N. White, 1986; Benston, 1989).

While this "knee-jerk" approach to bank regulation has offered great flexibility in times of need, it also has led to myopic and simplistic applications of the lessons of the past. These reactions often have lasting effects, given that important changes are infrequent. Consider the most important changes wrought in the 1930s. An alternative to deposit insurance as a means to stabilize banking – one that was understood and considered – was a movement toward nationwide branch banking. Why was it rejected? One explanation for the failure to move in that direction was the weakening of support for branching by an influential policymaker (Marriner Eccles, the Chairman of the Federal Reserve System) during the debate over the 1935 Banking Act. Doti and Schweikart (1991, pp. 133–34, 139–40, 171–72) argue that Eccles' change of heart regarding branching was attributable in part to his desire to constrain the growth of the Bank of America, possibly due to Eccles' personal dislike of A. P. Giannini (who would have stood to benefit greatly from the reform) or to Eccles' hope to maximize the influence of the Federal Reserve Board by maintaining a fragmented banking system. In the absence of a strong supporter of branch banking in the Roosevelt Administration, congressional hostility to branch banking faced no significant opposition. Once the crisis had passed, any real opportunity for branching reform had disappeared, as well. Eccles' support at a crucial juncture could have made a difference. The lessons of this episode seem to be that the window of opportunity for policymaking is often brief, and the guiding principles of policymakers during such opportune moments often may have little to do with the optimal allocation of scarce resources.

Not only has the accident of the Great Depression had a lasting regulatory effect through the inertia of policy, it has provided selective "lessons from history" that continue to exert a death grip on the imaginations of academics and policymakers, providing seemingly incontrovertible evidence of the inherent instability of banking and the need for constant government intervention to prevent a "meltdown." A better set of lessons would have been how preventable and unusually bad the Great Depression was, even from the jaundiced perspective of earlier American banking history; and more important, that the fragility of

American banking has always been an artifact of a fragmented, inefficient, and uncoordinated unit banking system.

A similar sort of regime-specific tunnel vision has preoccupied much of the recent academic literature on economies of scale and scope in banking. It simply does not make sense to reject the efficiency of a nationwide branching system, or the efficacy of relaxing Glass-Steagall (the economies of which could not possibly show themselves in a restrictive regulatory environment) on the basis of failing to find large economies of scale or scope for banks because the gains from expanded powers and size may be highly regime-dependant (Litan, 1987, pp. 110–11; Brewer, 1989, 1995; Kaufman and Mote, 1989, 1990; Brewer and Mondschean, 1991). Here our own history and the experiences of other countries are a much better guide to the advantages of deregulation.

1.6.1 Which lessons, which cures?

If reform is to be more modest, successful advocates must be selective in the enthusiasm with which they advocate particular reforms. Before suggesting a cure, or a triage ordering – even one informed by history – it helps to know which disease is likely to kill the patient first. There is much that is wrong with U.S. banking today, and there are many competing priority lists for which things to "fix" first. Which historical episodes are most relevant for the current declines and high failure rates of banks? Have banks taken on too much risk in the face of the perverse incentives of deposit insurance, as in the agricultural boom of the 1910s? If so, then a reform of bank capital regulations or a move to "narrow banking" might be sufficient to reverse the trend (for a discussion of the relative merits of these views, see Calomiris, 1991c, 1991d). In contrast, simply allowing bank consolidation or branching as a means to stability, without reforming deposit insurance, may be highly inappropriate in the current context, and may lead to even greater losses. As Boyd and Graham (1991) point out, in today's economy large banks do not seem less likely to fail, possibly because the incentives to take on risk (due to the mispricing of deposit insurance) are largest for these banks. Calomiris (1991c) suggests a means for simultaneously reforming (partly privatizing) deposit insurance and expanding bank branching and other bank powers while avoiding the potential problems of moral hazard due to mispriced deposit insurance.

But there may be bigger problems to address than insurance reform. While there is an accumulating body of evidence that deposit insurance has increased the risk taking and losses from failure of savings and loans (Barth, et al., 1989; Brewer, 1995), there is little evidence of this as a cause of the current distress of commercial banks, with the significant exception of Texas (Horvitz, 1991) and possibly some large, low-capital, "too-big-to-fail" banks in the East.

Gorton and Rosen (1995) propose a different explanation for bank distress, which sees banks as a protected industry with entrenched management. Declining lending opportunities, a captive deposit base, and bank managements' unwillingness to shrink, according to their view, reduced the portfolio quality of commercial banks in the 1980s. In the absence of a means for banks to be acquired more readily (thus disciplining managers) banks continued to operate inefficiently and failed. The closest historical parallel to this case is banking in the 1880s and 1890s. Lamoreaux's (1991a, 1991b) discussion of the entrenchment of some New England bank managements in the 1890s and their resistance to profitable consolidation is informative. By limiting branching and consolidation in the 1890s and by allowing expansion through lowered capital requirements, bank regulation set the stage for the increased fragmentation and subsequent collapse of the next four decades.

Another pitfall from historical learning in bank regulation is the selective application of lessons, which can be counter productive. For example, the trend in bank consolidation in the 1980s has been to allow within-state, rather than interstate mergers. In some states (notably California) this may reduce the number of competitors so much that the system becomes monopolistic. Aside from the inefficiency of creating monopoly, such a development would tend to reinforce the unfortunate incorrect association between large-scale banking and bank monopolization that has plagued U.S. regulatory history for 200 years. If Bresnahan and Reiss's (1991) findings regarding competition in local retail service markets is applicable to banks, somewhere between 3 and 5 competitors in any local market is adequate for competition. Indeed, Shaffer (1991) applies a similar method to measure the extent of market power in the current highly concentrated Canadian branch banking system and strongly rejects its existence. Thus the concentration ratios for some statewide-branching systems as of 1979, reported in L. J. White (1986, p. 187), probably did not pose a great problem for competition. Within-state mergers with barriers to entry by out-of-state banks, however, would threaten to restrict the field in some states to one or two major banks or bank holding companies, and this is worrisome.

A final caveat to applying the lessons of the past is the mutability of the economic environment. For example, Gorton and Pennacchi (1991) suggest that the technology of banking has changed significantly in the last decade and that securitization of loans and loan sales indicate a reduction in the asymmetric information problem that gives rise to banking panics (which has motivated deposit insurance, or alternatively, bank consolidation and branching). To the extent that banks increasingly can diversify risk *ex ante* through loan sales and securitization, the historical problems of fragility and inefficient capital allocation associated with fragmentation in banking are reduced.

This reduction does not mean that restrictions on the industrial organization of intermediaries have become irrelevant. So long as there are some links between bank loan portfolios and bank customer bases, entry restrictions will continue to be important impediments to diversification. Despite the important growth of loan sales without recourse, I remain skeptical that loans of many small- and medium-scale industrial and commercial borrowers of commercial banks, and even those of some larger firms, can be sold without recourse to passive investors. For example, the recent empirical findings of Hoshi, Kashyap, and Schartstein (1990b); Gilson, John, and Lang (1990); and Brown, James, and Mooradian (1993) all point to a continuing role for financial intermediaries to manage renegotiations of debt in distress states (rather than simply to screen borrowers initially). In particular, bank recontracting of debt can provide signals to other debt holders as to whether they should force liquidation of the firm or accept a particular form of renegotiation. What is not clear from any of these studies is whether the benefits of bank control over recontracting might depend, at least for some firms, on bank ownership of loans. For some firms an impediment to loan sales may be the incentive problem of delegating recontracting decisions to relatively informed bank agents who do not themselves own the loans. If this were the case, then for some firms and their banks it would be beneficial to allow bank diversification directly through new products and locations.

References

Aharony, Joseph, and Itzhak Swary (1983). "Contagion Effects of Bank Failures: Evidence from the Capital Markets." *Journal of Business* 56 (July), 305–22.

Alston, Lee J., Wayne A. Grove, and David C. Wheelock (1994). "Why Do Banks Fail? Evidence from the 1920s." *Explorations in Economic History* 30 (October), 409–31.

American Bankers Association (1933). *The Guaranty of Bank Deposits.* New York: The Association.

(1935). *The Bank Chartering History of the United States.* New York: The Association.

Asquith, Paul, and David W. Mullins, Jr. (1986). "Equity Issues and Offering Dilution." *Journal of Financial Economics* 15 (January/February), 61–89.

Baer, Herbert L., and Larry R. Mote (1991). "The United States Financial System." Federal Reserve Bank of Chicago working paper.

Bagehot, Walter (1873). *Lombard Street: A Description of the Money Market.* New York: Scribner, Armstrong.

Bankers Encyclopedia Co. *The Bankers Encylcopedia.* New York, semiannual.

Barth, James R., Philip F. Bartholomew, and Carol J. Labich (1989). "Moral Hazard and the Thrift Crisis: An Analysis of 1988 Resolutions." Federal Home Loan Bank Board Research Paper No. 160.

Benston, George J. (1989). *The Separation of Commercial and Investment Banking: The Glass-Steagall Act Revisited and Reconsidered.* Norwell: Kluwer Academic.

Benveniste, Lawrence M., and Paul A. Spindt (1989). "Bringing New Issues to Market: A Theory of Underwriting." Federal Reserve Board Finance and Economics Discussion Paper No. 39.

Bernanke, Ben S. (1983). "Nonmonetary Effects of the Financial Crisis in the Propagation of the Great Depression." *American Economic Review* 73 (June), 257–76.

Bernanke, Ben S., and Mark L. Gertler (1990). "Financial Fragility and Economic Performance." *Quarterly Journal of Economics 105* (February), 87–114.

Bernanke, Ben S., and Harold James (1991). "The Gold Standard, Deflation, and Financial Crisis in the Great Depression: An International Comparison." In *Financial Markets and Financial Crises*, ed. R. Glenn Hubbard, Chicago: University of Chicago Press, pp. 33–68.

Binder, John J., and Anthony T. Brown (1991). "Bank Rates of Return and Entry Restrictions, 1869–1914." *Journal of Economic History* 51 (March), 47–66.

Board of Governors of the Federal Reserve System (1929). "Branch Banking Developments, June 30 1928." *Federal Reserve Bulletin* (February), 97–105.

  (1959). *All Bank Statistics.* Washington, D.C.: Board of Governors.

  (1976). *Banking and Monetary Statistics, 1914–1941.* Washington, D.C.: Board of Governors.

Bodenhorn, Howard N. (1990). "Banking and the Integration of Antebellum American Financial Markets, 1815–1859." Rutgers University, Ph.D. diss.

Bogue, Allan G. (1955). *Money at Interest: The Farm Mortgage on the Middle Border.* Lincoln: University of Nebraska Press.

Bordo, Michael D. (1985). "The Impact and International Transmission of Financial Crises: Some Historical Evidence, 1870–1933." *Revista di Storia Economica* 2, 41–78.

Bordo, Michael D., and Angela Redish (1987). "Why Did the Bank of Canada Emerge in 1935?" *Journal of Economic History* 47 (June), 405–18.

Boyd, John H., and Stanley L. Graham (1986). "Risk, Regulation, and Bank Holding Company Expansion into Nonbanking." *Federal Reserve Bank of Minneapolis Quarterly Review 10* (Spring), 2–17.

(1988). "The Profitability and Risk Effects of Allowing Bank Holding Companies to Merge with Other Financial Firms: A Simulation Study." In *The Financial Services Industry in the Year 2000: Risk and Efficiency, Proceedings of a Conference on Bank Structure and Competition*, pp. 476–514.

(1991). "Investigating the Banking Consolidation Trend." *Federal Reserve Bank of Minneapolis Quarterly Review* 15 (Spring), 3–15.

Boyd, John H., Stanley L. Graham, and R. Shawn Hewiitt (1988). "Bank Holding Company Mergers with Nonbank Financial Firms: Their Effects on the Risk of Failure." Federal Reserve Bank of Minneapolis Working Paper No. 417.

Boyd, John H., and Edward C. Prescott (1986). "Financial Intermediary-Coalitions." *Journal of Economic Theory* 38, 211–32.

Bradford, Frederick A. (1940). *The Legal Status of Branching in the United States.* New York: American Bankers Association.

Brandeis, Louis D. (1914). *Other People's Money and How the Bankers Use It.* New York: Frederick A. Stokes.

Breckenridge, Roeliff M. (1899a). "Bank Notes and Branch Banks." *Sound Currency* 6 (April), 49–56.

(1899b). "Branch Banking and Discount Rates." *Sound Currency* 6 (January), 1–14.

(1910). *The History of Banking in Canada.* National Monetary Commission. 61st Congress, 2nd Session. Senate Document 332. Washington, D.C.: U.S. Government Printing Office.

Bremer, C. D. (1935). *American Bank Failures.* New York: Columbia University Press.

Bresnehan, Timothy F., and Peter C. Reiss (1991). "Entry and Competition in Concentrated Markets." *Journal of Political Economy* 99 (October), 977–1009.

Brewer, Elijah (1989). "Relationship between Bank Holding Company Risk and Nonbank Activity." *Journal of Economics and Business* 41, 337–53.

(1995). "The Impact of Deposit Insurance on S&L Share-holders' Risk/Return Trade-offs." *Journal of Financial Services Research* 9, 65–89.

Brewer, Elijah, and Thomas H. Mondschean (1991). "An Empirical Test of the Incentive Effects of Deposit Insurance: The Case of Junk Bonds at Savings and Loan Associations." Federal Reserve Bank of Chicago Working Paper WP-91-18.

Brewer, Elijah, Diana Fortier, and Christine Pavel (1988). "Bank Risk from Nonbank Activities." Federal Reserve Bank of Chicago Economic Perspectives (July/August), 14–26.

Brock, Leslie (1975). *The Currency of the American Colonies, 1700–1764: A Study of Colonial Finance and Imperial Relations.* New York.

Brown, David T., Christopher James, and Robert M. Mooradian (1993). "The Information Content of Distressed Restructurings Involving Public and Private Debt Claims." *Journal of Financial Economics* 33 (February), 93–118.

Bryan, Alfred C. (1899). "History of State Banking in Maryland." *Johns Hopkins University Studies in Historical and Political Science* (January), 1–144.

Bullock, Charles J. (1895). "The Finances of the United States from 1775 to 1789, with Especial Reference to the Budget." *Bulletin of the University of Wisconsin; Economics, Political Science, and History Series I*, 117–273.

(1900). *Essays on the Monetary History of the United States*. New York: Macmillan.

Butters, J. Keith, and John Lintner (1945). *Effect of Federal Taxes on Growing Enterprises*. Boston: Harvard University.

Calomiris, Charles W. (1988a). "Institutional Failure, Monetary Scarcity, and the Depreciation of the Continental." *Journal of Economic History* 48 (March), 47–68.

(1988b). "The Depreciation of the Continental: A Reply." *Journal of Economic History* 48 (September), 693–98.

(1989). "Deposit Insurance: Lessons from the Record." *Federal Reserve Bank of Chicago Economic Perspectives* (May/June), 10–30.

(1990). "Is Deposit Insurance Necessary? A Historical Perspective." *Journal of Economic History* 50 (June), 283–95.

(1991a). "The Motives of U.S. Debt-Management Policy, 1790–1880: Efficient Discrimination and Time Consistency." *Research in Economic History* 13, pp. 67–105.

(1991b). "Comment on 'Information Problems and Banks' Specialization in Short-Term Commercial Lending: New England in the Nineteenth Century'." In *Inside the Business Enterprise: Historical Perspectives on the Use of Information*, ed. Peter Temin Chicago: University of Chicago Press, pp. 195–203.

(1991c). "Getting the Incentives Right in the Current Deposit Insurance System: Successes from the Pre-FDIC Era. "In *Reform of Deposit Insurance and the Regulation of Depository Institutions in the 1990s*, eds. James Barth and Dan Brumbough. New York: Harper Business, 13–35.

(1991d). "Comment on International Bank Capital Standards." *Research in International Business and Finance*, 9, pp. 75–81.

(1992). "Do Vulnerable Economies Need Deposit Insurance? Lessons from U.S. Agriculture in the 1920s." In *If Texas Were Chile: A Primer on Bank Regulation*, ed. Philip L. Brock. San Francisco: The Sequoia Institute.

Calomiris, Charles W., and Gary Gorton (1991). "The Origins of Banking Panics: Models, Facts, and Bank Regulation." In *Financial Markets and Financial Crises*. ed. R. Glenn Hubbard Chicago. University of Chicago Press, pp. 107–73.

Calomiris, Charles W., and R. Glenn Hubbard (1989). "Price Flexibility, Credit Availability, and Economic Fluctuations: Evidence from the United States, 1894–1909." *Quarterly Journal of Economics* 104 (May), 429–52.

(1990). "Firm Heterogeneity, Internal Finance, and 'Credit Rationing'." *The Economic Journal* 100 (March), 90–104.

(1995). "Internal Finance, and Investment: Evidence from the Undistributed Profits Tax of 1936–1937." *Journal of Business* 68 (October), 443–482.

(1996) "International Adjustment Under the Classical Gold Standard: Evidence for the U.S. and Britain, 1879–1914." In *Modern Perspectives on the Gold Standard*, eds. T. Boyonmi, B. Eichengreen, and M. Taylor. Cambridge: Cambridge University Press, 186–217.

Calomiris, Charles W., R. Glenn Hubbard, and James H. Stock (1986). "The Farm Debt Crisis and Public Policy." *Brookings Papers on Economic Activity* 2, 441–79.

Calomiris, Charles W., and Charles M. Kahn (1991). "The Role of Demandable Debt in Structuring Optimal Banking Arrangements." *American Economic Review* 81 (June), 497–513.

Calomiris, Charles W., and Charles M. Kahn (1996). "The Efficiency of Self-Regulated Payments Systems: Learning from the Suffolk System." *Journal of Money, Credit and Banking* 28 (November), Part 2, 766–97.

Calomiris, Charles W., Charles M. Kahn, and Stefan Krasa (1991). "Optimal Contingent Bank Liquidation Under Moral Hazard." Federal Reserve Bank of Chicago, Working Paper WP-91-13.

Calomiris, Charles W., and Larry Schweikart (1988). "Was the South Backward? North-South Differences in Antebellum Banking." Columbia University working paper.

(1991). "The Panic of 1857: Origins, Transmission, and Containment." *Journal of Economic History* 51 (December), pp. 807–34.

Campbell, Tim, and William Kracaw (1980). "Information Production, Market Signalling and the Theory of Financial *Intermediation.*"*Journal of Finance* 35 (September), 863–81.

Cannon, James G. (1910). *Clearing Houses.* National Monetary Commission. 61st Congress, 2nd Session. Senate Document 491. Washington. D.C.: U.S. Government Printing Office.

Capie, Forrest, and Alan Webber (1985). *A Monetary History of the United Kingdom, 1870–1982, Volume I.* London: George Allen and Unwin.

Carosso, Vincent P. (1970). *Investment Banking in America.* Cambridge: Harvard University Press.

Cartinhour, Gaines T. (1931). *Branch, Group and Chain Banking.* New York: Macmillan.

Champ, Bruce, Bruce D. Smith, and Stephen D. Williamson (1991). "Currency Elasticity and Banking Panics: Theory and Evidence." Cornell University, CAE Working Paper No. 91-14.

Chandler, Alfred D. (1977). *The Visible Hand: The Managerial Revolution in American Business.* Cambridge: Harvard University Press.

Chapman, John M. (1934). *Concentration of Banking: The Changing Structure and Control of Banking in the United States.* New York: Columbia University Press.

Chapman, John M., and Ray B. Westerfield (1942). *Branch Banking: Its Historical and Theoretical Position in America and Abroad.* New York: Harper and Brothers.

Chari, V. V. (1989). "Banking Without Deposit Insurance or Bank Panics: Lessons from a Model of the U.S. National Banking System." *Federal Reserve Bank of Minneapolis Quarterly Review* (Summer), 3–19.

Davis, Andrew M. (1900). *Currency and Banking in the Province of the Massachusetts Bay.* New York: Macmillan.

   (1911). *Colonial Currency Reprints. Boston.* Reprinted in New York by Augustus Kelley, 1970.

Davis, Lance E. (1965). "The Investment Market, 1870–1914: The Evolution of a National Market." *Journal of Economic History* 25 (September), 355–93.

DeLong, J. Bradford (1991). "Did J. P. Morgan's Men Add Value? In *Inside the Business Enterprise: Historical Perspectives on the Use of Information*, ed. Peter Temin. Chicago: University of Chicago Press, 205–36.

Dewey, Davis R. (1910). *State Banking Before the Civil War.* National Monetary Commission. 61st Congress, 2nd Session. Senate Document 581. Washington, D.C.: U.S. Government Printing Office.

Diamond, Douglas (1984). "Financial Intermediation and Delegated Monitoring." *Review of Economic Studies* 51 (July), 393–414.

Dornbusch, Rudiger, and Jacob A. Frenkel (1984). "The Gold Standard and the Bank of England in the Crisis of 1847." In *A Retrospective on the Classical Gold Standard, 1821–1931*, eds. Michael D. Bordo and Anna J. Schwartz. Chicago: University of Chicago Press, 233–64.

Doti, Lynne P., and Larry Schweikart (1991). *Banking in the American West: From the Gold Rush to Deregulation.* Norman: University of Oklahoma Press.

Duncombe, Charles (1841). *Duncombe's Free Banking.* Cleveland: Sanford and Co.

Dutton, John (1984). "The Bank of England and the Rules of the Game under the International Gold Standard: New Evidence." In *A Retrospective on the Classical Gold Standard*, eds. Michael D. Bordo and Anna J. Schwartz. Chicago: University of Chicago Press, pp. 173–95.

Eichengreen, Barry (1984a). "Currency and Credit in the Gilded Age." *Research in Economic History* 3 (supplement), 87–114.

   (1984b). "Mortgage Interest Rates in the Populist Era." *American Economic Review* 74 (December), 995–1015.

   (1992). *Golden Fetters: The Gold Standard and the Great Depression, 1919–1939.* Oxford: Oxford University Press.

Ernst, Joseph (1973). *Money and Politics in America, 1755–1775.* Chapel Hill: University of North Carolina Press.

Evanoff, Douglas D. (1988). "Branch Banking and Service Accessibility." *Journal of Money, Credit and Banking* 20 (May), 191–202.

Fama, Eugene F. (1980). "Banking in the Theory of Finance."*Journal of Monetary Economics* 6 (January), 39–58.

Federal Deposit Insurance Corporation (1956). *Annual Report.* Washington, D.C.: FDIC.

Fenstermaker, J. Van (1965). *The Development of American Commercial Banking, 1782–1837.* Kent, Ohio: Kent State University.

Fisher, Irving (1933). "The Debt-Deflation Theory of Great Depressions." *Econometrica* 1, 337–57.

Fishlow, Albert (1965). *American Railroads and the Transformation of the AnteBellum Economy.* Cambridge: Harvard University Press.

Foulke, Roy A. (1941). *The Sinews of American Commerce.* New York: Dunn and Bradstreet.

Franklin, Benjamin (1729). "A Modest Inquiry into the Nature and Necessity of a Paper Currency." In *The Works of Benjamin Franklin, II*, ed. Jared Sparks. p. 1840.

Friedman, Milton, and Anna J. Schwartz (1963). A *Monetary History of the United States. 1867–1960.* Princeton: Princeton University Press.

Gage, Lyman J. (1906). "Currency Reform a Necessity." *Moody's Magazine*, 457–67.

Gale, Douglas, and Martin Hellwig (1985). "Incentive-Compatible Debt Contracts: The One-Period Problem." *Review of Economic Studies* (October), 647–63.

Gendreau, Brian (1990). "Federal Reserve Policy and the Great Depression." University of Pennsylvania working paper.

Gillett, A. D. S. (1900). "Better Credit Facilities for our Rural Communities." *Sound Currency* 7. 183–208.

Gilson, Stuart C., Kose John, and Larry H. P. Lang (1990). "Troubled Debt Restructurings." *Journal of Financial Economics* 27, 315–53.

Golembe, Carter H. (1960). "The Deposit Insurance Legislation of 1933: An Examination of Its Antecedants and Its *Purposes." Political Science Quarterly* (June), 189–95.

Golembe, Carter H., and Clark S. Warburton (1958). *Insurance of Bank Obligations in Six States During the Period 1829–1866.* Washington, D.C.: Federal Deposit Insurance Corporation.

Gorton, Gary (1985). "Clearing Houses and the Origin of Central Banking in the U.S." *Journal of Economic History* 45 (June), 277–83.

(1989). "Self-Regulating Bank Coalitions." University of Pennsylvania working paper.

(1990). "Free Banking, Wildcat Banking, and the Market for Bank Notes." University of Pennsylvania working paper.

Gorton, Gary, and Donald Mullineaux (1987). "The Joint Production of Confidence: Endogenous Regulation and Nineteenth-Century Commercial Bank Clearinghouses." *Journal of Money, Credit and Banking* 19 (November), 458–68.

Gorton, Gary, and George Pennacchi (1991). "Banks and Loan Sales: Marketing Non-Marketable Assets." NBER Working Paper No. 3551.

Gorton, Gary, and Richard Rosen (1995). "Corporate Control, Portfolio Choice and the Decline of Banking," *Journal of Finance* 50 (December), 1377–420.

Govan, Thomas (1936). "The Banking and Credit System in Georgia." Vanderbilt University, Ph.D. dissertation.

Grammatikos, Theoharry, and Anthony Saunders (1990). "Additions to Bank Loan-Loss Reserves: Good News or Bad News?" *Journal of Monetary Economics* 25 (March), 289–304.

Greef, Albert O. (1938). *The Commercial Paper House in the United States.* Cambridge: Harvard University Press.

Hamilton, James (1987). "Monetary Factors in the Great Depression." *Journal of Monetary Economics* 19 (March), 145–69.

Hammond, Bray (1957). *Banks and Politics in America from the Revolution to the Civil War.* Princeton: Princeton University Press.

Handlin, Oscar, and Mary F. Handlin (1947). *Commonwealth: A Study of the Role of Government in the American Economy, Massachusetts, 1774–1861.* New York: New York University Press.

Hartz, Louis (1948). *Economic Policy and Democratic Thought: Pennsylvania, 1776–1860.* Cambridge: Harvard University Press.

Haubrich, Joseph G. (1990). "Nonmonetary Effects of Financial Crises: Lessons from the Great Depression in Canada." *Journal of Monetary Economics* 25 (March), 223–52.

Horvitz, Paul M. (1991). "The Causes of Texas Bank and Thrift Failures." In *If Texas Were Chile: A Primer on Bank Regulation*, ed. Phillip L. Brock. San Francisco: The Sequoia Institute.

Horwitz, Morton J. (1971). "The Emergence of an Instrumental Conception of American Law, 1780–1820." *Perspectives in American History* 5, 285–326.

(1977). *The Transformation of American Law, 1780–1860.* Cambridge: Harvard University Press.

(1985). "Santa Clara Revisited: The Development of Corporate Theory." *West Virginia Law Review* 88, 173–224.

Hoshi, Takeo, Anil Kashyap, and David Scharfstein (1990a). "Bank Monitoring and Investment: Evidence from the Changing Structure of Japanese Corporate Banking Relationships." In *Asymmetric Information, Corporate Finance, and Investment*, ed. R. Glenn Hubbard. Chicago: University of Chicago Press, pp. 105–26.

(1990b). "The Role of Banks in Reducing the Costs of Financial Distress." *Journal of Financial Economics* 27 (September), 67–88.

(1991). "Corporate Structure, Liquidity, and Investment: Evidence from Japanese Industrial Groups." *Quarterly Journal of Economics* 106 (February), 33–60.

Hughes, Jonathan R. T. (1960). *Fluctuations in Trade, Industry, and Finance: A Study of British Economic Development, 1850–1860.* Oxford: Oxford University Press.

(1976). *Social Control in the Colonial Economy.* Charlottesville: University of Virginia Press.

(1984). "Comment on 'The Gold Standard and the Bank of England in the Crisis of 1847.'" In *A Retrospective on the Classical Gold Standard, 1821–*

1931, eds. Michael D. Bordo and Anna J. Schwartz. Chicago: University of Chicago Press, pp. 265–71.

(1991). *The Governmental Habit Redux.* Princeton: Princeton University Press.

Hunt's Merchants' Magazine. New York: G. W. and J. A. Wood.

Hurst, James W. (1970). *The Legitimacy of the Business Corporation.* Charlottesville: University of Virginia Press.

(1973). *A Legal History of Money in the United States, 1774–1970.* Lincoln: University of Nebraska Press.

James, Christopher (1987). "Some Evidence on the Uniqueness of Bank Loans." *Journal of Financial Economics* 19, 217–35.

James, Christopher, and Peggy Wier (1989). "Are Bank Loans Different? Some Evidence from the Stock *Market." Journal of Applied Corporate Finance,* 46–54.

(1990). "Borrowing Relationships, Intermediation, and the Cost of Issuing Public Securities." *Journal of Financial Economics* 28 (November/December), 149–72.

James, John A. (1976a). "The Development of the National Money Market, 1893–1911." *Journal of Economic History* 36 (December), 878–97.

(1976b). "Banking Market Structure, Risk, and the Pattern of Local Interest Rates in the United States, 1893–1911." *Review of Economics and Statistics* 58 (November), 453–62.

(1978). *Money and Capital Markets in Postbellum America.* Princeton: Princeton University Press.

James, Marquis, and Bessie R. James (1954). *Biography of a Bank: The Story of Bank of America.* New York: Harper and Brothers.

Jauncey, L. C. (1933). *Australia's Government Bank.* London: Cranley and Day.

Johnson, Joseph F. (1910). *The Canadian Banking System.* National Monetary Commission. 61st Congress, 2nd Session. Senate Document 583. Washington, D.C.: US. Government Printing Office.

Kaufman, George G., and Larry Mote (1989). "Securities Activities of Commercial Banks: The Current Economic and Legal Environment." Federal Reserve Bank of Chicago working paper.

(1990). "Glass-Steagall Repeal by Regulatory and Judicial Reinterpretation." *Banking Law Journal* (September–October), 388–421.

Kindleberger, Charles P. (1984). *A Financial History of Western Europe.* London: George Allen and Unwin.

Klebaner, Benjamin J. (1990). *American Commercial Banking: A History.* Boston: Twayne Publishers.

Knox, John J. (1900). *A History of Banking in the United States.* New York: Bradford Rhodes.

Korajczyk, Robert A., Deborah Lucas, and Robert L. McDonald (1990). "Understanding Stock Price Behavior Around the Time of Equity Issues." In *Asymmetric Information, Corporate Finance, and Investment,* ed. R. Glenn Hubbard. Chicago: University of Chicago Press, pp. 257–78.

Kryzanowski, Lawrence, and Gordon S. Roberts (1989). "The Performance of the

Canadian Banking System, 1920–1940." In *Banking System Risk: Charting a New Course, Proceedings of the 25th Annual Conference on Bank Structure and Competition.* Chicago: Federal Reserve Bank of Chicago.

Laderman, Elizabeth S., Ronald H. Schmidt, and Gary C. Zimmerman (1991). "Location, Branching, and Bank Portfolio Diversification: The Case of Agricultural Lending." *Federal Reserve Bank of San Francisco Economic Review* (Winter), 24–37.

Lamoreaux, Naomi R. (1991a). "Information Problems and Banks' Specialization in Short-Term Commercial Lending: New England in the Nineteenth Century." In *Inside the Business Enterprise: Historical Perspectives on the Use of Information*, ed. Peter Temin. Chicago: University of Chicago Press, pp. 154–95.

    (1991b). "Bank Mergers in Late Nineteenth-Century New England: The Contingent Nature of Structural Change." *Journal of Economic History* 51 (September), 537–58.

Lamy, Robert, and G. Rodney Thompson (1986). "Penn Square, Problem Loans, and Insolvency Risk." *Journal of Financial Research* 9 (Summer), 167–83.

Lee, Everett S., Ann Ratner Miller, Carol P. Brainerd, and Richard A. Easterlin (1957). *Population Redistribution and Economic Growth, United States 1870–1950.* Philadelphia: American Philosophical Society.

Leland, Hayne, and David Pyle (1977). "Informational Asymmetries, Financial Structure, and Financial Intermediation." *Journal of Finance* 32 (May), 371–87.

Lester, Richard A. (1939). *Monetary Experiments: Early American and Recent Scandinavian.* Princeton: Princeton University Press.

Litan, Robert E. (1985). "Evaluating and Controlling the Risks of Financial Product Deregulation." *Yale Journal on Regulation* 3 (Fall), 1–52.

    (1987). *What Should Banks Do?* Washington, D.C.: The Brookings Institution.

Martin, David (1974). "Metallism, Small Notes, and Jackson's War with the B.U.S." *Explorations in Economic History* 11 (Spring), 227–47.

McCusker, John J. (1978). *Money and Exchange in Europe and America, 1600–1775: A Handbook.* Chapel Hill: University of North Carolina Press.

Meinster, David R., and Rodney D. Johnson (1979). "Bank Holding Company Diversification and the Risk of Capital Impairment." *Bell Journal of Economics* 10 (Autumn), 683–94.

Mengle, David L. (1990). "The Case for Interstate Branch Banking." *Federal Reserve Bank of Richmond Economic Review* 76 (November/December), 3–17.

Michener, Ronald (1987). "Fixed Exchange Rates and the Quantity Theory In Colonial America." *Carnegie-Rochester Conference Series on Public Policy* 27 (Autumn), 233–308.

Michener, Ronald (1988). "Backing Theories and the Currencies of Eighteenth-Century America: A Comment." *Journal of Economic History* 48 (September), 682–92.

Miron, Jeffrey A. (1986). "Financial Panics, the Seasonality of the Nominal Interest Rate, and the Founding of the Fed." *American Economic Review 76* (March), 125–40.

Moen, Jon, and Ellis W. Tallman (1992). "The Bank Panic of 1907: The Role of Trust Companies." *Journal of Economic History* 52 (September), 610–630.

Mullineaux, Donald J. (1987). "Competitive Moneys and the Suffolk Bank System: A Contractual Perspective." *Southern Economic Journal* (April), 884–97.

Munn, Charles W. (1981). *The Scottish Provincial Banking Companies. 1747–1864.* Edinburgh: John Donald.

Musumeci, James, and Joseph Sinkey (1988). "The International Debt Crisis and the Signalling Content of Bank Loan-Loss-Reserve Decisions." University of Georgia working paper.

Myers, Margaret G. (1931). *The New York Money Market: Origins and Development.* New York: Columbia University Press.

Myers, Stewart, and Nicholas Majluf (1984). "Corporate Financing and Investment Decisions When Firms Have Information That Investors Do Not Have." *Journal of Financial Economics* 13, 187–221.

Nettles, Curtis P. (1934). *The Money Supply of the American Colonies Before 1720.* Madison: University of Wisconsin Press.

Neuberger, Hugh, and Houston H. Stokes (1974). "German Banks and German Growth, 1883–1913: An Empirical View." *Journal of Economic History* 34 (September), 710–32.

Osterweis, Steven L. (1932). "Security Affiliates and Security Operations of Commercial Banks." *Harvard Business Review* 11 (October), 124–31.

Peach, W. N. (1941). *The Security Affiliates of National Banks.* Baltimore: Johns Hopkins Press.

Pippenger, John (1984). "Bank of England Operations, 1893–1913." In *A Retrospective on the Classical Gold Standard, 1821–1931*, eds. Michael D. Bordo and Anna J. Schwartz. Chicago: University of Chicago Press, pp. 203–27.

Pope, David (1989). "Free Banking in Australia Before World War I." Australian National University working paper.

Pozdena, Randall J. (1991). "Is Banking Really Prone to Panics?" *Federal Reserve Bank of San Francisco Weekly Letter 91-35* (October 11).

Ransom, Roger L., and Richard Sutch (1977). *One Kind of Freedom: The Economic Consequences of Emancipation.* Cambridge: Cambridge University Press.

Redlich, Fritz (1951). *The Molding of American Banking: Men and Ideas.* New York: Hafner Publishing.

Riefler, Winfield W. (1930). *Money Rates and Money Markets in the United States.* New York: Harper and Brothers.

Riesser, Jacob (1911). *The Great German Banks and Their Concentration, in Connection with the Economic Development of Germany.* Translation of third edition. Washington, D.C.: United States Government Printing Office.

Robb, Thomas B. (1921). *The Guaranty of Bank Deposits.* Boston: Houghton Mifflin.

Rockoff, Hugh (1972). "The Free Banking Era: A Re-Examination." University of Chicago, Ph.D. dissertation.

Root, L. Carroll (1897). "Canadian Bank-Note Currency." *Sound Currency* 4 (May), 1–16.

Root, L. Carroll (1901). "Twenty Years of Bank Currency Based on General Commercial Assets." *Sound Currency* 8 (December), 209–32.

Schembri, Lawrence L., and Jennifer A. Hawkins (1988). "The Role of Canadian Chartered Banks in U.S. Banking Crises: 1870–1914." Carleton University working paper.

Schultz, William J. (1949). *Credit and Collection Management.* New York: Prentice Hall.

Schweikart, Larry (1988a). *Banking in the American South from the Age of Jackson to Reconstruction.* Baton Rouge: Louisiana State University Press.

Schweikart, Larry (1988b). "Jacksonian Ideology, Currency Control and Central Banking: A Reappraisal." *The Historian* (November), 78–102.

Schweitzer, Mary M. (1989). "State-Issued Currency and the Ratification of the U.S. Constitution." *Journal of Economic History* 49 (June), 311–22.

Schweitzer, Robert (1989). "How Do Stock Returns React to Special Events?" *Federal Reserve Bank of Philadelphia Business Review* (July/August), 17–29.

Sheard, Paul (1989). "The Main Bank System and Corporate Monitoring and Control in Japan." *Journal of Economic Behavior and Organization* 11, 399–422.

Sklar, Martin J. (1988). *The Corporate Reconstruction of American Capitalism, 1890–1916: The Market, the Law, and Politics.* Cambridge: Cambridge University Press.

Smith, Bruce D. (1985a). "Some Colonial Evidence on Two Theories of Money: Maryland and the Carolinas." *Journal of Political Economy* 93 (December), 1178–1211.

Smith, Bruce D. (1985b). "American Colonial Monetary Regimes: The Failure of the Quantity Theory of Money and Some Evidence in Favor of an Alternate View." *Canadian Journal of Economics* 18 (August), 531–65.

Smith, Hilary H. (1987). "Agricultural Lending: Bank Closures and Branch Banking." *Federal Reserve Bank of Dallas Economic Review* (September), 27–38.

Snowden, Kenneth A. (1987). "Mortgage Rates and American Capital Market Development in the Late Nineteenth Century." *Journal of Economic History 47* (September), 671–91.

Steiner, William H. (1922). *The Mechanism of Commercial Credit: Terms of Sale and Trade Acceptances.* New York: D. Appleton.

Stiglitz, Joseph E., and Andrew Weiss (1981). "Credit Rationing in Markets with Imperfect Information." American *Economic Review 71* (June), 393–410.

Sumner, William G. (1896). A *History of Banking in the United States.* New York: Journal of Commerce and Commercial Bulletin.

Sushka, Marie E., and W. Brian Barrett (1984). "Banking Structure and the National Capital Market, *1869–1914.*" *Journal of Economic History* 44 (June), 463–77.

Swary, Itzhak (1986). "Stock Market Reaction to Regulatory Action in the Continental Illinois Crisis." *Journal of Business* 59 (July), 451–73.

Sylla, Richard (1969). "Federal Policy, Banking Market Structure, and Capital Mobilization in the United States, 1863–1913." *Journal of Economic History* 29 (December), 657–86.

Sylla, Richard (1975). *The American Capital Market, 1869–1914.* New York: Arno Press.

Sylla, Richard, John B. Legler, and John J. Wallis (1987). "Banks and State Public Finance in the New Republic: The United States, 1790–1860." *Journal of Economic History* 47 (June), 391–404.

Temin, Peter (1969). *The Jacksonian Economy.* New York: W. W. Norton.

Thies, Clifford F., and Daniel A. Gerlowski (1989). "Deposit Insurance: A History of Failure." *Cato Journal* 8 (Winter), 677–93.

Tilly, Richard H. (1966). *Financial Institutions and Industrialization in the Rhineland, 1815–1870.* Madison: University of Wisconsin Press.

Treman, R. H. (1919). *Trade Acceptances, What They Are and How They Are Used.* New York: American Acceptance Council.

U.S. Department of Commerce (1975). *Historical Statistics of the United States: Colonial Times to 1970.* Washington, D.C.: U.S. Government Printing Office.

U.S. House of Representatives (1930). Branch, Chain, and Group Banking. Hearings Before the Committee on Banking and Currency, 71st Congress, 2nd Session. Washington, D.C.: U.S. Government Printing Office.

Vreeland, Edward B., John W. Weeks, and Robert W. Bonynge (1910). *Interviews on the Banking and Currency Systems of Canada.* National Monetary Commission. 61st Congress, 2nd Session. Senate Document 584. Washington, D.C.: U.S. Government Printing Office.

Wall, Larry D. (1987). "Has Bank Holding Companies Diversification Affected Their Risk of Failure?" *Journal of Economics and Business* 39 (November), 313–26.

Wall, Larry D., and David R. Petersen (1990). "The Effect of Continental Illinois' Failure on the Financial Performance of Other Banks." *Journal of Monetary Economics* 26 (August), 77–100.

White, Eugene N. (1982). "The Political Economy of Banking Regulation, 1864–1933." *Journal of Economic History* 42 (March), 33–40.

White, Eugene N. (1983). *The Regulation and Reform of the American Banking System, 1900–1929.* Princeton: Princeton University Press.

White, Eugene N. (1984a). "A Reinterpretation of the Banking Crisis of 1930." *Journal of Economic History* 44 (March), 119–38.

White, Eugene N. (1984b). "Voting for Costly Regulation: Evidence from Banking Referenda in Illinois, 1924." *Southern Economic Journal,* 1084–98.

White, Eugene N. (1985). "The Merger Movement in Banking, 1919–1933." *Journal of Economic History* 45 (June), 285–91.

White, Eugene N. (1986). "Before the Glass-Steagall Act. An Analysis of the Investment Banking Activities of National Banks."*Explorations in Economic History* 23 (January), 33–55.

White, Horace (1902). "Branch Banking: Its Economies and Advantages." *Sound Currency* 9 (June), 51–64.

White, Lawrence H. (1984). *Free Banking in Britain: Theory, Experience, and Debate, 1800–1845.* Cambridge: Cambridge University Press.

White, Lawrence J. (1986). "The Partial Deregulation of Banks and Other Depository Institutions." In *Regulatory Reform: What Actually Happened.* Boston: Little, Brown, eds. Leonard W. Weiss and Michael W. Klass. pp. 169–209.

Wicker, Elmus (1985). "Colonial Monetary Standards Contrasted: Evidence from the Seven Years' War."*Journal of Economic History* 45 (December), 869–84.

Williamson, Stephen D. (1986). "Costly Monitoring, Financial Intermediation, and Equilibrium Credit Rationing." *Journal of Monetary Economics* 18 (September), 159–80.

Williamson, Stephen D. (1989). "Bank Failures, Financial Restrictions, and Aggregate Fluctuations: Canada and the United States, 1870–1913." *Federal Reserve Bank of Minneapolis Quarterly Review* (Summer), 20–40.

Willit, Virgil (1930). *Selected Articles on Chain, Group and Branch Banking.* New York: H. W. Wilson.

Withers, Hartley, R. H. Inglis Palgrave, and others (1910). *The English Banking System.* National Monetary Commission. 61st Congress, 2nd Session. Senate Document 492. Washington, D.C.: U.S. Government Printing Office.

Wright, Gavin (1979). "Cheap Labor and Southern Textiles Before 1880."*Journal of Economic History 39* (September), 655–80.

Wright, Gavin (1986). *Old South, New South.* New York: Basic Books.

## CHAPTER 2

The origins of banking panics
Models, facts, and bank regulation

Charles W. Calomiris and Gary Gorton

2.1   Introduction

The history of U.S. banking regulation can be written largely as a history of government and private responses to banking panics. Implicitly or explicitly, each regulatory response to a crisis presumed a "model" of the origins of banking panics. The development of private bank clearing houses, the founding of the Federal Reserve System, the creation of the Federal Deposit Insurance Corporation, the separation of commercial and investment banking by the Glass-Steagall Act, and laws governing branch banking all reflect beliefs about the factors that contribute to the instability of the banking system.

Deposit insurance and bank regulation were ultimately successful in preventing banking panics, but it has recently become apparent that this success was not without costs. The demise of the Federal Savings and Loan Insurance Corporation and state-sponsored thrift insurance funds and the declining competitiveness of U.S. commercial banks have had a profound effect on the debate over proper bank regulatory policy. Increasingly, regulators appear to be seeking to balance the benefits of banking stability against the apparent costs of bank regulation.

This changing focus has provided some of the impetus for the reevaluation of the history of banking crises to determine how banking stability can be achieved at a minimum cost. The important question is: What is the cause of banking panics? This question has been difficult to answer. Theoretical models of banking panics are intertwined with explanations for the existence of banks and, particularly, of bank debt contracts which finance "illiquid" assets while containing American put options giving debt holders the right to redeem debt on demand at par. Explaining the optimality of this debt contract, and of the put option, while simultane-

The authors thank George Benston, Ben Bernanke, John Bohannon, Michael Bordo, Barry Eichengreen, Joe Haubrich, Glenn Hubbard, and Joel Mokyr for comments.

ously explaining the possibility of the apparently suboptimal event of a banking panic has been very hard.

In part, the reason it is difficult is that posing the problem this way identifies banks and banking panics too closely. In the last decade attempts to provide general simultaneous explanations of the existence of banks and banking panics have foundered on the historical fact that not all countries have experienced banking panics, even though their banking systems offered the same debt contract. Empirical research during this time has made this insight more precise by focusing on how the banking market structure and institutional differences affect the likelihood of panic. Observed variation in historical experience which can be attributed to differences in the structure of banking systems provides convincing evidence that neither the nature of debt contracts nor the presence of exogenous shocks which reduce the value of bank asset portfolios provides "sufficient conditions" for banking panics.

Empirical research has demonstrated the importance of such institutional structures as branch bank laws, bank cooperation arrangements, and formal clearing houses, for the probability of panic and for the resolution of crisis. The conclusion of this work and cross-country comparisons is that banking panics are not inherent in banking contracts – institutional structure matters. This observation has now been incorporated into new generations of theoretical models. But, while theoretical models sharpen our understanding of how banking panics might have occurred, few of these models have stressed testable implications. In addition, empirical work seeking to isolate precisely which factors caused panics historically has been hampered by the lack of historical data and the fact that there were only a relatively small number of panics. Thus, it is not surprising that research on the origins of banking panics and the appropriate regulatory response to their threat has yet to produce a consensus view.

While the original question of the cause of banking panics has not been answered, at least researchers appear to be looking for the answer in a different place. Our goal in this essay is to evaluate the persuasiveness of recent models of the origins of banking panics in light of available evidence. We begin, in Section 2.2, with a definition of a banking panic, followed by a discussion of panics in U.S. history. A brief set of stylized facts which a theory must confront is developed. In Section 2.3, recent empirical evidence on panics which strongly suggests the importance of the institutional structure is reviewed. Theories of panics must be consistent with this evidence.

Theoretical models of panics are discussed in section 2.4, where we trace the evolution of two competing views about the origins of banking panics. In the first view, which we label the "random withdrawal" theory, panics were caused historically by unexpected withdrawals by bank depositors associated primarily with real location-specific economic shocks, such as seasonal demands for currency due to agricultural payment procedures favoring cash. The mechanism that causes the panic in this theory suggests that the availability of reserves, say through central bank open market operations, would eliminate panics.

The second view, which we label the "asymmetric information" theory, sees panics as being caused by depositor revisions in the perceived risk of bank debt when they are uninformed about bank asset portfolio values and receive adverse news about the macro economy. In this view, depositors seek to withdraw large amounts from banks when they have reason to believe that banks are more likely to fail. Because the actual incidence of failure is unknown, they withdraw from all banks. The availability of reserves through central bank action would not, in this view, prevent panics.

The two competing theories offer different explanations about the origins and solutions to panics. A main goal of this essay is to discriminate between these two views, so we focus on testing the restrictions that each view implies. Section 2.5 describes the empirically testable differences between the competing hypotheses and provides a variety of new evidence to differentiate the two views. We employ data from the National Banking period (1863–1913), a single regulatory regime for which data are easily available for a variety of variables of interest. The two hypotheses have three testable implications that are explored in this paper. First, with respect to the shock initiating the panic, each theory suggests what is special about the periods immediately preceding panics. Second, the incidence of bank failures and losses is examined. Finally, we look at how crises were resolved.

Isolating the historical origins of banking panics is an important first step toward developing appropriate policy reforms for regulating and insuring financial intermediaries. In this regard, it is important to differentiate between the two views of the causes of panics because each has different policy implications. While we do not make any policy recommendations, in the final section, Section 2.6, we discuss policy implications.

2.2   Definitions and preliminaries

Essential to any study of panics is a definition of a banking panic. Perhaps surprisingly, a definition is not immediately obvious. Much of the empirical debate turns on which events are selected for the sample of panics.

This section begins with a definition, which is then applied to select events from U.S. history which appear to fit the definition. In doing this we suggest a set of facts which theories of panics must address.

2.2.1   What is a "banking panic"?

The term banking panic is often used somewhat ambiguously and, in many cases, synonymously with events in which banks fail, such as a recession, or in which there is financial market turmoil, such as stock market crashes. Many researchers provide no definition of a panic, relying instead on the same one or two secondary sources for an identification of panics.[1] But it is not clear whether these sources are correct nor whether the definitions implicit in these sources apply to other countries and periods of history.

One result of the reliance on secondary sources is that most empirical research has restricted attention to the U.S. experience, mostly the post-Civil War period, and usually with more weight placed on the events of the Great Depression. Moreover, even when using the same secondary sources, different researchers consider different sets of events to be panics. Miron (1986), for example, includes fifteen "minor" panics in his study. Sobel (1968) discusses twelve episodes, but mentions eleven others which were not covered. Donaldson (1989a) equates panics with unusual movements in interest rates.

Historically, bank debt has consisted largely of liabilities which circulate as a medium of exchange – bank notes and demand deposits. The contract defining this debt allowed the debt holder the right to redeem the debt (into hard currency) on demand at par. We define a banking panic as follows: A banking panic occurs when bank debt holders at all or many banks in the banking system suddenly demand that banks convert their debt claims into cash (at par) to such an extent that the banks suspend convertibility of their debt into cash or, in the case of the United States, act collectively to avoid suspension of convertibility by issuing clearing-house loan certificates.[2]

---

[1] The two secondary sources which are widely used are Kemmerer (1910) and Sprague (1910). Neither author provides a definition of a banking panic. Both works are concerned with the U.S. National Banking Era. Sprague details what occurred during the events of 1873, 1884, 1890, 1893, and 1907. Kemmerer arbitrarily identifies panics, finding six major and fifteen minor panics during the period 1890–1908 (see pp. 222–23, 232).

[2] Clearing-house loan certificates were the joint liabilities of all members of the clearing house. They were issued during banking panics. See Gorton (1985) and Gorton and Mullineaux (1987) for further discussion.

Several elements of this definition are worth discussing[3]. First, the definition requires that a significant number of banks be involved. If bank debt holders of a single bank demand redemption, this is not a banking panic, though such events are often called "bank runs." The term banking panic is so often used synonymously with "bank run" that there is no point attempting to distinguish between the two terms. Whether called a "bank run" or a "bank panic," the event of interest involves a large number of banks and is, therefore, to be distinguished from a "run" involving only a single bank. Thus, the events surrounding Continental of Illinois do not constitute a panic. On the other hand, a panic need not involve all the banks in the banking system. Rarely, if ever, have all banks in an economy simultaneously been faced with large demands for redemption of debt. Typically, all banks in a single geographical location are "run" at the same time, and "runs" subsequently occur in other locations.

The definition requires that depositors suddenly demand to redeem bank debt for cash. Thus, protracted withdrawals are ruled out, though sometimes the measured currency-deposit ratio rises for some period before the date taken to be the panic date. In the United States, panics diffused across the country in interesting ways. Panics did not occur at different locations simultaneously; nevertheless, at each location the panic occurred suddenly.

A panic requires that the volume of desired redemptions of debt into cash be large enough that the banks suspend convertibility or act collectively to avoid suspension. There are, presumably, various events in which depositors might wish to make large withdrawals. Perhaps a single bank, or group of banks at a single location, could honor large withdrawals, even larger than those demanded during a panic, if at the same time other banks were not faced with such demands.[4] But, if the banking system cannot honor demands for redemption at the agreed-upon exchange rate of one dollar of debt for one dollar of cash, then suspen-

---

[3] The definition is in terms of bank debt which circulates as a medium of exchange and which contractually allows redemption on demand at par. But, the definition does not otherwise distinguish between different types of bank liabilities. There may have been an important difference, however, between bank notes, which were non-interest-bearing bearer liabilities, and bank deposits, which bore interest and were not bearer liabilities, being checking accounts of the type familiar. Since banks often issued both types of liabilities, especially in the United States, effects of the distinction are difficult to detect empirically. But theoretically, different theories make important distinctions. The main difference, discussed later, concerns the existence or nonexistence of secondary markets. In the United States, such markets existed for bank notes but not for demand deposits. On this point, however, the definition is left vague.

[4] Nicholas (1907) provides evidence that idiosyncratic money-demand shocks to a particular bank were offset by interbank loans.

sion occurs. Suspension signals that the banking system cannot honor the redemption option.

It is important to note that a banking panic cannot be defined in terms of the currency-deposit ratio. Since banks suspend convertibility of deposits into currency, the measured currency-deposit ratio will not necessarily show a sharp increase at, or subsequent to, the panic date. The desired currency-deposit ratio may be higher than the measured number, but that is not observable. Also, clearing-house arrangements (discussed below) and suspension allowed banks to continue loans that might otherwise have been called.[5] In fact, in some episodes lending increased. Thus, there is no immediate or obvious way to identify a banking panic using interest rate movements related to credit reductions. Moreover, since panics in the United States have tended to be associated with business cycle downturns, and also with fall and spring, interest rate movements around panics may be quite complicated. Associations between interest rate movements and panics as part of a definition seem inadvisable.

2.2.2   Panics in the United States

Even if there was agreement on a definition of a banking panic, it is still difficult to determine practically which historical events constitute panics. Many historical events do not completely fit the definition. Thus, there is some delicacy in determining which historical events in American history should be labelled panics. Table 2.1 lists the U.S. events which arguably correspond to the definition of panics provided above.

Consider, first, the pre-Civil War period of American history. During this period, bank debt liabilities mostly consisted of circulating bank notes. We classify six events as panics during this period: the suspensions of 1814, 1819, 1837, 1839, 1857, and 1861. Data limitations prevent a detailed empirical analysis of the earliest panics. Moreover, some of these are associated with "special" historical circumstances, and this

---

[5] Suspension of convertibility did not mean that banks ceased to clear transactions or make loans. Indeed, suspension was usually the beginning of the end of the contraction, and marked a period of loan and deposit recovery, albeit at slow rates initially as banks strived to accumulate specie reserves to facilitate resumption. Sprague (1910, pp. 56–58, 186–91, 280–82) documents the existence of a secondary market for bank deposits during suspensions under the National Banking System as early as 1873. Certified checks of suspended banks typically traded at slight discounts of no more than 4 percent and usually less than 1 percent. Thus, while suspension placed limits on the movement of specie out of the banking system, it allowed depositors and merchants to exchange one form of bank liability for another, both within a locality and, to a lesser extent, across localities.

Table 2.1. *Banking panics and business cycles*

Height of panic	Nearest previous peak	Notation
August 1814 January 1817[a]	January 1812	War-related
April–May 1819	November 1818	
May 1837	April 1837	
October 1839–March 1842[b]	March 1839	
October 1857	May 1857	
December 1861	September 1860	War-related
September 1873	September 1873	
May 1884	May 1884	
November 1890	November 1890	
June–August 1893	April 1893	
October 1896	March 1896	
October 1907	September 1907	
August–October 1914	May 1914	War-related

[a] Suspension of convertibility lasted through February 1817. Discount rates of Baltimore, Philadelphia, and New York banks in Philadelphia roughly averaged 18, 12 and 9 percent, respectively, for the period of suspension prior to 1817. See Gallatin (1831, p. 106).
[b] Bond defaults by states in 1840 and 1841 transformed a banking suspension into a banking collapse.
Sources: Peaks are defined using Burns and Mitchell (1946, p. 510) and Frickey (1942, 1947), as amended by Miron and Romer (1990). For pre-1854 data we rely on the Cleveland Trust Company Index of Productive Activity, as reported in Standard Trade and Securities (1932, p. 166).

argues against their relevance to the general question of the sources of banking instability. The Panics of 1814 and 1861 both followed precipitous exogenous declines in the value of government securities during wartime (related to adverse news regarding the probability of government repayment). Mitchell (1903) shows that bad financial news in December 1861 came at a time when banks in the principal financial centers were holding large quantities of government bonds (also see Dewey 1903, pp. 278–82).

During the National Banking Era, there were four widespread suspensions of convertibility (1873, 1893, 1907, 1914) and six episodes where clearinghouse loan certificates were issued (1873, 1884, 1890, 1893, 1907, 1914). In October 1896 the New York Clearing House Association authorized the issuance of loan certificates, but none were actually issued. Thus, one could rank panics in order of the severity of the coordination problem faced by banks into three sets: suspensions (1873, 1893, 1907, 1914); coordination to forestall suspensions (1884, 1890); and a perceived need for coordination (1896). We leave it as an open question whether to view 1896 as a panic, as our results do not depend on its inclusion or exclusion.

The panics during the Great Depression appear to be of a different character than earlier panics. Unlike the panics of the National Banking Era, these events did not occur near the peak of the business cycle and did result in widespread failures and large losses to depositors. The worst loss per deposit dollar during a panic (from the onset of the panic to the business cycle trough) in the National Banking Era was 2.1 cents per dollar of deposits. And the worst case in terms of numbers of banks failing during a panic was 1.28 percent, during the Panic of 1893. The panics during the Great Depression resulted in significantly high loss and failure rates. During the Great Depression the percentage of national banks which failed was somewhere between 26 and 16 percent, depending on how it is measured. The losses on deposits were almost 5 percent (see Gorton 1988).

Many authors have argued that the panics during the 1930s were special events explicable mainly by the pernicious role of the Federal Reserve (Friedman and Schwartz 1963) or, at least, by the absence of superior preexisting institutional arrangements or standard policy responses which would have limited the persistence or severity of the banking collapse (Gorton 1988; Wheelock 1988). From the standpoint of this literature, the Great Depression tells one less about the inherent instability of the banking system than about the extent to which unwise government policies can destroy banks. For this reason we restrict attention to pre-Federal Reserve episodes.

As can be seen in Table 2.1, the National Banking Era panics, together with the Panic of 1857, all happened near business cycle peaks. Panics tended to occur in the spring and fall. Finally, panics and their aftermaths did not result in enormously large numbers of bank failures or losses on deposits. These observations must be addressed by proposed explanations of panics.

A final interesting fact about panics in the United States during the National Banking Era is their peculiarity from an international perspective. Bordo (1985) concludes, in his study of financial and banking crises in six countries from 1870 to 1933, that "the United States experienced banking panics in a period when they were a historical curiosity in other countries" (p. 73). Explanations of the origins of panics must explain why the U.S. experience was so different from that of other countries.

2.3   Market structure and bank coalitions

Proposed explanations of panics must also be consistent with, if not encompass, the abundant evidence suggesting that differences in branch-banking laws and interbank arrangements were important determinants of the likelihood and severity of panics. International comparisons frequently emphasize this point. Also, within the United States the key observation is that banking systems in which branch banking was allowed or in which private or state-sponsored co-operative arrangements were present, such as clearing houses or state insurance funds, displayed lower failure rates and losses. Since there now seems to be widespread agreement on the validity of these conclusions, theories of banking panics must be consistent with this evidence.

The institutional arrangements that mattered were of three types. First, there were more or less informal cooperative, sometimes spontaneous, arrangements among banks for dealing with panics. These were particularly prevalent in states that allowed branch banking. Secondly, some states sponsored formal insurance arrangements among banks. And finally, starting in the 1850s in New York City there were formal agreements originated privately by clearing houses. We briefly review the evidence concerning the importance of these institutional arrangements in explaining cross-country and intra-U.S. differences in the propensity of panics and their severity.

2.3.1   International comparisons

Economies in which banks issue circulating debt with an option to redeem in cash on demand (demandable debt) have historically had a wide range of experiences with respect to banking panics. While some of these countries did not experience panics at all, other countries experienced panics in the seventeenth and early eighteenth centuries but not thereafter. In the United States and England, panics were persistent problems. This heterogeneous experience is a challenge to explanations of panics.

In England, panics recurred fairly frequently from the seventeenth century until the mid nineteenth century. The most famous English panics in the nineteenth century are those associated with Overend, Gurney & Co. Ltd. in 1866, and those of 1825, 1847, and 1857. Canada experienced no panics after the 1830s. Bordo (1985) provides a useful survey of banking and securities-market "panics" in six countries from

1870 to 1933. Summarizing the literature, Bordo attributes the U.S. peculiarity in large part to the absence of branch banking.

Recent work has stressed, in particular, the comparison between the U.S. and Canadian performance during the National Banking Era and the Great Depression. Unlike the United States, Canada's banking system allowed nationwide branching from an early date and relied on coordination among a small number (roughly forty in the nineteenth century, falling to ten by 1929) of large branch banks to resolve threats to the system as a whole. Haubrich (1990) and Williamson (1989) echo Bordo's emphasis on the advantages of branch banking in their studies of the comparative performance of U.S. and Canadian banks. Notably, suspensions of convertibility did not occur in Canada. The Canadian Bankers' Association, formed in 1891, was the formalization of cooperative arrangements among Canadian banks which served to regulate banks and mitigate the effects of failures. As in Scotland and other countries, the largest banks acted as leaders during times of crisis. In Canada the Bank of Montreal acted as a lender of last resort, stepping in to assist troubled banks (see Breckenridge 1910; Williamson 1989).

The incidence of bank failures and their costs were much lower in Canada. Failure rates in Canada were much lower, but they do not accurately portray the situation since the number of banks in Canada was so small. However, calculation of failure rates based on the number of branches yields an even smaller failure rate for Canada. The failure rate in the United States for national banks during the period 1870–1909 was 0.36, compared to a failure rate in Canada, based on branches, of less than 0.1 (see Schembri and Hawkins 1988). Comparing average losses to depositors over many years produces a similar picture. Williamson (1989) compares the average losses to depositors in the United States and Canada and finds that the annual average loss rate was 0.11 percent and 0.07 percent, respectively.

Haubrich (1990) analyzes the broader economic costs of bank failures and of a less-stable banking system more generally. He investigates the contribution of credit market disruption to the severity of Canada's Great Depression. In sharp contrast with Bernanke's (1983) and Hamilton's (1987) findings for the United States, international factors rather than indicators of financial stress in Canada (commercial failures, deflation, money supply) were important during Canada's Great Depression. One way to interpret these findings is that, in the presence of a stable branch-banking system, financial shocks were not magnified by their effects on bank risk and, therefore, had more limited effects on economic activity.

2.3.2   Bank cooperation and institutional arrangements in the United States

Redlich (1947) reviews the history of early interbank cooperation in the northern United States, arguing that this cooperation was at a nadir in the 1830s. Govan (1936) studies the antebellum southern U.S. branch-banking systems, describing cooperative state- and regional-level responses to banking panics as early as the 1830s. The smaller number of banks, the geographical coincidence of different banks' branches, and the clear leadership role of the larger branching banks in some of the states allowed bankers to coordinate suspension and resumption decisions, and to establish rules (including limits on balance sheet expansion) for interbank clearings of transactions during suspension of convertibility. The most extreme example of bank cooperation during the antebellum period was in Indiana, from 1834 to 1851.[6] Golembe and Warburton (1958) describe the innovative "mutual-guarantee" system in that state, which was later copied by Ohio (1845) and Iowa (1858). In this system, banks made markets in each other's liabilities, had full regulatory powers over one another through the actions of the Board of Control, and were liable for the losses of any failed member banks.

As early as the Panic of 1839, these differences in banking structure and potential for coordination seem to have been an important determinant of the probability of failure during a banking panic. Hunt's Merchants' Magazine reports the suspension and failure propensities of various states from the origin of the panic on 9 October 1839 until 8 January 1840. Banks in the centralized, urban banking systems of Louisiana, Delaware, Rhode Island, and the District of Columbia all suspended convertibility during the panic, and none failed in 1839. Similarly, the laissez-faire, branch-banking states of the South (Virginia, North Carolina, South Carolina, Georgia, and Tennessee) saw nearly universal suspension of convertibility (with 92 out of 100 banking facilities suspending) and suffered only four bank failures in 1839, all small newly organized unit banks in western Georgia.[7] Indiana's mutual-guarantee banks all suspended, but would never suffer a single failure from their origin in 1834 to their dissolution in 1865, and after suspending in 1839 would never again find it necessary to suspend convertibility (see Golembe and Warburton 1958; Calomiris 1989a).

---

[6] In 1851 a free-banking statute created a second group of uncoordinated banks in the state.

[7] As Schweikart (1987) argues, the performance of Mississippi, Florida, and Alabama banks during this period mainly reflected government use of banks as a fiscal tool. These states are excluded from the comparison.

Other states typically had fewer suspensions, less uniformity among banks in the decision to suspend, and a higher incidence of bank failure. In New England, outside of Rhode Island, only four out of 277 banks suspended and remained solvent, while eighteen (6.5 percent) failed by the end of 1839. In the mid-Atlantic states, outside of Delaware and the District of Columbia, 112 out of 334 banks suspended and remained solvent, while 22 (6.6 percent) failed. In the southeastern states of Mississippi and Alabama, 23 of 37 banks suspended and two (5.4 percent) failed. In the northwestern states of Ohio, Illinois, and Michigan, 46 out of 67 banks suspended, while nine (13.4 percent) failed.

Calomiris and Schweikart (1991) and Calomiris (1989a) demonstrate that the importance of branch-banking laws and banking cooperation is just as apparent in the experiences of banks during the crisis of 1857. They document that the branch-banking South and the mutual-guarantee coinsurance systems of Indiana and Ohio enjoyed a lower *ex ante* risk evaluation on their bank notes and suffered far lower bank failure rates than the rest of the country during the Panic of 1857.[8]

None of Indiana's or Ohio's mutual-guarantee banks failed or suspended convertibility during the Panic of 1857. Both Ohio and Indiana chartered free banks, in addition to the coinsuring systems of banks. During the regional crisis of 1854–55, 55 of Indiana's 94 free banks failed, and during the Panic of 1857, 14 out of Indiana's 32 free banks failed. In Ohio, failure rates were lower, with only one bank failing in the Panic of 1857. The difference between Ohio's and Indiana's free banks cannot be attributed to observed differences in the size of the shocks affecting the two locations. For example, the magnitudes of the declines in bond prices were roughly comparable.[9] What set Indiana's newer free banks apart from those of Ohio was their failure to coordinate suspension or to obtain aid from the coinsuring banks.

Ohio banks received assistance from the coinsuring banks during the panic. In Indiana, the free banks and the coinsuring banks did not cooperate. Moreover, the free banks had not had the time to establish an independent coordination mechanism. Ironically, just prior to the

---

[8] Bank failure rates were low throughout the South and, unlike the North, confined almost entirely to small rural banks. Recovery of bank balance sheets was relatively rapid in the South, and many banks continued operations in an atmosphere of relative normalcy in comparison to the North. These differences can be traced to differences in bank coordination, particularly interbank lending during the crisis, rather than to a different incidence of fundamental shocks in the North and South.

[9] Rolnick and Weber (1984) argue that free bank failures were caused by exogenous asset depreciation. During banking panics, however, coordination among banks, or a lack thereof, also seems important.

Panic of 1857, Indiana free banks began to discuss forming a clearing association for their mutual benefit.[10]

Branch-banking systems tended to be less prone to the effects of panics. Evidence on the importance of branch banking in the United States is provided by Calomiris (1990, 1992) in a detailed, state-by-state examination of the response of banks in agricultural states to the large adverse asset shocks of the 1920s. Controlling for differences in the severity of shocks, states that allowed branch banking weathered the crisis much better than unit-banking states. Bank failure rates for (grand-fathered) branching banks in unit-banking states, and for branching banks in free-entry branching states, were a fraction of those of unit banks. Furthermore, in states that allowed branching it was much easier for weak banks to be acquired or replaced by new entrants.

Private banking associations in the form of clearing houses provided mechanisms for coordinating bank responses to banking panics. During the nineteenth century, starting in New York City in 1853, clearing houses evolved into highly formal institutions. These institutions not only cleared interbank liabilities but, in response to banking panics, they acted as lenders of last resort, issuing private money and providing deposit insurance. As part of the process of performing these functions, clearing houses regulated member banks by auditing member risk-taking activities, setting capital requirements, and penalizing members for violating clearing-house rules.

During banking panics, clearing houses created a market for the illiquid assets of member banks by accepting such assets as collateral in exchange for clearing-house loan certificates which were liabilities of the association of banks. Member banks then exchanged the loan certificates for depositors' demand deposits. Clearing-house loan certificates were printed in small denominations and functioned as a hand-to-hand currency. Moreover, since these securities were the liability of the association of banks rather than of any individual bank, depositors were insured against the failure of their individual bank.[11] Initially, clearing-house loan certificates traded at a discount against gold. This discount presumably

[10] Interestingly, *ex ante* pricing of bank note risk prior to the Panic of 1857 mirrored these *ex post* differences in the relative performance of free banks in Indiana and Ohio. Ohio's mutual liability and free banks, and Indiana's mutual liability banks, all enjoyed a common discount rate in New York City of 1 percent, while the Indiana free banks were discounted at 1.5 percent. For data on bank note discount rates in the Philadelphia market and a model of bank note risk pricing, see Gorton (1990, 1989a).

[11] Clearing houses created significant amounts of money. During the Panic of 1893, clearing houses issued $100 million of loan certificates, about 2.5 percent of the money stock. During the Panic of 1907, about $500 million was issued, about 4.5 percent of the money stock. This private money circulated as hand-to-hand currency, initially at a slight discount from par. See Gorton (1985) and Gorton and Mullineaux (1987).

reflected the chance that the clearing house would not be able to honor the certificates at par. When this discount went to zero, suspension of convertibility was lifted. Cannon (1910) and Sprague (1910) trace these increasingly cooperative reactions of city bank clearing houses to panics during 1857–1907. Gorton (1985, 1989b) and Gorton and Mullineaux (1987) also analyze these clearing arrangements.

Bank clearing houses, and their cooperative benefits, were limited to citywide coalitions in the United States because of branching restrictions. The sharing of risk inherent in these cooperative arrangements required effective monitoring and enforcement of self-imposed regulations. Banks could only monitor and enforce effectively if they were geographically coincident. Moreover, as the number of banks in a self-regulating coalition increases, the incentives for effective supervision decline because the cost of monitoring is borne individually, while the benefits are shared among all members of the group.

2.3.3   Summary

The variety of institutional arrangements discussed above resulted in different propensities for panics and different abilities to respond to panics when they occurred. Internationally, not all countries experienced panics, even when the banking contracts appeared similar to those present in the United States. In the case of the United States, as reviewed above, there is direct evidence that these institutional arrangements resulted in different loss and failure experiences. Also, there is evidence from the Free Banking Era (1838–63), during which bank notes traded in markets, that these differences were priced by markets. As shown by Gorton (1989a, 1990), the note prices varied depending on the presence or absence of arrangements such as insurance, clearing house, and so on.

The evidence on the importance of market and institutional structure strongly suggests the importance of asymmetric information in banking. If full information for all agents characterized these markets, then institutional differences would not matter. We interpret this evidence as implying a set of stylized facts with which a theory of banking panics must be consistent. A theory must not only explain why such institutional structure matters, but also the origins of such structures as responses to panics.

2.4   Models of banking panics

A decade ago, theoretical work on banks and banking panics was aimed at addressing the following questions: How can bank debt contracts be optimal if such contracts lead to banking panics? Why would privately issued circulating bank debt be used to finance nonmarketable assets if this combination leads to socially costly panics? Posed in this way, explaining panics was extremely difficult. In the last decade, two distinct theories have developed to explain the origins of banking panics. While these two lines of argument do not exhaust the explanations of panics, they seem to be the explanations around which research has coalesced.[12] In this section we briefly review the evolution of this research, stressing the testable implications of each.

One line of argument, initiated by the influential work of Diamond and Dybvig (1983), began by arguing that bank contracts, while optimal, necessarily lead to costly panics. Banks and banking panics were seen as inherently intertwined. Over the last decade, confronted with the historical evidence that panics did not accompany demandable-debt contracts in all cases, this view has evolved to include institutional structure as a central part of the argument. Nevertheless, as we trace below, the essential core of the theory remains unchanged, namely, that panics are undesirable events caused by random deposit withdrawals. We, therefore, label this view the "random withdrawal" theory of panics.

The second line of argument on the origins of panics emphasizes the importance of market structure in banking when depositors lack information about bank-specific loan risk. While it is important to explain the existence of banks as institutions, the second view essentially starts with the unit-banking system as given. In this view, runs on banks may be an optimal response of depositors. A key to this argument is the hypothesis that bank depositors cannot costlessly value individual banks' assets. In other words, there is asymmetric information. In such a world, depositors may have a difficult time monitoring the performance of banks. A panic can be viewed as a form of monitoring. If depositors believe that there are some under-performing banks but cannot detect which ones may become insolvent, they may force out the undesirable banks by a systemwide panic. This line of argument, then, emphasizes sudden, but rational, revisions in the perceived riskiness of bank deposits when nonbank-specific, aggregate information arrives. We label this view the "asymmetric information" theory of panics.

These two lines of thought have different visions of why banks exist, though there are also important overlaps in the arguments. These theoretical considerations are discussed in the final subsection.

---

[12] Other panic theories are provided by Bryant (1980), Donaldson (1989b), and Waldo (1985). Also, see Minsky (1975) and Kindleberger (1978).

2.4.1   Random withdrawal risk

The model of Diamond and Dybvig (1983) was the first coherent explanation of how bank debt contracts could be optimal and yet lead to banking panics. An essential feature of the Diamond and Dybvig model is the view of banks as mechanisms for insuring against risk. In their model, agents have uncertain needs for consumption and face an environment in which long-term investments are costly to liquidate. Agents would prefer the higher returns associated with long-term investments, but their realized preferences may turn out to be for consumption at an earlier date. Banks exist to insure that consumption occurs in concert with the realization of agents' consumption preferences. The bank contract, offering early redemption at a fixed rate, is interpreted as the provision of "liquidity." This idea, further developed by Haubrich and King (1984), will not suffice, by itself, to explain panics.

In order for panics to occur, two further, related ingredients were needed. First, as Cone (1983) and Jacklin (1987) made clear, markets had to be incomplete in an important way, namely, agents were not allowed to trade claims on physical assets after their preferences for consumption had been realized.[13] Thus, stock markets or markets in bank liabilities were assumed to be closed. Second, deposit withdrawals were assumed to be made according to a first-come-first-served rule, or sequential-service constraint. These two assumptions, particularly the latter, were able to account for panics which were caused by random withdrawal risk.

A panic could occur as follows. In the Diamond and Dybvig model, a bank cannot honor all its liabilities at par if all agents present them for redemption. The problem is that liquidation of the bank's long-term assets is assumed to be costly. But, the essential mechanism causing the possibility of panic is the sequential-service constraint. With this rule, a panic can occur as a self-fulfilling set of beliefs. If agents think that other agents think there will be many withdrawals, then agents at the end of the sequential-service line will suffer losses. Thus, all agents, seeking to avoid losses associated with being at the end of the line, may suddenly decide to redeem their claims, causing the very event they imagined. The first-come-first-served rule prevents allocation of the bank's resources on a pro rata basis, which would have prevented the panic.

---

[13] Jacklin (1987) shows that dividend-paying equity shares dominate demand deposits in the Diamond and Dybvig (1983) model, but that this depends on the specific nature of the preferences assumed by Diamond and Dybvig. It does not hold for fairly general preference structures. Nevertheless, trading restrictions are a necessary ingredient to the Diamond and Dybvig argument, as Jacklin shows.

A key question for the original Diamond and Dybvig model concerned the causes of panics. Why would agents sometimes develop beliefs
leading to a panic, while at other times believe that there would be
no panic? This question, the answer to which was essential for any empirical test of the theory, was not really addressed. Diamond and Dybvig
suggested that such beliefs may develop because of "a random earnings
report, a commonly observed run at some other bank, a negative
government forecast, or even sunspots" (1983, p. 410).

In the Diamond and Dybvig model, panics are due to random withdrawals caused by self-fulfilling beliefs. The difficulties with this hypothesis were quickly recognized. As mentioned above, Cone (1983) argued
that panics would be eliminated if banking was conducted without the
sequential-service constraint. Wallace (1988) observed that the explanation for the existence of the crucial sequential-service constraint was
"vague." Jacklin (1987) made the observation about the required market
incompleteness. Postlewaite and Vives (1987) observed that the optimality of the Diamond and Dybvig bank could not be demonstrated if
probabilities could not be attached to the possibilities of self-fulfilling
beliefs occurring. Gorton (1988) pointed out that the model was
untestable because it did not specify how beliefs were formed or changed
as a function of observables.

These difficulties with the Diamond and Dybvig model motivated
further research along two lines. First, some justification for the sequential-service constraint had to be found. In Diamond and Dybvig this constraint, clearly not optimal from the point of view of the agents in the
model, was assumed to be part of the physical environment. Without the
constraint, panics would not arise. Second, the model had to be refined
to make clear what types of events would cause beliefs to change such
that a panic would occur. The Diamond and Dybvig model theoretically
equated the existence of banks as providers of liquidity with the possibility of banking panics. But, in reality, not all banking systems experienced panics. Consequently, as argued by Smith (1987), explaining what
shocks would cause agents to withdraw would require more attention to
market structure in banking.

Wallace (1988) addressed the issue of the existence of the sequential-
service constraint by introducing spatial separation of agents. The
assumed isolation of agents prevents them from coordinating their withdrawals. In particular, they cannot organize a credit market at the time
when withdrawal choices must be made.[14] This interpretation formally

---

[14] A market would allow for agents' beliefs to be coordinated, eliminating panic-causing
conjectures about other agents' beliefs. Pre-Civil War America, with active markets for
bank liabilities, appears to contradict this view of spatial separation.

rationalized the existence of the constraint, but it was difficult to recognize as an historical phenomenon. Bhattacharya and Gale (1987), Smith (1987), and Chari (1989) interpreted the spatial separation of agents as corresponding to the institutional features of the U.S. banking system during the nineteenth century. While differing in some important respects, the common thread among these papers is the recognition that the United States had a large number of geographically separated banks due to prohibitions on interstate banking. Banks were linked by the regulatory structure of the National Banking System which required small country banks to hold reserves in specified reserve-city banks. New York City, deemed the central reserve city, was at the top of the reserve pyramid.

This reinterpretation remedied the two defects of the Diamond and Dybvig model in one stroke. The sequential-service constraint appeared to be imposed on the system by the three-tiered reserve system.[15] Isolation corresponded to the spatial separation of the country banks. Reinterpreting the Diamond and Dybvig model in this historical context meant locating a causal panic shock in the countryside. The gist of the causal mechanism now was that country banks, facing a withdrawal shock, would demand that their reserves from city banks be shipped to the interior. If enough country banks in various locations faced problems at the same time, then they would demand their reserves from their reserve-city banks. The reserve-city banks, in turn, would demand their reserves from their central reserve-city banks in New York City. Thus, panics were not inherent to banking, but were linked to a particular institutional structure, namely, unit banking and reserve pyramiding.

Vulnerability to panics was identified with the spatial separation of banks. But, in order for a panic to occur, the spatially separated banks must be unable to form an effective interbank insurance arrangement. If a coalition of banks could form, then banks could self-insure, moving reserves about through interbank loan markets. Chari (1989) argues that difficulties in unit banks monitoring each other's holdings of reserves vitiated credible interbank arrangements. In the absence of effective monitoring, banks will have an incentive to hold too little in reserves (and place reserves in interest-bearing loans), thus making coinsurance of withdrawal risk infeasible. According to Chari (1989), geographically separate unit banks should be forced to hold reserves by government

---

[15] Typically, in these models the sequential-service constraint still applies to the depositors of each individual bank. But, while the initiating shock may thus be the same as in the original Diamond and Dybvig model, the main point is the reserve pyramiding which causes country banks to essentially behave as individual depositors with respect to the central-reserve city bank.

regulation. The government would then enforce this regulation, and thereby make interbank lending feasible.

In the refined version of Diamond and Dybvig an important question still remained: What was the shock which caused the panic? In order to confront the data, this question must be answered. Unfortunately, not much of an answer has been provided. Bhattacharya and Gale (1987) refer only to "local" shocks in a model of spatially separated banks. Smith (1987) is also vague. Only Chari (1989) explicitly provides an explanation:

> The idea that the demand for currency can vary within communities is not implausible. In the second half of the 19th century an important source of these variations was agriculture. The demand for farm loans rose during the planting season and fell in the harvest. Since cash was required for many farm transactions, the demand for currency in agricultural communities was high at both planting and harvesting times and low at other times of the year. (p. 11)

Indeed, there is a long literature on the seasonality of the demand for currency in the United States.[16] And, the identification of unexpectedly large demands for currency in the countryside as the cause of panics also has a long history.[17] Thus, the modern theory of panics which associates panics with random withdrawal risk due to seasonal fluctuations theoretically rationalizes a traditional view of panics.

To summarize, the theoretical development of the random-withdrawal risk theory of panics has resulted in a view which assigns the origin of the panic-causing shock to the countryside. Only one kind of shock has been proposed, namely, seasonally related demand for money shocks. This has testable implications for the random-withdrawal theory, which are developed below.

2.4.2   Asymmetric information

The alternative theory of banking panics is based on identifying the conditions under which bank depositors would rationally change their

---

[16] The importance of seasonality is discussed by Andrew (1907) and Kemmerer (1910). Goodhart (1969) writes: "Financial crises were attributed, with a great deal of truth, not so much to cyclical factors as to the natural results of the recurring autumnal pressures upon the money market; these seasonal pressures were so extreme that it took only a little extra strain – in the form of overheated boom conditions or the bursting bubbles of Wall Street speculation – to turn tightness into distress."

[17] See Eichengreen (1984) for a review. Eichengreen finds substantial interregional variation in the propensity to hold cash relative to demand deposits. Thus, variations across regions in the demand for money would be associated with interregional flows of currency. Furthermore, seasonal demands for money in the West (where cash-to-deposit ratios were high) would cause an aggregate contraction in the money supply (shrinkage in the money multiplier).

beliefs about the riskiness of banks. Then the theoretical task is to identify banking system features under which such changes in beliefs are manifested in panics. The core of the theory is that banking panics serve a positive function in monitoring bank performance in an environment where there is asymmetric information about bank performance. Panics are triggered by rational revisions in beliefs about bank performance.

Banks are not viewed as providing insurance in the asymmetric information theory. Rather, banks are seen as providing valuable services through the creation of nonmarketable bank loans together with the provision of a circulating medium.[18] Since banks are involved in the creation of nonmarketable assets, they may be difficult to value, and bank managements difficult to monitor. There is, thus, asymmetric information between banks and depositors concerning the performance of bank managements and portfolios. In an environment where there are many small, undiversified banks, these problems may be particularly severe.[19] Arguments for the existence of banks' value-creating activities in making loans depend on depositors' abilities to monitor the unobservable performance of bank managements.[20] The view of the asymmetric information theory of panics is that the sequential-service constraint and, indeed, panics themselves, are mechanisms for depositors to monitor the performance of banks.

In an environment with asymmetric information, a panic can occur as follows. Bank depositors may receive information leading them to revise their assessment of the risk of banks, but they do not know which individual banks are most likely to be affected. Since depositors are unable to distinguish individual bank risks, they may withdraw a large volume of deposits from all banks in response to a signal. Banks then suspend convertibility, and a period of time follows during which the banks themselves sort out which banks among them are insolvent. Indeed, it is possible to view panics as a means for depositors to force banks to resolve asymmetries of information through collective

---

[18] The appropriate literature discussing bank activities on the asset side of the balance sheet consists of Diamond (1984), Boyd and Prescott (1986), Campbell and Kracaw (1980), among others. On bank liabilities as a circulating medium see Gorton (1989b), Gorton and Pennacchi (1990), and Calomiris and Kahn (1991). These ideas are discussed further in subsection 2.4.3.

[19] In the United States, most banks have not had traded equity claims historically because the overwhelming number of banks were small institutions. Thus, there were no markets in any bank assets or liabilities.

[20] Diamond's (1984) argument explains how it is possible for depositors to monitor the monitor, that is, how the depositors can rely on the bank to monitor the borrowers.

action (i.e., monitoring and closure). The efficiency of this mechanism derives from a supposed comparative advantage (low monitoring costs) that banks possess.

No single model has given rise to the view that banking panics are essentially due to revisions of the perceived risk of bank debt in an environment where there is asymmetric information about bank asset portfolios. A number of researchers, including Calomiris (1989a); Calomiris and Schweikart (1991); Chari and Jagannathan (1988); Gorton (1987, 1989b); Gorton and Mullineaux (1987); Jacklin and Bhattacharya (1988); Williamson (1989); and others, have argued for this asymmetric information-based view of banking panics. These models are broadly consistent with the arguments of Sprague (1910) and Friedman and Schwartz (1963) which stress real disturbances, causing erosion of trust in the banking system, as precursors to panics. Although these viewpoints differ in important respects, they seem to have a similar idea at core.

The evolution of the asymmetric-information view is not as straightforward as the random withdrawal theory, but there is some logic to its development. To see how the asymmetric-information view differs from the random-withdrawal theory and to trace some of its development, we will focus on the sequential-service constraint. The asymmetric-information theory of banking panics views the sequential-service constraint in a fundamentally different way than the random-withdrawal theory.

A convenient beginning point is Chari and Jagannathan (1988). They assumed a setting in which depositors are uninformed about the true values of banks. In their model, depositors randomly fall into one of three groups: those who become informed about the state of bank portfolios; those who withdraw because they wish to consume, independently of the state of banks; and those who are uninformed and do not wish to consume. Their basic idea was that some bank depositors might withdraw money for consumption purposes while other depositors might withdraw money because they knew that the bank was about to fail.[21] In this environment, the group of depositors which cannot distinguish whether there are long lines to withdraw at banks because of consumption needs or because informed depositors are getting out early may also withdraw. The uninformed group learns about the state of the bank only by observing the line at the bank. If there happens to be a long line at

---

[21] In Chari and Jagannathan (1988), as in Diamond and Dybvig (1983), bank liabilities have no discernible role as a circulating medium of exchange. Thus, in Chari and Jagannathan it is not clear why agents withdraw from the bank if they want to consume. Apparently, bank liabilities do not function to satisfy cash-in-advance constraints.

the bank, they infer (rightly or wrongly) that the bank is about to fail and seek to withdraw also.[22]

This view of panics assumes the sequential-service constraint and asymmetric information, but introduces the idea of heterogeneously informed depositors (also see Jacklin and Bhattacharya 1988). Heterogeneously informed depositors became the basis for Calomiris and Kahn's (1991) and Calomiris, Kahn, and Krasa's (1991) argument that a debt contract, together with the sequential-service constraint, is an optimal arrangement in banking when depositors are uninformed about the bank's assets and managers' actions. To see the basic idea, suppose that information about the bank is costly to obtain. In order to monitor bank performance, some depositors must be induced to undertake costly information production. A sequential-service constraint rewards those who arrive first to withdraw their money because their deposit contracts are honored in full. Since informed agents would know when to withdraw, they would arrive first, receiving a larger return; those at the end of the line, the uninformed, would get less since the bank would have run out of cash. Thus, the sequential-service constraint induces efficient monitoring of banks by depositors.

In this context, however, the sequential-service constraint does not inevitably lead to banking panics. Instead, the above scenario would occur at specific banks which faced problems, but would not necessarily occur at many banks simultaneously. Banking panics do not occur unless there are a large number of undiversified banks. Some details about the reasons for this were provided by Gorton (1989b). He argued that a bank debt contract and sequential-service constraint, as implied by Calomiris and Kahn (1991), can be a costly way to monitor banks if it requires a large equity-to-debt ratio. (Equity is owned by the managers, so the managers' stake in the bank can be threatened by withdrawal.) For Gorton, bank debt has a role independent of the banks' value-adding activities in creating loans. Bank debt circulates as a medium of exchange. In that setting there must be some mechanism to clear bank liabilities. Gorton compares two institutional arrangements for clearing in the banking industry. The first was similar to American free banking in that bank debt liabilities were like bank notes. That is, bank debt traded in secondary markets. The market prices of these notes revealed information about bank-specific risks. Hence, there is no asymmetric information in this setting. As a result, bank managers are induced to perform their tasks of

---

[22] There is no explanation in Chari and Jagannathan (1988) for why this would be a systemic event affecting the entire banking system, rather than an event producing a run on a single bank.

monitoring or information production because of the threat of redemption. But, optimal performance is only achieved if enough equity is at stake.

Now consider a second way of organizing the banking industry in which there is no market in which bank debt is traded. Instead of clearing bank debt through trade in a market, suppose that bank liabilities clear through a clearing house. This arrangement would create an information asymmetry since there are no publicly observed market prices of different banks' debts. The market incompleteness, assumed in some other models, arises endogenously if this clearing arrangement is chosen. Gorton shows that panics can occur under this second system, but that the costs of monitoring banks can be reduced. The reason is that, with the information asymmetry, banks are forced to internalize the monitoring. The threat of a panic induces banks to form clearing houses which monitor member banks and act as the lender of last resort. The equity–debt ratio can be reduced, economizing on resources. In this view, panics are part of an optimal arrangement for monitoring banks.

While the assumption of information-revealing note prices, revealing bank-specific risk, may be a bit extreme, the essential point is that the need for bank debt holder to place a collective burden on banks to resolve information asymmetries is much greater under deposit banking than under note banking.[23] The clearing-house coalition is the natural group to resolve asymmetric information problems. Banks as a group have a collective interest in the smooth functioning of the payments system and comparative advantage in monitoring and enforcement.

Notice that there is a subtle difference between the arguments of Calomiris and Kahn (1991) and Gorton (1989b). Calomiris and Kahn argue that the sequential-service constraint provides an efficient way for depositors to monitor individual banks, though it may have the disadvantage of allowing systemic panics to occur. Gorton, however, sees the operation of the sequential-service constraint during panics as adding to the advantages of demandable debt.

The asymmetric information theory argues that insufficient diversification of asset risk among banks occurs under unit banking. Bank depositors do not know the value of bank asset portfolios. A panic may occur when depositors observe a public signal correlated with the value of

---

[23] The assumption of full revelation of bank-specific risk may be extreme for the following reasons. Note brokers sometimes refused to make markets in individual banks' notes, particularly during panics. Furthermore, earlier banking panics, for example, one in Indiana in 1854, took the form of runs by note holders rather than depositors. Gorton's (1990) evidence on the information content of bank notes pertains to state-specific, not bank-specific, risk. The extent to which bank-specific note risk was information revealed by the note market prices remains an area for future research.

banking-system assets. In Gorton (1988) the signal is an increase in a leading indicator of recession. In Calomiris and Schweikart (1991) the signal is a decline in the net worth of a particular class of bank borrowers. The signal may imply very slight aggregate losses to banks as a whole, but depositors are unable to observe the incidence of the shock across the many banks in the banking system. Conditional on the signal, deposits are riskier.[24] At some point, as the risk associated with asymmetric information rises, depositors prefer to withdraw their funds or force a suspension of convertibility which will resolve the information asymmetry.

2.4.3   Theoretical considerations

The competing theoretical constructs discussed above propose different visions of the nature of banks and banking, though there is some common ground. The varying perspectives on the nature of banking are not unrelated to the resulting different theories of panics. From a purely theoretical point of view, there are desirable and undesirable features of the two theories. In this section we indicate these differences and commonalities.

Banks are unique institutions because of services that are provided on each side of the balance sheet. Examining the asset side of the balance sheet first, the two theories appear to agree on the nature of banks' value-adding activities with respect to the creation of bank loans. Monitoring borrowers and information production about credit risks are activities that banks undertake that cannot be replicated by capital markets. The arguments for this are articulated by Diamond (1984) and Boyd and Prescott (1986), among others. The essential idea is that bank production of these activities requires that the bank loan which is created be nonmarketable or, synonymously, illiquid, that is, that it not be traded once created. If the loan could subsequently be sold, then the originating bank would not face an incentive to monitor or produce information. This argument depends on the banks' activities being unobservable, so that the only way of insuring that banks undertake the activities they promise is by forcing them to maintain ownership of the loans they create. This need for incentive compatibility makes bank loans nonmarketable.

---

[24] Moreover, the expected losses on deposits may be expected to occur when consumption is highly valued, during a recession, for example. As shown in Gorton (1988), losses per se cannot explain panics. But, losses occurring during a recession would receive more weight in utility terms. The combination of these events can cause panics. See Gorton (1988) for a model.

The nonmarketability or illiquidity of bank loans plays an essential role in each theory of banking panics. The random-withdrawal risk theory requires that the liquidation of long-term bank assets be costly. Though never clearly stated, presumably the reason for this cost assumption is that bank loans are not marketable. The asymmetric-information theory also assumes that bank loans are nonmarketable. If banks' monitoring and information production activities were observable, then there would be no information asymmetry. Bank loans are not traded because bank activity is hard to observe and monitor.

The two theories significantly differ concerning the nature of bank liabilities. The key question concerns the meaning of "liquidity." The random-withdrawal theory sees banks as institutions for providing insurance against random consumption needs. The high-return, long-term investment can only be ended, and transformed into cash or consumption goods, at a cost (for the reasons discussed above). While agents prefer the high-return, long-term investment project, they may want to consume at an earlier date. The bank, by pooling the long- and short-term investments in the right proportions, can issue a security which insures against the risk of early consumption. The idea, articulated by Diamond and Dybvig (1983, p. 403), is that "banks are able to transform illiquid assets by offering liabilities with a different, smoother pattern of returns over time than the illiquid assets offer." Thus, the insurance feature of the bank contract is interpreted as the provision of "liquidity."

In the random-withdrawal theory the illiquidity or nonmarketability of bank assets provides the rationale for the special feature of bank liabilities. In fact, precisely because the long-term investments are illiquid, the bank is needed. The banks' liabilities do not circulate as a medium of exchange in this model, so there is no sense in which demand deposits function like money. This appears to be a weakness of the model. But, the model provides a rationale for banks appearing to be financing illiquid assets with liabilities which have a redemption option. In the random-withdrawal theory, liquidity means inter-temporal consumption flexibility.

The asymmetric-information theory also offers a definition of the "liquidity" of bank liabilities. This notion of liquidity refers to the ease with which a security can be valued and, hence, traded. (This definition of liquidity is based on Akerlof 1970.) Importantly, this notion of liquidity is related to explaining the combination of nonmarketable or illiquid bank loans with liabilities offering the redemption option. As mentioned above, Calomiris and Kahn (1991) argue that the illiquidity of bank loans makes bank debt, together with the sequential-service constraint, optimal. Here, uninformed depositors learn about the state of the bank by observing whether informed depositors have run the bank. Thus, information about the value of bank debt is created. An implication would be that bank debt can be used as a medium of exchange. Gorton (1989b) and Gorton and Pennacchi (1990) also argue that bank liabilities are special because they circulate as a medium of exchange. In Gorton and Pennacchi (1990) the same notion of liquidity is articulated. The basic point is that bank debt is designed to be valued very easily because it is essentially riskless. This makes it ideal as a medium of exchange.

Gorton and Pennacchi consider a set-up similar to Diamond and Dybvig (1983) in that consumption needs are stochastic for some agents. But, other agents do not have random consumption and are informed about the state of the world. The informed agents can take advantage of the uninformed agents who have urgent needs to consume. This is accomplished by successful insider trading. Insiders can profit at the expense of the uninformed agents because these agents need to trade to finance consumption and do not know the true value of the securities they are exchanging for consumption goods. Gorton and Pennacchi show that market prices do not reveal this information. This problem creates the need for a privately produced trading security with the feature that its value is always known by the uninformed. A bank can prevent such trading losses by issuing a security which is riskless.

Banks can design a riskless security by creating liabilities which are, first of all, debt, and secondly, backed by a diversified portfolio. Debt contracts reduce the variance of the security's price. In addition, banks are in a relatively unusual position to back these liabilities with diversified portfolios, because banks make loans to many firms and, thus, hold large portfolios against which debt claims can be issued. For this reason, it is banks which issue trading securities, such as demand deposits.

The asymmetric-information theory articulates a notion of liquidity that corresponds closely to the idea that bank liabilities have unique properties making them suitable as a circulating medium. Banks create securities with the property that they can be easily valued because they are riskless. The property of risklessness makes these securities desirable as a medium of exchange. The random-withdrawal theory has a notion of liquidity corresponding to a type of insurance that banks are viewed as being in a unique position to offer. Bank debt does not circulate, but functions to insure against the liquidation of bank assets which would be costly. We leave it to the reader to judge whether any weight should be attached to these theoretical distinctions.

2.5   Confronting the data: The United States during the national banking era

Having established the importance of banking institutions and market structure in generating banking panics, we proceed, in this section, to an examination of the comparative empirical performance of the two competing theories of the origins of banking panics. At the outset it is worth noting the substantial overlap in the predictions of the two views.

First, both views predict widespread banking contraction coinciding with suspension of convertibility. Second, the order in which suspension occurs in different regions (that is, typically moving from East to West) is consistent with either view, as well. According to both views, because of interbank reserve pyramiding, a nationwide move to withdraw funds for whatever reasons will concentrate pressure on eastern financial centers first. Because peripheral banks had substantial deposits in New York, and because depositors often moved to withdraw funds from banks in one location to compensate for suspension elsewhere, suspension in New York City or Philadelphia would precipitate widespread suspension by banks elsewhere. Suspension of convertibility typically spread from eastern cities to other locations within a day or two of suspension in the financial centers (see Calomiris and Schweikart 1991, and Sprague 1910).

Third, as noted above, both views predict that branch banking or deposit insurance would be associated with an increase in banking stability, that is, a reduction in the incidence and severity of banking panics. Branch banking diversifies, and deposit insurance protects against, both asset and withdrawal risks, and either removes the incentive for preemptory runs by depositors which both the withdrawal-risk and asymmetric-information views predict.[25]

Fourth, the two approaches are consistent with the fact that bank panics occurred in certain months of the year. The withdrawal-risk approach views the seasonality of banking panics as evidence of the role of seasonal money-demand shocks in precipitating panics. According to the asymmetric-information view, seasonal patterns in the incidence of banking panics, noted by Andrew (1907), Kemmerer (1910), and Miron (1986), indicate that the banking system was more vulnerable to asset-side shocks during periods of low reserve-to-deposit and

---

[25] Chari (1989) argues that the reduction in the "bank failure" rate in the United States upon introducing deposit insurance supports the withdrawal-risk view over the asymmetric-information view. We do not agree. In an undiversified system of many unit banks, confusion over the incidence of an asset shock will lead depositors to withdraw, absent the ex post protection of deposit insurance. This will, in turn, cause suspensions of convertibility, disruptions in commerce, deflations, and increased bank insolvency rates.

capital-to-deposit ratios, but exogenous withdrawals by themselves were not the cause of panics. This is the argument for the seasonality of panics found in Sprague (1910) and Miron (1986). We provide further evidence for this argument below.

Despite the substantial agreement in the predictions of the two views, there are some important differences in their empirical implications. We have identified three verifiable areas of disagreement. First, because the two views differ over the sources of shocks, they differ in their predictions about what aspects of panic years were unusual, particularly the weeks or months immediately preceding the panic. The withdrawal-risk approach implies an unusual increase in withdrawals from banks typically combined with an unusually large interregional flow of funds at the onset of a panic. In particular, Chari (1989) argues that unusually large demands for money in the periphery for planting and harvesting crops were an important source of disturbance. Eichengreen (1984) provides some supporting evidence for this point by showing that the propensity to hold currency relative to deposits was higher in agricultural areas. During the planting and harvesting seasons, when the composition of money holdings shifted to the West, the money multiplier fell.

In contrast, the asymmetric-information approach predicts unusually adverse economic news prior to panics, including increases in asset risk, declines in the relative prices of risky assets, increases in commercial failures, and the demise of investment banking houses. The importance of this news for banking panics depends on the links between the news and the value of bank assets.

A second difference between the two approaches concerns predictions about the incidence of bank liquidations during panics. According to the asymmetric-information view of panics, the incidence of bank failures will reflect, in large part, the interaction between different bank loan portfolios and a systemic disturbance. Bank-failure propensities should vary according to the links between bank assets and the shock. For example, a shock which affects western land values or railroads' values clearly should tend to bankrupt banks holding western mortgages or railroad bonds more than other banks. According to models of random-withdrawal risk, banks should fail disproportionately in locations with pronounced idiosyncratic money-demand shocks. Or banks fail because they have connections to those regions through correspondent relationships (which transmit the money-demand shocks).[26] Furthermore, the

---

[26] One could argue, from an asymmetric-information perspective, that correspondents' asset risks are related and, therefore, the asymmetric-information approach could also explain increases in the probability of failure associated with correspondent relations. However, as demonstrated later in our discussion, the asymmetric-information approach does not rely on these linkages to explain variations in failure rates within a given region.

asymmetric-information view predicts that the aggregate ratio of bank failures to suspensions should depend on the severity of the shock that initiates suspension, while the withdrawal-risk approach would link the severity and suddenness of the withdrawal from banks to the ratio of suspensions to subsequent bank liquidations over different panics.

The third area of disagreement refers to sufficient conditions to resolve a panic. That is, the causes of banking panics can be inferred by the types of measures that are capable of resolving crises. (This has regulatory implications, discussed in the final section.) While both views of panics agree that bank coordination *ex ante* will probably mitigate the likelihood of panics and the effects of panics when they do occur, the two views have different implications for what efforts are sufficient to resolve panics. The withdrawal-risk model predicts that panics take time to resolve because of the difficulty banks face in transforming assets into cash quickly. Historically, however, a large proportion of bank assets took the form of internationally marketable securities, including bills of exchange and high-grade commercial paper which were convertible into gold in international markets (see Myers 1931). In some instances there were more immediate sources of funds available. We investigate whether the time it would have taken to perform this conversion corresponds to the duration of suspension.

Alternatively, the asymmetric-information view sees the duration of suspension as an indicator of how long it takes to resolve confusion about the incidence of asset shocks. The availability of specie per se may be insufficient to resolve panics, especially if many banks' assets are not "marked to market" and are viewed as suspect. Furthermore, the asymmetric-information view predicts that interbank transfers of wealth can resolve asset-risk concerns without necessarily taking the form of specie movements and, thus, can put an end to crises. We consider examples of private and public bailouts that took this form.

2.5.1   How were pre-panic periods unusual?

We begin by examining whether pre-panic periods were characterized by unusually large withdrawals and interregional flows of funds. Consistent with our definition of panics, we date the beginning of trouble by reference to the timing of a cooperative emergency response by banks, such as providing for the issue of clearing-house loan certificates. This will produce an upwardly biased measure of the withdrawals during panic years, since by the time banks had recognized and acted upon a problem, some endogenous pre-emptive withdrawals may already have occurred. Thus, our inter-year comparisons of shocks are biased in favor of finding large withdrawals in advance of panics. In other words, a negative finding would provide an a fortiori argument against the importance of random withdrawals.

All comparisons are made across years for the same week of the year. This allows one to abstract from predictable seasonal components of withdrawals.

Our first measures refer to the condition of New York City banks at the beginnings of panics so defined, using data compiled up to 1909 by the National Monetary Commission (see Andrew 1910). We focus on the percentage of deposits withdrawn and the ratio of reserves to deposits as indicators of the New York banks' vulnerability or illiquidity. The two measures are complementary. Because weekly disturbances in money demand are likely to be serially correlated within the year (the sine qua non of the seasonal withdrawal-risk approach), it is useful to focus not only on the reserve ratio but also on the amount actually withdrawn from banks, as an indication of how much is likely to be withdrawn for similar purposes in the following weeks. At the same time, a large withdrawal during times when banks are holding large reserves will be of little consequence, so one must also pay attention to the reserve ratio when comparing years of similar seasonal withdrawal shocks.

Introducing two complementary measures of seasonal "illiquidity risk" complicates matters slightly for determining the extent to which pre-panic episodes were unusual. How does one compare years where the two measures provide opposite results for the degree of "tightness"? We adopt the following conventions: A year is said to be unambiguously tighter than another year (during a particular week) if its reserve ratio is lower and the percentage of deposits withdrawn in the immediate past is higher during a given week. A year is defined as possibly tighter if the percentage of withdrawals is higher and the reserve ratio differs by less than 1 percent.

We also had to choose a definition of the immediate past. Seasonal withdrawals associated with planting and harvesting tend to be spread over periods of one to two months (more on this below). Clearly, protracted steady withdrawals of funds over a two-month period would not have posed nearly the threat to banks that a sudden withdrawal of the same amount would have posed. The transatlantic cable was in operation beginning in 1866, and it took roughly ten days for a steamship to cross the Atlantic to exchange European specie for marketable bills of exchange and commercial paper. Calomiris and Hubbard (1996) show that specie flows across the Atlantic and within the country responded extremely rapidly to specie demands, with most long-run adjustments to a shock occurring in the first month. We decided on four weeks as a reasonable time horizon for withdrawal risk since it would take at least two weeks after recognizing a threat to liquidity to retrieve the gold from abroad and distribute it.[27]

Table 2.2 is divided into five pairs of columns, which provide data from 1871 to 1909 on reserve ratios and the percentage change in deposits immediately prior to benchmark weeks that witnessed the onset of banking panics. Panics originated in week 19 (mid-May 1884), week 22 (early June 1893), week 37 (late September 1873), week 42 (late October 1907), and week 45 (mid-November 1890).

The "quasi panic" of 1896 is excluded from our list. Its inclusion would strengthen the conclusions reported below, since its onset did not correspond to unusually large seasonal withdrawals. Our conclusions would also be strengthened by extending comparisons to include weeks other than 19, 22, 37, 42, and 45. That is, one could seasonally adjust the complete data set on withdrawals and reserve ratios and perform comparisons across weeks, as well.[28] By restricting our attention to the five clear panic cases and to inter-year comparisons for panic weeks, we biased our results in favor of concluding that panic episodes were times of unusually large withdrawals. This will strengthen the interpretation of our findings below. We also chose not to detrend the reserve ratios in Table 2.2 for the same reason. Detrending the reserve ratio increases the number of episodes in which we find "unambiguously tighter" conditions than those preceding panics.

The measures reported in Table 2.3 do not support the notion that panics were preceded by unusually large seasonal shocks or that panics resulted from tripping a threshold of bank liquidity, as measured either by reserve ratios or rates of deposit withdrawal. As shown in Table 2.3, even using our extremely conservative methods, we find eighteen episodes in which panics did not occur, even though seasonal "liquidity risk" at New York City banks was unambiguously more acute than in periods preceding panics. Three additional episodes involved comparable or larger withdrawals than panic years, with only slightly higher reserve ratios (1900, p. 45; 1905, p. 42; 1909, p. 42). Measures of stringency just prior to the Panics of 1907 and 1893 were roughly at their median levels for the same weeks in other years.

Clearly, seasonal withdrawals from, and reserve ratios of, New York

---

[27] It is worth noting that experimentation confirms that our results are robust to variations in the choice of time horizon over the interval from two to five weeks.

[28] Three particularly large withdrawals (for their respective weeks) occurred before week 50 in 1880 (−15.5 percent, bringing the reserve ratio to 24.96 percent), week 10 in 1881 (−13.4 percent, bringing the reserve ratio to 25.15 percent), and week 33 in 1896 (−8.3 percent, bringing the reserve ratio to 27.01 percent).

Table 2.2. *Four-week percentage change in deposits and reserve ratios of New York city banks prior to weeks when panics occurred*

	Panic of 1884, week 19		Panic of 1893, week 22		Panic of 1873, week 37		Panic of 1907, week 42		Panic of 1890, week 45	
	%Δ	Reserve ratio	%Δ	Reserve ratio	%Δ	Reserve ratio	%Δ	Reserve ratio	%Δ	Reserve ratio
1871	7.4	34.67	5.7	35.06	−0.2	29.98	−16.4	29.50	−0.4	32.39
1872	11.0	30.98	6.4	33.14	−12.5	29.01	−0.0	32.38	6.7	30.28
1873	7.9	30.67	5.6	30.65	**−13.3**	**27.54**	—	—	—	—
1874	−1.0	35.56	−0.9	37.39	−0.0	35.78	−2.9	32.84	−3.0	31.71
1875	4.1	29.89	5.1	32.13	−2.2	32.38	−4.9	27.49	−3.7	29.09
1876	1.2	29.60	2.6	32.79	3.5	34.85	−4.7	29.99	−4.3	29.09
1877	3.2	32.70	−1.6	33.88	−2.4	30.64	−5.7	28.84	−1.9	29.56
1878	−0.4	32.86	0.4	32.14	0.2	30.90	−4.4	27.30	−0.3	31.09
1879	13.2	32.14	5.1	26.83	−10.2	26.31	2.0	25.54	−0.3	24.71
1880	0.8	27.35	3.9	31.13	−0.1	26.91	1.2	26.57	2.2	25.56
1881	3.6	29.67	10.2	27.79	−5.7	25.14	−9.7	25.66	0.2	26.02
1882	3.0	27.72	−1.3	26.32	−6.6	24.66	−4.3	25.97	−1.2	23.98
1883	6.4	26.64	1.3	27.91	−1.8	26.17	−1.7	24.99	−2.2	26.56
1884	**−4.4**	**26.35**	—	—	—	—	—	—	—	—
1885	2.1	40.28	0.9	41.81	1.0	38.28	−0.6	35.36	−0.2	32.39
1886	−0.2	27.37	−2.1	28.77	−6.8	27.20	−1.5	26.31	0.2	26.60
1887	−0.2	26.10	−1.4	26.16	−1.3	26.11	4.2	27.62	0.3	27.69
1888	NA	NA	NA	NA	NA	NA	NA	NA	NA	NA
1889	1.6	27.10	0.5	28.29	−1.4	26.21	−3.8	25.22	−1.4	24.56
1890	−0.9	25.36	−0.2	26.21	−4.3	24.13	−3.4	24.91	**−3.7**	**25.35**
1891	−3.1	26.18	−5.2	26.94	−0.7	27.15	1.6	27.19	2.9	26.19
1892	0.7	27.78	0.1	29.59	−5.0	25.95	−5.1	25.11	−3.6	25.57
1893	−1.1	29.09	**−0.3**	**29.84**	—	—	—	—	—	—
1894	2.7	38.92	−1.1	38.62	0.3	35.21	1.1	35.51	0.2	35.41
1895	6.3	30.77	6.9	32.28	−1.0	29.66	−5.0	27.88	−1.0	28.64
1896	2.4	29.08	0.8	29.45	−4.9	26.96	1.7	27.62	−4.6	27.10
1897	0.8	32.73	−0.2	33.09	1.8	29.15	−3.2	27.37	2.5	28.34
1898	0.5	32.04	7.0	32.35	−7.4	25.61	6.0	28.13	6.4	26.92
1899	1.4	28.00	−1.1	29.78	−3.9	25.03	−3.9	25.17	−4.0	24.62
1900	3.8	26.76	2.1	27.26	1.4	27.29	−6.0	25.34	−3.7	25.55
1901	0.8	25.83	−2.2	27.22	−3.6	25.76	1.6	26.63	0.8	25.89
1902	0.3	25.35	−2.1	26.25	−5.7	25.07	−2.1	25.64	1.5	27.00
1903	3.5	26.08	0.8	26.06	1.6	26.66	−2.0	26.95	−3.4	25.61
1904	4.1	27.00	−1.4	27.69	1.2	28.14	−2.6	26.33	−0.8	25.84
1905	0.9	26.44	0.7	25.53	−8.4	25.42	−5.8	26.22	0.2	24.75
1906	3.2	26.26	0.9	25.65	−4.8	25.34	3.7	25.57	−5.2	24.84
1907	2.1	25.75	0.7	26.13	−1.4	25.65	**−2.1**	**26.08**	—	—
1908	3.6	30.03	2.2	28.72	2.4	28.84	0.3	27.39	−0.4	27.33
1909	1.6	26.08	0.8	26.37	−3.8	25.58	−8.3	26.37	−2.6	25.59
Median	1.6	27.78	0.7	29.45	−1.8	26.96	−2.6	26.95	−0.8	26.92

Source: Andrew (1910, pp. 79–117).

Table 2.3. *Times of greater "seasonal withdrawal stress" than during panic years (within-week comparison)*

Unambiguously greater		Possibly greater	
Year	Week	Year	Week
1881	42		
1882	22		
1882	42		
1886	22		
1887	22		
1889	42		
1891	22		
1892	42		
1899	22		
1899	42		
1899	45		
1900	42		
		1900	45
1901	22		
1902	22		
1902	42		
1904	22		
1905	22		
		1905	42
1906	45		
		1909	42

Source: Table 2.2.

City banks were not "sufficient statistics" for predicting panics. Tables 2.4 and 2.5 provide additional evidence that pre-panic periods were not episodes of unusually large seasonal flows of funds to the interior. Andrew (1910) reports weekly data on shipments of gold between New York City banks and the interior beginning in 1899. These data were used to construct measures of net cash flows from New York to the interior for the four- and eight-week periods prior to the Panic of 1907, and prior to comparable weeks in earlier years. According to these measures, 1900, 1901, and 1906 witnessed greater or comparable withdrawals for both time horizons relative to 1907. For the eight-week period, six out of eight years witnessed larger seasonal net outflows.

Andrew (1910) compiled monthly data on cash shipments to and from New York City by region of origin and destination beginning in 1905.

Table 2.4. *Net flows of cash from New York city banks to interior,*
1899–1907

	For 4 weeks prior to October 21, or comparable dates[a]	For 8 weeks prior to October 21, or comparable dates[a]
1899	9,682	26,273
1900	25,190	34,836
1901	15,585	27,266
1902	6,973	16,050
1903	10,636	16,127
1904	9,968	22,962
1905	6,764	23,832
1906	21,649	37,076
1907	17,700	18,248

[a] Comparable dates are as follows: 20 October 1899; 19 October 1900; 18 October 1901;
24 October 1902; 23 October 1903; 21 October 1904; 20 October 1905; 19 October 1906;
18 October 1907.
Source: Andrew (1910, pp. 172–77).

Table 2.5. *Net shipments of cash for month of*
September 1905–1907, from New York City
clearing house banks to interior

Region	1905	1906	1907
New England	2,640	3,453	3,846
Eastern states	3,130	6,616	809
Southern states	8,035	3,921	4,834
Middle West	1,965	7,886	6,611
Western states	−5	−2	89
Pacific states	−496	−107	−95
Aggregate			
Sum of balances	15,269	21,767	16,094
Mean of balances	2,545	3,628	2,682

Source: Andrew (1910, pp. 232–39).

Data for September (the month in which harvesting payments are
most concentrated, as discussed below) are used to construct Table 2.5.
Again, 1906 shows a much larger outflow in September. Furthermore,
since the Chari (1989) model emphasizes regional variation, it is
interesting to note that both 1905 and 1906 show larger region-specific

outflows than any in 1907. In September 1906, two regions received net transfers of cash in excess of the largest amount received by any region in September 1907, while in September 1905 one region did.

Advocates of random withdrawal risk might object to these findings on the grounds that it was anticipated future seasonal withdrawals, not past withdrawals, that caused banking panics. To this objection we have four responses. First, anticipations of cash needs in the West and South for planting and harvesting should be closely related to previous weeks' withdrawals, since not all farmers plant or harvest crops in the same week. Thus, years of unusual expected withdrawals (e.g., large harvest years) typically will be years of unusual withdrawals in the immediate past.

Second, information on the volume of crops harvested, which provides independent information on the expected payments required for harvesting, indicates that years in which panics occurred in the fall (1873, 1890, 1907) were not years of unusually large harvests for corn, wheat, and cotton. Table 2.6 reports data on the percentage differences between the annual volume of these three crops compared to five-year moving averages centered in that year, from 1871 to 1907. As can be seen, in 1873, 1890, and 1907, the harvests were not unusually large. In fact, in many cases they were unusually small.

Third, the timing of panics (with the possible exception of the Panic of 1873) places them after weeks of seasonal shocks associated with planting and harvesting, so that any money flows for these purposes would have occurred prior to the dates when panics began. Kemmerer's (1910) and Swift's (1911) analyses of seasonal patterns for interregional currency transfers and agricultural trade make clear that planting was associated with large retentions of funds in the interior in February through April, with large seasonal flows to New York beginning in May. Similarly, late August through early October marked the height of the fall currency transfer. Average seasonal deviations reported by Swift and Kemmerer are given in Table 2.7. Data on seasonal variation in currency premia across cities within the United States point to the same seasonal pattern of currency scarcity as in New York, as shown in Table 2.8.

Swift (1911) and Allen (1913a) emphasize the difference between the early autumn movement of currency to finance harvesting and the late autumn increase in loans (associated with increased deposits in the banking system) to finance the movement of the crops. Allen cites the description of this difference given by the New York Chamber of Commerce Currency Committee:

Table 2.6. *Percentage difference between annual harvest of corn, wheat, and cotton and respective five-year moving averages centered in that year*[a]

	Corn (thousand bushels)	Wheat (thousand bushels)	Cotton (thousand bales)
1871	−0.5	−8.0	−19.3
1872	10.1	−4.2	2.0
1873	−9.7	3.3	6.7
1874	−22.4	8.5	−9.8
1875	15.3	−4.9	5.9
1876	3.7	−13.6	−1.8
1877	−2.5	0.3	−3.4
1878	−4.7	4.0	−4.9
1879	7.6	6.1	4.0
1880	15.0	−9.6	10.7
1881	−1.8	−15.1	−10.5
1882	2.7	8.6	14.2
1883	−4.2	−3.4	−6.0
1884	4.8	14.0	−7.7
1885	15.2	−19.0	4.2
1886	−5.8	3.9	−0.7
1887	−20.3	4.8	2.0
1888	14.1	−6.3	−5.3
1889	16.0	3.4	10.5
1890	−19.7	−18.1	11.5
1891	15.6	26.7	14.6
1892	1.6	8.2	−19.9
1893	−6.6	−19.2	−6.4
1894	−31.8	1.5	1.1
1895	17.3	2.4	−19.7
1896	17.0	−16.4	−9.3
1897	−8.0	0.0	16.9
1898	−6.6	25.0	10.6
1899	9.0	−9.4	−8.1
1900	3.6	−17.4	−0.1
1901	−27.3	19.7	−5.3
1902	16.2	7.0	0.6
1903	1.3	−3.2	−8.4
1904	−4.2	−16.1	1.6
1905	4.7	6.6	−0.8
1906	9.5	12.0	6.5
1907	−5.2	−8.5	−4.3

[a] Calculated as a percentage of the value of the moving average.
Source: Andrew (1910, p. 14).

Table 2.7. *Average seasonal currency flows, 1899–1906*[a]

	Average net inflow of funds from interior to New York City Banks ($ million)	Deviation from average monthly flow over the year ($ million)
January	23.8	18.8
February	10.0	5.0
March	4.1	−0.9
April	7.7	2.7
May	9.5	4.5
June	12.3	7.3
July	13.4	8.4
August	3.8	−1.2
September	−15.6	−20.6
October	−13.1	−18.1
November	−0.3	−5.3
December	3.9	−1.1
Average over the year	5.0	0.0

[a] Figures for weekly flows were compiled by the Commercial and Financial Chronicle and reported in Kemmerer (1910). Goodhart (1969) argues that these are the most reliable of available data. The data reported here do not include 1907 and 1908 (because of the panic, the last three months of 1907 witnessed unusual interbank outflows from New York, with correspondingly unusual inflows in early 1908). According to Kemmerer's (1910) definition of "months," some months contain five weeks, while others contain four. April, July, September, and December each contain five weeks.
Source: Kemmerer (1910, pp. 358–59).

These harvests and the marketing of the crops bring to bear upon the banks a two fold strain, one for capital, the other for currency. The demand for capital comes from the buyers and shippers of agricultural products and is in the main satisfied by an expansion of bank loans and deposits, most of the payments being made by checks and drafts. The demand for currency comes principally from the farmers and planters who must pay their help in cash. In the satisfaction of this demand the banks are unable to make use of their credit, but are obliged to take lawful money from their reserves and send it into the harvest fields. (Quoted in Allen 1913a, p. 128)

The upshot of this analysis is that, whatever seasonal currency outflows were associated with planting and harvesting, these flows preceded the Panics of May 1884, June 1893, (late) October 1907, and November 1890. Thus, it would be difficult to argue that at these dates people were expecting large seasonal withdrawals of cash to agricultural areas.

Fourth, the observation that a reversal of seasonal flows of cash from New York typically would have been expected beginning in May and late October implies that "illiquidity risk" thresholds consistent with the

Table 2.8. *Seasonal variations in the relative demand for money in Chicago, St. Louis, and New Orleans, as evidenced by exchange rates in New York City (average figures, 1899–1908, per $100)*

Month and week	Chicago average rate	St. Louis average rate	New Orleans average rate
January			
1	2.5¢p	7¢p	35.5¢d
2	5¢p	3¢d	15.5¢d
3	5¢p	7.8¢p	0.5¢d
4	10¢p	1.5¢p	8¢d
February			
5	2¢p	8¢d	19¢d
6	6¢d	13¢d	26.5¢d
7	9¢d	7¢d	24¢d
8	20¢d	4.5¢p	26¢d
March			
9	29.5¢d	5.5¢d	13¢d
10	23¢d	0.05¢d	18.5¢d
11	13¢d	2¢p	15.5¢d
12	14.5¢d	3.5¢p	17¢d
April			
13	5¢d	2¢p	22.5¢d
14	14¢d	5¢d	18.5¢d
15	7.5¢d	8¢d	18¢d
16	4¢p	4¢p	20¢d
17	9¢d	1.5¢d	21.5¢d
May			
18	3.5¢d	4.5¢d	45¢d
19	2.5¢p	7.5¢p	46¢d
20	16¢p	20.5¢p	45¢d
21	16¢p	35¢p	37.5¢d
June			
22	10¢p	24¢p	20¢d
23	5¢p	7¢p	8.5¢d
24	4¢p	8¢p	12.5¢d
25	10.5¢p	12¢p	33¢d
July			
26	11.5¢p	2.5¢d	33¢d
27	16.5¢p	18¢d	56.5¢d
28	7.5¢d	21.5¢d	50.5¢d
29	8¢d	11¢d	42¢d
30	10.5¢d	9.8¢d	26¢d
August			
31	11¢d	24.5¢d	35¢d
32	17.5¢d	23.5¢d	28.5¢d
33	19¢d	31.5¢d	42¢d
34	34.5¢d	27¢d	42¢d

130

Table 2.8. *(cont.)*

Month and week	Chicago average rate	St. Louis average rate	New Orleans average rate
September			
35	37.5¢d	32¢d	59.5¢d
36	36.5¢d	48¢d	65.5¢d
37	25¢d	40.5¢d	79.5¢d
38	26¢d	39¢d	82¢d
39	33¢d	55.5¢d	81¢d
October			
40	32¢d	54¢d	95.5¢d
41	29.5¢d	46.5¢d	85.5¢d
42	27.5¢d	45¢d	85.5¢d
43	31¢d	72.5¢d	82¢d
November			
44	29¢d	60.5¢d	$1.005d
45	20¢d	26.5¢d	$1.09d
46	4.5¢d	11.3¢p	$1.03d
47	13¢p	53.3¢p	91.5¢d
December			
48	2.5¢d	7.3¢p	81.5¢d
49	11.5¢d	2¢d	82.5¢d
50	5¢p	32¢p	74¢d
51	3.5¢p	11.8¢p	86.5¢d
52	3.5¢p	2¢d	66¢d

Note: "p" = premium; "d" = discount.
Source: Kemmerer (1910, pp. 94–95).

withdrawal risk approach should have been lower in early spring and autumn. That is, given the expected reversal of fund flows in the summer and winter, a liquidity shock in late spring or fall should have prompted less of a concern than in early spring or fall. Table 2.2 provided evidence that contradicts that implication. The withdrawal shock associated with the onset of the Panic of 1893 (week 22) indicates a lower threshold to initiate a panic than for the shock associated with the Panic of 1884 (week 19). Similarly, the panics in 1907 (week 42) and 1890 (week 45) were associated with lower previous percentage withdrawals than the Panic of 1873 (week 37). This evidence leads one to wonder why there were not many more panics in weeks 19 and 37. That is, using a cross-week comparison criterion to predict panics, we predict fifteen additional panics that never occurred, which are listed in Table 2.9. Thus, under the assumption that seasonal liquidity-shock thresholds should be smaller during weeks of higher risk of seasonal withdrawals from New York, the number of unrealized, predicted panics rises from 18 (or 21) to 33 (or

Table 2.9. *Times of greater "seasonal withdrawal stress" than during panic years (cross-week comparison)*

Year	Week	Year	Week	Year	Week
1881	37	1892	37	1901	37
1882	37	1893	19	1902	37
1890	19	1896	37	1905	37
1890	37	1898	37	1906	37
1891	19	1899	37	1909	37

Source: Table 2.2.

36). Furthermore, one could add to this list by considering unusual seasonal withdrawals prior to weeks other than (and before) weeks 19 and 37. One such case would be March 1881 (week 10), with withdrawals equal to 13.4 percent of deposits over the previous four weeks and a reserve ratio of 25.15. In summary, an emphasis on expected future withdrawal risk, rather than actual past withdrawals, strengthens the case against the random-withdrawal-risk approach.

We turn now to investigate whether pre-panic periods were unusual in a manner consistent with the predictions of the asymmetric information theory of panics. The accounts of Sprague (1910), Calomiris and Schweikart (1991), and Gorton (1988) emphasize various specific real disturbances prior to panics, some originating in particular markets (e.g., the western land market in 1893), or high-risk railroad securities in several cases, as well as general business contractions. The single time-series most likely to be systematically associated with all of these shocks is the stock price index. Thus, it seems reasonable to require that pre-panic periods be characterized by unusually adverse movements in stock prices. The extent to which such disturbances threaten the banking system, however, will depend on (1) their severity; (2) the extent to which they signal adverse circumstances in other markets; and (3) the extent to which banks are exposed to risk.

As a starting point it is interesting to compare real economic news prior to the 18 (21) "unrealized panics" (using the within-week criterion) to news preceding the five actual panics. Table 2.10 reports the three-month percentage change in nominal and real (WPI-deflated) stock prices prior to all 26 episodes. This time horizon is long enough to allow continuing bad news to become fully reflected in stock prices, but not too long as to include gradual price declines. Whether one focuses on

Table 2.10. *Stock price declines over three months prior to periods of "seasonal withdrawal stress" (within-week criterion)*

Actual panics	Predicted unrealized panics[a]	Nominal %Δ[b]	Real %Δ (WPI-deflated)[c]
1873 (37)		**−7.9**	**−7.9**
	1881 (42)	−3.2	−10.1
	1882 (22)	−1.6	−3.5
	1882 (42)	0.8	−1.1
1884 (19)		**−12.6**	**−8.5**
	1886 (22)	−5.0	−0.2
	1887 (22)	6.3	6.3
	1889 (42)	2.3	1.0
1890 (45)		**−8.4**	**−13.3**
	1891 (22)	1.2	−0.4
	1892 (42)	0.6	−0.7
1893 (22)		**−12.2**	**−7.4**
	1899 (22)	−1.9	−3.9
	1899 (42 and 45)	0.8	−5.9
	1900 (42 and [45])	2.7	3.6
	1901 (22)	6.6	7.7
	1902 (22)	3.2	0.4
	1902 (42)	−1.0	−7.9 (−3.7)[c]
	1904 (22)	0.0	3.6
	1905 (22)	−3.3	−0.5
	[1905 (42)]	5.4	4.6
	1906 (45)	10.0	4.8
1907 (42)		**−18.6**	**−19.8**
	[1909 (42)]	2.8	−0.6

[a] Episodes of "possibly greater" seasonal stress than preceding panics appear in brackets.
[b] Stock price changes are measured using monthly data as follows: for week 19 and week 22 we use February and May prices to calculate the percentage change; for week 37 we use June and September prices; and for week 42 and week 45 we use July and October prices. Evidence on daily stock price changes from the Commercial and Financial Chronicle indicates that most of the stock price declines measured in May 1884, September 1873, and October 1907 preceded the onset of panic. In the two remaining panics the monthly stock price changes reported here entirely predate the panics.
[c] The wholesale price index shows an unusually large upward movement in October 1902, which is reversed immediately thereafter. Real percentage change computed using November's price level is given in parentheses.
Source: U.S. Department of Commerce (1949), pp. 344–45, and Table 2.2.

real or nominal stock price changes depends on the extent to which the wholesale price index follows a random walk (i.e., whether short-run changes in commodity prices are a good indicator of long-run expectations). Barsky (1987) shows that, roughly speaking, price movements can be characterized this way, although Calomiris (1988) shows that 1869–79 (and especially 1876–79) was an exceptional period of deflationary expectations in anticipation of the resumption of greenback convertibility. Thus, with the exception of the 1870s, deflated stock price movements are probably the best indicator of real change. At the same time, the existence of measurement error in the wholesale price index argues against identifying a large real stock price movement that does not coincide with nominal movements in stock prices.

The evidence presented in Table 2.10 supports the view that large withdrawals only threatened the banking system when they were accompanied by (perhaps precipitated by) real disturbances. The five pre-panic episodes experienced the largest nominal declines in stock prices by far and were all associated with similarly large real declines in stock prices.

Thus far we have shown that adverse stock price movements preceded panics and that unusually large seasonal movements of cash or withdrawals from New York banks were neither necessary nor sufficient conditions for panics. We now ask whether adverse stock price movements by themselves provide sufficient conditions for predicting panics. Specifically, did all sufficiently large percentage declines in stock prices predict panics? Table 2.11 describes all periods of unusual three-month downturns in stock prices, that is, all non-overlapping three-month intervals in which stock prices fell by more than 5 percent.[29]

Of the 23 intervals of greater than 5 percent nominal decline in stock prices, nine preceded or coincided with panics. Another of these intervals preceded the "quasi panic" of 1896. As Table 2.11 shows, these ten pre- and post-panic intervals showed much larger nominal and real declines in stock prices than the remaining thirteen non-panic intervals. The average nominal and real percentage declines for the five pre-panic intervals were –11.9 and –11.4, respectively, while the averages for the thirteen non-panic intervals were 1.7 and 0.07 percent. There were only five non-panic intervals that showed real stock price declines as large as the minimum of ten pre- and post-panic intervals. In other words, assuming a threshold of 7.9 percent real decline in stock prices is sufficient to

[29] Each interval of decline is defined as follows. Moving forward in time we compare the price index of each month in the sample to the index three months before. Intervals are defined not to overlap. For example, if stock prices fell from February to May, then fell again in June and rebounded in July, we would register only the February-May interval (not the March-June interval).

Table 2.11. *Three-month periods of unusual stock price decline, 1871–1909*

	Nominal %Δ	Real %Δ	Seasonal difference (%Δ) in liabilities of commercial failures[a]
1873 (June–September)	**−7.9**	**−7.9**	**NA**
1874 (February–May)	−6.3	−4.0	NA
1876 (February–May)	−7.9	−3.3	30.0
1877 (January–April)	−17.2	−12.9	−8.1[b]
1880 (February–May)	−8.3	−2.6	−11.5
1882 (August–November)	−5.6	−1.1	26.6[c]
1883 (May–August)	−5.4	−0.5	115.8[d]
1884 (February–May)	**−12.6**	**−8.5**	**202.9**
1884 (August–November)	−8.8	−4.5	−6.3[c]
1886 (February–May)	−5.0	−0.2	−27.3
1887 (May–August)	−7.7	−6.5	168.4[d]
1890 (July–October)	**−8.4**	**−13.3**	**50.3[c]**
1893 (February–May)	**−12.2**	**−7.4**	**428.3**
1893 (May–August)	**−15.4**	**−6.6**	**389.2[d]**
1895 (September–December)	−10.2	−8.8	25.2
1896 (May–August)	**−13.1**	**−11.1**	**71.2**
1900 (April–July)	−7.4	−5.0	148.0
1902 (September–December)	−8.8	−13.6	−3.8
1903 (February–May)	−9.5	−4.7	23.3
1903 (May–August)	−12.9	−12.6	22.7
1907 (January–April)	−12.3	−13.1	−7.7
1907 (May–August)	−7.1	−7.9	110.0
1907 (August–November)	**−17.0**	**−14.7**	**143.5**

[a] Data on seasonal differences in liabilities of business failures are for four-month period ending the month after the corresponding stock decline, unless otherwise noted. Quarterly data exist for 1875–94; monthly data exist after 1894.
[b] Uses average of first- and second-quarter data.
[c] Uses average of third- and fourth-quarter data.
[d] Uses average of second- and third-quarter data.
Source: U.S. Department of Commerce (1949, pp. 344–45, 349).

produce a banking panic, one can predict all actual panics (including 1896) and falsely identify only five non-panics as panics.

Of course, the asymmetric-information view need not see stock price declines as a sufficient condition for producing panics. As already noted, it is the threat to banks that matters. Stock price declines will have more severe consequences for banks the more they are associated with widespread commercial defaults, and the more banks' portfolio positions expose themselves to loan-default risk.

In Table 2.11, we also present data on seasonal differences in the liabilities of business failures for the periods of stock market price declines beginning in 1875. These are the percentage change in the liabilities of business failures for the given interval relative to the previous year's interval. This allows us to abstract from the pronounced seasonality in the series owing to the seasonality in the settlement of debts (see Kemmerer 1910, p. 219; Swift 1911).[30] Not surprisingly, the intervals of the sharpest stock price declines also tend to be the intervals of greatest increase in the seasonal difference of the liabilities of commercial failures.

If one asks which periods (for which data are available, i.e., 1875 and after) of the most extreme adverse economic news (real stock price declines in excess of 7.4 percent) are also periods of unusually large business failure (seasonal differences of greater than 50 percent), one is left with only the actual panic episodes and the quasi-panic of 1896. In other words, if one posits that the simultaneous violations of thresholds for percentages of real stock price decline and commercial failure increase are sufficient conditions for panic, one can predict panics perfectly. Indeed, one would even be able to predict that the stock price decline of 1896 would not be as severe a threat to banks as the other episodes, since business failures increased by a somewhat smaller percentage.

An analysis of national bank portfolio risk exposure is also consistent with the predictions of the asymmetric information approach and helps explain why panics tended to occur when they did (near business-cycle peaks, in the fall and spring). According to the asymmetric information view, panics are most likely to occur when bad news immediately follows a period of high loan demand and sanguine expectations. These will be periods when the leverage of banks and their borrowers is highest. This explains why in panic periods, adverse news was translated into unusually large declines in securities' prices and high borrower-default rates.

Because the dates of call reports for national banks vary greatly across years, the potential for meaningful specific inter-year comparisons of bank balance sheet positions is limited. Nevertheless, two broad patterns are unmistakable. First, the risk exposure of banks is highest in spring and fall, and lowest in winter and summer. Second, years of cyclical peaks are associated with unusually high risk exposure. These patterns are demonstrated in Table 2.12.

Bank leverage was highest at cyclical peaks (including panic years). Reading down any column in panel A of Table 2.12, one compares

---

[30] Seasonal patterns for 1901–10 show the highest commercial failure rates in the months of October through February (see Swift 1911, p. 40).

average loan-to-reserve ratios at different cyclical points, holding the time of year constant. In every case, the ratio is higher at peaks than at troughs and, in most cases, peaks show the highest loan-to-reserve ratios. Clearly, the longer an economic downturn is maintained (as one approaches troughs), the lower is the ratio of loans to reserves. Table 2.12 also provides data on loan-to-reserve ratios at different times of the year and at different points in the business cycle.

Reading across panel A, one can see how seasonality influenced bank loan risk exposure. Typically, March, October, and November calls saw seasonal peaks in the ratio, with declines from March to June, and from November to December. Panics occurred at times of the year when banks were unusually vulnerable to loan-default risk.[31] While withdrawal risk was low during prepanic periods, loans (and hence, loan-default risk) were high in late autumn, when most panics occurred (see Allen 1913a; Swift 1911; Kemmerer 1910). It is interesting to note in Table 2.11, however, that periods of severe bad news in risky-asset pricing are typically confined to these same seasons. Notice how few of the precipitous declines in stock prices occur from November to February, or from April to July. Intervals ending in April or May account for nine incidents of severe decline, and declines for intervals ending in August through November account for eleven more. This leaves three episodes which occurred in other times of the year, namely, two intervals ending in December (1895 and 1902), and one in July (1900). No intervals of decline ended in January, February, March, and June. More formally, using a chi-squared test we were able to reject the null hypothesis that the probability of a severe decline in the stock market was randomly distributed over the year at the 0.004 significance level. More contemporary patterns are also consistent with these findings. The stock market crashes of 1929, 1987, and 1989 all occurred in mid to late October.

Thus, it is not possible to argue that bank or borrower leverage transformed normal disturbances into panics. From a cyclical perspective, bad news and high leverage are both associated with cyclical peaks. Furthermore, fundamental seasonal patterns in the economy seem to concentrate adverse news in the spring and fall, at times when leverage is also high. What can explain these patterns? It is not difficult to explain why cyclical peaks are times of bad news (*ex post*), otherwise they would not have been cyclical peaks, and the high leverage of banks in these times

---

[31] Banks, of course, would have understood the seasonal vulnerability induced by changes in leverage. One might expect that banks would have responded by importing and exporting reserves to offset seasonally related loan changes. Presumably, the costs of importing and exporting specie, to maintain constant asset risk (i.e., the ratio of risky to riskless assets), were high.

Table 2.12. *Cyclical and seasonal influences on the ratio of national bank loans to reserves, 1870–1909*

	A. Mean loan-to-reserve ratios					
	March 10[c]	May 17[d]	June 11[e]	October 3[f]	November 12[g]	December 13[h]
Trough and early recovery[g]	4.62	5.19	4.77	5.74	5.96	5.30
Recovery and expansion	NA	5.87	5.93	6.40	6.65	6.24
Peaks and early decline[b]	6.72	6.45	6.06	6.84	6.68	6.05
Decline	6.89	NA	NA	6.64	NA	6.54

	B. Data for specific calls	
Date	Business-cycle reference	Loan-to-reserve ratios
March 10 Calls[c]		
Comparable March calls		
10 March 1876	Decline	6.96
11 March 1881	Peak	6.57
11 March 1882	Early decline	6.72
13 March 1883	Decline	7.47
7 March 1884	Decline	6.23
10 March 1885	Trough	4.72
6 March 1893	Peak	6.88
9 March 1897	Trough	4.52
May 17 Calls[d]		
Comparable May calls		
19 May 1882	Early decline	6.30
13 May 1887	Peak	6.12
13 May 1889	Recovery	5.87
17 May 1890	Peak	6.94
17 May 1892	Early recovery	5.65
14 May 1897	Trough	4.72
June 11 Calls[e]		
Comparable June calls		
9 June 1870	Trough	4.25
10 June 1871	Early recovery	4.57
10 June 1872	Expansion	5.47
13 June 1873	Peak	5.89
14 June 1879	Recovery	6.21
11 June 1880	Expansion	5.64
9 June 1903	Peak	6.23
9 June 1904	Trough	5.50
October 3 Calls[f]		
Comparable October calls		
2 October 1871	Recovery	5.63
3 October 1872	Expansion	6.79
2 October 1874	Decline	5.81
1 October 1875	Decline	7.39
2 October 1876	Decline	6.91
1 October 1877	Decline	7.25
1 October 1878	Trough	6.53
2 October 1879	Early recovery	6.36
1 October 1880	Recovery	6.00

138

Table 2.12. *(cont.)*

Date	B. Data for specific calls	
	Business-cycle reference	Loan-to-reserve ratios
1 October 1881	Peak	6.74
3 October 1882	Early decline	7.11
2 October 1883	Decline	6.95
1 October 1885	Trough	4.96
5 October 1887	Early decline	6.48
4 October 1888	Early recovery	6.28
30 September 1889	Expansion	6.88
2 October 1890	Early decline	7.03
30 September 1892	Recovery	6.63
2 October 1894	Early recovery	4.98
6 October 1896	Decline	5.52
5 October 1897	Early recovery	5.31
30 September 1901	Recovery	6.49
November 12 Calls[g]		
Comparable November calls		
17 November 1903	Early decline	6.68
10 November 1904	Early recovery	5.96
9 November 1905	Expansion	6.54
12 November 1906	Expansion	6.97
16 November 1909	Expansion	6.45
December 13 Calls[h]		
Comparable December calls		
16 December 1871	Recovery	5.65
17 December 1875	Decline	8.10
12 December 1879	Expansion	6.46
12 December 1888	Recovery	6.34
11 December 1889	Expansion	6.85
13 December 1895	Peak	6.05
17 December 1896	Decline	4.98
15 December 1897	Early recovery	5.12
13 December 1900	Early recovery	5.48
10 December 1901	Recovery	5.92
Other dates of interest		
12 September 1873	Early decline	5.89
24 April 1884	Peak	6.52
4 May 1893	Peak	6.70
25 November 1902	Expansion	6.28

[a] Business cycles are defined relative to the Frickey (1942) index, reported in Burns and Mitchell (1946). "Early" recovery refers to a date no more than six months after the trough.
[b] "Early" decline refers to a date no more than six months after the peak.
[c] "March 10 calls" include all call reports from March 6 to March 13.
[d] "May 17 calls" include all call reports from May 13 to May 19.
[e] "June 11 calls" include all call reports from June 9 to June 14.
[f] "October 3 calls" include all call reports from September 30 to October 6, except for the unusual post-panic year 1893.
[g] "November 12 calls" include all call reports from November 9 to November 17.
[h] "December 13 calls" include all call reports from December 10 to December 17.
Sources: Andrew (1910, pp. 63–66); and Bums and Mitchell (1946, pp. 111–12), based on Frickey (1942, p. 328).

is explicable by reference to previous rosy circumstances (given the evidence that economic activity during this period was strongly autoregressive; see Calomiris and Hubbard 1989, pp. 442–43). The simplest explanation for the seasonal pattern is that seasons of greatest economic activity will witness both higher borrowing and more news.[32]

Of course, very bad news and high leverage were not always coincident, and these episodes reinforce the notion that both bad news and risk exposure are necessary to produce a panic. The (nominal and real) stock price declines of December 1895 and December 1902 were larger than the average declines that preceded panics, but these did not produce panics, occurred "off season" at times when bank and borrower leverage was low (see Table 2.12), and were associated with less-pronounced business failure increases.

Before moving on to the next section, it may be useful to make a methodological point regarding what we have not done in this section. We did not use linear regression analysis, with adjustments for seasonal factors, to test models. Given the oscillation between panic and non-panic episodes, it would be difficult to argue that bank balance sheet variables are a stationary process. Thus, direct comparison across plausibly comparable episodes seemed to us a better way to proceed. Moreover, as we have stressed, the implications of the two approaches are best stated in terms of responses to violations of thresholds and nonlinear combinations of such violations (news and leverage). More formal technical analysis of these nonlinearities would be possible, but given the conclusiveness of the simple approach, we found this was not necessary.

The results of this subsection suggest that seasonal money-demand shocks originating in the countryside cannot possibly be the cause of panics. Rather, the results are consistent with the view that "bad" macroeconomic news combined with the vulnerability of banks to shocks, a vulnerability which is associated with banking activities in a natural way, accounts for panics. These results confirm the time-series econometric work of Gorton (1988) which shows that panics are associated with a threshold level of news receipt concerning the growth in liabilities of failed businesses, which is a leading indicator of recession (see also Calomiris and Hubbard 1989). Gorton (1988) argued that panics in the

---

[32] There is an alternative explanation for these findings. High leverage during times when adverse news is relatively likely is consistent with the view of Minsky (1975) and Kindleberger (1978) that investors and banks were myopic. According to this view, the reason that large stock price declines, higher leverage, and panic are most likely coincident events is that they are all driven by myopic speculative frenzies. Such frenzies are most likely to occur in the months and cyclical phases of greatest economic activity.

United States occurred every time measures of the liabilities of failed businesses reached a critical threshold, and did not occur otherwise.

2.5.2   Bank liquidations and deposit losses during panics

We now analyze the data on bank failures during panics to compare the predictions of the asymmetric-information and random-withdrawal-risk views. Both predict that cooperation among banks (branching or coinsurance) reduces the incidence of bank failure during panics. As noted above, there is abundant evidence to support this view. But the two theories differ in many of their implications regarding which banks are mostly likely to fail, as well as the extent and regional distribution of bank failures in different panics.

The withdrawal-risk approach sees the greatest threat to banks as coming from regionally concentrated shocks transmitted through the correspondent network. Regionally concentrated shocks should be especially problematic for banks in the region of the shock, especially those in regional reserve centers and their correspondents in other regions. Episodes of greatest money-demand shocks or vulnerability to money-demand shocks should correspond to those with the highest incidence of bank failure. Finally, bank failures during panics are mainly attributable to the exogenous money-demand disturbance, rather than to the investment decisions of bankers.

The asymmetric-information approach has strong testable implications for bank failure, since it identifies asset shocks as the source of panics and sees panics as an attempt by the banking system as a whole to resolve asymmetric information by closing insolvent banks, that is, those which have suffered the greatest declines. Thus, there should be a direct link between ultimate bank failures and the asset shock that triggers the panic. Regions with relatively large asset shocks (such as region-specific agricultural commodity and land price declines) should show higher incidences of failure. Also, within regions, banks with the greatest exposure to the asset shocks that induce the panic should be more likely to fail (some shocks are more likely to affect city banks than country banks because of their different loan portfolios). Across panics, the aggregate failure rate should depend on the severity of the disturbance as well as its concentration (more regionally concentrated shocks induce higher average failure rates). Finally, individual banker behavior in undertaking risky investments could be an important determinant of within-region variation in failures.

Table 2.13 presents state and regional data on the number of national banks and national bank failures for intervals surrounding panics,

Table 2.13. *The number of national banks and national bank failures during panics, by state and region, 1873–1907[a]*

Region and state	1873 Banks	Failures	1884 Banks	Failures	1890 Banks	Failures	1893 Banks	Failures	1896 Banks	Failures	1907 Banks	Failures
New England												
ME	63	0	72	0	78	0	83	0	82	0	79	0
NH	42	0	49	0	51	0	53	2	50	0	57	0
VT	42	0	47	1	51	0	48	0	49	0	50	0
RI	62	0	63	0	59	0	59	0	57	0	23	0
MA	217	0	246	0	260	0	268	0	268	0	203	0
CT	80	0	88	0	84	0	84	0	82	0	80	0
	506	0	565	1	583	0	595	2	588	0	492	0
East												
NY	277	1*	314	2*	319	0	336	2*	330	3	401	0
NJ	62	0	69	0	94	0	99	0	102	0	168	0
PA	202	1	270	0	349	0	399	0	419	0	722	1
DE	11	0	15	0	18	0	18	0	18	0	24	0
MD	33	0	41	0	59	0	68	0	68	0	97	0
DC	5	1	6	0	12	0	13	0	14	0	12	0
	590	3	715	2	851	0	933	2	951	3	1,424	1
West												
ND	1	0	30	0	29	0	35	3	29	4	121	0
SD		0		0	39	0	39	2	31	1	83	0
NE	10	0	41	0	135	1	137	2	114	1	193	0
KS	26	1	35	0	159	7	138	1	105	2	199	0

142

											Total	
MT	5	0	10	1	25	0	28	3	26	1	37	0
WY	2	0	4	0	11	0	13	1	11	0	29	0
CO	7	0	22	0	46	0	53	1	42	0	97	0
NM	0	0	6	0	9	0	11	1	7	1	36	0
OK	0	0	0	0	5	0	6	0	13	0	294	0
	51	1	148	1	458	8	460	14	378	10	1,089	0
South												
VA	24	2	23	0	32	0	36	0	37	0	96	0
WV	17	0	19	0	21	0	30	0	33	0	88	0
NC	10	0	15	0	21	1	24	0	28	0	57	0
SC	12	0	13	0	16	0	14	0	15	0	25	0
GA	13	0	13	0	30	0	30	3	30	0	86	0
FL	0	0	2	0	15	0	18	1	17	0	35	0
AL	9	0	9	0	30	0	30	1	27	0	73	0
MS	0	0	3	0	12	0	13	0	10	0	26	0
LA	9	1*	8	0	19	0	20	4	21	1*	36	0
TX	8	0	44	0	189	0	226	0	209	3	510	1
AR	2	0	5	1	9	0	9	1	9	0	35	0
KY	36	0	64	0	76	0	81		77	2	139	0
TN	24	0	30	0	51	0	55	4	48	0	77	0
	164	3	248	1	521	1	586	15	561	6	1,283	1
Middle West												
OH	169	1	200	0	233	0	244	1	249	1	358	2
IN	93	1	97	2	100	0	120	2	113	0	219	1
IL	137	0	161	1	192	0	216	3**	220	2*	389	0
MI	77	0	87	0	110	0	102	2	92	4	91	0
WI	45	0	45	0	68	0	82	0	81	0	125	0
MN	32	0	43	0	60	0	77	0	76	2*	245	0
IA	75	0	108	0	139	0	170	1	168	2	301	1

Table 2.13. *(cont.)*

Region and state	1873 Banks	1873 Failures	1884 Banks	1884 Failures	1890 Banks	1890 Failures	1893 Banks	1893 Failures	1896 Banks	1896 Failures	1907 Banks	1907 Failures
MO	36	0	34	0	79	0	79	0	68	1*	113	0
	664	2	775	3	981	0	1,090	9	1,067	12	1,841	4
Pacific												
WA	0	0	12	0	51	1	66	5	41	2	41	0
OR	1	0	6	0	37	0	40	1	33	0	53	0
CA	5	0	13	0	37	0	37	1	31	1	126	0
ID	1	0	3	0	7	0	13	0	11	0	34	0
UT	3	0	4	0	10	0	14	0	11	0	18	0
NV	0	0	1	0	2	0	2	0	1	0	7	0
AZ	0	0	1	0	2	0	5	0	5	0	14	0
	10	0	40	0	146	1	177	7	133	3	293	0
Total	1,985	9	2,491	8	3,540	10	3,841	49	3,676	34	6,412	6
Reserve center banks		2		1		0		3		4		0

Notes: "Banks" means the number of banks in existence prior to panics. "Failures" means bank failures at or near the time of panic (only liquidated banks are included). Specifically, we include bank failures that occurred within the following intervals: June–December 1873; March–August 1884; August 1890–February 1891; April–October 1893; July 1896–January 1897; August 1907–February 1908.

*Denotes a reserve-center bank failure.

**Denotes two reserve-center bank failures.

Sources: U.S. Comptroller of the Currency, Annual Report (1873, 1884, 1890, 1893, 1920).

144

Table 2.14. *The causes of national bank failures during panics[a]*

	1873	1884	1890	1893	1896	1907
Total number of failures	9	6	10	49	34	6
Number attributed to asset depreciation alone	4	2	5	31	26	3
Number attributed to fraud alone	0	2	0	7	3	2
Number attributed to both asset depreciation and fraud	5	4	5	11	5	0
Asset depreciation attributed to monetary stringency	0	0	0	17	8	0
Asset depreciation only; attributed to real estate	0	1	2	0	4	0
Bank failure attributed to real estate depreciation and fraud	0	1	2	0	1	0
Bank failure attributed to run on bank	0	0	0	0	0	1

[a] Relevant intervals for bank failures are defined in Table 2.13.
Source: U.S. Comptroller of the Currency, Annual Report (1920, pp. 56–73).

including the quasi panic of 1896. Table 2.14 provides data on individual bank failures during panics and their causes, according to the brief summary of each case provided by the Comptroller of the Currency in his Annual Report of 1920.

With respect to the stated causes of bank failures, the data in Table 2.14 are strongly supportive of the asymmetric-information view and provide virtually no evidence that money-demand shocks provided necessary or sufficient conditions for banks to fail. Of the 116 bank failures that occurred during intervals surrounding panics, 101 were attributed to asset depreciation, with eleven of these cases mainly involving real estate-related investments (all from 1884 to 1896). Thirty of these 101 failures involved fraudulent activities. An additional fourteen failures were attributed solely to fraud. The single remaining failure was attributed to a bank run (in 1907). These data clearly indicate that bank failures during panics often involved shady activities by bankers (44 out of 116 cases), which typically made banks' assets especially vulnerable to bad news (hence the association between asset depreciation and fraud in most of the fraud cases). The fact that bank failure is linked to asset depreciation does not itself contradict the withdrawal-risk approach, since advocates of this view argue that panics themselves caused asset depreciation of banks. In 25 cases, asset depreciation was deemed the result of high market interest rates during the panics. Nevertheless, in the overwhelming majority of cases (91 of the 116), failure was not attributed to panic-induced stringency in the money market. Furthermore, the fact that the Comptroller only attributed one failure to a bank run per se shows that the direct link between bank runs and bank failures during panics was not important.

The withdrawal-risk and asymmetric-information views also differ in their implications regarding the relative severity of bank failure rates during the various panics. According to the withdrawal-risk approach, inadequacy of reserves to meet withdrawal needs is the key factor in causing suspensions and failures alike. Thus, the degree to which panics were associated with illiquidity in the banking system should be reflected in bank failure rates as well. In other words, the three widespread suspensions of convertibility (1873, 1893, and 1907) should be associated with the largest failure rates, followed by the Panics of 1884 and 1890 in which there was bank coordination without widespread suspension, with the quasi-panic of 1896 showing the least-severe failure experience of all. Moreover, within the group of suspensions, 1893 should have been milder than 1873 or 1907, since it followed especially small spring seasonal money flows and occurred in the middle of the year (rather than in the fall), when anticipated interregional flows favored New York City and reserve ratios of the system as a whole rose (as shown in Table 2.12). Thus, one should find that the failure rates are ranked in four groups roughly as follows: 1873 and 1907; 1893; 1884 and 1890; and 1896.

The predictions of the asymmetric-information approach regarding the relative severity of bank failures during these panics could be quite different. The asymmetric-information approach does not equate systemic illiquidity risk of banks with failure risk. It can envision cases in which the aggregate illiquidity of the banking system is severe but the *ex post* failures are relativity few. It can also envision cases where large observable shocks to a subset of banks could cause many failures without leading to a suspension of convertibility for the banking system as a whole. In particular, panics that are associated with large region-specific asset shocks may produce larger failure rates in one region, while posing a relatively small problem for systemic convertibility of deposits on demand. In the asymmetric-information approach, nationwide commercial-failure rate and production data, as well as other region-specific proxies for real shocks preceding panics, would be useful guides for ranking the likely consequences for bank failures.

For aggregate data we consider the new Miron and Romer (1990) monthly production index [augmented by Frickey (1942, 1947) for the period prior to 1884] and liabilities of commercial failures. A consistent monthly series of commercial failures at the national level is not available for the entire period from 1873 to 1907. Limited comparisons that are possible using quarterly and monthly data for 1875 to 1907, however, provide a rough ranking of commercial failure severity, again using seasonal difference as our measure. Table 2.15 reports data for the liabilities of commercial failures and industrial production growth for the bank failure intervals used to construct Table 2.13.

Interestingly, if one confines oneself to these two aggregate measures, the predicted ranking of bank failure severity for panics is very close to that of the withdrawal-risk view above. The ranking would be: 1893, 1907, 1873, 1884, 1890, 1896. If the positions of 1893 and 1873 are switched, the ranking becomes the same as that implied by the random-withdrawal approach.

The actual ranking of bank failure rate and depositor loss rate severity for national banks as a whole is different from the predicted ranking of the withdrawal-risk view and the predicted ranking from economy-wide measures of real shocks. The ranking, with the percentage of national banks failing given in parentheses, is: 1893 (1.28 percent), 1896 (0.92 percent), 1873 (0.45 percent), 1884 (0.32 percent), 1890 (0.28 percent), and 1907 (0.09 percent). The relative positions of 1893 and 1873 in this ranking correspond to the predictions of the asymmetric-information approach, but in other respects this ranking differs drastically from either of the two "predicted" rankings.

First, the Panic of 1907 is practically a non-event from the standpoint of national bank failures. Indeed, it was a time of unusually low bank failures during the National Banking Era. For the entire period of 1865 to 1909, there were 0.94 bank failures per month on average. There were only six failures during the seven-month interval we examined for the Panic of 1907, implying a rate of 0.86 failures per month. Considering the more than tripling of the number of banks over this period, this amounts to a substantially lower failure rate (per bank, per month) than the average rate for the entire period.

Second, the quasi-panic of 1896 was a time of substantially above-average bank failure, even though it did not result in suspension. According to the asymmetric-information approach, this would imply that the shocks of 1896 were not accompanied by a great deal of confusion regarding their incidence.

To summarize, the data on actual bank failures support the asymmetric-information approach more than the random-withdrawal approach, but they also pose a challenge, namely, to explain the lack of

Table 2.15. *Liabilities of commercial failures and industrial production during panic intervals*

	Liabilities	Industrial production (%Δ)
June–December 1873	NA	−6.9 (−12.9)[a]
April–September 1884[b]	140.8	−4.0
April–September 1883	77.9	
seasonal difference	80.7%	
October 1890–March 1891[b]	131.3	−2.9
October 1889–March 1890	80.6	
seasonal difference	62.9%	
April–September 1893[b]	204.0	−26.6
April–September 1892	41.7	
seasonal difference	389.2%	
July 1896–January 1897	146.7	2.0
July 1895–January 1896	106.2	
seasonal difference	38.1%	
August 1907–February 1908	169.6	−28.5
August 1906–February 1907	73.6	
seasonal difference	130.4%	

[a] Miron and Romer (1990) begin their index in 1884. Frickey's (1947) monthly index of production for transportation and communication is reported instead, as well as Frickey's (1942) quarterly index of economic activity (in parentheses).
[b] Intervals were dictated by the use of quarterly data for commercial failures prior to 1894 and differ slightly from bank-failure intervals reported in Table 2.13.
Sources: U.S. Department of Commerce (1949, p. 349); Miron and Romer (1990); Frickey (1947, p. 120; 1942, p. 328).

bank failures during the severe contraction of 1907 and the unusually large incidence of failure during the relatively mild business-cycle down-swing of 1896.

With respect to the low national bank failure rate during the Panic of 1907, a recent paper on the panic by Moen and Tallman (1992) points out that national banks and state banks fared much better than trusts in New York City during the panic:

Depositor runs on trust companies in 1907 occurred without similar runs on New York City national banks. . . . The balance sheets of trust companies in New York City suggest that their asset values were subject to greater volatility than the other intermediaries. . . . In addition, it is notable that the initial runs on intermediaries in 1907 occurred at the trust companies, institutions that were not eligible to hold legal reserve funds for interior banks. Thus, the onset of the Panic does not appear to be a result of the institutional structure of reserves held at national banks, often referred to as the "pyramid" of reserves.

Moen and Tallman show that trusts had much greater proportions of investments in securities and in call loans, which were collateralized by securities. This made them more vulnerable to the stock market decline that preceded the panic. They also find that practically all of the contraction in New York City loans during the panic is attributable to the trust companies. On the basis of this evidence, Moen and Tallman argue that the Panic of 1907 is best understood as a consequence of adverse news about the value of a subset of assets in the economy.

One does not need to search too hard to find reasons for the unusually high failure rates during 1896. Table 2.13 shows that failures were concentrated in a few states, while many other states avoided failures altogether during the panic. This was also true in 1890 and 1893. In 1890, eight out of ten failures occurred in Kansas and Nebraska, producing a combined failure rate in these states of 4.1 percent. In 1893 the outliers were the western states, with a 3.0 percent overall failure rate, and a combined failure rate for Montana and the Dakotas of 7.3 percent. Washington had a failure rate of 7.6 percent. The southern states (especially Texas, Tennessee, and Georgia) failed at a rate of 2.6 percent. In the Middle West during the Panic of 1893, the states of Illinois, Indiana, and Michigan experienced a combined failure rate of 1.6 percent.

In 1896 the pattern is quite similar. Western states' national banks failed at the rate of 2.6 percent, with a failure rate in the Dakotas of 13.8 percent. Texas and Kentucky, in the South, suffered a combined failure rate of 1.7 percent, while 4.9 percent of Washington's national banks failed. In Michigan, Iowa, and Illinois the combined failure rate was 1.7 percent. Explaining unusually high failure experiences of national banks during panics, therefore, reduces to explaining why scattered states in the Middle West, West, Pacific, and South regions experienced high failure rates during the 1890s.

The regional pattern of failures seems incompatible with the withdrawal-risk view of panics. States with high failure rates in any one panic were often quite distant, differed in planting and harvesting times, and were oriented toward different financial centers. Thus, it would be unlikely for them to experience simultaneous liquidity shocks. For example, Washington, Kentucky, Texas, Michigan, and the Dakotas (in 1896) are unrelated in terms of correspondent relations, harvest and planting timing, and geographical proximity. Georgia, Texas, Tennessee, the Dakotas, and Montana are similarly unrelated (in 1893).

What does explain the regional patterns of bank failure, and why is it that high regional bank failures in 1890 and 1896 were not associated with systemic illiquidity? The answer seems to be that the 1890s were a time of unusually adverse shocks concentrated in agricultural product and land markets. These shocks were known to be isolated to particular markets and had especially adverse consequences for borrowers and bankers whose portfolio values varied with the value of investments in newly cleared land.

Allan Bogue's (1955) classic study of the speculative land boom and bust of 1873–96 documents the changing fortunes of mortgage brokers who acted as intermediaries between western landowners and mortgage investors throughout the country. During the boom of the 1870s and early 1880s, agricultural prices and land prices rose, and many mortgages were bought by banks in other regions. A series of ever-worsening economic news for agriculture created waves of foreclosures, bankruptcy, and bank failure. Bogue writes:

Between 1888 and 1894 most of the mortgage companies failed. The causes of failure were closely interrelated. The officers of the mortgage agencies had misunderstood the climatic vagaries of the plains country. They had competed vigorously to finance the settlement of areas beyond the ninety-eighth meridian (e.g., western Kansas and Nebraska). Beginning in 1887 the plains country was struck by a series of disastrously dry years. The effects of drought and short crops are sometimes alleviated by high prices, but in these years the prices of agricultural products were depressed. Many of the settlers along the middle border failed to meet their obligations. The real estate holdings of the companies grew to unmanageable size; operating capital was converted into land at a time when the bottom had dropped out of the land market. (p. 267)

Panics in the 1890s were associated with large declines in productivity and the terms of trade for agriculture. In each of the years prior to the panics of 1890 and 1893, the terms of trade in agriculture, as measured by the ratio of the price of wheat to the wholesale price index, declined by approximately 30 percent.

The hypothesis that the unusual failure experience of certain states in the 1890s can be explained by the collapse of the high-risk mortgage market in certain agricultural areas has testable implications. First, the Comptroller of the Currency identifies cases of national bank failure that are primarily attributable to real estate depreciation. As Table 2.14 shows, almost all real-estate-related failures of national banks that accompanied panics occurred during the Panics of 1890 and 1896.

Of course, national banks faced restrictions on mortgage lending which limited their direct exposure to land price declines. State banks, however, tended to permit greater involvement in mortgage lending. Hence, another testable implication of the land-value-shock explanation of bank failures during the 1890s is that state banks in Kansas and Nebraska should have had unusually high rates of bank failure compared to their counterparts in the national banking system in those same states. In other panics, rates of failure in those states should have been lower and more similar between national and state banks.

As a first step toward testing this proposition, we collected data on state bank failures during panic intervals for the Panics of 1893 and 1907 from state banking reports available at the Library of Congress. These data are provided in Table 2.16. We find that state bank failure rates were high relative to national bank failure rates in Kansas and Nebraska in 1893. This same pattern is not visible in other states in 1893. Furthermore, in 1907, Kansas and Nebraska state banks had failure records similar to western national banks.

These data provide some support for the notion that region-specific asset shocks in western lands were important in explaining the peculiar regional patterns of bank failures in the 1890s. They also provide evidence supporting the general importance of asset risk in explaining the incidence of bank failure, which is essential to the asymmetric-information-approach. In future research we plan to extend our sample to include other states and episodes.

2.5.3   Sufficient conditions for ending panics

The mechanisms for resolving banking panics, by bringing suspension of convertibility to an end, provide a way of discriminating between the two hypotheses concerning the origins of banking panics. In this section we first ask whether physical inflows of gold or the availability of cash per se were sufficient to bring an end to suspensions of convertibility. Cash availability includes the possibility of borrowing from the discount window during the Great Depression. Then we ask whether coinsurance in the absence of aggregate increases in gold is sufficient to end banking panics. Here we consider some cooperative arrangements of banks to mitigate the effects of panics. We also examine the experiences of branches of Canadian banks in the United States during panics.

If suspension of convertibility is made necessary by a scarcity of cash in the banking system, then shipments of gold should be able to resolve the problem. The asymmetric information view also predicts that shipments of gold will occur during panics, in part as a means for banks to signal their creditworthiness to depositors. But according to the asymmetric information view, gold shipments into the country are neither a

Table 2.16. *State and national bank failure rates from available states during panic intervals in 1893 and 1907*[a]

	State bank failure rate[b] (%)		National bank failure rate (%)	
	1893	1907	1893	1907
Massachusetts	0	0	0	0
New Jersey	0[c]	0	0	0
New York	0.7	0.9	0.6	0
Kansas	8.1	0.1	0.7	0
Nebraska	2.0	0.3	1.5	0
Michigan	0.7	0	2.0	0

[a] Panic intervals are April–October 1893 and August 1907–February 1908.
[b] For 1893 the number of state banks is assumed to be roughly equal to the number in existence in 1896 for which data are available.
[c] One bank failed, but it was able to pay its depositors in full.
Sources: U.S. Comptroller of the Currency, Annual Report (1920); the reports of banking authorities of various states; Board of Governors of the Federal Reserve System (1959, passim).

necessary nor a sufficient condition for bringing panics to an end. Gold shipments are not a necessary condition for ending panics because a sufficient degree of asset insurance or coinsurance might itself resolve problems of asymmetric information, potentially even in the absence of gold inflows. Gold shipments are not a sufficient condition because it is the transfer of gold to banks, rather than the physical fact of gold availability per se, that brings an end to the panic.

As Myers (1931) shows, New York City banks held substantial amounts of internationally traded securities, including bills of exchange and commercial paper, in their portfolios in the nineteenth century. While the proportion of commercial paper to other investments declined over the period, even as late as 1909, banks in New York City held 30–40 percent of their interest-bearing assets in this form (Myers 1931, p. 336). From 1866 on, the transatlantic cable connected New York to the major financial centers of Europe and allowed financial transactions to take place at a moment's notice. Finally, it took approximately ten days for a steamship to travel from London to New York. Thus, upon suspending convertibility it should have been possible for New York City banks to wire to have a shipment of gold sent to alleviate any money-demand shocks. They could have paid for the gold with their substantial holdings of prime-grade paper. Allowing for railroad delivery lags within the United States, the process of shipping and distributing the currency should have taken no longer than two or three weeks. Calomiris and Hubbard (1996) show that international gold flows moved rapidly across the Atlantic during the Panic of 1907, and coincided with internal movements of gold, which indicates extremely rapid adjustment to changes in the demand for gold, most of which was accomplished within a month of the initial shock.

Yet the duration of suspensions of convertibility could be substantially longer than the time horizon for the delivery of gold. The durations of the suspensions of 1873 and 1893 were roughly a month (see Sprague 1910, pp. 53–58, 180–86), but the suspension during the Panic of 1907 lasted from 26 October 1907 until 4 January 1908 (pp. 277–82). While Sprague chides the New York banks for not resuming sooner, the currency premium on certified checks was still roughly 1 percent as late as December 20.

Another way to consider whether the availability of cash can end a panic, as suggested by the random-withdrawal theory, is to examine the behavior of banks during the Great Depression. A basic purpose of the Federal Reserve Act was to establish a lender of last resort that would provide cash when necessary. The Fed's discount window would appear to provide a mechanism for obtaining ample amounts of cash to banks, even if the Fed did not engage in open market operations. Yet, during the 1930s, bank runs and failures were not avoided by bank access to the discount window. This contradicts the random-withdrawal theory. Even if the Fed made discount window borrowings relatively expensive, as suggested by Gendreau (1990), banks suffering random withdrawals presumably would have preferred to pay a high price at the discount window rather than become insolvent. And yet, they did not.

The behavior of banks during the Great Depression is consistent with the asymmetric-information theory, however. In this view, the basic problem is that depositors do not know which banks are most likely to fail. A bank that went to the discount window would be publicly identifying itself as a weak bank, would immediately face a run, and could go bankrupt. The information asymmetry would be resolved if the weak banks went to the discount window. It was for precisely this reason that, during the panics of the National Banking Era, clearing houses never revealed the identities of banks that had received the largest quantities of loan certificates. The need for secrecy was paramount if the interests of all banks were to be protected (see Gorton 1985; Gorton and Mullineaux 1987). Also, to the extent that exogenous loan losses prompted runs in the 1930s, then the problem was one of insolvency risk, not illiquidity – a problem that is not resolved by access to the discount window.

In summary, monetary scarcity per se was not a sufficient condition for prolonging or avoiding suspensions of convertibility. On the other hand, the availability of cash, through gold flows or the discount window, was not a sufficient condition for ending a panic either. We now turn to the question of whether crises could be avoided or brought to an end by collective action that did not involve aggregate increases in specie. The clearest and most famous example is the resolution of the Baring crisis, as recounted by Kindleberger (1978).

The possible insolvency of Baring Brothers investment banking house in London in November 1890, to which Sprague (1910) attributed the Panic of 1890 in the United States, threatened a more general financial crisis in Britain, presumably because of asymmetric information about the precise causes and extent of its insolvency, and its possible links to commercial banks or their borrowers. Evidence on the importance of these information externalities comes mainly from the behavior of London bankers themselves. As it became clear that Baring was insolvent, London bankers cooperated to assume full mutual liability through an insurance fund to guarantee against any losses to Baring's creditors.

Three points deserve emphasis here. First, there was no money-demand shock and no bank run on Baring. Baring was not a commercial bank. Thus, there was no question of its failure resulting from money-demand shocks or low reserves. Second, the banks' commitment was sufficient to quell whatever incipient disturbance they had feared. Third, the banks voluntarily assumed liability without compensation for a firm that was clearly insolvent. If there were not substantial externalities associated with asymmetric information and if it did not pay the banks to dispel doubts about the incidence of the disturbance, then why would banks have volunteered to provide a bailout?

A final important experiment which helps to test the withdrawal-risk view against the asymmetric-information view concerns the role of Canadian banks in the United States during banking panics. Earlier we discussed the fact that Canadian banks were heavily branched and cooperated to regulate themselves through the Canadian Bankers' Association. The result was that Canada did not experience banking panics, and had significantly lower loss and failure rates compared to the U.S. experience. These Canadian banks also had American branches. If the withdrawal-risk theory is correct, then during a panic, branches of Canadian banks should have experienced specie withdrawals similar to those of American banks in the same location. However, Schembri and Hawkins (1988) argue that, rather than suffering the same disintermediation as their American counterparts, Canadian branches were viewed as a "safe haven" during the crisis and received net inflows at that time.

2.6   Bank regulation and financial history

Banking panics have long been a motivating factor in the development of financial regulation and monetary policy. Ideally, public policy should reflect the "lessons of history," once relevant differences between historical and contemporary environments are considered. Designing public policy is complicated not only because it is difficult to distill the appropriate lessons from history but also because banking and capital markets continue to be transformed by technological change. That is to say, history does not end. Possibly, the lessons of history are not relevant in the new environment. In this section we briefly consider some of these issues in the context of our conclusion that the historical evidence is consistent with the asymmetric information hypothesis. Since this conclusion contradicts a long history of received wisdom, we begin by asking why the alternative view – that seasonal money shocks cause panics – has had such a long history. It may be that the answer to this puzzle is very important for understanding public policy.

2.6.1   The politics of panics

Why does the previous literature on the origins of banking panics, including, in particular, some of the studies of the National Monetary Commission, view monetary shocks as a source of banking instability? We think there are two answers. The first reason for the misinterpretation of the importance of money-demand shocks in causing panics is the political usefulness of this distortion of the facts during the debate over the establishment of the Federal Reserve System, which included the possible regulation of commercial bank lending to securities brokers and of securities markets transactions of banks through underwriting and trust affiliates. The "interior money-demand shock" story exonerated New York City banks and Wall Street speculators from any blame for causing stock market collapses and banking panics. Instead, this story identified decentralized disturbances in the periphery as the cause of both (rather than "excessive" bank credit backed by stocks in New York).

In a series of articles criticizing the money-demand view and its proponents, W. H. Allen (1911, 1913a, 1913b) offered contrary evidence and questioned the motives of Aldrich, Andrew, Kemmerer, Vreeland, and the National Monetary Commission as a whole. He argued against Kemmerer's (1910) use of call loan interest rates (the rate charged to stock brokers) as a guide to general conditions in the money market, and pointed out that seasonal money flows were not large in panic years. He emphasized the difference between money movements in the early fall and credit growth in the late fall. Finally, Allen (1913b) accused the Commission of catering to the interests of Wall Street bankers:

Wall Street bankers originated the idea of making a financial bogie of crop demands; they also originated this theory of the cause and effect of the concentration of money at New York; and Congress, with all of its investigating, has never even tried to learn if there were not other possible causes of this concentration of money [in the stock market] and the resulting financial ills. . . . The currency committees of the present Congress are, it is believed, freer from outside control than any currency committees that we have had in many years. Nevertheless, they have lapsed into the old habit of looking to our big bankers as the sole depositaries of financial facts. (p. 105)

Allen was not alone in this view. In a speech to the Wisconsin State Bankers Association in 1903, Andrew J. Frame, president of a rural national bank in Wisconsin, disputed the claim that agriculture-related shocks in the periphery were the main cause of banking instability:

I challenge any man to prove that since 1893 there have been more than two fall seasons when the money market has been above a normal or reasonable level, and then speculation and not crop movements were the primary causes of trouble. (Frame 1903, p. 12)

Frame goes on to cite several prominent banking sources who agree with his view that the "excessive speculation" of New York City bankers is the greatest threat to banking stability. While the arguments of these various sources fall far short of proving their case, they do offer insight into the conflicting opinions and motivations of bankers, who tried to influence opinion on currency reform. Given the political benefits to New York City bankers of the National Monetary Commission's recommendations, one is led to wonder whether the Commission was "captured" by the most powerful group having a stake in its banking reform proposals.

A second reason for the persistence of the seasonal money-shock view is that authors frequently used the terms "money" and "money market" loosely, sometimes meaning cash, sometimes credit. This has led to confusion regarding the views of earlier scholars. As noted before, Sprague (1910) clearly focused on asset shocks, but saw seasonal money market strain as one of many factors influencing bank vulnerability. While Kemmerer (1910) did emphasize money-demand shocks in much of his discussion, he also discussed credit seasonality and was often unclear about whether he viewed seasonality as mainly influencing bank leverage (and hence vulnerability to asset shocks) or withdrawal risk per se.

His direct references to panics occupy only three pages of his 500-page statistical tome. Even there, in his reference to Jevons' (1884) discussion of seasonality, Kemmerer seems to emphasize credit risk rather than money demand as the primary determinant of the seasonality of panics.

2.6.2   Bank regulation and the historical record

What conclusions can be drawn from the evidence on the origins of panics for regulation of banks? We divide our discussion of the implications of the asymmetric-information view of the causes of historical banking panics into two parts. First, we describe the broad implications of the above analysis. Then we explore the general relevance of the historical record for today's financial system.

As we have noted, both views of banking panics agree that a banking system composed of a small number of nationwide branching banks would have been much more stable. According to Chari (1989), stability would have come from diversification of withdrawal risk. According to the asymmetric-information view, diversification *ex ante* and credible coinsurance *ex post* would have substantially reduced, if not eliminated entirely, the possibility and costliness of banking panics historically. Therefore, there is a consensus that a smaller number of larger, branched, more diversified banks, approximating the Canadian system, would likely prevent panics. Short of this conclusion, however, there is disagreement between the two views about appropriate public policies toward banks.

According to the random-withdrawal-risk view, under the historical conditions of the United States, with unit banking and before federal deposit insurance, the basic problem was that there were not enough reserves to go around in time of crisis. When there was a seasonal, unusually high desired currency-deposit ratio, the economy needed cash. Notably, the implication of this view is that an increase in cash through open market operations would have been effective in forestalling panics. During the National Banking Era the government was unable to conduct open market operations to inject cash. The U.S. Treasury was unable to purchase securities in sufficient amounts to prevent panics or effectively aid in their resolution.

Moreover, in the random-withdrawal-risk view, banks themselves were unable to form effective coalitions to mitigate the effects of panics. Banks as a group were unable to diversify withdrawal risk because reserves were unobservable. Taken literally, this view suggests intervention in the form of open market operations or reserve requirements, which may make feasible private bank coalitions for diversifying withdrawal risk.

The asymmetric-information view suggests different directions for future research. First, in this view, open market operations by themselves will not be effective in preventing or easing panics. The problem is not that depositors want cash for its own sake, as in the random-withdrawal view, but are concerned that their bank will fail. In this case, discount loans can (in the absence of deposit insurance) be an effective way to transform illiquid bank assets into an asset that depositors can easily value, namely cash. Private clearing houses historically provided the discount window through the issuance of clearing-house loan certificates. Both government lending to banks and deposit insurance share the same essential feature, namely, the government is willing to bear some risks that are peculiar to the banking system, either by making collateralized loans to banks or by guaranteeing bank deposits.

It is difficult to determine the potential importance of asymmetric-information problems for today's banks. The very fact that banks are regulated prevents a clear determination of how banks would have evolved in the absence of this regulation. To some extent, perhaps to an extreme degree, regulation prevents the evolution of the banking system in ways that may be very desirable. The fact that such evolution is not directly observable prevents us from finding persuasive evidence that it would not occur in a different regulatory environment. There are two final observations we wish to make about the current environment in this regard.

The first observation is that the historical efficacy of bank self-regulation seems (to us) not to have been well understood in the literature. Private bank coalitions were surprisingly effective in monitoring banks and mitigating the effects of panics, even if panics were not eliminated. While in today's thrift debacle we observe the costs of having eliminated panics through government deposit insurance, this does not imply that all insurance is undesirable. Private self-regulation may be quite effective, especially when combined with some government policies. One does find examples in other less-regulated financial markets of coinsurance arrangements and problems of asymmetric information. For example, futures-market clearing house members coinsure against each other's default by standing between all market transactions, as a group.[33]

The second observation is that the business of banking has changed in some important respects over the last decade, partly in response to regulation. The regulatory costs for financial intermediaries of increasing the size of their balance sheets (reserve requirements, insurance premia, etc.), along with the advantages of diversification, have encouraged them

---

[33] Also, Calomiris (1989b) describes cooperative arrangements between commercial paper issuers and banks that insure against similar problems.

to initiate and re-sell loans. While initially this was confined mainly to mortgages, commercial loan sales have become increasingly common in the last decade (see Gorton and Haubrich 1989). There still may be a substantial proportion of small- and medium-sized borrowers whose loans are not saleable. Nonetheless, to the extent that loans can be sold on the open market, asymmetric information is less of a concern. The fact that loans can be sold indicates that information-sharing technology has improved, and hence that asymmetries are likely to be less dramatic. The ability of banks to sell loans, even if only among themselves, provides an important means for asset diversification, as well. Investigating the extent to which loan sales by intermediaries reflect fundamental changes in information sharing and the regulatory implications of these changes is an important area for future research.

References

Akerlof, G. 1970. The Market for Lemons: Qualitative Uncertainty and the Market Mechanism. *Quarterly Journal of Economics* 84: 488–500.

Allen, W. H. 1913a. Seasonal Variations in Money Rates: A Reply to Professor Kemmerer. *Moody's Magazine* (February).

1913b. A False Diagnosis of Financial Ills. Moody's Magazine (November).

1911. The Lie in the Aldrich Bill. *Moody's Magazine* (April).

Andrew, A. Piatt. 1907. The Influence of Crops Upon Business in America. *Quarterly Journal of Economics* 20: 323–53.

1910. *Statistics for the United States*, 1867–1909. National Monetary Commission. 61st Cong. 2d sess. Senate Doc. 570. Washington D.C.: U.S. Government Printing Office.

Barsky, Robert B. 1987. The Fisher Hypothesis and the Forecastability and Persistence of Inflation. *Journal of Monetary Economics* 19(1): 3–24.

Bernanke, Ben. 1983. Nonmonetary Effects of the Financial Crisis in the Propagation of the Great Depression. *American Economic Review* 73: 257–76.

Bhattacharya, Sudipto, and Douglas Gale. 1987. Preference Shocks, Liquidity, and Central Bank Policy. In *New Approaches in Monetary Economics*, ed. William A. Barnett and Kenneth Singleton. New York: Cambridge University Press.

Board of Governors of the Federal Reserve System. 1959. *All-Bank Statistics*, 1896–1955.

Bogue, Allan G. 1955. *Money at Interest: The Farm Mortgage on the Middle Border.* Lincoln: University of Nebraska Press.

Bordo, Michael D. 1985. The Impact and International Transmission of Financial Crises: Some Historical Evidence, 1870–1933. *Revista di storia economica*, 2d ser., vol. 2: 41–78.

Boyd, John, and Edward Prescott. 1986. Financial Intermediary Coalitions. *Journal of Economic Theory* 38: 211–32.

Breckenridge, R. M. 1910. *The History of Banking in Canada*. National Monetary Commission. 61st Cong., 2d sess. Senate Doc. 332. Washington D.C.: U.S. Government Printing Office.

Bryant, John. 1980. A Model of Reserves, Bank Runs, and Deposit Insurance. *Journal of Banking and Finance* 4: 335–44.

Burns, Arthur, and Wesley C. Mitchell. 1946. *Measuring Business Cycles*. NBER Studies in Business Cycles, no. 2. New York: Columbia University Press.

Calomiris, Charles W. 1988. Price and Exchange Rate Determination During the Greenback Suspension. *Oxford Economic Papers* 40: 719–50.

1989a. Deposit Insurance: Lessons from the Record Federal Reserve Bank of Chicago, *Economic Perspectives* (May–June).

1989b. The Motivations for Loan Commitments Backing Commercial Paper. *Journal of Banking and Finance* 13: 271–7.

1990. Is Deposit Insurance Necessary?: A Historical Perspective. *Journal of Economic History* 50, no. 2 (June): 283–95.

1992. Do "Vulnerable" Economies Need Deposit Insurance?: Lessons from the U.S. Agricultural Boom and Bust of the 1920s. In *If Texas Were Chile: A Primer on Bank Regulation*, ed. Philip L. Brock, 237–349, 450–58. San Francisco: Sequoia Institute.

Calomiris, Charles W., and R. Glenn Hubbard. 1989. Price Flexibility, Credit Availability, and Economic Fluctuations: Evidence from the United States, 1894–1909. *Quarterly Journal of Economics* 104(3): 429–52.

1996. International Adjustment Under the Classical Gold Standard: Evidence for the U.S. and Britain, 1879–1914. In *Modern Perspectives on the Gold Standard*, eds. T. Bayoumi, B. Eichengreen, and M. Taylor. Cambridge: Cambridge University Press, 186–217.

Calomiris, Charles W., and Charles M. Kahn. 1991. The Role of Demandable Debt in Structuring Optimal Banking Arrangements. *American Economic Review*, June, pp. 497–513.

Calomiris, Charles W., Charles M. Kahn, and Stefan Krasa. 1991. Optimal Contingent Bank Liquidation Under Moral Hazard. Federal Reserve Bank of Chicago, Working Paper WP-91-13.

Calomiris, Charles W., and Larry Schweikart. 1991. The Panic of 1857: Origins, Transmission, and Containment. *Journal of Economic History* 51 (December), pp. 807–34.

Campbell, Tim, and William Kracaw. 1980. Information Production, Market Signalling and the Theory of Financial Intermediation. *Journal of Finance* 35(4): 863–81.

Cannon, J. G. 1910. *Clearing Houses*. National Monetary Commission. 61st Cong., 2d sess. Senate Doc. 491. Washington D.C.: U.S. Government Printing Office.

Chari, V. V. 1989. Banking Without Deposit Insurance or Bank Panics: Lessons from a Model of the U.S. National Banking System. Federal Reserve Bank of Minneapolis, *Quarterly Review* (Summer): 3–19.

Chari, V. V., and Ravi Jagannathan. 1988. Banking Panics, Information, and Rational Expectations Equilibrium. *Journal of Finance* 43: 749–60.

Cone, Kenneth. 1983. Regulation of Depository Institutions. Ph.D. diss., Stanford University.

Dewey, Davis R. 1903. *Financial History of the United States.* New York: Longman's Green and Company.

Diamond, Douglas. 1984. Financial Intermediation and Delegated Monitoring. *Review of Economic Studies* 51: 393–414.

Diamond, Douglas, and Phillip Dybvig. 1983. Bank Runs, Liquidity and Deposit Insurance. *Journal of Political Economy* 91: 401–19.

Donaldson, R. Glenn. 1989a. Sources of Panics: Evidence From the Weekly Data. Princeton University, typescript.

1989b. Money Moguls, Market Corners and Cash Collusion During Panics. Princeton University, typescript.

Eichengreen, Barry. 1984. Currency and Credit in the Gilded Age. *Research in Economic History*, supp. 3: 87–114.

Frame, Andrew J. 1903. *Sound vs. Soft Money.* Waukesha: Wisconsin State Bankers' Association.

Frickey, Edwin. 1942. *Economic Fluctuations in the United States.* Cambridge: Harvard University Press.

1947. *Production in the United States*, 1860–1914. Cambridge: Harvard University Press.

Friedman, Milton, and Anna Schwartz. 1963. *A Monetary History of the United States, 1867–1960.* Princeton: Princeton University Press.

Gallatin, Albert. 1831. *Considerations on the Currency and Banking System of the United States.* Philadelphia: Carey and Lea.

Gendreau, B. 1990. Federal Reserve Policy and the Great Depression. University of Pennsylvania, typescript.

Golembe, Carter, and Clark Warburton. 1958. Insurance of Bank Obligations in Six States During the Period 1829–1866. Federal Deposit Insurance Corporation, typescript.

Goodhart, C. A. E. 1969. *The New York Money Market and the Finance of Trade*, 1900–1913. Cambridge: Harvard University Press.

Gorton, Gary. 1985. Clearing Houses and the Origin of Central Banking in the U.S. *Journal of Economic History* 45(2): 277–83.

1987. Bank Suspension of Convertibility. *Journal of Monetary Economics* 15(2): 177–93.

1988. Banking Panics and Business Cycles. *Oxford Economic Papers* 40: 751–81.

1989a. An Introduction to Van Court's Bank Note Reporter and Counterfeit Detector. The Wharton School, University of Pennsylvania, typescript.

1989b. Self-Regulating Bank Coalitions. The Wharton School, University of Pennsylvania, typescript.

1990. Free Banking, Wildcat Banking, and the Market for Bank Notes. The Wharton School, University of Pennsylvania, typescript.

Gorton, Gary, and Joseph Haubrich. 1989. The Loan Sales Market. In *Research in Financial Services*, ed. George Kaufman. Greenwich, Conn.: JAI Press.

Gorton, Gary, and Donald Mullineaux. 1987. The Joint Production of Confidence: Endogenous Regulation and 19th Century Commercial Bank Clearinghouses. *Journal of Money, Credit and Banking* 19(4): 458–68.

Gorton, Gary, and George Pennacchi. 1990. Financial Intermediation and Liquidity Creation. *Journal of Finance* 45(1): 49–72.

Govan, Thomas. 1936. The Banking and Credit System in Georgia. Ph.D. diss., Vanderbilt University.

Hamilton, James. 1987. Monetary Factors in the Great Depression. *Journal of Monetary Economics* 19: 145–69.

Haubrich, Joseph. 1990. Non-Monetary Effects of Financial Crises: Lessons from the Great Depression in Canada. *Journal of Monetary Economics*, 25, no. 2 (March): 223–52.

Haubrich, Joseph, and Robert King. 1984. Banking and Insurance. National Bureau of Economic Research Working Paper no. 1312.

Jacklin, Charles. 1987. Demand Deposits, Trading Restrictions, and Risk Sharing. In *Contractual Arrangements for Intertemporal Trade*, ed. Edward D. Prescott and Neil Wallace. Minneapolis: University of Minnesota Press.

Jacklin, Charles, and Sudipt Bhattacharya. 1988. Distinguishing Panics and Information-Based Bank Runs: Welfare and Policy Implications. *Journal of Political Economy* 96(3): 568–92.

Jevons, Stanley. 1884. *Investigations in Currency and Finance*. London: Macmillan.

Kemmerer, E. W. 1910. *Seasonal Variations in the Relative Demand for Money and Capital in the United States*. National Monetary Commission. 61st Cong., 2d sess. Senate Doc. 588. Washington, D.C.: U.S. Government Printing Office.

Kindleberger, Charles. 1978. *Manias, Panics, and Crashes: A History of Financial Crises*. New York: Basic Books.

Minsky, Hyman P. 1975. *John Maynard Keynes*. New York: Columbia University Press.

Miron, Jeffrey A. 1986. Financial Panics, the Seasonality of the Nominal Interest Rate, and the Founding of the Fed. *American Economic Review* 76(1): 125–40.

Miron, Jeffrey A., and Christina D. Romer. 1990. A New Monthly Index of Industrial Production, 1884–1940. *Journal of Economic History* 50 (June): 321–38.

Mitchell, Wesley. 1903. *A History of the Greenbacks*. Chicago: University of Chicago Press.

Moen, Jon, and Ellis W. Tailman. 1992. The Bank Panic of 1907: The Role of Trust Companies. *Journal of Economic History* 52 (September): 611–30.

Myers, Margaret G. 1931. *The New York Money Market*. New York: Columbia University Press.

Nicholas, Henry C. 1907. Runs on Banks. *Moody's Magazine* (December).

Postlewaite, Andrew, and Xavier Vives. 1987. Bank Runs as an Equilibrium Phenomenon. *Journal of Political Economy* 95: 485–91.

Redlich, Fritz. 1947. *The Molding of American Banking: Men and Ideas*. Reprint. New York: Augustus Kelley, 1968.

Rolnick, Arthur, and Warren E. Weber. 1984. The Causes of Free Bank Failures: A Detailed Examination. *Journal of Monetary Economics* 14: 267–91.

Schembri, Lawrence L., and Jennifer A. Hawkins. 1988. The Role of Canadian Chartered Banks in U.S. Banking Crises: 1870–1914. Carleton University, typescript.

Schweikart, Larry. 1987. *Banking in the American South from the Age of Jackson to Reconstruction*. Baton Rouge: Louisiana State University Press.

Smith, Bruce. 1987. Bank Panics, Suspension, and Geography: Some Notes on the "Contagion of Fear" in Banking. Cornell University, typescript.

Sobel, Robert. 1968. *Panic on Wall Street: A History of America's Financial Disasters*. New York: Macmillan.

Sprague, O. M. W. 1910. *A History of Crises Under the National Banking System*. National Monetary Commission. Washington, D.C.: U.S. Government Printing Office.

Standard Trade and Securities. 1932. *Base Book of the Standard Statistical Bulletin*.

Swift, W. Martin. 1911. The Seasonal Movements of Trade. *Moody's Magazine* (July).

U.S. Comptroller of the Currency. Various issues. *Annual Report*. Washington, D.C.: U.S. Government Printing Office.

U.S. Department of Commerce. 1949. *Historical Statistics of the United States*. Washington, D.C.: U.S. Government Printing Office.

Waldo, Douglas. 1985. Bank Runs, the Deposit-Currency Ratio and the Interest Rate. *Journal of Monetary Economics* 15(3): 269–78.

Wallace, Neil. 1988. Another Attempt to Explain an Illiquid Banking System: The Diamond and Dybvig Model With Sequential Service Taken Seriously. Federal Reserve Bank of Minneapolis, *Quarterly Review* (Fall): 3–16.

Wheelock, David C. 1988. The Fed's Failure to Act as Lender of Last Resort During the Great Depression, 1929–1933. University of Texas, typescript.

Williamson, Steven. 1989. Bank Failures, Financial Restrictions, and Aggregate Fluctuations: Canada and the United States, 1870–1913. Federal Reserve Bank of Minneapolis, *Quarterly Review* (Summer): 20–40.

## CHAPTER 3

The origins of federal deposit insurance

Charles W. Calomiris and Eugene N. White

3.1   Introduction

The insurance of bank deposits has become a common feature of bank-ing regulation in many countries, but until recently it was strictly an American phenomenon. Many countries adopted deposit insurance in imitation of the United States, where – with the exception of many econ-omists – it is regarded as an institution necessary for the stability of the banking system and the protection of depositors. In the current debate about how to reform the U.S. banking system, most argue on economic or political grounds that deposit insurance must be retained in some form, despite the enormous costs it has imposed. Federal deposit insur-ance may thus be the only enduring legacy of the New Deal's banking legislation.

The widespread support for deposit insurance in the United State rep-resented a remarkable change of public opinion. Until the early 1930s, there was no general interest in deposit insurance. Even after the 1933 banking crisis, a bitter struggle was waged over deposit insurance legis-lation. As Carter Golembe (1960, pp. 181–82) pointed out over thirty years ago, "Deposit insurance was not a novel idea; it was not untried; protection of the small depositor, while important, was not its primary purpose; and finally it was the only important piece of legislation during the New Deal's famous 'one hundred days' which was neither requested nor supported by the new administration."

On the one hand, the answer to the question why the United States passed long-dormant deposit insurance legislation is simple. In 1933, the United States had just suffered the worst economic contraction in its history, and proponents of deposit insurance offered it as a prophylactic against a repetition of the disruption and depositor loss that plagued America in the early 1930s. Had there been no Great Depression, it seems unlikely that the United States would have adopted deposit

The authors are grateful to Claudia Goldin and Gary Libecap, for helpful comments, and to Greg Chaudoin and Ronald Drennan for research assistance.

insurance. On the other hand, although the Great Depression may have constituted a necessary condition for deposit insurance's success, it is not clear why it was sufficient. There were many formidable obstacles to its passage, and there were alternative means to stabilize the banking system.

The obstacles included the Roosevelt Administration and the bank regulatory agencies, all of which opposed deposit insurance. Bankers were divided on the issue, but the banks that traditionally favored deposit insurance – small, rural, single-office (unit) banks in states that prohibited bank branching – had been in retreat economically since 1921 and had lost ground politically. Agricultural distress in the post-World War I years hastened the movement toward larger, more diversified banks, which had less need of protection. Experiences with deposit insurance at the state level had proved disastrous. Eight state-level deposit insurance systems had been created since 1908 at the behest of small unit banks in those states. In the 1920s, all collapsed under the weight of excessive risk taking and fraud, encouraged by the protection of deposit insurance. The experiences of these states were widely discussed at the time (American Bankers Association 1933; White 1983; Calomiris 1992).

Deposit insurance cannot be explained as an emergency measure conceived in haste to resolve an ongoing crisis. The legislation had been debated for years, the banking crisis of 1933 had been over for months prior to the implementation of the new insurance plan, and prior losses of banks and depositors were unaffected by the plan. Finally, there was an alternative long-run solution to the instability of the American banking system – nationwide branch banking – and it had been gaining ground politically in the 1920s, partly in response to widespread failures of agricultural unit banks and the failures of state deposit insurance schemes.

The purpose of our paper is to explain how and why federal deposit insurance – special-interest legislation that had failed in Congress for nearly fifty years – was adopted with near unanimity in 1933. We consider the forces in favor of, and against, federal deposit insurance from the nineteenth century to 1933. We argue that, even though the traditional supporters of federal deposit insurance had suffered repeated defeats and their power was at its nadir in 1933, the nature of the political struggle over deposit insurance changed in the 1930s from a battle waged in Congress among special interests to one that engaged the general public. The banking collapse focused the attention of the public on the otherwise esoteric political issue of banking reform and offered the supporters of deposit insurance the opportunity to wage a campaign to convince the public that federal deposit insurance was the best solution to banking instability.

Throughout the history of the debate over federal deposit insurance, advocates and opponents agreed that an alternative solution to bank instability would be to reduce the number of banks and increase their geographic scope by repealing limits on bank branching and consolidation.[1] Advocates of insurance – including small banks – opposed allowing greater bank concentration, while opponents of deposit insurance saw concentration as the best means to promote stability. A key factor in the passage of federal deposit insurance was the discrediting of large-scale banking by the advocates of deposit insurance.

3.2   The historical context of the struggle over federal deposit insurance

3.2.1   *Unit banking, bank instability, and deposit insurance in the United States*

The debate over federal insurance of deposits was conducted with reference to earlier efforts to insure bank liabilities. Insurance schemes were enacted by six states prior to the Civil War, and by eight states between 1907 and 1917. In all of these cases, insurance of banknotes or deposits was the mutual responsibility of banks, not the state governments.[2] The instability of small, unit banks and the desire to insulate the economy from recurrent disruptions of bank failures and suspensions of convertibility motivated all of the deposit insurance systems created by the various states (Golembe 1960). Thus the

---

[1] It was widely understood that fractional-reserve banking, in and of itself, was not the source of the peculiar instability of banking in the United States. Other countries with fractional-reserve banking. but which lacked the fragmented banking system of the United States, avoided the episodes of widespread bank failure and suspension of convertibility that characterized the U.S. experience (Bordo 1985; Calomiris and Gorton 1991; Calomiris 1993a).

[2] The National Banking Acts of the 1860s provided federal government insurance of national banknotes. But this insurance was redundant protection because notes always were secured by 100 percent (or more) of their value in the form of deposits of U.S. government bonds held at the Treasury. Unlike the antebellum free-banking systems on which it was modelled, bond backing under the national banking system eliminated default risk on notes. The National Banking Acts were motivated by the financial exigencies of the Civil war, as well as long-standing Jacksonian policy proposals to create a uniform national currency backed by government bonds (Duncombe 1841). Of course, government bonds and national banknotes did suffer numeraire risk, notably during the period of greenback suspension and silver agitation (Calomiris 1993b).

evolution of the structure of the banking system is closely tied to the history of deposit insurance.

The fragmentation and consequent instability of the American banking system are without parallel in the international history of banking. Experiments with large-scale banking – including the antebellum South and the federally chartered Banks of the United States – were early exceptions to reliance on local, unit banks. Despite increasing interest by banks in consolidating and expanding branching networks, by the late nineteenth century restrictive state and federal regulations combined to make unit banking the norm. The U.S. banking system expanded until 1920 primarily by adding banks rather than by increasing the size of banks. By 1920, there were more than thirty thousand banks operating in the United States, or one bank for every 3,444 people. Thirteen years later less than half that number remained, as banks disappeared in the wake of the severe agricultural distress of the 1920s and the Great Depression. The structure of the American banking industry – thousands of mostly small banks operating in geographical isolation of one another – produced its propensity for panics and bank failures by reducing opportunities for diversification of portfolios and by making it difficult for banks to coordinate their joint response to financial crises.

The origins of unit banking and its persistence have been widely debated by historians. One of the most important preconditions for bank fragmentation was federalism and the early judicial and legislative precedents giving individual states authority to design their own banking systems and limit competition from institutions outside their state. In particular, the Supreme Court's decision not to apply the commerce clause to banks and the Congress's deference to state chartering powers set the stage for a banking system in which individual states could determine the industrial organization of banking within their borders. Why states would choose unit banking is less clear. Here attention has focused on the role of populist propaganda by rent-seeking unit bankers (White 1984) and on the benefits to some farmers from tying banks to particular locations as a form of loan insurance (Calomiris 1993a).

The inherent fragility of a unit-banking system set the stage for further regulations to stabilize the system, notably deposit insurance. Every one of the fourteen states that enacted deposit insurance legislation from 1829 to 1917 was a unit-banking state seeking to find a means of stabilizing its banking system. States that chose to imitate wholly or even partly the standard international practice of allowing branch banking eschewed insurance.

Of the six antebellum state mutual-guarantee schemes, three had short lives and suffered large losses, while the other three suffered virtually no losses and survived for long periods (Golembe and Warburton 1958; Golembe 1960; Calomiris 1990). The varying degrees of success of these two groups of systems can be traced to the incentives created under their different regulatory regimes. The successful systems of Indiana, Ohio, and Iowa included limited numbers of banks (typically about thirty) with strong incentives to police one another and with broad powers of self-regulation and enforcement. Banks provided substantial mutual protection to one another without encouraging excessive risk taking. These systems were eliminated by federal legislation that imposed a 10 percent annual tax on state banknote issues (their primary liabilities) to foster the newly created national banking system.

The other antebellum insurance experiments (of New York, Vermont, and Michigan) all had become insolvent by the 1840s as the result of common problems of design that induced adverse selection and moral hazard, encouraging risk taking within the insured system. The large numbers of members and limited mutual liability encouraged free riding, and the government provided little effective supervision and regulation. Protection to noteholders and depositors under these three mutual-guarantee systems was limited; protection rested on the ability and willingness of surviving banks to remain in the systems to fund the losses of failed banks. Bank failures resulted in substantial losses to noteholders and depositors.

Stimulated by the disruptions from the Panic of 1907, states began a second round of experimentation with mutual-guarantee systems (White 1983; Calomiris 1990, 1992).[3] Like the antebellum systems, all the post-1907 state insurance systems arose in unit-banking states dominated by large numbers of small, rural banks. White (1983, p. 200) found that the

---

[3] At the federal level, protection was offered to depositors via the postal savings system, which was also established in the wake of the Panic of 1907 (Kemmerer 1917). Postal savings was the limited remedy to banking instability offered by the victorious Republicans after the election of 1908. The Democratic platform had contained a proposal for federal deposit insurance (O'Hara and Easley 1979, pp. 742–43). To limit competition between postal savings and bank deposits, postal savings paid low interest, was restricted to small deposits, and was largely reinvested in the banking system. While the government stood behind postal savings deposits (many of which were deposited in commercial banks), this did not expose the government to significant risk because banks were required to secure postal savings account deposits with municipal, state, and federal bonds specified by Congress (Zaun 1953, pp. 27–28). Thus government backing for postal savings was redundant in the same way as the backing for national banknotes. Banks profited from the spread they earned on postal savings deposits (equal to the yield on collateral bonds, less the 2 percent interest paid to the post office on the accounts). This profit turned negative during the Great Depression, as bond yields fell. The result was a switch from the investment of postal savings deposits in banks (who refused them) to direct investment of postal savings in government bonds.

probability of passage of deposit insurance at the state level was positively affected by the presence of unit-banking laws, small bank size, and a high bank-failure rate.

Unfortunately, the postbellum systems all adopted the design features of the failed antebellum systems, including limited mutual liability and government rather than private regulation. In a sense, this imitation is not surprising. A successful system of self-regulating banks with unlimited mutual liability – like those of Indiana, Ohio, and Iowa – would not have been feasible for state unit-banking systems of hundreds of unit banks like those of the postbellum deposit insurance states. In systems of hundreds of banks, banks would have little incentive to expend resources policing one another, since the benefits one bank would receive from monitoring another would be shared with too many others banks, while the costs of monitoring would be borne privately. Thus the decision to imitate the design of the failed antebellum systems was consistent with the industrial structure of banking in these large, agricultural states dominated by large numbers of unit banks.

These systems suffered large losses and went bankrupt in the 1920s. Calomiris (1990, 1992) and Wheelock (1992) trace these large losses to the excessive risk taking of banks in insured states during the World War I agricultural boom. Insured banking systems grew at an unusually high rate in the form of small banks with relatively low capital. In the face of the post-1920 agricultural bust, insured banks failed at a high rate and with the lowest asset values relative to deposit claims of any banks in the 1920s. State banks in agricultural states all suffered from the large price and land-value declines of the 1920s, but the risk taking encouraged by deposit insurance added greatly to the costs state banks suffered in the face of the decline.

At the same time that the post-1907 state insurance systems collapsed, conditions in the banking industry began to change in a direction that threatened the future of unit banking. Up to 1914, the banking system had been expanding rapidly, which, under the prohibition of branch banking in most states, resulted in the proliferation of small unit banks. Beginning with the postwar recession, many banks failed in agricultural areas. They continued to fail at historically high rates, even as the rest of the economy thrived in the mid-1920s. Surviving banks faced tougher competition as legal barriers to branching were weakened under pressure from larger urban banks and by efforts to allow surviving banks a means to fill the gaps created by the many rural bank failures. The proven survivability of branching banks during the 1920s in contrast to the failures of the insured unit-banking systems also favored expanded branching and consolidation (White 1983; Calomiris 1992, 1993a). Table 3.1

Table 3.1. *Bank mergers, branching, and securities affiliates, 1900–1931*

Year	Bank mergers	Total assets acquired ($mil)	Banks operating branches	Number of branches	Branch banks loans and investments ($mil)	Securities affiliates of banks	Number of banks
1900	20		87	119			
1901	41						
1902	50						
1903	37						
1904	63						
1905	69		196	350			
1906	56						
1907	54						
1908	97						
1909	80						
1910	127		292	548	1,272		
1911	119						
1912	128						
1913	118						
1914	142						25,510
1915	154		397	785	2,187		25,875
1916	134						26,217
1917	123						26,831
1918	119						27,457
1919	178	650					27,859
1920	181	874	530	1,281	6,897		29,087
1921	281	710	547	1,455	8,354		29,788
1922	337	750	610	1,801	9,110	277	29,458
1923	325	1,052	671	2,054	10,922	314	29,201
1924	350	662	706	2,297	12,480	372	28,372
1925	352	702	720	2,525	14,763	413	27,858
1926	429	1,595	744	2,703	16,511	464	27,235
1927	543	1,555	740	2,914	17,591	493	26,149
1928	501	2,093	775	3,138	20,068	561	25,330
1929	571	5.614	764	3,353	21,420	591	24,504
1930	699	2,903	751	3,522	22,491	566	23,251
1931	706	2,757	723	3,467	20,681	525	21,309

Sources: Data on the number of bank mergers from Chapman 1934, p. 56; the assets of banks absorbed by merger from White 1985, p. 286; the number of banks operating branches, the number of branches in operation, and the loans and investments of branching banks from Board of Governors 1976, p. 297; the securities affiliates of banks from Peach 1941, p. 83; and the number of state and national commercial banks from Board of Governors 1976, p. 19.

provides data on bank industry trends during the 1920s. As the number of banks declined, the number of branches began to rise and mergers became more common. Banks began to diversify their activities, moving into a variety of financial services, including trust services, brokerage, and investment banking. A larger, more diversified, and safer portfolio

(White 1986) and the availability of a variety of new services attracted customers (Calomiris 1995). Smaller unit banks found it hard to compete in this environment and turned to the political arena to secure economic protection.

3.2.2   Constituent interests and federal deposit insurance

From an early date, advocates of deposit insurance pushed for federal legislation. From 1886 through 1933, 150 bills were introduced into either the House or the Senate, proposing to establish federal deposit insurance. These proposals differed in their particulars regarding the range of membership (i.e., whether to restrict members to national banks, all Federal Reserve member banks, or all national and qualifying state banks), the form of protection for deposits (mutual bank guarantee or government guarantee), and the charges to participating banks, but they shared common fundamental features. All the proposed systems would have established a national system of insurance in which all banks would pay identical premiums and receive identical protection. Such a national system would have extended to the national level the model of deposit insurance adopted at the state level by the eight postbellum insurance systems.

In economic terms, regardless of whether insurance was funded by banks or backed by a government guarantee, such a scheme necessarily involves cross-subsidization of risk across states. States with banks that suffered higher risks of failure would gain at the expense of other states' banks, and in the case of government guarantees, at the expense of the rest of the nation's taxpayers. From this standpoint, one would expect that the states most likely to favor national insurance would be those with the most vulnerable banking systems. For these states, the common costs of insurance would be more than reimbursed by the expected bailouts of failed banks by relatively stable banks (and taxpayers) from other states. Compared to state-level deposit insurance, federal deposit insurance was particularly attractive to unit bankers located in the high-risk rural states because it offered greater protection at lower cost. But this same fact made federal insurance legislation less likely to succeed. Rural unit banks wielded more power in theuir states than they wielded in Congress, where banks from states with relatively stable banking systems would oppose cross-subsidization of risky banks.

One way to test this special-interest, rent-seeking view of support and opposition for federal deposit insurance would be to compare each state's banking system's vulnerability with its support for federal legislation creating deposit insurance.

3.2.3   *Inferring constituent interest from congressional behavior*

Difficult conceptual issues and empirical pitfalls arise in inferring constituents' interests from politicians' support for particular legislation. Conceptually, it is not always clear how to map from congressional behavior to the probable interests of constituents. There is a large and growing literature on the difficulty of measuring constituent interest from voting records (e.g., Poole and Rosenthal 1994). Elected representatives often trade votes on issues, so that a negative vote on one bill does not necessarily indicate that constituents would be opposed to that bill. Political parties often play an important role in enforcing intertemporal trade-offs in voting across different bills. Party discipline can encourage a representative to vote against his constituent interests on one bill in exchange for promised votes on another bill, or perhaps in exchange for party support for introducing a "private" bill to benefit a select group of his supporters. Poole and Rosenthal suggest that party discipline is likely to be most important in close votes. In votes that are not close, the party will free members to vote their constituents' interests, since there is no benefit from trading votes. These considerations suggest that voting patterns, particularly in close votes, may reveal little about constituent interests, especially on issues that are not viewed as the highest priorities of one's constituents.

In the case of congressional voting on deposit insurance bills, there is an even better reason to look for an alternative to representatives' voting records as a measure of constituent interests – namely, the scarcity of voting data. Of the 150 bills that were introduced into Congress to establish federal deposit insurance between 1886 and 1933, only one bill ever came to a roll call vote (amended HR 7837 in December 1913). Of these 150 bills, 147 never emerged from the House or Senate committees that were given the responsibility of considering them. This is a very poor batting average. From the 49th to the 73d Congress (from 1886 to 1933), 5 percent of bills introduced were enacted into law, of which roughly one-third were "private" bills, that is, bills benefitting particular named individuals (Bureau of the Census 1975, pp. 108, 1–82). Thus deposit insurance bills suffered an unusually low chance of emerging from committee, much less being enacted into law.

To understand these facts, it is useful to review the procedures for the consideration of bills by Congress.[4] The process in the House begins with bills being dropped into a "hopper" on the clerk's desk. In the Senate,

---

[4] For additional details see Berman 1964; Froman 1967; Davidson and Oleszek 1981; Morrow 1969; Reid 1980.

the sponsor must gain recognition on the floor and make the announcement of the bill's introduction. These bills are then assigned to a committee to analyze and perhaps amend the bill. Most bills die in committee. If a bill makes it out of committee, the House or Senate can vote on the bill or send it back to committee, where, as before, it typically dies. Once bills reach the House or Senate after making it out of committee, there are several possibilities. In the House, a bill gets placed before the Committee as a Whole (which is made up of at least one hundred representatives). A bill must pass through the Committee as a Whole before the House of Representatives can vote on the bill. The Committee as a Whole, assuming there is a quorum of one hundred members, cannot have a roll call vote. Instead they vote by voice, division (standing), or teller (lining up and being counted on a pro or con side of the aisle). If a bill makes it out of the Committee as a Whole, it can be voted on by voice, division, or roll call. However, it takes a one-fifth approval – assuming there is a quorum – to be granted a roll call. In the House, roll calls are time-consuming events and do not happen often.

In the Senate, roll call votes occur relatively more often because there are fewer members and it does not use up much time. But the Senate also utilizes voice votes and division votes. As in the House, it takes one-fifth of senators present to approve a roll call. This minimum can be hard to achieve sometimes, as senators can be present at a quorum call but exit soon after, leaving only a handful of senators on the floor for the vote on the motion for yeas and nays.

It is likely that the authors of deposit insurance bills (prior to 1932) were aware that their efforts would fail. One indication of their unlikely success is that deposit insurance bills were typically not introduced by the chairmen of committees that would consider the bills, or even by members of the committees. Committee members, and particularly their chairmen, enjoy considerable power in determining whether a bill will be successful. Bills not introduced by committee chairmen, or subcommittee chairmen, stand little chance of emerging from the committee.[5] From 1886 through 1931, 120 bills were introduced on deposit insurance.

---

[5] The power of the committee chairmen is difficult to exaggerate (Berman 1964, p. 212). One of their key powers lies in their ability to hold up a bill in committee. They can do this by refusing to schedule a bill for a hearing or by setting meeting times when the bill's proponents cannot possibly attend. Committee chairmen also hire and fire most of the committee's staff, assign members to subcommittees, and lead floor debates on bills reported from their committees, among other things. They can form subcommittees in such a way that they can kill a bill by sending it to a subcommittee stacked with members opposed to the bill, or they can push through bills they support by sending the bill to a committee stacked in its favor.

In only twenty-one of these cases were they introduced by members of the committees that would consider them, and in only one case (notably in 1908) was a bill introduced by a committee chairman.

Congressmen and senators who introduced these unpromising bills often did so repeatedly over many years, possibly as a signal to constituents that the failure of such legislation was not due to a lack of effort on their part. If this is correct, then it seems reasonable to suppose that the identities of those introducing legislation are a good indicator of strong constituent interests in that legislation. In the empirical patterns we report, we focus on the differences between states whose representatives authored bills and other states, examining correlations between authorship and economic indicators at the state level. We confine most of our analysis to the period prior to the national banking crises of September 1931–March 1933. In 1932 and 1933, when nine of the thirty bills introduced were authorized by committee members (including three by Chairman Steagall and one by Senator Glass), the likelihood of passage was known to be higher, and the link between the identity of authors and constituent interests may have been weaker (given the compromises being engineered, authors may have been chosen to maximize the chance of successful passage). We also discuss voting patterns for the 1913 roll call votes in the House and Senate.

3.2.4   Empirical evidence on the characteristics of states with authors of bills

We define states whose congressmen or senators authored deposit insurance bills as "authoring states," and the remaining states as "nonauthoring states." Appendix table 3.A.1 presents the full list of bills introduced; their date and congressional session; their authors; each author's house of Congress, party affiliation, and state; and whether the author (if a congressman) represents a "large-city" constituency or its complement, which we call a "rural" constituency. If the author is a "large-city" congressman, we state the name of the city contained within his congressional district. Table 3.A.1 also indicates whether the bill specified mutual guarantee or government guarantee of deposits, and which banks would have been included in the insurance system.

The committee chairman, or ranking minority committee member, will customarily agree as a matter of courtesy to introduce a bill originating in the White House. The bills from the executive branch typically get the most attention from committees. Deposit insurance bills introduced into the House of Representatives between 1886 and 1933 were referred to the Committee on Banking and Currency. Senate deposit insurance bills were referred to the Committee on Finance until 1919, and thereafter referred to the Senate Committee on Banking and Currency.

Both major parties account for large numbers of proposals, with fifty-eight bills introduced by Republicans and ninety introduced by Democrats, but the relative authorship of Democrats and Republicans shifted somewhat over time. Eleven Republicans authored bills from 1886 to 1906, compared to only six authored by Democrats. From 1907 through 1933, thirty-six Democrats and twenty-eight Republicans authored bills.

One interesting pattern shown in Table 3.A.1 is the changing regional composition of authoring states over time. For the first twenty-five bills introduced (covering 1886–1906), the regional composition of authors is very diverse. Eastern states (Pennsylvania, New York, New Jersey, and Ohio) account for eleven of the twenty-five bills and six of the nineteen authors, ten authors hailed from the Middle West and West (Wisconsin, Missouri, Kansas, Nebraska, Washington, and North Dakota), and three were southerners (Virginia, Mississippi, and Alabama). For the next eighty-nine bills (covering 1907–February 1931), authorship is highly concentrated in the West and Middle West, which accounts for sixty-six of the bills introduced, with the South accounting for the remaining nineteen bills (thirteen of which are authored by Mississippians and Alabamans). During this period, bills introduced by easterners are confined to four bills introduced by Pennsylvanians in 1907 and 1908.

For the final period (covering December 1931–May 1933), the regional mix again becomes more diverse. Of the thirty-six bills introduced during this period, seven states that had not been "authoring" states in the previous twenty years (New York, Ohio, California, Michigan, Tennessee, Florida, and Virginia) account for eighteen of the bills introduced. This change in 1931 is also visible in the change from a nearly universal rural identity of authors prior to 1931 to a mixture of rural and urban authors from 1931 through 1933. Of the eighty bills introduced in the House prior to December 1931, only four were authored by congressmen who could be regarded as coming from major cities (Omaha, Denver, Chicago, and Atlanta). From December 1931 through 1933, five of twenty-six bills were introduced by House members from Chicago, New York City, Columbus, Detroit, and Tulsa.

What explains the changes over time in the locational composition of authors? Tables 3.2 through 3.4 present evidence on differences in the characteristics of these two sets of states for various time periods. In analyzing cross-sectional characteristics of authoring and nonauthoring states, we focus on the period before December 1931, prior to the emergence of a congressional consensus in favor of federal insurance. The dates over which variables are defined often are indicated by data availability. Given the small sample size, we emphasize median comparisons,

Table 3.2. *Bank characteristics in authoring and nonauthoring states*

| | State Banks | | | | | | National Banks | | | | | |
| | Authoring | | | Nonauthoring | | | Authoring | | | Nonauthoring | | |
	Mean	Med.	S.D.	Mean	Med.	S.D.	Mean	Med.	S.S.	Mean	Med.	S.D.
Bank-failure rate (%)[a]												
1864–96	0.54	0.45	0.47	0.51	0.43	0.29	0.39	0.37	0.27	0.32	0.24	0.32
1907–10	0.13	0.04	0.20	0.20	0.04	0.46	0.12	0.10	0.12	0.15	0.00	0.21
1921–29	4.23	4.67	2.86	1.98	1.07	2.36	2.25	1.76	1.76	0.96	0.37	1.45
Average bank size												
1896	465	212	553	408	207	565	837	697	656	596	491	312
1910	448	251	594	1,008	430	1,720	1,030	857	630	1,202	864	925
1919	813	449	963	1,768	847	2,727	1,969	1,681	1,067	2,409	1,720	2,041
1929	729	545	703	3,113	940	5,243	2,025	1,615	859	3,335	2,634	2,456
Small-Town bank suspensions relative to total[b]												
1920–31	0.94	0.97	0.07	0.85	0.90	0.19	0.95	0.97	0.07	0.86	0.92	0.21
Deposit-loss rate (%)												
For failed banks.												
1920–31[c]	44.8	40.6	11.2	30.3	31.6	22.4	40.9	49.3	18.6	35.1	31.4	18.4
For all banks, 1920s[d]	1.77	2.19	1.05	0.73	0.04	1.29	1.07	0.91	0.92	0.41	0.08	0.84

Notes: Authoring states are those where one or more of the state's representatives or senators introduced a federal deposit insurance bill. Authorship is categorized into three periods: 1886–98, 1905–19, and 1920–February 1931. The authoring states in each of these periods are matched by date with items listed in the table. For example, average bank size (1910) is matched with authoring during 1905–19.

[a] Bank-failure rates for 1921–29 are defined as the ratio of the sum of each years liquidated banks to the sum of each years surviving banks. For the periods prior to the 1920s, bank-failure rates are defined as the ratio of average annual failures during the period divided by the number of banks in 1896 plus the number of failures during the period.

[b] Small towns had populations of under twenty-five thousand.

[c] The deposit-loss rate for failed banks is one minus the ratio of payments from assets to proven claims.

[d] The deposit-loss rate for all banks is the product of the bank-failure rate for 1921–29 and the deposit-loss rate for failed banks.

Sources: Data on bills introduced are from Table 3.A.1. Bank-failure rates for 1864–96 are from Upham and Lanke 1934, p. 246. For 1896–1929, data on numbers of national and stare banks for each state are reported in Board of Governors 1959. Data on bank failures after 1896 are given in Comptroller of the Currency 1907–29. Data on bank suspensions, their location, and deposit loss rates are constructed from Goldenweiser et al. 1932, pp. 5; 183–97.

176

Table 3.3. *Characteristics of authoring and nonauthoring states*

	Authoring states			Nonauthoring states		
	Mean	Median	S.D.	Mean	Median	S.D.
Branching indicator unit = 0, branch = 1						
1910[a]	0.29	0	0.47	0.52	1	0.51
1925[b]	0.22	0	0.44	0.41	0	0.50
Branching ratio[c]						
1910	0.03	0.00	0.04	0.07	0.03	0.09
1920	0.03	0.00	0.03	0.10	0.02	0.13
1930	0.07	0.01	0.11	0.17	0.02	0.22
Non-Fed members relative to all banks						
1919	0.70	0.73	0.16	0.61	0.63	0.17
1929	0.66	0.69	0.11	0.61	0.61	0.17
Business-failure[d] rate (%)						
1909–13	0.81	0.81	0.28	0.99	0.94	0.37
1921–29	1.09	1.13	0.29	1.05	0.96	0.39
Farm to total population						
1920	0.47	0.46	0.13	0.32	0.31	0.18

Notes: Authoring states are those where one or more of the state's representatives or senators introduced a federal deposit insurance bill. Authorship is categorized into three periods: 1886–98, 1905–19, and 1920–February 1931. The authoring states in each of these periods are matched by date with items listed in the table. For example, the branching ratio (1910) is matched with authoring during 1905–19.
[a] The branching indicator distinguishes states that allow new branches to open from other states.
[b] The branching indicator equals one if at least one branch exists, and if continuing branching (however limited) is allowed, as described in Board of Governors 1926.
[c] The ratio of bank offices operated by branching banks relative to total bank offices in the state.
[d] Business failure rates are annual averages for commercial enterprises.
Sources: Data on bills introduced are from Table 3.A.1. These data, as well as data on Federal Reserve members and nonmembers, are taken from Board of Governors 1976, pp. 298, 24–33. Branching indicator for 1910 is constructed from Calomiris 1993a, pp. 86–87. Business-failure rates are derived from U.S. Bureau of the Census 1909–29. Data on farm and nonfarm populations are from Leven 1925, p. 259.

which provide a better gauge than means because they are relatively insensitive to outliers.

For the twentieth century, the authoring states tend to differ from other states in ways consistent with the view that special interest groups in those states, which stood to benefit from cross-subsidization of risk, encouraged deposit insurance proposals by their elected officials in

Table 3.4. *Deposit insurance bills and their authors*

	All states		Authoring states[a]	
Bills/Authors per state	Mean	Median	Mean	Median
Bills introduced, 1886–98 (18 bills)	0.4	0	1.8	2
Authors of bills, 1886–98 (15 authors)	0.3	0	1.5	1
Bills introduced, 1905–19 (63 bills)	1.7	0	5	3
Authors of bills, 1905–19 (32 authors)	0.6	0	1.8	1
Bills introduced, 1920–Feb. 1931 (29 bills)	0.9	0	4.3	3
Authors of bills, 1920–Feb. 1931 (15 authors)	0.5	0	2.2	1

[a] An authoring state is one in which one or more of its representatives introduced a federal deposit insurance bill.
Source: Data on bills introduced are from Table 3.A.1.

Washington. The banking systems of authoring states were more vulnerable than those of nonauthoring states by several of the measures reported in Tables 3.2 through 3.4. Authoring states had much higher bank-failure rates and higher deposit loss rates on failed banks in the 1920s.

The greater vulnerability of authoring states' banking systems in the 1920s is partly explained by the structure of their banking systems, which tended to be dominated by small, unit banks. There is a strong association between unit banking and the support for deposit insurance legislation. States committed to unit banking tended to be supporters of deposit insurance. Nonauthoring states tended to rely relatively more on branch banking. Furthermore, consistent with standard historical writings on the links between agrarian populism and deposit insurance, we find that states promoting federal deposit insurance legislation had a higher ratio of rural-to-total population and a greater proportion of bank failures in towns of less than twenty-five thousand inhabitants.

Comparisons across states for the nineteenth century reveal no apparent difference between authoring and nonauthoring states. The increase in the regional concentration of support for deposit insurance in the twentieth century is mirrored in starker differences between the authoring and nonauthoring states. In the nineteenth century, within-state differences may have been as important as cross-state differences in risk, making it difficult to detect the role of special interests at the state level. Later, differences across states seem to be more important than differences within states. This is largely explained by the changes in various states' regulations of branching, and the stability branching brought to these states' banking systems. From 1900 to 1930, the number of branching banks in the United States rose from 87 to 751, and the number of branches rose from 119 to 3,522. This movement toward branching was concentrated in a few states, and many of these had been states with early supporters of deposit insurance legislation (notably Ohio, New York, Pennsylvania, and New Jersey). During the first decade of the twentieth century, as the branching movement took hold in these states, their elected officials disappeared from the list of congressmen and senators authoring deposit insurance bills. These four states alone saw increases in the number of banking offices operated by branching banks from 56 in 1900 to 1,534 in 1930.

The branch-banking movement of the early twentieth century created profound differences across states in the propensity for failure, which encouraged high-risk unit-banking states to attempt to free ride on the stability of branch-banking states through the establishment of national deposit insurance. As the agricultural banking crisis wore on in the grain and cotton belts in the 1920s, those states became the staunchest advocates of deposit insurance legislation. Not surprisingly, representatives of states that had passed state-level deposit insurance between 1907 and 1917 (Oklahoma, Texas, Nebraska, North Dakota, South Dakota, Washington, Texas, and Mississippi) were among the most frequent authors of bills for national insurance from 1907 through 1931, accounting for fifty-five of ninety-five bills introduced during this period. The collapse of the state insurance systems in the 1920s created a new urgency for protection at the national level in the face of the collapse of so many state banks.

Nebraska and Oklahoma, whose banks were among the smallest, least-diversified, and lowest-capitalized banking systems in the country during the 1920s, led the movement for national insurance plans. Of the thirty-four bills proposed between 1921 and 1931, fourteen were introduced by representatives of Oklahoma and Nebraska.

3.2.5   The 1913 roll call votes

The only federal deposit insurance bill on which roll call votes were taken was amended HR 7837, which was voted on by both houses of Congress in December 1913. The bill was proposed as an addition to the Federal Reserve Act, and it originated in the Senate. The bill passed the Senate with 54 yeas, 34 nays, and 7 not voting. It then went to the House, where it was defeated with a vote of 295 nays, 59 yeas, 78 not voting, and 2 "present." These votes are described in detail in Table 3.5.

In the Senate, where the vote was close, party discipline was enforced

Table 3.5. *House and Senate voting patterns on amended HR 7837, December 1913*

| | House voting | | | | | | | | | | | | Senate voting | | | | | | | | |
| | Democrats | | | Republicans | | | Other Parties | | | State total | | | Democrats | | | Republicans | | | State total | | |
	Y	N	N/V	Y	N	N/V	Y	N	N/V	Y	N	N/V	Y	N	N/V	Y	N	N/V	Y	N	N/V
AL		8	2								8	2	1						1		
AR		7									7		2						2		
AZ		1									1		2						2		
CA		4		4	2	1				4	6	1				1	1		1	1	
CO		4									4		2						2		
CT		4	1								4	1					2	1		2	1
DE		1									1		1				1		1	1	
FL	1	3								1	3		2						2		
GA	6	6								6	6		2						2		
IA		2	1		7	1					9	2					2			2	
ID				1	1					1	1						1			1	
IL	3	9	8	2	1	2	1	1		6	11	10	1				1		1	1	
IN		11	1			1					11	2	2						2		
KS		4		1	1	1				1	5	1	1				1		1	1	
KY		7	2	1		1				1	7	3	1				1		1	1	
LA		6	2								6	2	1		1				1		1
MA		7	1		6	2					13	3				1		1	1		1
MD		5	1								5	1	1						1		
ME		1			2	1					3	1	1						1		
MI		2		1	8	1	1			2	10	1					1	1		1	1
MN		1			8	1					9	1									
MO		12	2		2						14	2		2						2	
MS	6	3								6	3		2						2		
MT	1	1								1	1		2						2		

NC	2	8							2	8	2	2			2		2		2
ND						3				3					2	2	2	2	
NE	1	2		3					4	2	1	1	1		1	1	1	1	
NH		2	3		1					2	1	1			1		2	2	
NJ		7			1					8	2	2			1		2		1
NM		1								1			1	1				1	
NV						1				1	2		1		2		2		
NY	2	21	10	7	1	5	1			28	15	1	1		1	1	1	1	
OH	3	15	2	2	5	1			2	17	3	1	1		1	1	1	1	
OK		3		2	1				3	5		2			2		1		
OR				2		1			1	2		2			2	2			
PA	1	8	3	9	9	1			5	17	12	2	2		2	2		2	
RI		1	1	1	1					2	1		2				2	2	
SC	1	6							1	6		2							
SD										1			2		2	2			
TN		7	1	1	2				1	8	2	2	1		2			2	1
TX	11	5	3	1					11	5	1	1		1		1			
UT					2					2			2				1		
VA		9	1							9	1	2			2	2		2	
VT		2		2	1			1		2			2		2	2		2	
WA				2						3									
WI		3		8						11	1		2		2	2	2	2	
WV		1	1	3	1					4	2	1	1	1	1	1	1	1	
WY				1						1							1	1	1
Totals	38	207	48	17	85	32	4	3	59	295	80	47	7	3	34	4	54	34	7

Note: Y, N, and N/V correspond to yea, nay, and no vote.

a Includes the Progressive Republicans, Progressives, and Independents.

Source: Voting records are taken from Roll Call Voting records available through the Inter-University Consortium for Political and Social Research.

more rigorously, and the vote was essentially along party lines. Forty-seven of fifty-four yeas were cast by Democrats, and all nays were cast by Republicans. Four Republicans and three Democrats declined to vote. While votes along party lines provide little evidence of state constituent interests, the states of the senators casting "renegade" votes (those who went against their party) are interesting to examine. Five of the seven Republican senators who voted yea were from states that had enacted or soon would enact deposit insurance at the state level (Nebraska, South Dakota, and Washington).

The other two Republican senators who voted yea were from California and Massachusetts. While both of these states allowed some branch banking by 1913, they were both essentially unit-banking states at that time, and both states had suffered unusually high recent spates of bank and business failures, as shown in table 3.6. Unlike the rural states supporting deposit insurance, bank failures in these two states (and in Pennsylvania) were associated with substantial commercial distress. Massachusetts saw three of its national banks fail from 1907 to 1913. From 1907 through 1913, sixteen banks were liquidated by order of the superintendent of banking in California, and one national bank was placed into receivership by the comptroller. These rates of bank failure had not been seen in California since the mid-1890s. California law did not explicitly disallow branching, but banks were only allowed to branch with the permission of the state superintendent of banking, and the superintendent would not grant permission without the approval of local banks in the town where the proposed branch would be located. When economic distress threatened the solvency of unit banks, A. P. Giannini's requests to open branches were granted, beginning with the San Jose branch of the Bank of Italy in 1909, which received the explicit endorsement of local bankers and planters. Progress remained slow until 1916, when the revealed benefits of branching and the precedents established by Giannini helped to encourage widespread approval for branching. Similarly, in Massachusetts only fourteen banks had branches in 1910, with a total of sixteen branches in operation. By 1930, fifty-eight banks were operating 128 branches.

The House vote was not nearly as close as that in the Senate, and there is little evidence of any attempt to enforce party discipline in the House. Thus the House vote should provide a better indication of constituent interests. The fact that roll call votes divide into three categories – yea, nay, and abstention – complicates any attempt to measure support and opposition for a bill. As a first step toward measuring support for the legislation, we divide states into two groups according to their degree of opposition to the bill. We designate states as relatively strong supporters (weak opponents) if the proportion of nay votes in that state is less than two-thirds and the proportion of yea votes is greater than 20 percent. We chose these thresholds to place a sufficient number of states in the supportive group for purposes of comparison. Changes in the choice of thresholds will affect our relative sample sizes but not our qualitative results. By our measure, there are thirteen states designated as relatively strong supporters of the legislation. These include California, Florida, Georgia, Idaho, Illinois, Kansas, Mississippi, Missouri, Montana, Nebraska, Oklahoma, Pennsylvania, and Texas. Five of these states are among the eight states that passed deposit insurance legislation at the state level (Kansas, Mississippi, Nebraska, Oklahoma, and Texas). These thirteen states are not the same as the fourteen states whose congressmen introduced deposit insurance legislation between 1905 and 1919 (the definition of interest in deposit insurance used in Table 3.2), but there is substantial overlap. Seven states are in both groups, including the five "supporting" states that enacted state-level deposit insurance, as well as Missouri and Pennsylvania. Table 3.6 shows that supporting states (the thirteen from the House vote) had more fragile banking systems than did other states, as measured by median comparisons of bank size, branching ratios, rural population ratios, and business- and bank-failure rates.

The relative strength of voting support in the House by the congressmen from states that had passed insurance legislation at the state level may reflect a variety of factors, including a fragile unit-banking system, recent high rates of bank failure and business failure, and competitive considerations. On the latter point, national banks in insured states (which had been excluded from participation in state insurance plans by a ruling of the Comptroller of the Currency) may have desired to have access to a national insurance plan to be able to compete with the existing state insurance systems in their states, and may have lobbied harder than national banks in other states for the bill.

By the same token, in noninsured state systems, small rural unit banks may have opposed the bill more than similar banks in insured states. The reason small state unit banks in many other states might have opposed amended HR 7837 is that it stipulated that membership in the federal insurance system was restricted to *Federal Reserve member banks,* and many of them would not be Fed members. The original intent of the Federal Reserve Act was to encourage all banks (through the benefits of access to the discount window) to join the Federal Reserve System, but the costs of compliance with Fed regulations – especially reserve requirements – kept many small banks from joining (White 1983, pp. 64–125, 177–87). A small rural bank that may have expected to opt out

Table 3.6. *House of Representatives vote on federal deposit insurance in 1913: Comparison of characteristics of thirteen "supportive" and thirty-five "unsupportive" states*

	Relatively supportive states			Relatively unsupportive states		
	Mean	Median	S.D.	Mean	Median	S.D.
State bank–failure rate (%), 1907–10	0.13	0.12	0.12	0.19	0	0.45
National bank–failure rate (%), 1907–10	0.14	0.10	0.19	0.14	0	0.19
Average state bank assets. 1910	434	211	493	949	387	1,648
Average national bank assets, 1910	1,107	759	766	1,154	873	862
Business–failure rate (%), 1909–13	1.07	1.03	0.31	0.87	0.78	0.35
Branching indicator unit = 0, branch = 1, 1910	0.31	0	0.48	0.49	0	0.51
Branching ratio, 1910	0.03	0	0.05	0.62	0.03	0.09
Farm to total population 1920	0.39	0.42	0.17	0.33	0.31	0.18

Note: A supportive state is defined as one for which at least 20 percent of its representatives voted yea, and no more than two-thirds nay on the December 1913 bill to establish federal deposit insurance (HR 7837). Other definitions are given in Tables 3.2 and 3.3. *Sources*: See Tables 3.2 and 3.3.

of the Federal Reserve System in 1913 would not have wanted its competitors who were Fed members to have access to federal insurance. The presence of state insurance, therefore, would reduce the incentives of small banks to lobby against the federal insurance plan, since state insurance offered a means to have insurance without joining the Fed. Indeed, as we discuss below, some small banks may have opposed federal deposit insurance in the 1930s initially because it did not extend membership to non-Fed members. Congressional supporters of rural unit banks eventually succeeded in the 1930s in opening up membership in the Federal Deposit Insurance Corporation (FDIC) to state banks that were not members of the Fed.[6]

[6] As a first attempt to test the importance of the Fed membership provision in limiting support for the legislation in the House, we compared the Fed membership ratios in 1919 of the "supporting" states with those of twenty-five other "similar" states with stronger voting opposition to insurance in 1913. Given the importance of bank size for the Fed membership decision, we controlled for this influence by excluding from the group of "similar" states the relatively large-bank, high-population density states of New York,

Thus far we have shown that prior to 1931 state support for federal deposit insurance legislation, measured either by the propensity to author legislation or to vote for it, was related to the benefits that a state could expect to receive from the legislation. Unit banking, small average bank size, and high rates of bank failure all were associated with support for legislation. Initially, support was not regionally concentrated, and not correlated with banking performance at the state level. But by the 1920s, many states that previously had been supportive of deposit insurance legislation changed course. They liberalized their branching laws, developed more concentrated and stable banking systems, and became opponents rather than supporters of national deposit insurance. The "stability gap" across states widened in the 1920s due to regionally concentrated depression in the agricultural sector, and to differences in branch-banking laws at the state level. These developments reduced the relative importance of within-state variation in the costs and benefits of deposit insurance and increased the across-state variation in the degree of support for deposit insurance. By the twentieth century, we find evidence consistent with the view that states that stood to benefit from the cross-subsidization of risk in a national deposit insurance plan supported legislation, while those that enjoyed relatively stable banking systems opposed it. The widening "stability gap" between unit and branch-banking systems during the 1920s made it unlikely that deposit insurance legislation would be passed in Congress.

In light of this evidence, which is consistent with the standard Olson-Stigler-Posner-Peltzman view of the role of special interest groups in pushing through legislation, the 1930s are a surprising aberration. According to the standard political-economy paradigm, declining power of special interests should result in the elimination of special interest regulations (or in this case, reductions in the probability of passage). By this logic, the continuing failure of unit banks in the early 1930s should have extended the trend toward bank consolidation. The continuing erosion

---

New Jersey, Delaware, and all New England. We also compared the group of twenty-five states with the eight supporting states that did not have state-level deposit insurance plans. If the Fed membership requirement was important for explaining opposition to the bill in the House on the part of some rural states, one should expect to find that Fed membership ratios were higher for the eight "supporting" states than for the rural states that strongly opposed federal legislation. The comparison may not be as relevant for the five supporting states with state-level insurance because small rural state banks in those states might not have been harmed as much by the membership limitation. Comparisons of means and medians between the eight noninsured "supporting" states and the twenty-five-state control group provided weak evidence in favor of the view that states with more banks that expected to remain outside the Fed system would have been more likely to oppose deposit insurance.

of the relative economic and political capital of unit bankers should have meant a further decline in the likelihood of federal deposit insurance.

Neither of these predictions was fulfilled. By late 1931, representatives of eastern states that had not supported deposit insurance for decades introduced federal deposit insurance bills. Many of these authors represented urban, not rural, constituencies. Federal banking legislation providing for deposit insurance passed by nearly unanimous consent in 1933. This and other federal legislation slowed or reversed the trends toward greater bank consolidation, expansion of branching, and expanded bank powers, all of which had been hailed as great progress in light of the bank failures of the 1920s. What explains this reversal in direction and the puzzling increase in the breadth of support for federal deposit insurance in the 1930s? The detailed narrative of the next section shows how events and political strategy by the proponents of federal deposit insurance turned the tide in favor of its passage.

3.3   The debate over federal deposit insurance during the depression

3.3.1   Bank distress, 1930–1932

Following the 1929 stock market crash, interest in bank reform, which had moved slowly in the twenties, stirred. In his December 1929 annual message to Congress, President Herbert Hoover called for Congress to establish a joint commission to consider banking reform. The House and the Senate ignored the president's request for a cooperative effort and passed resolutions to initiate their own investigations. However, 1930 was an election year and little was accomplished after Congress adjourned on 3 July (Burns 1974, pp. 7–9). The elections of 1930 split control of Congress, giving the Democrats control of the House. For deposit insurance's future, there was also a crucial change in the chairmanship of the House Banking and Currency Committee. The new Democratic chairman would have been Otis Wingo (D-AR), but his sudden death in 1930 allowed Henry B. Steagall (D-AL) to take control and alter the course of banking reform. A devoted follower of William Jennings Bryan, one of the first post-Civil War proponents of deposit insurance, Steagall had already introduced bills for deposit insurance in 1925, 1926, and 1928. Although Wingo's position on deposit insurance is unclear, he never authored a bill. Wingo and Steagall agreed on most issues and fought hard to contain branch banking, but they approached the problem differently. In the struggle over the McFadden Act in 1926–27, Wingo was willing to compromise to place new limits on branching, whereas Steagall demanded that branching be eliminated entirely.[7] For Steagall, deposit insurance was essential to the survival of unit banks; the House committee now had a chairman whose position on deposit insurance was unyielding and who would use the power of his office to secure it.

The many bank failures of late 1930 pushed the issue of banking reform to the fore and led President Hoover and Congress in January 1931 to consider establishing the Reconstruction Finance Corporation (RFC) to support smaller banks and financial institutions. Congress and the President did not immediately act. Hoover organized a series of meetings with bankers and businessmen in October 1931, which resulted in the establishment of the National Credit Corporation. Through this private corporation, banks pooled funds to lend to weak banks on assets not eligible for discount at the Federal Reserve banks. Although $500 million in funds was made available, the corporation had only lent out $155 million to 575 banks by the end of the year (Burns 1974, pp. 14–15; Upham and Lamke 1934, p. 7; Jones 1951, p. 14).

The rise in bank failures beginning in late 1930 spurred congressional action on two fronts to increase bank liquidity. First, Congress passed the Glass Steagall Act of 1931, which liberalized the Federal Reserve's discounting rules as of 21 February 1932. Second, Congress passed the Reconstruction Finance Corporation Act on 22 January 1932. The RFC was authorized to make collateralized loans to financial institutions for up to three years. The RFC moved faster than its private predecessor. By the end of the first quarter of 1932, it had disbursed $124 million, and by 31 December it had provided 7,880 loans totaling $810 million. In addition to improving the liquidity of open banks, the RFC was empowered to make loans to closed banks to speed the process of liquidation and repayment of depositors. During 1932, the RFC disbursed $42 million in loans to closed banks (Upham and Lamke 1934, pp. 145–87). Thus the RFC improved the confidence of depositors in open banks and the pace of payment to depositors in suspended banks. These actions indirectly reduced the demand for deposit insurance.

While these two acts of Congress may have alleviated some pressures on the banks, and some analysts concluded that the RFC helped to arrest the number of suspensions (Upham and Lamke 1934, pp. 150–51), bank failures continued at an alarmingly high level. But the RFC could not combat the effects of the Federal Reserve's persistently deflationary policy. The decline in bank failures was assisted by the Federal Reserve's open market purchase of $1 billion from April to July 1932, a policy that

---

[7] See the *Congressional Record* 1926, pp. 2854, 3226–27.

Friedman and Schwartz (1963, pp. 347–48) have emphasized was not continued after Congress adjourned.

Pressure on banks continued unabated, as all banks could not qualify for RFC assistance. As in previous financial crises, locally declared moratoria and holidays were used to offer banks protection from anxious depositors. Oregon acted first in 1930, passing a law that allowed banks to suspend payments for sixty days, during which they were to arrange for longer voluntary restrictions with depositors. In 1931, Florida banks were granted the power to restrict withdrawals to 20 percent of deposits. By mid-1932, Massachusetts, Michigan, and Virginia adopted similar laws. As the crisis deepened in 1932, mayors in small towns and cities in the Midwest declared holidays when restriction on withdrawals were set in place. The Indiana Commission for Financial Institutions surveyed the number of banks restricting payment as of May 1932. Replies were obtained from thirty-five states that indicated that 658 banks in their jurisdiction had restricted payments, a number that certainly understates the total (Upham and Lamke 1934, pp. 11–13).

3.3.2   Initial attempts at insurance and the deepening banking crisis

The number of bills submitted to both the House and Senate for deposit insurance began to rise in late 1931. In the 71st Congress (April 1929–March 1931), six bills were submitted to the House of Representatives, where they died in committee. Between the opening of the first session of the 72d Congress in December 1931 and its closure in July 1932, five bills were submitted to the Senate and fifteen to the House of Representatives. The only bill to leave committee was Steagall's second bill introduced on 14 April 1932. The House passed the bill quickly on 27 May 1932, when, after a voice vote, it was given unanimous assent. Despite this success, the bill died in the Senate Banking and Currency Committee, where Senator Glass, an adamant opponent of deposit insurance, held sway. Pushing his own panacea, the separation of commercial and investment banking, Glass sponsored banking reform bills that made no progress in Congress, especially the House, where there was strong sentiment for some form of deposit insurance. By the end of the year, Glass would not accede to deposit insurance, but he did include a provision for a Liquidation Corporation to speed up the liquidation of failed banks (Burns 1974, p. 25).

An impasse had been reached in Congress where Congressman Steagall would not agree to any bill that failed to include deposit insurance, and Senator Glass would not consent to any bill that included it. There was little in the elections of 1932 to encourage the supporters of deposit insurance. Sensing victory in the elections, the Democratic Party adopted several planks on bank reform, but these all bore the imprimatur of Senator Glass. The party called for quicker methods of realizing on assets for the relief of deposits in suspended banks, more rigid supervision to protect deposits, and the separation of commercial and investment banking. Roosevelt supported these planks and took Glass's side. The presidential candidate was himself strongly opposed to the idea of guaranteeing deposits (Burns 1974, pp. 22–24). Clearly, the Democratic landslide did not make the adoption of deposit insurance certain.

The banking situation continued to deteriorate in late 1932. The most important source of trouble, the continued deflationary monetary policy, was not reversed. In addition, the effectiveness of the RFC may have been compromised. In July 1932, Congress required that the names of banks receiving RFC loans be published beginning in August. Banks may have feared damage to their reputation or a run if they borrowed from the RFC. The problem became worse when, in January 1933, after a House resolution, the RFC made public all loans extended before 1933. Although the law only required reports to be made to the President and the Congress, the Speaker of the House, John Nance Garner, instructed the clerk to make the reports public on the grounds that they wanted to prevent favoritism in the loans. Availability of funds was not reduced, but new loans to open banks in the fourth quarter of 1932 were smaller than in any of the previous three quarters (Friedman and Schwartz 1963, 325; Upham and Lamke 1934, p. 148).

As more banks failed, the crisis in the payments systems intensified. Restrictions on withdrawals that had been local or voluntary proved insufficient. The first state banking holiday was declared in Nevada on 31 October 1932, when runs on individual banks threatened to involve the whole state. This holiday was originally set for a twelve-day period but was subsequently extended (Friedman and Schwartz 1963, p. 429). Iowa declared a holiday on 20 January 1933, and Louisiana declared a holiday to help the banks in New Orleans on 3 February. Grave banking problems spread to the industrial Midwest. The Detroit banks were on the verge of collapse with over a million depositors, and Michigan declared a bank holiday 14 February. In the second week of the holiday, depositors were permitted to draw out only 5 percent of their balances. In Cleveland, all but one bank suspended payments on 27 February, restricting withdrawals to under 5 percent (Jones 1951, pp. 69–70). Even when the RFC stepped in, it could not halt suspensions. By July 1932, sixty-five Chicago banks had obtained RFC loans, but by February 1933 only eighteen remained open (Upham and Lamke 1934, p. 156). Declarations of holidays and moratoria picked up momentum. By 3 March, holidays limiting withdrawals had been declared by executive order or legislation in thirty-six states. On 4 March, the banking-center states of Illinois, Pennsylvania, New York, and Massachusetts were among six more states that declared holidays (Patrick 1993, p. 132).

The holidays increased withdrawal pressures on banks in other states, especially on the New York City banks. There was also fear of a run on the dollar, as many believed the new administration would devalue the dollar (Wigmore 1987). The Federal Reserve responded by raising discount rates in February 1933, and it failed to offset this contractionary move, scarcely increasing its total holdings of government securities (Friedman and Schwartz 1963, p. 326).

3.3.3   The national banking holiday, RFC policy, and the rejection of a bailout

In this crisis atmosphere, Franklin D. Roosevelt immediately ordered the suspension of all banking transactions on 6 March 1933. Transactions were suspended for a period of four days, during which banks could make change, cash government checks, and conduct other activities where no cash payment was required. The President's authority for this action was based on the Trading with the Enemy Act, but he sought specific authority from Congress as soon as it reopened on 9 March 1933. Within an hour of its receipt, Congress passed the Emergency Bank Act, which confirmed the proclamation of 6 March and gave the President and the Secretary of the Treasury the authority to regulate the business of banks during any such emergency period as the President might designate. The President issued a proclamation on 9 March extending the previous proclamation until further notice. The next day an executive order authorized the Secretary of the Treasury and the supervisory authorities in each state to permit the opening of banks after they obtained a license either from the Secretary or from the state supervisory authority if they were not Fed members. On 11 March, Roosevelt announced a schedule for reopening the commercial banks. Licensed member banks in the twelve Federal Reserve Bank cities could open on 13 March. Licensed member banks in 250 cities with clearinghouse associations could open on 14 March, and all other licensed member banks could open on 15 March. The schedule for opening nonmember state banks was left to the discretion of state banking authorities.

Although most banks were reopened, a significant fraction of the industry remained shut down. At the end of 1932, two months before the banking holiday, there were 17,796 active commercial banks in operation with $28.2 billion in deposits (seasonally adjusted). Between 31

December 1932 and 15 March 1933, 447 banks were suspended, merged, or liquidated. When the holiday ended, the 11,878 licensed banks had $27.4 billion in deposits on 14 March 1933 while the 5,430 unlicensed banks held $4.5 billion. The unlicensed banks included 1,621 Fed member banks and 3,709 nonmember banks with $2.9 and $1.6 billion in deposits, respectively. The unlicensed banks were left in limbo to be opened later or finally closed (Friedman and Schwartz 1963, pp. 421–27. and Tables 13 and 14). Their depositors had only extremely limited access to funds – 5 percent of their total deposits (Upham and Lamke 1934, p. 5). The decline in deposits was tied to the closing of banks. Between December 1932 and 15 March 1933, deposits in banks open for business fell by one-sixth, and 70 percent of this decline was accounted for by the deposits on the books of banks not licensed to open (Friedman and Schwartz 1963, pp. 426–28).[8]

The licensing process was not very rapid. Between 15 March and 30 June, the number of unlicensed banks fell from 5,430 to 3,078, reducing the deposits in suspended banks from $4.5 billion to $2.2 billion. Of the 2,352 banks processed, 1,964 banks with deposits of $642 million were reopened, and 388 banks with deposits of $1,189 million were suspended, liquidated, or merged. By 30 December 1934, there were still 1,769 unlicensed banks with $1 billion in deposits, and it took until December 1936 to dispose of these institutions. Overall, of the banks unlicensed on 15 March 1933, 3,298 reopened for business with $1.5 billion in deposits, while 2,132 with deposits of $2.5 billion were closed or merged.

The RFC seems to have played a modest role in stabilizing the banking system. The banks that were immediately opened were very strong and required little assistance. In fact, RFC outstanding loans to open banks declined continuously from $677 million at the end of the first quarter of 1933 to $462 million by the end of the year, and its purchases of capital obligations remained small until December 1933 (Upham and Lamke 1934, pp. 149, 188–206). The RFC shifted its activity to providing capital for the reopening of weak banks and making loans to speed up the process of liquidating insolvent banks.[9]

---

[8] Friedman and Schwartz (1963, pp. 328–30) have thus argued that the banking holiday was far more restrictive than any of the earlier suspensions as far back as 1814. Banks had not been closed down entirely for a day, but now they were closed for a minimum of six business days. In the earlier episodes, banks had continued most activities except the unlimited payment of deposits on demand, and sometimes were able to expand loans under these circumstances. In 1933, access to all deposits was denied. Friedman and Schwartz conclude that "the 'cure' was close to being worse than the disease" (p. 330).

[9] The RFC was financed by the Treasury. By 30 June 1934, the Treasury had subscribed to $50 million of the RFC's capital and bought $3.3 billion of its notes, bearing interest ranging from 1/8 to 3 percent (Upham and Lamke 1934, pp. 229–32).

The RFC Act had given authority to the corporation to make loans to closed banks for liquidation or reorganization, and empowered receivers to borrow from the corporation, setting a ceiling of $200 million on these types of loans. Loans were offered on the estimated recovery from pledged assets. Loans outstanding for this purpose rose from $48 million at the end of the first quarter 1933 to $100 million by the end of the second quarter. In June, the ceiling was lifted, and by the end of the year loans totaled $292 million (Upham and Lamke 1934, pp. 162–87). These loans were intended to speed up the process of paying out depositors of closed institutions.

There were attempts to force the RFC to liberalize its loan procedure. Numerous bills were introduced to Congress to provide for partial or complete payoff of bank depositors. Representatives from Michigan and Ohio, where some of the largest banks had been closed, pushed for this legislation. The most active sponsor of these proposals was Representative Clarence J. McLeod of Michigan. His first bill, introduced on 13 April 1933, mandated the RFC to loan 70 percent of the book value of bank assets. In the next session of Congress, McLeod introduced a bill to purchase all assets of closed national banks at a price sufficient to pay all depositors in full and liquidate the assets over a ten-year period. The 73d Congress was pressed to pass a new McLeod bill, lobbied by the Hearst newspapers and the governors of several states. While President Roosevelt opposed these measures, Speaker Rainey, Majority Leader Burns, and Chairman Steagall were reportedly in favor of some form of payoff. Finally, in May 1934, 119 members of the House signed a petition to force the bill to a vote (53 Democrats, 61 Republicans, and 5 Farmer-Laborites). Testifying against this proposal in the House Banking Committee, the Secretary of the Treasury estimated that a payoff of deposits of $2,500 or less in banks that had failed since 1 January 1930 would cost the Treasury over $1 billion (Upham and Lamke 1934, pp. 181–87). The bill failed to win passage. Thus, while Congress would become willing in mid-1933 to vote for deposit insurance, it was never willing to countenance a bailout.

3.3.4   How federal deposit insurance was won

While Congress rejected a bailout of depositors, a battle ensued over whether deposit insurance would be included in a reform bill. Flood's (1991) survey of the contemporary deposit insurance debate reveals that it was extremely well informed and considered all the issues that are today believed to be pertinent to deposit insurance. This is not surprising in light of the collapses of state deposit insurance systems in the

1920s, which had been observed and commented upon frequently. Indeed, the American Bankers Association (1933) provided a detailed quantitative analysis of the state insurance system failures as part of its campaign against federal deposit insurance. Opponents of deposit insurance used this evidence as an example of the moral-hazard costs of providing government guarantees to depositors.

Proponents of deposit insurance did not try to dismiss the potential importance of such costs. Rather, they argued that deposit insurance could avoid moral-hazard costs if properly designed. Furthermore, they argued that deposit insurance was necessary and fair. Supporters of deposit insurance argued it was a matter of simple justice that depositors not be forced to bear the losses from bankers' mistakes or folly. On the other side, bankers argued that it was unjust for well-managed banks to subsidize poorly run banks. The president of the American Bankers Association pointed out that deposit insurance would mean a net transfer from big banks, where most deposits were, to smaller state-chartered banks, where most of the losses were. The money center banks all emphasized that it was not an actuarially sound insurance plan, as premiums were not set by exposure to risk.

The character of the bank failures of the 1930s and the widespread losses suffered by depositors throughout the country were a new and important ingredient in the political debate after 1932. Figure 3.1 reports data on the number of failing national banks, and Figure 3.2 shows the percentage of proven claims paid one, two, and three years after national banks were placed in receivership. From 1929 to 1933, as the number of banks failing increased, the percentage of deposit claims recovered fell dramatically. In prior decades, bank failures had sometimes been numerous, but never had there been so many bank failures at such high cost, and never had this cost been so dispersed throughout the country. In the recession of 1920–21, there were large losses for the relatively few banks that failed. In the 1920s, the number of failures rose, but recoveries were fairly high, and losses were concentrated in a few states. But in the 1930s, failures rose and recoveries fell; few people in the country did not know someone who had lost substantial wealth as the result of the banking collapse. Thus the expected value of a dollar deposit fell precipitously.

The severity of these costs, however, by itself was not enough to produce success for the proponents of deposit insurance. Even after the banking crisis of 1933, there still was formidable opposition to deposit insurance. President Roosevelt, Secretary of the Treasury Woodin, Senator Carter Glass, the American Bankers Association, and the Association of Reserve City Bankers all remained opposed to deposit insurance. While not offering any formal position, the leading officials of the

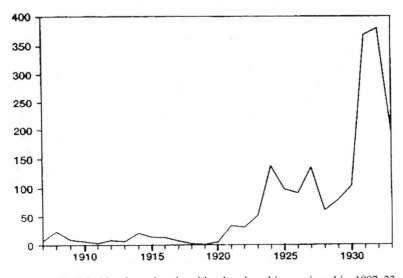

Fig. 3.1. Number of national banks placed in receivership, 1907–33.
Source: Comptroller of the Currency 1907–36.
Note: The data for 1933 cover the period from 1 January to 31 August.

Federal Reserve did not favor insurance. On the other side, Vice President John Nance Garner, Jesse Jones of the RFC, and Chairman Steagall favored deposit insurance.

Perhaps most important, the severity of losses during the early 1930s changed the *location* of the debate over deposit insurance. For decades, deposit insurance had been one of the hundreds of issues coming before Congress repeatedly. Like most others, it received relatively little attention from the general public, and its fate was determined by the relative weights of special interests measured on hidden scales in smoke-filled rooms. The banking crisis had the attention of the public, and the costs of the crisis were one of the major public concerns of the time. The debate over banking reform thus moved from the smoke-filled room to the theater of public debate. Once it became a focal issue of relevance for the election of 1934, the contest between proponents and opponents became a struggle for the hearts and minds of the public. Public support would be courted, and public support – not just special interests – would govern congressional voting.

Public attitudes were shaped in part by events and debates of the 1930s other than those that pertained directly to deposit insurance. People's perceptions of banks had been changed by the events of the Great Depression, and the way those events were interpreted at the time. In

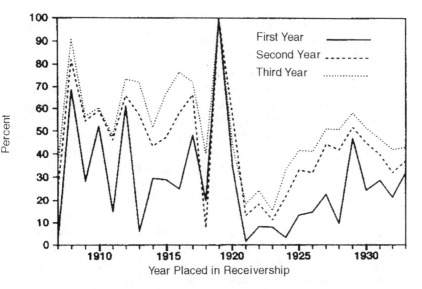

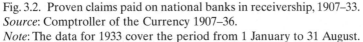

Fig. 3.2. Proven claims paid on national banks in receivership, 1907–33.
Source: Comptroller of the Currency 1907–36.
Note: The data for 1933 cover the period from 1 January to 31 August.

particular, many influential contemporaries were arguing that banks
were the perpetrators rather than the victims of the Great Depression.
Bankers were sometimes referred to as gambling "banksters" in the
popular press. Some critics of banks argued simply that bankers were to
blame because depositors placed funds with bankers for safekeeping,
and such funds should not have been risked at the depositors' expense.
By 1933, it had become commonplace to blame the stock market crash
and the Depression on the recklessness and greed of large, reserve-
center banks. The press and the Pecora hearings blamed the speculative
excesses of the 1920s on the big-city bankers, depicting the depositor –
and to some extent the bank shareholder – as a victim of bankers'
greed.[10] The Pecora hearings, which were widely covered in the press.
involved little evidence or systematic discussion, and their conclusions

[10] Stockholders of national banks were liable for extended (double) liability on their
capital contributions in the event of asset shortfall when the bank failed. Double liability was repealed for new national bank share issues in 1933. and for all outstanding issues
in 1935 (Macey and Miller 1992, p. 38). The earlier repeal of double liability for new
shares reflected the perceived need to spur new investment to replenish bank capital
stock. But the repeal of double liability for bank stockholders reflected other currents
of thought that also favored federal deposit insurance. Prior to the 1930s, extended liability of shareholders was deemed an adequate means of protecting depositors, and there

have been questioned by subsequent scholarship (White 1986; Benston 1989; Kroszner and Rajan 1994). The hearings provided scapegoats for the financial collapse of 1929–33 and a springboard for new regulation.

The challenge for Steagall and his allies was to break the deadlock with Glass by wooing the public, and by offering Glass something he wanted – namely, the separation of commercial and investment banking. Steagall's strategy for winning the public debate was to respond to the actuarial and fairness concerns of critics of deposit insurance, while stressing the evils of large-scale banking and the unfairness of making depositors pay for bankers' errors. Steagall responded to critics by emphasizing that his system would only cover the small depositor because of the ceilings on deposits insured. The actual ceiling set in 1933 for insured deposits of $2,500 covered 97 percent of depositors and 24 percent of deposits (Board of Governors 1933, p. 414). Moreover, his bill provided for less than 100 percent coverage even of small deposits, which he argued would reduce problems of moral hazard. Finally, in comparison to the state systems, a federal system with its broader geographic coverage (including industrial areas) would diversify and strengthen the plan.

Steagall also wanted to allow membership in the insured system for state banks who were not members of the Federal Reserve System. As Keeton (1990, p. 31) points out, this may have been a crucial ingredient for receiving support from small rural banks who were not members of the Fed. Many of these banks earlier had joined forces with big-city banks to oppose deposit insurance legislation. Apparently, for many small, rural banks, the value of the cross-bank subsidy from flat-rate federal deposit insurance was not as great as the costs of complying with Fed regulations, and so their support for insurance hinged on allowing state nonmember banks to join.

On 11 March, Glass introduced a bill that was very similar to his previous bank reform bill – once again, without deposit insurance. The President called a White House conference attended by Treasury officials, representatives of the Federal Reserve Board, and Senator Glass. Working on the basis of the Glass bill, there were further conferences

was little concern for shareholders, possibly because bank shares (like other stock) were much more closely held prior to the mid-1920s. In the 1930s, bank stockholders' losses were large (with recoveries totaling roughly half their capital contributions to the bank), and these losses did not prevent the collapse of the banking system or large losses to depositors (Macey and Miller 1992, p. 34). Stockholders, who by now tended to be largely firm "outsiders" were viewed as innocent victims of bank management. Thus the double-liability provision was deemed both unfair and ineffectual in limiting bank runs by the mid-1930s (Macey and Miller 1992, pp. 34–38).

and consultations for the next six weeks, with Glass a frequent visitor. Senator Duncan Fletcher, chairman of the Banking and Currency Committee, and Steagall were also polled (Burns 1974, p. 80). The most hotly contested issue was deposit insurance, which neither the President nor Glass wanted included in the bill. But congressional pressure was building. Twenty-five Democratic house members signed a petition in support of a guarantee in early March (Burns 1974, pp. 89–90). Key legislators, like Senator Arthur Vandenberg (R-ML), became outspoken insurance advocates after local bank failures generated enormous constituent pressure.[11] Patrick (1993, p. 176) argues that mounting public pressure in support of deposit insurance at this juncture partly reflected anti-big-bank sentiment due to the coincident resumption of the Pecora hearings, with testimony from J. P. Morgan and George Whitney that made front-page news. Glass reportedly told the White House that, if insurance was not put into the administration bill, Congress would include it anyway. Glass reportedly yielded to public opinion because "Washington does not remember any issue on which the sentiment of the country has been so undivided or so emphatically expressed as upon this."[12]

In mid-May, Glass and Steagall each introduced their own bills with changes in the structure of the Federal Reserve, separation of commercial and investment banking, equal branching rights for national banks (which had more limited rights than state banks), and a plan for the creation of the FDIC (Burns 1974, p. 81). Both bills included specifications made by the Roosevelt Administration that deposit coverage be based on a sliding scale and that there be a one-year delay in the start of the insurance corporation. Accounts were to be 100 percent insured up to $10,000, 75 percent for deposits between $10,000 and $50,000, and 50 percent for funds in excess of $50,000. Deposit insurance was to be financed by assessments levied on banks, the Federal Reserve Banks, and $150 million from the Treasury. It would begin on 1 July 1934 (Burns 1974, p. 90).

Glass's original bill required all FDIC member banks to join the Federal Reserve, but he was blocked by a coalition led by Steagall in the

[11] The large bank failures of Detroit had converted Vandenberg into a supporter of deposit insurance. His switch reveals a response to the more general interests of his constituents rather than the special interests of bankers. He had come on board Steagall's ship, but he did not change his basic beliefs. In his testimony on the Federal Deposit Insurance Act of 1950, he opposed raising the insurance limit from $5,000 to $10,000 because "there is no general public demand for this increased coverage. It is chiefly requested by banker demand in some quarters for increased competitive advantage in bidding for deposits" (Senate 1950, pp. 50–51).

[12] "Deposit Insurance." *Business Week.* 12 April 1933, 3.

House and Huey Long in the Senate, joined by Senator Vandenberg, who feared this would end state-chartered banking. Long, who had blocked Glass's bill in the previous Congress with a ten-day filibuster, virulently opposed Glass's branching provisions. Long and Steagall extolled deposit insurance as a means of survival for the small banks and the dual banking system (Flood 1991, pp. 51–52). Eager for a bill to separate commercial and investment banking, Glass finally agreed to support deposit guarantee and the coverage of nonmember banks in exchange for more Federal Reserve authority. The prohibition of interest payments on deposits appears to have been another part of this elaborately crafted compromise. Glass argued that the pro- hibition of interest was necessary to reduce the flow of inter- bank deposits to reserve centers, where funds were often invested in securities. Consistent with his desire to break the link between commercial and investment banking, Glass viewed the investment of interbank deposits in the securities market as a destabilizing influence on banks.[13]

This carefully crafted compromise bill reflected the tenuous balance of power between the dominant factions in the House and Senate. However, in a maneuver reflecting the ability of individuals to use congressional rules to alter the balance of power, the bill was radically amended by a proposal of Senator Vandenberg. His amendment proposed to create a temporary deposit insurance fund, thereby offering deposit insurance more quickly. The amendment of the bill was engineered by Vice President Garner, who was presiding over the Senate, while it sat as a court of impeachment in the trial of a district judge. In a surprise move that enabled him to seize control of the agenda, Garner temporarily suspended the court proceedings and ordered the Senate into regular session to consider the amendment presented by Vandenberg. The amendment – establishing a temporary fund effective 1 January 1934 to provide 100 percent coverage up to $2,500 for each depositor until a permanent corporation began operation on 1 July 1934 – was overwhelmingly adopted (Federal Deposit Insurance Corporation 1984, pp. 41–43). The bill was almost derailed in a joint con- ference committee on 12 June, but survived to pass both houses of

---

[13] Golembe (1975, p. 64) rejects Glass's stated motivation for restriction of interest rates on deposits and argues that interest rate restrictions were simply a payoff to big banks to reduce their opposition to the Banking Act of 1933. Golembe provides no evidence in support of this interpretation. Moreover, big banks continued to devote energy to overturning deposit insurance during and after the inclusion of a provision for an inter- est rate ceiling, so it is hard to see any effect of interest rate restrictions on big bankers' willingness to accept deposit insurance.

Congress the next day. Glass was forced to make another concession and permit nonmember banks to join under the amendment's terms. The American Bankers Association urged its members to telegraph the President to veto the bill. Although the President was opposed to the Vandenberg amendment, Glass warned him not to delay, and Roosevelt signed the Banking Act of 1933 on 16 June 1933.

Under the provisions of the Banking Act, the Temporary Deposit Insurance Fund would begin operations on 1 January 1934. Only those banks certified as sound could qualify for insurance (Burns 1974, p. 120). The capital required to establish the FDIC was contributed by the Treasury and the twelve Federal Reserve banks. Banks joining the FDIC were assessed 0.5 percent of insurable deposits, of which one-half was payable immediately and the remainder on call. All Federal Reserve member banks were required to join the FDIC; other licensed banks could receive FDIC protection upon approval of the FDIC so long as they became Fed members within two years.

Throughout 1933, many banks still were adamant in their opposition to insurance. The American Bankers Association at its annual meeting adopted a resolution to recommend that the Administration postpone initiation of deposit insurance (Burns 1974, p. 125). They hoped that Congress would reconvene and make some adjustment, but they were sorely disappointed. When the Temporary Deposit Insurance Fund was given a one-year extension in 1934 and permanent deposit insurance was postponed, Steagall pushed his agenda further. Steagall wanted to increase the deposit coverage from $2,500 to $10,000. Although Roosevelt opposed this change and pointed out that 97 percent of depositors already were protected, Congress followed Steagall's lead and set the account limit at $5,000 (Burns 1974, pp. 127–28). In addition, compulsory membership in the Fed was postponed from 1 July 1936 until 1 July 1937. Bankers gradually gave up their opposition and accepted that deposit insurance would remain in place (Burns 1974, p. 129).

The temporary system was extended to 1 July 1935 by an amendment in 1934, and to 31 August 1935 by a congressional resolution signed by the President. On 23 August, 1935, the permanent system finally became effective under Title 1 of the Banking Act of 1935, which created the FDIC and superseded the original permanent plan, liberalizing many of its provisions. All members of the Federal Reserve System were required to insure their deposits with the FDIC. Nonmember banks with less than $1 million in deposits could obtain insurance upon approval of the FDIC, but were required to submit to examination by the FDIC. The insurance limit was set at $5,000 for each depositor. Insured banks were charged a premium of one-twelfth of 1 percent of their deposits payable semian-nually. This was a substantial reduction from 0.5 percent, half of which was paid to the temporary fund, which was returned to banks upon its closure.

3.3.5   *Winners, losers, and political entrepreneurs*

By 1935, it had become clear who had won and who had lost from the provisions of the permanent deposit insurance plan. Small, rural banks, and lower-income individuals (with small deposit accounts) were clear winners, while large, big-city banks, wealthy depositors, and depositors in failed banks were the losers. Depositors of relatively stable urban banks effectively subsidized the deposits in less stable rural banks. Under the 1935 law, wealthy depositors contributed premiums as a fraction of all their deposits (through their banks), but only received protection on deposits up to $5,000, providing an effective subsidy from the rich to the poor. Depositors in failed banks were not bailed out despite the strenu-ous efforts by some congressmen on their behalf. Furthermore, the pres-ence of deposit insurance removed one of the main motivations for allowing further consolidation and branching in banking, which would have mainly benefited larger banks. Small, rural banks now had access to federal government insurance at low cost. In particular, access to federal insurance did not require small banks to pay the high regulatory cost of joining the Fed, and insurance protected virtually all of their deposits.

Some who benefited most from federal deposit insurance – small depositors and small, rural banks – were not very visible advocates of insurance from the beginning of the insurance debate. As Keeton (1990) points out, not all small, rural banks supported deposit insurance, as some insurance plans would have created more costs than benefits for small banks. In particular, small banks were concerned that Fed membership might be a requirement for deposit insurance, or that the fee structure of deposit insurance might be designed in a way that would put them at a disadvantage. Similarly, the gains small depositors received did not reflect any initial active lobbying effort on their part, although their voice was clearly heard after the banking crises. Small depositors were not a well-organized, coordinated special interest pushing for legislation to create a transfer of resources from the rich to the poor. The public's role was important, but it was not the initiator of the legislation. The public reacted to overtures by congressional advocates of deposit insurance who sought to use public support as a lever against their opponents in Congress.

Without the "political entrepreneurship" of Steagall and others, the beneficiaries of deposit insurance would not have played an important role in influencing legislation. Steagall, Long, and other politicians with populist constituencies made deposit insurance a focal issue, and thus made public opinion an important ingredient in the outcome. They also shepherded bills through Congress, making sure the details of the bills (premiums, membership limitations, deposit coverage) would protect the interests of small, unit banks, and they knew that these banks would be grateful for the help, even if they had not pushed for it. In the Olson-Stigler-Posner-Peltzman view of the political economy of regulation, rent-seeking special interest groups typically are identified as the political entrepreneurs who define which issues are important and push for their passage. In the case of federal deposit insurance, entrepreneurial politicians defined an issue they thought would be beneficial to their constituents, structured the forum in which it would be debated to serve their purposes, and organized constituent support for their proposals.

3.4   Lessons for models of political economy

What general lessons for the political economy of regulation can be culled from the fifty-year struggle over federal deposit insurance? We would emphasize three general caveats to the standard Olson-Stigler-Posner-Peltzman view that rent-seeking special interests define and determine regulatory outcomes.

First, there is more than one theater of action in the political process. If the proponents of regulation can succeed in drawing sufficient public attention to their issue, then politicians will respond to public pressure, not just to special interests. Second, influential politicians, not just special interests, may be instigators of regulation and may play an especially important role in determining which issues become "focal" to the general public, and in winning public support. Third, while public opinion may have been somewhat informed, it is not likely that the public anticipated all the changes wrought by its support for federal deposit insurance. Furthermore, once public support had been won during the debate of 1932–34, the theater of debate predictably shifted back to the smoke-filled room as the attention of the public moved on to other issues. After the hurdle of establishing deposit insurance had been cleared and the public was no longer easily mobilized, the special interests within banking struggled among themselves over changes in the law. The Federal Deposit Insurance Act of 1950 was a compromise that offered something to all banks and looks more like a creature of the Olson-Stigler-Posner-Peltzman paradigm. The act increased the insurance limit, as desired by small banks, and introduced a scheme for a partial rebating of assessments that pleased large banks. Once unit bankers had been given a new lease on life by deposit insurance, they were able to exert influence over other regulation, as well. Progress in permitting expanded scope and scale of banking was stalled.[14]

It is interesting to contrast the deposit insurance debate of the 1930s with that of the 1990s. Deposit insurance reform to protect the interest of the taxpayers has fallen far short of the ambitious plans outlined by many would-be reformers. In part, this seems due to the fact that the issue simply has not captured the imagination of the population, even in the face of a $200 billion loss in the savings and loan industry, and the possibility of large losses to the FDIC. It was hardly mentioned in the election of 1992. Why has no political entrepreneur in the House or Senate come forward as Steagall did, with a bold plan to make reform a focal issue in the public eye? One possible explanation is that hard-headed economic arguments about incentives do not play as well in the public theater as soft-hearted populist arguments about fairness. Another explanation is that politicians do not see big benefits for their most influential constituencies from supporting a major reform. No political entrepreneur has yet appeared who can assemble a powerful enough coalition to upset the existing balance of special interests.

---

[14] For a discussion of the political and regulatory reversal of interest in expansion of branching after 1933, see Doti and Schweikart (1991).

Table 3.A1. *Characteristics of authors of federal deposit insurance bills and amendments*

Item	Intro date	Cong.	Title	Author	Party -state	City district[a]	Type[b]	Banks covered in bills provisions
1	1886/1/11	49th	Rep.	Price	R-WI		B	National
2	1886/2/1	49th	Rep	Sawyer	R-NY		B	National
3	1886/2/15	49th	Rep.	Hutton[c]	D-MO		B	National
4	1886/3/1	49th	Rep.	Brumm	R-PA		B	National
5	1888/1/4	50th	Rep.	Brumm	R-PA		B	National
6	1891/12/10	52nd	Sen.	Hiscock[c]	R-NY		B	National
7	1892/3/23	52nd	Rep.	Clover	O-KS		G	National
8	1893/8/14	53rd	Sen.	Hunton	D-VA		G	National
9	1893/9/9	53rd	Rep.	Babcock	R-WI		B	National
10	1893/9/22	53rd	Rep.	Bryan	D-NE		B	National
11	1894/3/26	53rd	Rep.	Mercer	R-NE	Omaha	B	National
12	1895/1/3	53rd	Sen.	George	D-MS		G	National
13	1897/1/5	54th	Sen.	Peffer	O-KS		G	National
14	1897/3/15	55th	Rep.	Fowler[c]	R-NJ		B	National and state
15	1897/7/15	55th	Rep.	Lewis	D-WA		G	National
16	1897/7/15	55th	Rep.	Jenkins	R-WI		G	National
17	1898/1/5	55th	Rep.	Jenkins	R-WI		B	National
18	1898/2/1	55th	Rep.	Fowler[c]	R-NJ		B	National
19	1905/2/27	58th	Rep.	Webber	R-OH		G	National
20	1905/12/4	59th	Rep.	Bates	R-PA		B	National
21	1906/1/19	59th	Rep.	Bates	R-PA		B	National
22	1906/2/14	59th	Rep.	Bates	R-PA		B	National
23	1906/3/5	59th	Rep.	Gronna	R-ND		B	National
24	1906/12/13	59th	Rep.	Underwood	D-AL		B	National
25	1906/12/17	59th	Rep.	Bates	R-PA		B	National
26	1907/12/12	60th	Rep.	Candler	D-MS		B	National
27	1907/12/2	60th	Rep.	Norris	R-NE		B	National
28	1907/12/2	60th	Rep.	Sheppard	D-TX		B	National

Table 3.A1. *(cont.)*

Item	Intro date	Cong.	Title	Author	Party-state	City district[a]	Type[b]	Banks covered in bills provisions
29	1907/12/2	60th	Rep.	Russell	D-TX		B	National
30	1907/12/2	60th	Rep.	Gronna	R-ND		B	National
31	1907/12/2	60th	Rep.	Underwood	D-AL		B	National
32	1907/12/2	60th	Rep.	Bates	R-PA		B	National
33	1907/12/16	60th	Rep.	Campbell	R-KS		G	National
34	1907/12/16	60th	Rep.	Reeder	R-KS		B	National
35	1907/12/19	60th	Rep.	Chaney	R-IN		B	National
36	1907/12/19	60th	Rep.	Underwood	D-AL		B	National
37	1907/12/21	60th	Sen.	Owen	D-OK		B	National
38	1908/1/6	60th	Rep.	Hinshaw	R-NE		B	National
39	1908/1/6	60th	Rep.	DeArmond	D-MO		B	National
40	1908/1/8	60th	Sen.	Culberson	D-TX		B	National
41	1908/1/7	60th	Sen.	Brown	R-NE		B	National
42	1908/1/8	60th	Rep.	Fulton	D-OK		B	National
43	1908/1/8	60th	Rep.	Fowler[d]	R-NJ		B	National
44	1908/1/8	60th	Rep.	Davidson	R-WI		B	National
45	1908/1/8	60th	Rep.	McHenry[c]	D-PA		G	National and state
46	1908/1/9	60th	Sen.	Nelson	R-MN		B	National
47	1908/1/14	60th	Rep.	Adair	D-IN		B	National
48	1908/1/15	60th	Sen.	Owen	D-OK		B	National
49	1908/1/27	60th	Rep.	Bates	R-PA		B	National
50	1908/1/27	60th	Sen.	Gore	D-OK		B	National
51	1908/1/30	60th	Rep.	Crawford[c]	D-NC		G	National and state
52	1908/2/7	60th	Rep.	Williams	D-MS		B	National and state
53	1908/2/12	60th	Sen.	Owen	D-OK		B	National
54	1908/2/17	60th	Sen.	Brown	R-NE		B	National
55	1908/3/15	60th	Sen.	McCumber	R-ND		B	National
56	1908/3/13	60th	Sen.	Nelson	R-MN		B	National

204

	Date	Congress	Chamber	Name	Party-State		Members	
57	1908/3/16	60th	Rep.	Bates	R-PA		National	B
58	1908/3/25	60th	Sen.	Owen	D-OK		National	B
59	1909/3/18	61st	Rep.	Sheppard	D-TX		National	B
60	1909/3/24	61st	Rep.	DeArmond	D-MO		National	B
61	1909/5/3	61st	Rep.	Underwood	D-AL		National	B
62	1909/12/10	61st	Rep.	Candler	D-MS		National	B
63	1909/12/10	61st	Rep.	Russell	D-TX		National	B
64	1910/2/28	61st	Rep.	Rucker	D-CO	Denver	National	B
65	1910/6/16	61st	Sen.	Jones	R-WA		National	G
66	1911/7/26	62nd	Rep.	Candler	D-MS		National	B
67	1911/12/12	62nd	Rep.	Sheppard	D-TX		National	B
68	1913/11/10	63rd	Sen.	Williams[c]	D-MS		National	B
69	1913/11/25	63rd	Sen.	Hitchcock	D-NE		Federal Reserve Members	B
70	1913/12/1	63rd	Sen.	Owen	D-OK		National	B
71	1913/12/18	63rd	Sen.	Owen	D-OK		National	B
72	1913/12/23	63rd	Sen.	Williams[c]	D-MS		Federal Recerve Members	B
73	1914/1/16	63rd	Rep.	Kinkaid	R-NE		National	B
74	1914/3/10	63rd	Sen.	Owen	D-OK		Federal Reserve Members	B
75	1914/9/12	63rd	Rep.	Barton	R-NE		Federal Reserve Members	B
76	1915/12/6	64th	Rep.	Kinkaid	R-NE		National	B
77	1915/12/7	64th	Sen.	Williams[c]	D-MS		National	B
78	1915/12/10	64th	Sen.	Owen	D-OK		Federal Reserve Members	B
79	1917/4/4	65th	Sen.	Owen	D-OK		Federal Reserve Members	B
80	1917/4/6	65th	Sen.	Williams[c]	D-MS		National	B
81	1918/2/18	65th	Rep.	Shouse[c]	D-KS		National	G
82	1918/2/18	65th	Sen.	Owen	D-OK		National	G
83	1918/4/23	65th	Sen.	Shaforth	R-CO		National	G
84	1919/5/26	66th	Sen.	Williams	D-MS		National	B
85	1919/5/26	66th	Sen.	Owens[c]	D-OK		Federal Reserve members	B
86	1920/12/13	66th	Rep.	McClintic	D-OK		National Federal Reserve members	B
87	1921/4/11	67th	Rep.	McClintic	D-OK		National Federal Reserve members (in approving Federal Reserve districts)	B
88	1922/9/16	67th	Rep.	Smith	R-ID		National Federal Reserve members (in approving Federal Reserve districts)	B

Table 3.AI. (cont.)

Item	Intro date	Cong.	Title	Author	Party-state	City district[a]	Type[b]	Banks covered in bills provisions
89	1923/2/3	67th	Sen.	Brookhart	R-IA		B	Cooperative national
90	1923/12/5	68th	Rep.	McClintic	D-OK		B	National Federal Reserve members (in approving Federal Reserve districts)
91	1924/1/1	68th	Sen.	Brookhart	R-IA		B	Cooperative national
92	1924/3/1	68th	Sen.	Jones	R-NM		B	Federal Reserve members
93	1924/3/10	68th	Rep.	Thomas	D-OK		B	Federal Reserve Members
94	1924/4/30	68th	Rep.	Doyle	D-IL	Chicago	G	National
95	1925/2/9	68th	Rep.	Steagall[c]	D-AL		B	Federal Reserve members
96	1925/12/14	69th	Rep.	Hastings	D-OK		G	Federal Reserve members
97	1926/3/6	69th	Rep.	Thomas	D-OK		B	Federal Reserve members
98	1926/3/23	69th	Rep.	Steagall[c]	D-AL		B	Federal Reserve members
99	1926/12/6	69th	Rep.	Brand[c]	D-GA		B	Federal Reserve members (except banks in states with insurance)
100	1926/12/6	69th	Rep.	Howard	D-NE		B	National
101	1926/12/11	69th	Rep	Brand[c]	D-GA		B	Federal Reserve members (except banks in states with insurance)
102	1927/12/5	70th	Rep.	Hastings	D-OK		G	Federal Reserve members
103	1927/12/5	70th	Rep.	Howard	D-NE		B	Federal Reserve members
104	1927/12/13	70th	Rep.	Brand[c]	D-GA		B	Federal Reserve members (except banks in states with insurance)
105	1928/2/16	70th	Rep.	Hastings	D-OK		G	Federal Reserve members
106	1928/2/20	70th	Rep.	Hastings	D-OK		G	Federal Reserve members
107	1928/5/26	70th	Rep.	Steagall[c]	D-AL		B	Federal Reserve members
108	1929/4/15	71st	Rep.	Howard	D-NE		B	Federal Reserve members
109	1929/12/12	71st	Rep.	Brand[c]	D-GA		B	Federal Reserve members (except banks in states with insurance)
110	1930/1/6	71st	Sen.	Brookhart[c]	R-IA		B	Cooperative National
111	1930/3/26	71st	Rep.	Steagall[c]	D-AL		B	Federal Reserve members

#	Date	Congress	Chamber	Name	State-Party	City	G/B	Description
112	1930/6/12	71st	Rep.	Hastings	D-OK		G	Federal Reserve members
113	1930/1/10	71st	Rep.	Hare	D-SC		B	Federal Reserve members
114	1931/2/28	71st	Rep.	Ramspeck	D-GA	Atlanta	B	National
115	1931/12/8	72nd	Rep.	Howard	D-NE		B	National
116	1931/12/8	72nd	Rep.	Beam	D-IL	Chicago	G	National
117	1931/12/8	72nd	Rep.	Hastings	D-OK		G	Federal Reserve members
118	1931/12/9	72nd	Rep.	Hare	D-SC		B	Federal Reserve members
119	1931/12/9	72nd	Sen.	Brookhart^c	R-IA		B	Cooperative national
120	1931/12/17	72nd	Rep.	Lanneck	D-OH	Columbus	B	Federal Reserve members
121	1932/1/4	72nd	Rep.	LaGuardia	R-NY	New York	B	Federal Reserve members; state members have option to with draw
122	1932/1/26	72nd	Sen.	Lewis	D-IL	Chicago	G	Federal Reserve Members
123	1932/2/8	72nd	Rep.	Shallenberger	D-NE		B	Federal Reserve Members
124	1932/2/20	72nd	Rep.	Jenkins	R-OH		B	Federal Reserve Members
125	1932/2/26	72nd	Sen.	Fletcher^c	D-FL		G	Federal Reserve Members
126	1932/3/2	72nd	Rep.	Disney^c	D-OK	Tulsa	B	Federal Reserve Members
127	1932/3/5	72nd	Rep.	Cable	R-OH		B	Banks and DIs; non-Federal Reserve have withdrawal option
128	1932/3/7	72nd	Sen.	Fess	R-OH		B	Banks and DIs; non-Federal Reserve have withdrawal option
129	1932/3/7	72nd	Rep.	Steagall^c	D-AL		B	Federal Reserve members
130	1932/3/7	72nd	Rep.	McClintic	D-OK		B	Federal Reserve members
131	1932/3/21	72nd	Rep.	Taylor	R-TN		G	Federal Reserve members
132	1932/4/13	72nd	Rep.	Strong^c	R-KS		G	National
133	1932/4/14	72nd	Rep.	Steagall^c	D-AL		B	Federal Reserve members and sound nonmembers
134	1932/5/21	72nd	Sen.	Fletcher	D-FL		B	Federal Reserve members and sound nonmembers
135	1932/12/23	72nd	Sen.	Vandenberg	R-MI		B	Federal Reserve members and sound nonmembers
136	1933/3/9	73rd	Rep.	Jenkins	R-OH		B	Federal Reserve members
137	1933/3/9	73rd	Rep.	Taylor	R-TN		G	Federal Reserve members
138	1933/3/10	73rd	Sen.	Vandenberg	R-MI		B	Federal Reserve members and sound nonmembers

Table 3.A1. (cont.)

Item	Intro date	Cong.	Title	Author	Party -state	City district[a]	Type[b]	Banks covered in bills provisions
139	1933/3/10	73rd	Sen.	McAdoo	D-CA		B	Federal Reserve members and sound nonmembers
140	1933/3/11	73rd	Sen.	Fletcher	D-FL		B	Federal Reserve members and sound nonmembers
141	1933/3/14	73rd	Rep.	Hastings	D-OK		G	Federal Reserve members
142	1933/3/14	73rd	Rep.	Johnson	D-TX		B	Federal Reserve members and sound nonmembers
143	1933/3/15	73rd	Rep.	Whitely	R-NY		B	Federal Reserve members and sound nonmembers
144	1933/3/16	73rd	Rep.	Church[c]	D-CA		B	Federal Reserve members and sound nonmembers
145	1933/3/17	73rd	Rep.	Shallenberger	D-NE		B	Federal Reserve members
146	1933/4/20	73rd	Rep.	Carter	R-CA		B	Federal Reserve members
147	1933/5/9	73rd	Rep.	McLeod	R-MI	Detroit	B	Federal Reserve members
148	1933/5/10	73rd	Rep.	Steagall[d]	D-AL		B	Federal Reserve members and sound nonmembers
149	1933/5/15	73rd	Sen.	Glass[c]	D-VA		B	Federal Reserve members
150	1933/5/17	73rd	Rep.	Steagall[d]	D-AL		B	Federal Reserve members and sound nonmembers

[a] City district refers to the large-city congressional districts of representatives introducing bills.
[b] B: bill in which banks provide mutual insurance; G: bill in which the government provides a guarantee.
[c] Member of the House or Senate committee to which the bill was referred.
[d] Chair of the House or Senate committee to which the bill was referred.
Source: Data are available through the Inter-University Consortium for Political and Social Research.

208

References

American Bankers Association. 1933. *The Guaranty of Bank Deposits.* New York: American Bankers Association.

Benston, George J. 1989. *The Separation of Commercial and Investment Banking. The Glass-Steagall Act Revisited and Reconsidered.* Norwell, Mass.: Kiuwer Academic.

Berman, Daniel M. 1964. *In Congress Assembled. The Legislative Process in the National Government.* New York: Macmillan.

Board of Governors of the Federal Reserve System. 1926. Branch Banking in the United States. *Federal Reserve Bulletin* 12(40) (June): 1–8.

1933. *Federal Reserve Bulletin* 19 (January–June).

1959. *All Bank Statistics.* Washington, D.C.: Board of Governors of the Federal Reserve System.

1976. *Banking and Monetary Statistics, 1914–1941.* Washington, D.C.: Board of Governors of the Federal Reserve System.

Bordo, Michael D. 1985. The Impact and International Transmission of Financial Crises: Some Historical Evidence, 1870–1933. *Revista di Storia Economica* 2: 41–78.

Burns, Helen M. 1974. *The American Banking Community and New Deal Banking Reforms, 1933–1935.* Westport, Conn.: Greenwood Press.

Calomiris, Charles W. 1990. Is Deposit Insurance Necessary? *Journal of Economic History* 50 (June): 283–95.

1992. Do Vulnerable Economies Need Deposit Insurance? Lessons from U.S. Agriculture in the 1920s. In *If Texas Were Chile: A Primer on Bank Regulation,* ed. Philip L. Brock, 237–349, 450–58. San Francisco: Sequoia Institute.

1993a. Regulation, Industrial Structure, and Instability in U.S. Banking: An Historical Perspective. In *Structural Change in Banking,* eds. Michael Klausner and Lawrence J. White, 19–116. Homewood, Ill.: Business One Irwin.

1993b. Greenback Resumption and Silver Risk: The Economics and Politics of Monetary Regime Change in the United States, 1862–1900. In *Monetary Regimes in Transition,* eds. Michael D. Bordo and Forrest Capie, 86–132. Cambridge: Cambridge University Press.

1995. The Costs of Rejecting Universal Banking: American Finance in the German Mirror, 1870–1914. In *Coordination and Information: Historical Perspectives on the Organization of Enterprise,* eds. Naomi Lamoreaux and Daniel M. G. Raff. Chicago: University of Chicago Press, pp. 257–315.

Calomiris, Charles W., and Gary Gorton. 1991. The Origins of Banking Panics: Models, Facts, and Bank Regulation. In *Financial Markets and Financial Crises,* ed. R. Glenn Hubbard, 107–73. Chicago: University of Chicago Press.

Chapman, John M. 1934. *Concentration of Banking: The Changing Structure and Control of Banking in the United States.* New York: Columbia University Press.

Comptroller of the Currency. 1907–36. *Annual Report.* Washington, D.C.: U.S. Government Printing Office.

Congressional Record. 1926. 69th Cong., 1st sess. Vol. 67, pt. 3.

Davidson, Roger H., and Walter J. Oleszek. 1981. *Congress and Its Members.* Washington, D.C.: Congressional Quarterly Press.

Doti, Lynne P., and Larry Schweikart. 1991. *Banking in the American West: From the Gold Rush to Deregulation.* Norman: University of Oklahoma Press.

Duncombe, Charles. 1841. *Duncombe's Free Banking.* Cleveland: Sanford and Co.

Federal Deposit Insurance Corporation. 1984. *The First Fifty Years: A History of the FDIC, 1933–1983.* Washington, D.C.: Federal Deposit Insurance Corporation.

Flood, Mark D. 1991. The Great Deposit Insurance Debate. *Federal Reserve Bank of St. Louis Review* 74 (July–August): 51–77.

Friedman, Milton, and Anna J. Schwartz. 1963. *A Monetary History of the United States, 1867–1960.* Princeton: Princeton University Press.

Froman, Lewis A., Jr. 1967. *Strategies, Rules, and Procedures.* Boston: Little, Brown.

Goldenweiser, E. A., et al. 1932. *Bank Suspensions in the United States, 1892–1931.* Prepared for the Federal Reserve System by the Federal Reserve Committee on Branch, Group, and Chain Banking.

Golembe, Carter H. 1960. The Deposit Insurance Legislation of 1933. *Political Science Quarterly* 76 (June): 181–95.

    1975 (first published). Memorandum re Interest on Demand Deposits. Reprinted in *The Golembe Reports. Twenty-fifth Anniversary Edition, 1967–1992.* Delray Beach, Fla.: CHG Consulting, 1992.

Golembe, Carter H., and Clark S. Warburton. 1958. *Insurance of Bank Obligations in Six States during the Period 1829–1866.* Washington, D.C.: Federal Deposit Insurance Corporation.

Jones, Jesse H. 1951. *Fifty Billion Dollars.* New York: Macmillan.

Keeton, William R. 1990. Small and Large Bank Views of Deposit Insurance: Today vs. the 1930s. *Federal Reserve Bank of Kansas City Economic Review* 75 (September–October): 23–35.

Kemmerer, Edwin W. 1917. *Postal Savings. An Historical and Critical Study of the Postal Savings System of the United States.* Princeton: Princeton University Press.

Kroszner, Randall S., and Raghuram G. Rajan 1994. Is the Glass-Steagall Act Justified? A Study of the U.S. Experience with Universal Banking before 1933. *American Economic Review* 84 (September): 810–32.

Leven. Maurice. 1925. *Income in the Various States: Its Sources and Distribution, 1919, 1920, and 1921.* New York: Columbia University Press.

Macey, Jonathan R., and Geoffrey P. Miller. 1992. Double Liability of Bank Shareholders: History and Implications. *Wake Forest Law Review* 27(1): 31–62.

Morrow, William L. 1969. *Congressional Committees.* New York: Scribners.

O'Hara, Maureen, and David Easley. 1979. The Postal Savings System in the Depression. *Journal of Economic History* 39 (September): 74: 1–53.

Patrick, Sue C. 1993. *Reform of the Federal Reserve System in the Early 1930s. The Politics of Money and Banking.* New York: Garland Publishing.

Peach, W. Nelson. 1941. *The Security Affiliates of National Banks.* Baltimore: Johns Hopkins University Press.

Poole, Keith T., and Howard Rosenthal. 1994. Congress and Railroad Regulation: 1874 to 1887. In *The Regulated Economy*, eds. Claudia Goldin and Gary D. Libecap, 81–120. Chicago: University of Chicago Press.

Reid, T. R. 1980. *Congressional Odyssey: The Saga of a Senate Bill.* San Francisco: W.H. Freeman and Co.

U.S. Bureau of the Census. 1909–30. *Statistical Abstract of the United States.* Washington, D.C.: U.S. Government Printing Office.

1975. *Historical Statistics of the United States: Colonial Times to 1970.* Washington, D.C.: U.S. Government Printing Office.

U.S. Senate Committee on Banking and Currency. 1950. *Amendments to the Federal Deposit Insurance Act: Hearings before a Subcommittee of the Committee on Banking and Currency* 81st Cong., 2d Sess. 11, 23, 30, January.

Upham, Cyril B., and Edwin Lamke. 1934. *Closed and Distressed Banks: A Study in Public Administration.* Washington, D.C.: Brookings Institution.

Wheelock, David C. 1992. Deposit Insurance and Bank Failures: New Evidence from the 1920s. *Economic Inquiry* 30 (July): 530–43.

White, Eugene N. 1983. *The Regulation and Reform of the American Banking System, 1900–1929.* Princeton: Princeton University Press.

1984. Voting for Costly Regulation: Evidence from Banking Referenda in Illinois, 1924. *Southern Economic Journal* 51, 1084–98.

1985. The Merger Movement in Banking, 1919–1933. *Journal of Economic History* 45 (June): 285–91.

1986. Before the Glass-Steagall Act: An Analysis of the Investment Banking Activities of National Banks. *Explorations in Economic History* 23 (January): 33–55.

Wigmore, Bane A. 1987. Was the Bank Holiday of 1933 Caused by a Run on the Dollar? *Journal of Economic History* 47 (September): 739–56.

Zaun, Adam J. 1953. The Postal Savings System. Diss., American Bankers Association Graduate School of Banking, Rutgers University.

## CHAPTER 4

The costs of rejecting universal banking
American finance in the German mirror, 1870–1914

Charles W. Calomiris

4.1   Introduction

The American financial system has been an outlier internationally in virtually every important respect for the past century. It has been the most geographically fragmented and the most susceptible to financial crises (Calomiris and Gorton 1991; Calomiris 1993). It has been among the most restrictive of combinations of financial services within intermediaries, although in recent years some of these restrictions have begun to be relaxed (Kaufman and Mote 1989, 1990). The American system has also been the most persistently innovative financial system in the world. Often, important innovations have been induced by regulatory restrictions that raised the cost of finance under preexisting financial technology.

These observations are commonplace. Other unusual aspects of American financial history have received less attention, including the relative lack of bank involvement in industrial finance, the heavy reliance on corporate bonds as a means of finance, the high costs of securities underwriting, and the high cost of capital in American industry.

The main goal of this paper is to weave these peculiar features of the American system into a single interpretive tapestry. The central argument of the paper is that regulatory limitations on the scale and scope of banking in America hampered financial coordination and substantially increased the cost of capital for industrialization, particularly in the period of the growth of large-scale industrial enterprises prior to World War I. This may seem a strange claim in light of American growth and financial innovativeness. The claim is not that America failed to grow and

The author thanks Henning Bohn, Nancy Calomiris, Marco Da Rin, Barry Eichengreen. John James, Charles Kindleberger, Naomi Lamoreaux, Daniel Raff, Carlos Ramirez, Jay Ritter, Kenneth Snowden, Peter Temin, Richard Tilly, Lawrence White, seminar participants at Brandeis University, participants at the NBER Conference on Financial Institutions and Macroeconomic Stability, and participants at the NBER Conference on Microeconomic History for helpful suggestions. Jurgen Wiesmann, Susanne Hellmann, and Sandra Gerling provided invaluable assistance as translators.

prosper, but that large-scale industrial investment was stunted relative to its potential by a faulty financial system.

To gauge the costs of American banking regulation, I compare and contrast the American and German financial systems. Rapid industrial growth in new industries and the increasing importance of large-scale enterprises are common features of the German and American experience in the pre-World War I era. The second industrial revolution witnessed rapid growth in industries that exploited new technological breakthroughs and produced entirely new products. The scale of firms was much larger than during earlier episodes of industrial expansion. Large-scale production of new products using new technologies created unprecedented challenges for the financial system. Large-scale production implied greater reliance on external funding, and the novelty of the products and techniques made it especially difficult for uninformed "outsiders" with available funds to judge the merits of the various investment opportunities. The ability of the financial system to mobilize and direct large amounts of funds into new firms was a prerequisite to rapid industrialization.

The means of financing industrial expansion during this period in the United States and Germany were quite different. The German universal banks *(Kreditbanken)* – sometimes referred to as the joint-stock or credit banks – were large-scale, externally financed, limited-liability banks. These banks operated nationwide branching networks and provided an unrestricted range of services, including lending, underwriting, trust services, and deposit taking. They held and underwrote securities issued by clients and made conventional loans for industrial purposes. They maintained close ties with the firms they financed and exerted control over corporate decision making in their combined role as lenders, stockholders, trustees of stock portfolios, and members of boards of directors.

The American banking system, in contrast, was shaped by restrictions on branching and consolidation that protected unit (single-office) banks.[1] The fragmentation of commercial banking limited American banks' involvement in supplying credit to large-scale firms. Over the nineteenth century, as industrial firm size grew, the role of banks as suppliers of industrial credit waned, and commercial banks focused increasingly on financing commerce (Lamoreaux 1994). Private bankers operating partnerships (also known as investment bankers) filled the gap in American finance, but because they had limited resources, they relied on under-

---

[1] Direct restrictions on the types of activities banks could finance – notably, attempts to confine bank lending to the financing of commerce, which is often referred to as the "real bills doctrine" – appear not to have been a binding constraint on bank lending activities (Lamoreaux 1994).

writing syndicates, funded in a decentralized way by an elaborate network of commercial banks, trust companies, and brokers, to raise funds for the firms they financed. Like universal bankers in Germany, investment bankers established methods for monitoring and controlling corporate management of the firms they financed.

Clearly, these are two very different ways of coordinating the flow of funds from savers to investors. But did these differences matter? In Section 4.2, I review general theoretical and empirical perspectives that suggest why they may have mattered. Here the review is selective, and serves to introduce concepts that will be emphasized in section 4.3's detailed discussion of the German and American financial systems and economies. Section 4.3 compares and contrasts the German and American experiences, argues that the various differences between them are mutually consistent, and points to evidence of higher costs of industrial finance in the United States. That section closes with a brief historical review of the different evolution of financial regulations and institutions in the two countries.

Section 4.4 offers some conjectures on why inefficient restrictions on banking have persisted in the United States. Limitations on branching and restrictions on joint production of financial services did not disappear as their costs became apparent. Indeed, the Great Depression saw an increase in restrictions, most notably the separation of commercial and investment banking, many new restrictions on securities transactions, a reversal of direction in the regulatory trend toward branching and consolidation of the 1920s, and the subsidization of unit banking by the creation of federal deposit insurance. Political considerations, as well as endogenous changes in financial technology that lowered the costs of regulation, may help to explain persistently poor banking regulation in the United States.

4.2   General perspectives on universal banking

This section provides an overview of general theoretical and empirical perspectives on universal banking, which will serve as a basis for the discussion of Section 4.3. I begin with a discussion of the role of various intermediaries and contracting arrangements for mitigating financing costs. Second, I argue that the form of financial instrument and the intermediation arrangement chosen by a firm reflect its place in the financial "pecking order" which is largely determined by the stage it has reached in its financial "life cycle." Third, I examine the role played by universal banking in reducing firm financing costs. Universal banking is defined as a combination of activities performed by banks, including deposit taking, trust services, direct lending, equity holding, and underwriting. Informational economies account for economies of scope among the three forms of intermediary financing of firms (lending, equity holding, and underwriting). These economies of scope are driven by considerations of time consistency, the reusability of information over the firm's life cycle, and improvements in the quality of signals generated by underwriters. Fourth, I consider the effect of restrictions on bank branching on the efficiency of universal banking. The benefits of universal banking are enhanced in a system that allows banks to branch. Direct access to sources of funds through deposit and trust accounts reduces the costs of marketing securities by facilitating the flow of information and limiting the number of layers of securities transactions.

This four-part summary of the economics of universal banking places universal banking in the context of theoretical literature on the role of banks and the financing structure of corporations. The changing needs of corporations over time correspond to different financial products produced by the universal bank. The advantages of a long-term relationship between a firm and an intermediary are best achieved by allowing the intermediary to perform a variety of tasks. The advantages of universal banking are best achieved in the context of large-scale banking, where transactions and information costs of syndications are minimized.

The theoretical discussion closes by linking these arguments to others made in the existing literature, both for and against universal banking. My emphasis on benefits of universal banking from reductions in corporate finance costs is also related to the question of portfolio diversification benefits under universal banking. Much of the recent policy debate over universal banking in the United States has focused on potential advantages from diversification from allowing commercial banks broader powers. A weakness of some of these studies has been the implicit assumption that available market assets are invariant to the establishment of universal banking. Potential benefits from diversification depend on the effect universal banks have on the feasible set of externally financed investments. If universal banking reduces corporate finance costs, then it enlarges the set of investments available to "outsiders."

Common theoretical arguments against universal banking are considered in light of theory and history. These include destabilization of the financial system, conflicts of interest, and inefficiency from lack of competition in banking or in industry. Theory and history support the view that universal banking is a stabilizing influence on banking. Furthermore, potential problems of conflict of interest can be overcome if universal banks are allowed to hold or manage equity as well as to underwrite and lend. Finally, while bank concentration and long-term links between firms and their banks may encourage lack of competition among banks or firms, Germany's universal banking system had many observable advantages, and was not a necessary condition for the formation of industrial cartels.

4.2.1   The roles of financial intermediaries

Financing investment is fundamentally a problem of coordination. Savers and investors need a low-cost means to transact. Of course, ultimate savers and investors virtually never meet. Rather, each deals with an intermediary, and often ultimate savers and investors do not use the same intermediary. In many transactions, complex hierarchies of intermediation may be employed. For example, many individuals own securities primarily through pension funds. Pension-fund managers might purchase securities through local bankers or dealers, who in turn may be marketing these securities for an investment banking syndicate formed and financed by a small group of banks, and managed by a lead investment bank who negotiates the deal with the issuing firm.

The links separating the individual saver and the firm issuing the security in this case are many, and involve substantial costs. These costs can be divided usefully into two categories: costs of information collection and transmittal – that is, costs of creating and enforcing mechanisms that lead to credible monitoring of firms and revelation of the true state of firm finances – and physical transactions costs – costs associated with legal and accounting paperwork, and with physically distributing securities to ultimate holders.

Recent contributions to the literature in banking and corporate finance have drawn attention to the ways various institutional arrangements can economize on such costs. For example, the costs to investment banking syndicates of collecting information about the proper pricing of new issues may be affected by the mechanism chosen for the initial marketing of the securities. Rationing of issues to a select group of securities purchasers who have repeated contact with the investment banking house may encourage truthful revelation of information about the value of the securities by those purchasers prior to the issue. Benveniste and Spindt (1989) argue that this beneficial revelation effect explains various otherwise puzzling features of the marketing and pricing of initial public offerings (IPOs). More generally, investment banks are valuable to the economy because they provide a low-cost means of generating and disseminating credible information about firms' characteristics, which benefits both securities issuers and purchasers in deciding on the form and price of the security used to finance an investment.

The recent literature on banking also views commercial banks as solving problems that arise from physical transactions costs and information asymmetry, and sees the form of intermediaries' contracts as a key determinant of the cost of finance. Banks economize on physical costs of transacting (clearing payments, liquidating insolvent firms), costs of generating information (monitoring firms' actions and outcomes), and costs of enforcing contractual compliance on the part of firms and bankers (disciplining borrowers and protecting against improper behavior by the banker at the expense of those funding the bank).

Models of banking stress the economies of concentrating funds in banks and appointing the banker as the "delegated monitor" of bank borrowers (Campbell and Kracaw 1980; Diamond 1984; Calomiris and Kahn 1991; Calomiris, Kahn, and Krasa 1991). Banking arrangements can avoid duplication in monitoring bank borrowers and thus reduce banking costs. Enforcement of contracts (monitoring and discipline) is also less costly if a single agent with proper incentives can specialize in the task.

Empirical evidence on the characteristics of firms choosing banks as financing sources confirms the view that banks specialize in performing ongoing monitoring and contractual enforcement for firms whose access to outside funding otherwise would be limited (Butters and Lintner 1945; Fazzari, Hubbard, and Petersen 1989; James and Wier 1988, 1990; Mackie-Mason 1990). Other firms – older, better-known firms – have access to securities markets on better terms and can avoid the costs of bank finance. These firms typically still use intermediaries (like investment banks) to assist them in determining what types of securities to issue and in credibly signaling the value of their securities (Benveniste and Spindt 1989; Ramakrishnan and Thakor 1984), but they avoid at least some of the ongoing costs of bank finance. Costs of bank finance include regulatory costs (like reserve requirements), monitoring costs, and rents the bank may extract from firms it finances by virtue of its possession of private information, as in Rajan (1992a).

Empirical studies of the effects of bank lending decisions on the prices of existing securities or bank borrowers also provide evidence of the role of banks as "insiders" with respect to information relevant for valuing claims on firms to which they lend. Announcing financing arrangements between banks and firms increases firms' stock prices (James 1987; James and Wier 1988). Bank participation in working out corporate distress increases the value of distressed firms' stock (Gilson, John, and Lang

1990), especially when banks are willing to take a junior position in the firm (Brown, James, and Mooradian 1993). Japanese firms with close, long-term banking relationships are better able to maintain investment levels than other firms during episodes of financial distress (Hoshi, Kashyap, and Scharfstein 1990a, 1990b).

4.2.2   The financial "pecking order" and the "life cycle" of firms

The growing theoretical literature in corporate finance focuses on how particular financing arrangements mitigate some costs at the expense of others. In some cases, using an investment bank may be desirable because it provides a low-cost means of signaling the value of securities. In other cases, bank loans may be the appropriate financing vehicle, possibly because of banks' low costs of managing financial distress or of monitoring managers' actions and enhancing corporate control.

The new "information-based" approach to corporate finance revolves around the financial "pecking order" – a continuum of financing instruments defined according to the elasticity of their cost with respect to problems of asymmetric information (Myers 1984; Myers and Majluf 1984; Diamond 1991). Firms progress up the pecking order of finance as they mature. Firms just starting out may be forced to rely exclusively on retained earnings and the wealth of insiders. After a successful beginning, the firm can rely on "inside debt" in the form of bank loans. The bank spends resources to monitor the firm, and protects itself against "lemons" problems by holding a debt claim on the firm.[2] As the firm

---

[2] Given the general predominance of debt finance, particularly in banking, recent contracting models try to explain the optimality of debt. Debt claims are often a desirable means of finance when claimants are relatively uninformed about firm opportunities or outcomes, or when outcomes are difficult to demonstrate to a third party. As Myers and Majluf (1984) show, in a world where firms' opportunities are unobservable *ex ante*, debt suffers less of a "lemons premium" than equity because the payoffs to debt depend less on the unobservable information. Townsend (1979), Diamond (1984), Gale and Hellwig (1985), Williamson (1986), and others have argued that costs of *ex post* monitoring and third-party verification favor the use of debt contracts. Lacker (1991) shows that debt is especially useful in these environments as a means to penalize firms by threatening to take collateralized assets that have special value to the firms' operators.

These arguments for the optimality of debt contracting may help explain the reliance by banks on deposits and banknotes as the primary means of "outsider" financing of bank activities historically (as argued above), and the use of debt as the primary means of "outsider" finance of many corporations. But these arguments do not suggest that bank financing of firms will always, or even mainly, occur in the form of debt. Indeed, the pecking-order theory of corporate finance – which emphasizes the role of debt as an optimal means of financing outsiders' contributions to the firm – suggests advantages from insiders' avoidance of debt, as argued below.

matures and develops a track record, its financing will change. Informed intermediaries will be willing to take equity positions in the firm (as in the venture capital market), which will reduce the leverage of the firm and its exposure to financial distress, and provide a positive signal to outside investors. Outside finance through securities may initially take the form of closely held senior instruments (e.g., private placements). Later, firms will graduate to issuing bonds and preferred and common stock on the open market to outsiders, using underwriters as a means for providing credible signals of the firm's value to outsiders.

The maturity of debt instruments chosen can reflect a trade off between the information and transactions costs of finance. Short-term debt mitigates incentive problems between banks and firms. As Jensen and Meckling (1976, pp. 334–37) show, debt contracts create a potential agency problem known as the "asset substitution effect." Once debt contracts are entered into, managers with an equity interest in the firm may have an incentive to take on greater risk, because they are only concerned with expanding the upper tail of the asset returns distribution. Short term debt can be useful as a means to restrict such risk-taking. Firms that increase risk face the threat that their loans will not be rolled over, or will be rolled over only at a higher interest rate. If lenders keep debt short-term and monitor borrowers' actions, borrowers will find little benefit in increasing risk, so long as the threat of the bank's rollover response is credible (e.g., see Pennacchi 1983; Gorton and Kahn 1992). Similarly, bank-loan contracts typically allow acceleration of the maturity of debt when the firm's position deteriorates. This right of acceleration is particularly powerful in restricting borrower risk taking when combined with compensating balance requirements (which force firms to hold their checking accounts in the bank) and the option of deposit setoff (bank seizure of deposits), as Garber and Weisbrod (1991) argue.

Despite the advantages of short-term debt in protecting lenders and encouraging proper behavior by borrowers, short-term debt has higher transactions costs than long-term debt. The costs of renegotiation and rollover are especially large for *nonbank* debt, which must be physically redeemed and reissued to a widely dispersed group of creditors.[3] For example, the costs of issuing bonds (costs charged for paperwork and for

---

[3] Another reason why banks may be in a better position to offer short-term debt is suggested in recent work by Diamond (1992). He argues that short-term debt can be costly when held by uninformed lenders because they may be too quick to liquidate a solvent, but illiquid, firm. One could argue that, if banks are better informed about firms, they will be able to reap the disciplinary advantages of short-term debt without creating losses through excessive liquidations.

fees to the investment banking syndicate marketing the bonds) averaged 6 percent of the size of the issue in the United States during 1925–29 (Securities and Exchange Commission 1940, pp. 10–11). If the maturity of these bonds had been, say, one year rather than the actual fifteen-to-twenty-year average maturity (Hickman 1960, p. 152), this would have entailed a significant increase in the cost of funds. Thus, short-term debts of firms typically take the form of bank loans (with low rollover costs) or short-term trade credit.[4]

In summary, banks, investment banks, and other intermediaries can be seen as "optimal mechanisms" for connecting particular groups of savers and investors in a world of costly transactions and asymmetric informa-tion. Informational characteristics of firms (the availability of a track record, the costs to outsiders of monitoring and controlling activities of the firm) are important determinants of whether firms choose to finance themselves with securities issues or with bank lending, and of the form and maturity of the financing instrument. This approach emphasizes the importance of financing through banks in the early stages of the life cycle of the firm, and sees other forms of intermediation (investment banking) as depending on earlier information creation by the firm's track record with inside lenders. Choice variables for minimizing financ-ing costs include the intermediation technology used, the forms of the claims issued (e.g., debt or equity) by firms and intermediaries, their maturity, covenants on behavior and options granted to holders or issuers of claims on firms or banks, liquidation rules, allocation of voting authority, agreements that ensure a long-term relationship between or among contracting parties (and thereby solve problems of time incon-sistency), and the voluntary formation of coalitions (of banks, investment banks, or informed IPO purchasers), which regulate the behavior of members.[5]

---

[4] In addition to bank loans, the United States developed an important innovation in com-mercial and industrial finance, which became known as the commercial paper market. For reasons related to its fragmented banking system, bankers' acceptances and foreign bills of exchange never reached the level of importance in the United States that they did elsewhere (Calomiris 1993). The commercial paper market developed as a means for banks to transfer their lowest-risk customers to other intermediaries, to take advantage of lower costs of finance in other locations. The commercial paper market was a unique feature of the American financial system, which grew substantially in importance during the last quarter of the nineteenth century.

[5] An important contributor to minimizing finance costs has been coalitions of banks, whose function includes cooperation in underwriting networks, interbank correspondent rela-tions, cost-effective payment clearings, and perhaps most important, coalitions for mutual protection. Such coalitions are more easily organized, managed, and self-regulated in a concentrated banking system. For discussions of several examples, see Gorton 1985, 1989; Gorton and Mullineaux 1987; Calomiris 1989, 1990, 1993; Calomiris and Kahn 1991, 1996; and Calomiris and Schweikart 1991.

4.2.3   The advantages of universal banking

The pecking-order framework implies that financing arrangements that accelerate the process of seasoning a firm and economize on the costs of information production and corporate governance can stimulate investment by reducing the costs of external finance. In this light, the main advantage of universal banking is that it encourages a long-term relationship to develop between a firm and its intermediary by allowing the intermediary to vary the form of firm financing as the firm matures, in keeping with the optimal financing arrangement, which changes over the life cycle of the firm. Initially, the intermediary lends directly to the firm. Later, it will be best for the same intermediary to underwrite the firm's securities issues (either by itself or as a leader of a syndicate of universal banks). Underwriting will require that the bank be allowed to own (and act as trustee for) shares of the firm. Without the flexibility to vary the form of the bank-firm relationship, relationships between firms and banks are unlikely to persist over the firm's life cycle.

By "long-term" I mean that the firm and bank have a credible implicit contract to continue to do business in the future. The firm cannot switch banks costlessly. The advantage of a credible long-term relationship is that it encourages banks to lend to firms on favorable terms in anticipation of a continuing relationship. The costs of gathering information about a firm's credit risk is high for unseasoned firms, which pay for bank monitoring in the form of higher interest cost on loans. If banks can spread the cost of monitoring over many periods, this reduces the initial costs of borrowing and allows firms to pay less for credit during their early years when investment needs are high and cash flow is low. Despite the advantages of a long-term relationship for smoothing the cost of credit to firms, there is a potential "time-inconsistency" problem that makes it difficult for banks to postpone charging firms for high early monitoring costs. Firms receiving low-interest loans in their early years may opt out of the initial banking relationship once they become seasoned and have opportunities to borrow from other intermediaries. Competing intermediaries may be able to provide credit at lower cost in the later stage of the firm life cycle because the costs of monitoring the firm have fallen as the result of its observable credit history with the initial bank (James and Wier 1990). Thus, competing banks may be able to "free ride" on the initial bank's efforts.

In practice, long-term exclusivity can be enforced in two ways. First, to the extent that competing banks are unable to learn relevant information about the firm from the initial bank's lending decisions, the initial bank's investment in information about the firm at an early stage reduces future costs of granting credit or underwriting only for the initial bank, so the firm and bank are naturally drawn to one another for repeat business.[6] Second, banks may prohibit "their" firms from doing business with other banks (Neuburger and Stokes 1974, p. 713). Presumably, such prohibitions would be enforced by cooperation among the banks to limit deviation from this rule. While finance historians have argued that banks in Germany and the United States were not successful in enforcing exclusivity once clients became large, well-known firms (Tilly 1992, p. 109), nevertheless, for a limited period of time such enforcement may have been important.

Given the benefits to borrowers from interest cost smoothing, such collusion among banks is not necessarily a bad thing. Although it may allow banks to extract rent from firms, without it the advantages of a long-term relationship may not be available to young, growing firms. Mayer (1988) cites post-World War II Japan as an example of successful elimination of information externalities among banks through credible long-term contracting, made feasible by limits on period-by-period competition among banks. Without a credible long-term relationship between firms and banks, banks may have been unwilling to pay fixed costs initially and bear risk during early stages of industrialization of infant industries.

Another important avenue for internalizing externalities for banks lending to young, growing firms is to allow banks to take equity positions in these firms. This allows banks to benefit fully from the positive signal they create when they finance firms. Also, by making banks junior

---

[6] Given the evidence of disadvantages from not creating a long-term bank relationship, or of deciding to discontinue one (Hoshi, Kashyap, and Scharfstein 1990a, 1990b; De Long 1991; Ramirez 1992), it may seem puzzling that some firms did not opt for such a close, long-term relationship. A simple example will help to fix ideas, and help one to understand why some firms may choose not to borrow from universal banks, or to discontinue borrowing eventually. Suppose that the costs to a bank at time zero of starting a relationship with a firm consist of monitoring costs, which decline over time. To be concrete, assume the initial cost to the bank is X, and the costs for all subsequent periods is m per period. Furthermore, assume that, if the firm cannot borrow from a bank, it must rely only on retained earnings to finance investment, and that this entails a reduction in profitable investment (alternatively, one could assume the firm will borrow from nonbanks at a higher cost, reflecting a lemons premium on uninformed lending). For simplicity, assume the firm will need external funding for only 10 periods, after which its investment opportunities can be completely financed from its (larger) stream of retained earnings. The bank will charge a fee for the ten periods of z per period, which includes reimbursement for X and m costs, and possibly additional rents extracted by the bank (if the bank has an initial information advantage over its competitors). The firm compares the value of joining the bank (the present value of firm assets if it joins the bank minus the z fees), with the present value of firm assets if it does not join the bank. Firms that require a large X and m investment *relative to the advantages they would receive from rapid access to finance through a banking relationship* will prefer autarky.

claimants on the firm, equity holding provides a strong incentive for continuing diligence by the banker (Pozdena 1991).[7] Equity financing has other advantages as well. It reduces financial distress costs for firms by reducing leverage, and by concentrating ownership stakes (which reduces bargaining and coordination costs among creditors during distress). Also, in distress states, firms may need their banker to credibly signal that the firm's prospects are good to other firm creditors. A bank's willingness to exchange debt for equity in the firm during distress can be a strong signal of the bank's confidence in the firm (Brown, James, and Mooradian 1993). Several recent studies of Japanese banking have emphasized the advantages of stock ownership by banks as a means of promoting monitoring and reducing costs of financial distress.[8] A final advantage of allowing equity finance is that this avoids potential conflicts of interest between the firm and its creditors. Reliance on debt can lead to an "underinvestment problem" (Myers 1977). Positive net present value (NPV) projects with relatively low risk may not be undertaken on the margin because undertaking the project generates a transfer of wealth from the firm's stockholders to its debtholders. Similarly, debt finance entices firms to substitute relatively high-risk assets for existing low-risk assets, since such substitution leads to a wealth transfer from creditors to stockholders.

These advantages from equity contracting may be offset by costs associated with equity finance. If the riskiness of firms is unobservable, those

---

[7] By holding equity in the firm, the bank may also be able to exert influence over the firm's future choice of a bank to act as purchaser and underwriter of securities. Thus equity can help solve Mayer's (1988) time-inconsistency problem, in part, by allowing banks to control firm financing decisions in the future. As argued below, there is little evidence for this sort of monopoly control by banks in Germany or the United States, at least after the 1890s.

[8] Sheard (1989) points out that a "main" bank's debt position in a firm often takes a junior position to other debt effectively, and is written down during financial distress to avoid bankruptcy. Thus Japanese banks' "equity" positions in firms are effectively larger than their balance-sheet statements would indicate. Kim (1992) finds that equity stakes by Japanese banks are higher for growing firms with high external finance ratios and high risk. In Japan, the incidence of bankruptcy is much lower, and the costs of bankruptcy when it does occur are also much lower, than in the United States Kim shows that these advantages in Japan depend on the ownership structure of firms – specifically, the concentration of ownership in the firm (or equivalently, the proportion of the firm owned by banks). Hoshi, Kashyap, and Scharfstein (1990b) find that firms with close ties to Japanese banks suffer much lower reduction in investment levels during periods of financial distress, but they do not find an effect from bank's equity interest on the costs of financial distress once one has controlled for other characteristics of the firms' financing sources. The upshot of their findings is that there are substitute means for achieving the desirable features of inside equity, which take the form of concentrating lending in the hands of few borrowers, or allowing banks to hold junior debt positions that have equity-like features. Further support for this interpretation comes from Prowse (1992) and Hoshi, Kashyap, and Loveman (1992).

who finance firms must charge all firms the same cost of finance. For good firms, this entails a lemons premium on their cost of finance. The premium will be largest for junior securities, since their payoffs are the riskiest (Myers and Majluf 1984). Also, as Jensen and Meckling (1976) and others have stressed, if managerial effort depends on managers' stakes in the firm, or if management's objectives conflict with shareholders', then equity issues can reduce managerial incentives and encourage non-profit-maximizing behavior by management (by reducing the concentration of ownership in the firm, and hence the ability to discipline managers).

Thus, reaping the advantages of equity depends on constructing mechanisms that provide adequate control over the firm's management to avoid prohibitive lemons premiums and managerial incentive problems. Bankers may sit on corporate boards of directors and exert direct control over managerial decisions. This entails large fixed costs to the bank, which may be prohibitive for small firms with uncertain prospects. Alternatively, firms could avoid equity issues and rely on debt. In this case, banks use debt covenants and short-term debt as a disciplinary device on management. Managers who behave improperly will find their credit lines discontinued by the bank, through either the "calling" of the bank's loan or the bank's decision not to rollover its debt. As discussed below, the history of German universal banking – in which both enforcement technologies were available to banks – suggests that banks began lending to firms via protected short-term debt. Once the firm had matured and the bank had become an informed insider, both parties benefited from a conversion of short-term debt into equity finance. The transition from debt to equity finance also entailed an increased role of the bank in controlling corporate decision making through the board of directors. The life cycle of "corporate governance" arrangements with intermediaries parallels the life cycle of the firm's financial structure.

Thus, the economies of scope from a single intermediary being able to lend, hold equity, exert corporate discipline, and underwrite securities for a firm may be entirely unrelated to conventional technological economies of scope (or transactions costs) in providing these services. Rather, the main advantages of allowing a single intermediary to perform all these activities revolve around information and control economies. First, in the context of the pecking-order approach outlined above, because lending to a firm precedes underwriting in the firm's life cycle, a bank that has lent to the firm in the past will have access to private information that will reduce the costs of underwriting. Second, consistent with Mayer's (1988) emphasis on time consistency, it may be important to allow the bank to hold equity and underwrite securities for the mature firm as an efficient means for the firm to pay for earlier bank investments in information with capital gains on stock and underwriting fees at later dates when the firm's cost of funds is lower. Third, when banks take long-term positions in a firm, by lending or holding the equity of the firm, their signals as underwriters may be more credible. This is particularly true if banks are allowed to hold equity; or alternatively, if the securities they underwrite are senior to preexisting claims on the firm.[9]

4.2.4 Universal banking and bank concentration

The recent literature on commercial banking has stressed advantages of allowing banks to be large. A concentrated banking system permits greater portfolio diversification of banks and allows banks to coordinate their response to crises by forming credible mutual-insurance arrangements, which would not be possible in a system of many geographically isolated banks. These theoretical propositions receive ample support from the comparative history of banking systems and their performance (see Calomiris 1993 for a review).

In the context of universal banking, there are further advantages to becoming a large bank operating a branching network. First, if industrial firms find it advantageous to operate large-scale enterprises over a wide geographic area (as Chandler 1977 argues), then monitoring the activities of the firm will be easier if a bank has similarly wide geographic scope. Second, large branching banks are better able to take advantage of long-term relationship economies of financing firms through a universal bank because of their access to both securities purchasers and depositors. Unit banking laws that prohibit the establishment of deposit-taking branches effectively limit banks' access to deposits on a large scale and, therefore, limit large-scale lending to firms.

Furthermore, given the overhead costs of setting up a bank office, restrictions on commercial bank branching limit branching in securities retailing, too, and this raises the costs of bringing securities to market.[10]

---

[9] It is possible that universal banking can involve a conflict of interest. Banks with existing claims on a firm might use underwriting as a means of reducing losses on their existing claims on the firm by attracting outside investors, or, conversely, banks may discourage outside investors to keep a good-risk firm to themselves. These problems can be overcome if banks are allowed to have a stake in the securities they underwrite, or if the security being underwritten is senior to the bank's existing claim on the firm. For both of these reasons, it is important to allow banks to take equity positions in firms or manage equity holdings by bank trust customers.

[10] Implicit in this argument are the realistic assumptions that the depositors and holders of trust accounts required a branch to be located near them, and that depositors were not indifferent to holding claims on banks in nontransactable form; otherwise, unit banking laws would not have been a binding constraint.

Without access to a large number of securities purchasers, a bank may not be able to internalize all the benefits of collecting information about issuing firms' prospects and about the ultimate demand for firms' securities. The lack of retail branching also creates transactions and signaling costs associated with setting up networks of banks that collect and credibly transmit such information. Finally, branching reduces the physical cost of distributing securities.[11] Riesser (1911, pp. 756–57) writes that the German banks are "able to find a wider and safer market for the sale of securities which [they] proposed to float. [They] can, therefore, acquire such securities on a larger scale and with greater confidence, knowing beforehand that such securities will go into good hands as permanent investments, and not be thrown back at once upon the market, to be taken up again by the bank." Riesser also argues that large-scale banking concentrates voting power (proxies from trust accounts), which can be useful for disciplining management of firms that banks finance. Jeidels (1905, pp. 164–76) argues that industry-specific knowledge was important in evaluating the creditworthiness of German firms, and that economies of information gathering encouraged concentration and specialization by underwriters in particular industry niches.

Commentators on the emergence of some large-scale universal banking in the United States in the 1920s noted that one of the chief advantages of securities affiliates of commercial banks relative to investment banks was their larger size, which was due to their large branching networks. Chicago's growth as an investment-banking center in the 1920s was encouraged by the growth of regional correspondent relations centering in Chicago, which increased the deposit and securities accounts managed by Chicago commercial banks operating investment banking affiliates (Bureau of Business Research 1928, p. 40).

Preston and Finlay (1930a, p. 1154) argue that American investors were more confident of securities underwritten by a single bank, since concentration of underwriting "centers responsibility" for the issue in one bank. They also argue that research into the creditworthiness of a firm "must involve more than simply a study of statistics: it must include continuous contact with the management of companies whose equities are selected." These large fixed costs imply that stock offerings and underwriters' resources must be large.

---

[11] White (1985) argues that economies of scale and scope in providing investment banking and trust activities, as well as the nonbank corporate merger wave, encouraged bank mergers in the 1920s. Peach (1941, p. 86) notes that affiliates often operated large branching networks, nationally or internationally. These networks no doubt reduced transactions costs of placing issues; however, they were not substitutes for full-fledged branch banking, which involves the taking of deposits, clearing of checks, management of trust accounts, and placing of securities within the same organization.

Despite the advantages of concentration for universal banks, regulations limiting branch banking made large-scale universal banking impossible. Long before the 1914 Clayton Act restrictions on bank involvement on corporate boards or the 1933 Glass-Steagall restrictions on universal banking activities, branching restrictions hampered the development of long-term relationships between firms and banks and made large-scale underwritings by commercial banks very rare. In the United States, after Jay Cooke's bond campaign to finance the Union during the Civil War, underwriting syndicates relied on a complex hierarchy of banks and brokers to coordinate securities transactions. This network became an important vehicle for funding underwriting, defining securities holders' demand schedules (to set prices and determine types of securities underwritten), and distributing securities once they were underwritten (Carosso 1970). The network of interbank relationships established for this purpose was an important financial innovation of the post-Civil War era. Nevertheless, in the absence of regulations prohibiting branching and consolidation across states, such coordination of information could have been accomplished (as in Germany) within syndicates of a few nationwide banks, with far fewer transactions, and with stronger incentives to collect accurate information about firms' prospects and securities holders' demands. This system also would have enhanced control over the management of public firms by concentrating voting rights in the hands of a few agents.

4.2.5 Diversification and universal banking

My discussion of universal banking has focused on corporate-finance cost reductions that come from information and transactions cost savings under a universal banking system. Much of the current discussion of the economies of allowing universal banking has focused on a different issue. Empirical studies of the United States in the post–World War II era have examined primarily the potential benefits of diversification that would come from combining the activities of commercial and investment banks, as well as other intermediaries. Diversification lessens the chance of costly liquidation of intermediaries and reduces transactions costs of constructing diversified portfolios for wealth holders. Some of these studies examine the relative performance of firms with diverse activities (Meinster and Johnson 1979; Boyd and Graham 1986; Litan 1985, 1987, pp. 105–11; Wall 1987; Brewer 1989), while others consider random combinations of firms actually pursuing separate activities (Boyd and Graham 1988; Litan 1987, pp. 112–18; Boyd, Graham, and Hewitt 1988; Brewer, Fortier, and Pavel 1988). The results from this literature have been mixed, though on balance they indicate small benefits of diversification. Not only do these studies focus too narrowly on the issue of portfolio structure, but by design they are ill-suited to measure the portfolio-diversification advantages of universal banking.

The studies of random, counterfactual combinations of different activities suffer from the obvious problem that combining firms is not the same as combining balance sheets. The behavior of financial firms might change as the result of combining activities; indeed, this underlies the arguments of economies of scope outlined above. But even the studies that analyze the comparative performance of actual combinations of financial activities will understate the potential diversification advantages from universal banking for two reasons. First, the observed combinations have occurred in the existing regulatory environment, in which many potentially beneficial combinations are prohibited by law. Second, universal banking might enlarge the feasible set of traded assets in the economy in ways that cannot be observed under the current regulatory regime.

Obviously, a better measure of the diversification benefits from universal banking would examine diversification opportunities across regulatory regimes, and within regimes that permitted universal banking. In the latter category, White's (1986) findings for the United States in the 1920s are of interest. National banks with securities affiliates had lower risk of failure than other banks. This may reflect greater portfolio opportunities for banks that could establish credible long-term relationships with borrowers. White also found that securities affiliates reduced the overall risk to bank stockholders, since the incomes from affiliates and parent banks were uncorrelated.

In a series of interesting studies, Tilly (1980, 1984, 1986, 1992) analyzes the risk-return characteristics of the portfolios created by Germany's universal banks in the pre–World War I era, and compares them with a constructed "efficient" portfolio (the efficient frontier of risk-return tradeoffs available). He finds German universal banks' portfolios remarkably close to the efficient frontier of the economy, and interprets this as evidence against the suggestions of some (e.g., Neuburger and Stokes 1974; Gerschenkron 1962, p. 15) that German banks may have preferred some industries over others for reasons unrelated to efficient capital allocation.

Cross-regime comparisons for this period are also possible. Tilly (1984, 1986, 1992) and Kennedy and Britton (1985) compare British (nonuniversal) and German bank portfolios for the pre–World War I period. They argue that British portfolios were much more distant from the efficient frontier of the British economy and far inferior to Germany in the risk-return trade-offs they achieved.

The results of the studies of Germany and Britain are controversial, since they rely on rather heroic assumptions to measure both the efficient portfolio frontier and the portfolio created by the banks. But they draw attention to the importance of a universal banking system's ability to produce, not merely to combine, investment opportunities. As Tilly (1986, p. 117; 1992) emphasizes, and as is too often ignored in the empirical studies of diversification from combining banking activities in the United States today, the banking system's achievement of an efficient portfolio in Germany did not merely reflect wise choices by passive money managers of the portfolio weights to attach to a set of exogenously given investment opportunities. The German banking system, with its ability to economize on a variety of costs, was essential to making investment opportunities available to the market, and hence to expanding the feasible portfolio frontier. Opportunities for efficient construction of portfolios through universal banking depended on the ability of the banks to mitigate information, control, and transaction costs (Tilly 1992, p. 110).

4.2.6   Criticisms of universal banking

Perspectives on universal banking have not always been favorable. Historically, in the United States, there has been substantial opposition to allowing both the concentration of banking and the combination of commercial lending, underwriting, and equity holding by financial intermediaries. Indeed, as will be discussed in Section 4.3, for most of the period prior to the legal separation of commercial and investment banking in 1933, which forced the closing of state-chartered underwriting affiliates of commercial banks, lending and underwriting were performed mainly by different intermediaries. In particular, because banks typically were not allowed to branch or merge, they could not take advantage of the economies from internalizing the functions of the securities marketing network within a single intermediary. Changes in bank branching and consolidation permitted in the 1920s were an important precondition for the encroachments made by commercial banks into investment banking in the 1920s.

Thus, the time-honored tradition of American restrictions on the scale of banking effectively limited universal banking prior to Glass-Steagall in 1933. The outright prohibitions on investment banking affiliates of commercial banks in Glass-Steagall were justified by two accusations.

First, banks were accused of taking advantage of conflicts of interest in securities dealings. Second, it was claimed that links between affiliates and parent banks contributed to the banking collapse of the Great Depression.

Scholars who have investigated these claims have found no supporting empirical evidence, and have disputed them on theoretical and empirical grounds (Carosso 1970; White 1986; Benston 1989; Kaufman and Mote 1989, 1990; Kroszner and Rajan 1994). On the question of whether affiliates weakened banks, White (1986) found that national banks with securities affiliates had lower failure propensities, and he linked these to diversification advantages. White also pointed out that, as documented in Peach (1941), affiliates were wholly owned by banks, and thus strategies to strengthen affiliates at the expense of parent banks would not have been chosen knowingly by management.

Benston (1989) argues that the presumed link between bank failures and securities activities of affiliates, on which much of the reasoning of the various banking committees relied, never received careful scrutiny in any of the many congressional "studies" of banking from 1931 to 1940. Nevertheless, this presumption underlay the drastic changes of the separation of investment and commercial banking in the Banking Act of 1933.

Conflicts of interest are unlikely to occur. In equilibrium, investment bankers – whether operating out of private investment banking houses or national bank affiliates – will not be able to attract customers if they cannot credibly signal the quality of securities they underwrite. If bank affiliates could not overcome potential investors' concerns over conflicts of interest (for example, by purchasing or managing some of the new issues), then they would lose business to private investment banks. The fact that affiliates were able to provide underwriting services on a large scale for many years in open competition with other underwriters indicates that conflicts of interest were not significant. Evidence against conflict of interest is provided by Kroszner and Rajan (1994). They analyze default costs for bonds issued by affiliates and their competitors prior to Glass-Steagall and conclude that the performance of affiliate-underwritten securities of a given *ex ante* class was at least as good as that of securities underwritten by their competitors.

Two other common criticisms of universal banking are that it increases inefficient bank rent extraction from firms, and encourages the development of industrial cartels. Coordination, of course, is not always efficient. In a concentrated banking system where firms have exclusive relationships with intermediaries, would collusion among banks in setting fees and interest rates increase the cost of finance in the economy? And

would close corporate monitoring and control, along with long-term relationships between firms and universal banks, encourage the development
of industrial cartels by providing a credible enforcement mechanism for
collusive behavior within industries?

On the first point, it is doubtful that universal banking raises financing costs by allowing banks to extract greater rent from firms. As Rajan
(1992a) shows, a banking relationship that involves the production of
private information about firms may give banks access only to quasi-
rents (which are transferred back to the firm *ex ante*). The interesting
question is whether universal banking will increase or decrease the distortions that come from asymmetric information. Here the point to
emphasize is not the *extent* of quasi- or true rents, but the way they are
extracted. As argued above, universal banking may be beneficial for
solving the time-inconsistency problem because it allows banks to reap
long-term gains from large initial costs of investing in information. Thus,
for example, banks will be able to "charge" for underwriting services
partly by relying on long-term gains from their relationship with firms.
In the absence of universal banking, banks may have to recover costs
over a shorter horizon. This will require "front-loading" of financing
costs, which will distort the firm's investment decision by making finance
excessively costly in the near term. Thus, if universal banking allows
banks to design compensation schemes that eliminate such distortions,
then even if it increases the share of firms' rents that accrue to banks (as
opposed to firms' entrepreneurs), this rent extraction may be relatively
efficient. Empirical evidence (De Long 1991; Ramirez 1992) discussed
below suggests that banking relationships added value to firms, and that
investment bankers' fees reflected costs of providing information and
transaction services, rather than simply rents.[12]

On the question whether investment banks promoted inefficient
industrial cartels, two points are worth emphasizing. First, the development and enforcement of industrial cartels by intermediaries is not a
weakness peculiar to concentrated universal banking systems. Indeed,
such accusations were the hallmark of the Pujo committee hearings of
1912–13 in the United States (Carosso 1970, chap. 6). According to his

---

[12] A separate question is whether the universal bank's possibly higher share of its client
firms' rents will discourage entrepreneurial investment. Universal bankers should vary
the amount of rent, and the variables on which it depends, to ensure that the entrepreneur receives his reservation level of rent, and that the entrepreneur's incentives will be
minimally distorted by rent extraction. In other words, a perfectly discriminating monopolistic banker with access to a "lump-sum tax" will not discourage entrepreneurial investment. Indeed, if universal banks are better able to gauge the total rents of the firm
because of better information, then they will make fewer mistakes than other intermediaries in determining how much rent to extract from entrepreneurs.

critics, J. P. Morgan managed to exert as much control over "other people's money" in the context of the fragmented American banking system as would a universal bank in a concentrated banking industry. According to Louis Brandeis and Samuel Untermyer, Morgan oversaw a complex "money trust" involving corporate boards of directors dominated by investment bankers who effectively enforced collusion among firms, limited competition by commercial banks (which were controlled by the investment bankers as well), and extracted rents for investment banking firms. From this jaundiced perspective, bankers' corporate-control services were really just selling protection, Mafia-style (Brandeis 1914). With respect to the German experience, Riesser (1911) argues that bank involvement in firms was neither a necessary nor a sufficient condition for enforcing cartels. Riesser claims that the influence of the banks was "decisive in some cases, less so in others, and hardly perceptible in some cases" (p. 712). Notably, in the chemical industry, industrial cartels were enforced with great apparent success despite the absence of bank involvement (pp. 721–25). Jeidels (1905, pp. 199–252) provides a much more detailed accounting of the role of German banks in industrial cartels. He argues that banks focused on individual customers and were not instigators in organizing cartels. Only after firms moved to establish cartels did banks assist in enforcing those arrangements. Both German and American history shows that bank discipline was not a unique means of enforcing industrial cartels. Policies other than prohibitions on universal banking are likely to be superior for facilitating competition within industries.

Second, it is not clear that an important or primary function of German universal banks or the American "money trust" was the enforcement of inefficient industrial cartels.[13] There have been many recent chal-

[13] To the extent cartels were inefficient in Germany, it was through monopolistic restriction of output. Another possible inefficiency associated with cartels – lack of innovation – does not seem to have been relevant in Germany. Indeed, Webb (1980) argues to the contrary that cartelization of the steel industry encouraged innovation. Furthermore, the ability to solve information problems efficiently is especially important to spurring innovation, as Schumpeter (1939), Butters and Lintner (1945), and many others have recognized. Here, too, German industry was at a distinct advantage, as the discussion in Section 4.3 will show. Tilly (1982) also points out that acquisitions within industries by best-practice producers were frequent, and this too can be credited to financing elasticity. Financing new ideas quickly may have increased competition within industries and quickly driven out inefficient firms. One should exercise caution in interpreting comparisons of the rate of start-up of new firms in the United States and Germany as a measure of innovativeness (and costs of cartels). New firms may have been more necessary to innovation in the United States because of a lack of corporate discipline, exercised in part through intermediaries (Berle and Means 1932). As the record of post-World War II Japan shows, innovativeness can be a feature of relatively concentrated industries, particularly if the management of firms in those industries are "disciplined" (Japan Development Bank 1994).

lenges to the notion that the Morgan syndicate was exclusively or mainly a device for extracting rent. Carosso (1970) and Huertas and Cleveland (1987) dispute the "findings" of the Pujo committee, arguing that investment banking was a competitive, contestable business. Entry was not blocked, and firms in need of finance did not feel compelled to use the same investment banker repeatedly. There was active competition for business, and repeated contacts reflected economies of information. If these authors are right, it follows that attempts by banks to restrict competition within industries would have encouraged entry by intermediaries to finance competing industrial firms. With respect to Germany, even Alexander Gerschenkron, a staunch advocate of the notion that banks enforced industrial cartels during the period of early industrialization, argued that this was not possible after 1900 because of ease of entry into banking (1962, pp. 15, 21, 88–89, 139). Jeidels (1905, pp. 122–30), Whale (1930, p. 35), and Tilly (1992, p. 109) support this view, arguing that German banking was a competitive industry after 1890, particularly in financing large, mature industrial firms.

Quantitative studies have been helpful, but not conclusive, in resolving the question of whether industrial cartel enforcement was historically an important function of intermediaries. De Long (1991) finds that the presence of a Morgan partner on a firm's board of directors increased the value of the firm's common stock by 30 percent. More importantly, he traces this increase in stock value to the superior earnings performance of Morgan companies: "The Morgan partnership and its peers saw themselves – and other participants saw them – as filling a crucial 'monitoring' and 'signaling' intermediary role between firms and investors in a world where information about firms' underlying values and the quality of their managers was scarce. . . . The presence of Morgan's men meant that when a firm got into trouble – whether because of 'excessive competition' or management mistakes – action would be taken to restore profitability" (1991, p. 209). De Long shows that investment banking firms were not simply vehicles for extracting rent, but he is not able to distinguish whether investment bankers increased the productivity of firms, or simply helped firms by eliminating their competition. "The relative roles of monopoly and efficiency in the 'Morganization premium' cannot be determined in a fashion convincing enough to overcome prior beliefs" (pp. 224–25). Another recent study, by Ramirez (1992), connects Morgan involvement with increases in the elasticity of credit supply for firms. Ramirez finds similar advantages in reducing cash-flow sensitivity of investment for German firms with universal banking connections. While these studies show that at least some of Morgan's contribution, and those of German universal banks, involved a credit relationship with the firm, they do not refute the notion that banks helped their clients by limiting competition within industry. Indeed, by giving client firms "deep pockets," Morgan may have helped them effectively threaten competitors with potential price wars.

In sum, the role of intermediaries in developing and enforcing industrial cartels remains a murky area in economic history. But to the extent such accusations have been made, they apply more broadly to the problems of all forms of interbank coalitions (notably to the American "money trust") and are not a peculiar feature of a concentrated universal banking system. Clearly, eliminating industrial cartels requires more draconian measures than restrictions on universal banking. These would include limits on cooperation, communication, and oversight among firms, banks, and securities dealers. Some of these were adopted in the United States as early as the 1890s, culminating in the 1914 Clayton Act prohibitions on interlocking directorates, the 1933 separation of commercial and investment banking, and the new trend toward fragmentation of both investment banking and commercial banking under the restrictive regulations of the New Deal. To the extent that these changes undermined monitoring and control networks, such drastic action may have caused more problems than it solved, by increasing financing costs of firms and by allowing firms' managers to escape the discipline of their stockholders and the marketplace (Berle and Means 1932; De Long 1991; Calomiris and Hubbard 1995). The most important point for the purposes of the German-American comparison in section 4.3 is that allowing a concentrated universal banking system in the United States during the pre–World War I era would have had little *marginal* effect on industrial cartelization.

4.2.7   Summary

This review of general perspectives on universal banking has argued that there are significant advantages of allowing banks to combine lending, equity holding, underwriting, trust activities, and deposit taking in the same intermediary, and thus significant costs to restricting this combination of activities. The advantages of universal banking arise from a combination of three factors. First, the corporate financial life cycle (or pecking order) entails a progression in which a firm's external financing evolves from short-term debt directly held by banks to widely held equity finance underwritten by banks. The optimal form of corporate finance and governance changes as firms become seasoned. Initially, banks discipline firms and limit their exposure to risk by holding short-term senior debt. As firms become seasoned, they come to rely on junior claims for their financing needs, and intermediaries underwriting firms' stock issues protect their interests by exercising direct control over firms through boards of directors. Second, there are economies of establishing long-term relationships between firms and intermediaries that revolve around the reusability of information and the smoothing of costs of external finance over the firm's life cycle (which may only be possible within the context of a long-term relationship).

Together, firms' changing financial needs over the life cycle and the advantages of long-term relationships between firms and intermediaries imply benefits to allowing intermediaries to engage in both underwriting and lending. A universal bank's ability to provide funds to firms at low cost requires a third factor – that the bank be allowed to operate a network of branches for collecting deposits and placing and managing securities. Widespread branching allows banks to diversify when making large loans to customers. It also economizes on information and transactions costs of placing and managing securities. The costs of credibly communicating the condition of firms to outsiders, and of gauging the market demand for new securities issues, are particularly large for equity issues. Large-scale universal banking reduces these costs by placing a single intermediary between ultimate holders and securities issuers. True universal banking allows banks to combine underwriting, lending, trust activities, and deposit taking within a single branching intermediary. Thus, despite the fact that national banks operated investment banking and trust affiliates in the 1920s, true universal banking never was permitted in the United States because of limitations on branching that effectively limited a bank's direct access to funds, and hence its ability to finance large-scale industry.

The next section is devoted to measuring German-American differences in financial structure and costs and relating them to theoretical perspectives on the advantages of universal banking. I argue that the absence of universal banking in the United States, and its presence in Germany, resulted in different methods and higher costs of financing American industrialization in the pre-World War I period.

4.3   Banking and Finance in Germany and America, 1870–1914

By the outbreak of World War I, Germany and the United States had developed financial systems that bore little resemblance to one another. The role of banks in corporate finance and corporate control, the types of financial instruments that dominated the scene, the way financial instruments were underwritten and sold, the combinations of activities that banks performed, and the financial structure of industrial firms and banks differed sharply between the two countries. This section reviews these differences in detail along dimensions suggested in Section 4.2, focusing on consequences for the cost of industrial finance. The evidence suggests substantially higher costs of industrial finance in the United States.

In light of these differences, I describe and attempt to explain the "inversion" that took place from 1850 to World War I in German and American financial institutions. American financial institutions circa 1850, like their German counterparts circa 1900, played a much greater role in industrial finance, especially in New England's early industrialization. In antebellum New England, a financial system flourished that bore much resemblance to the mature German system. The German financial system circa 1850 was more fragmented and less integrated than New England's, but rapidly progressed after 1870, and quickly developed a concentrated universal banking system. At the same time, New England's financial system moved away from its early structure, and from financing industrial activities of those closely involved with the banks. The "regressive" history of American banking from 1850 to 1920 reflected the increasing scale of industrial borrowers and their credit needs and the restrictions on bank branching and consolidation, which kept banks' size and geographical scope small while the size and scope of their customers grew. These restrictions on U.S. banks prevented them from reaping advantages of universal banking long before the separation of commercial and investment banking in 1933.

4.3.1   Relative factor intensity and capital scarcity in U.S. and German industrialization

The second industrial revolution, beginning in the mid-nineteenth century, saw rapid industrial expansion especially in the areas of railroads, steel, chemicals, and electricity. Germany and the United States were among the most impressive examples of industrial growth during this period, although Germany's heyday of industrial expansion began later than that of the United States. As Table 4.1 shows, in the United States, nonagricultural output grew most rapidly from 1850 to 1870, while in Germany rapid growth was more concentrated in the period from 1870 to the First World War. In the United States, value added in manufacturing, mining, and construction more than doubled from 1849 to 1869. Nonagricultural income grew by less than half from 1869 to 1889 and doubled from 1890 to 1913. In Germany, nonagricultural net product increased by less than half from 1850 to 1870, then doubled from 1870 to 1890, and more than doubled from 1890 to 1913.

Table 4.1. *Nonagricultural growth in Germany and the United States*

	Germany		United States		
	Nonagricultural NNP 1913 prices (millions of marks)	Nonagricultural labor (thousands)	Nonagricultural VA 1879 prices (millions of $)	Nonagricultural NI 1869 prices (millions of $)	Nonagricultural labor (thousands)
1849			670		
1850	5,052				
1869			1,550	5,325	6,193
1870	8,431				
1871		8,796			
1889				7,543	12,540
1890	15,857	12,807			
1910–13				16,519	20,871
1913	37,210	20,267			

Notes: NNP = net national product; VA = value added; NI = national income.
Sources: Real nonagricultural activity in the United States was calculated using value added in mining, manufacturing, and construction for 1849–69, from Gallman, as reported in U.S. Department of Commerce 1975, p. 239. For 1869–1913, I used Martin's data on current national income outside of agriculture (U.S. Department of Commerce 1975, p. 240), deflated by a nonagricultural output deflator. This deflator was constructed as follows. Romer's (1989, p. 22) GNP deflator is assumed to equal a weighted average of the nonagricultural deflator and the agricultural deflator (from Warren and Pearson for 1869–1890 and BLS for 1890 to 1910–13), as reported in U.S. Department of Commerce 1975, pp. 200–201, using Martin's weights for agricultural and nonagricultural income. For Germany, nonagricultural net national product and labor are derived from Hoffmann 1965, pp. 205, 454–55.

Despite the similarity in nonagricultural output growth rates in Germany and the United States from 1870 to 1913, the way growth was achieved was quite different. In the United States, employment in the nonagricultural sector grew by the same rate as output, while in Germany nonagricultural employment grew at half the rate of output. Relative to Germany, American industrialization relied more intensively on labor.

Goldsmith (1985) defines three capital-to-output ratios, using broad, intermediate, and narrow definitions of capital. The intermediate measure excludes land, and the narrow measure also excludes consumer durables and residential structures. A comparison for all three measures, for Germany and the United States at selected dates from 1850 to 1913, is provided in Table 4.2. The German capital-to-output ratio is substantially higher than that of the United States regardless of which measure is chosen, but the proportionate difference between the United States

Table 4.2. *Ratios of capital to GNP*

	Narrow capital measure		Intermediate capital measure		Broad capital measure	
	United States	Germany	United States	Germany	United States	Germany
1850	1.24	4.20	1.66	5.04	2.83	9.29
1875		3.29		4.26		7.12
1880	1.78		2.45		3.56	
1895		2.70		3.79		5.68
1900	1.81		2.91		4.56	
1912	1.71		2.69		4.17	
1913		3.42		4.82		6.58

Notes: Narrow capital is nonresidential structures, equipment, inventories, and livestock. Intermediate capital is narrow measure plus residential structures and consumer durables. Broad capital is intermediate measure plus land.
Source: Goldsmith 1985, pp. 39–42.

and Germany is greatest for the narrow measure, which focuses on the reproducible capital of producers. On average, from 1850 to 1913, the U.S. narrow capital-to-output ratio is half that of Germany.[14]

Field (1983, 1987) and Wright (1990) have emphasized the reliance placed by the United States on substitutes for fixed capital in the production process, especially natural resources. As Cain and Paterson (1981) document, materials prices fell sharply in the United States after the Civil War. Continuing discoveries of new resources, especially metals and oil fields, kept resource costs low throughout the pre-World War I period. Wright (1990, p. 658) notes that U.S. exports had far higher resource content than imports and that the resource intensity of exports increased substantially during late-nineteenth-century industrialization. By 1928, resource intensity of exports was 50 percent higher than its 1879 level. Wright follows Piore and Sabel (1984) and Williamson (1980) in linking the American utilization of resources with the "high-throughput" system of manufacture emphasized by Chandler (1977), which Field (1987) points out is a means to economize on capital costs. Wright and others also emphasize that the reliance on resources in the United States

[14] The capital intensity of the German economy in 1850 cannot be attributed to universal banking, since universal banking under limited liability laws began in 1870. Centralized government subsidization and planning of railroads, built ahead of demand, may account for the large capital-to-output ratio in the pre-1870 period (Dunlavy 1993).

Table 4.3. *Components of tangible reproducible assets*

	Germany (1913) (%)	United States (1912) (%)
Dwellings	25	24
Other structures	31	35
Equipment	26	13
Inventories	10	10
Livestock	5	5
Consumer durables	3	13

Source: Goldsmith 1985, p. 111.

was not exogenously determined. America's natural resource base is not among the richest in the world. Rather, the American reliance on natural resources, the development of production techniques that were resource intensive, and the emergence of high-throughput production and distribution processes were induced in part by the high cost of raising capital.

Goldsmith's (1985) breakdown of the components of the capital stock also provides interesting evidence about differences between the United States and Germany in the allocation of capital across different uses. Table 4.3 compares the shares of various components of tangible reproducible assets for Germany in 1913 and the United States in 1912. The shares of livestock, inventories, and structures are quite similar. The principal difference is the relative importance of equipment and consumer durables. In Germany, equipment is 26 percent of reproducible assets, while in the United States, it is half that percentage. Conversely, in the United States, consumer durables account for 13 percent of the total, while in Germany they make up only 3 percent. Comparisons for other years during the interval 1850 to 1900 lead to similar results, although in Germany the relative importance of equipment in reproducible assets grew during the pre-World War I era.

While there are many possible interpretations of the different weights for equipment in Germany and the United States, two points warrant emphasis. First, the greater relative weight in Germany is unlikely to be the result of measurement error. Both countries' data are derived from the same individual's work – Goldsmith 1955–56, 1976; and Goldsmith, Lipsey, and Mendelson 1963. Thus, gross incomparabilities across categories or insensitivity to data source differences are unlikely to explain the differences. One problem worth worrying about is whether the German data on equipment include items that would have been excluded from consumer durables in Germany, but included in consumer durables in the United States. I examined the items included in U.S. consumer durables to see whether production equipment located at home might explain the observed differences. Goldsmith (1955–56, 1: p. 680) reports nonfarm individuals' expenditures on the main categories of consumer durable goods. These categories include "furniture, household appliances, house furnishings, china etc., musical instruments, books, passenger cars, passenger car accessories, medical appliances, and miscellaneous." None of these sounds like production equipment. Even if "household appliances" or "miscellaneous" includes some producer durables, these constitute such a small share of total consumer durables (16 percent in 1913) that they could not account for the difference between German and American equipment shares.

The second point to emphasize, in anticipation of the discussion that follows, is that the greater reliance on equipment in Germany is consistent with a lower cost of financing industrial expansion, particularly in the form of large-scale factory production.[15] Equipment-intensive production is more capital-intensive because of its lower "throughput" rate (Field 1987). Also, equipment is less liquid than materials, which makes it harder to collateralize and finance.

4.3.2   Interregional and intersectoral capital allocation in the United States

The cost of capital was not uniform within the United States across locations, sectors, or time. Interregional and intersectoral differences in rates of return on capital in the United States (a measure of inefficiency in capital allocation) were largest during the mid- to late-nineteenth-century. But even as late as the 1920s, Federal Reserve surveys show that interest rates on like bank loans in provincial U.S. cities could be 4 or 5 percent higher than rates in eastern financial centers (Riefler 1930, p. 79). Breckenridge (1899, p. 5) contrasted the enormous interregional variation in low-risk U.S. interest rates with those of European countries, including Germany. For Germany, he cites evidence that the interest rates in 260 provincial towns were identical to those charged in Berlin for loans of a standard quality. As Bodenhorn (1992) shows, the ante-

---

[15] It is also interesting to note that the production of producer durables is relatively capital-intensive. Creamer and Borenstein (1960, p. 52) show that the capital-output ratios of capital-equipment industries were 1.05 in 1900, compared to 0.68 for consumption-goods industries.

bellum United States did not suffer from large interregional differences in costs of funds. The integration of capital markets seems to have worsened during the geographical expansion and industrialization of the post-bellum era. In their study of the profitability of American enterprises from 1850 to 1880, Atack and Bateman (1992) find that interregional profit-rate differentials in the United States were largest in the industrial sector, that industrial profit rates were far above profit rates in other sectors, and that convergence in profit rates for manufacturing was most protracted. They attribute this to capital immobility across regions and across sectors that kept the capital stock of manufacturing enterprises low.

4.3.3   The different roles of banks in industrial finance

Qualitative discussions of the importance of German banks to industrial progress date from Jeidels (1905), Riesser (1911), Schumpeter (1939), and Gerschenkron (1962). Goldsmith (1985) provides detailed comparative analyses of many countries, and quantitative measures of important features of German finance from an international comparative perspective. Goldsmith (1958) and Goldsmith, Lipsey, and Mendelson (1963) analyze the funding sources of American industrialization in detail.

Goldsmith (1985, p. 135) defines the "financial intermediation ratio" as a rough, general measure of the economy's reliance on intermediation for the creation of wealth. The financial intermediation ratio for Germany rose from 20.3 in 1850 to 30.1 in 1913. Over this same period, the U.S. ratio rose from 12.5 to 21.3. By this measure, the United States was fifth from the lowest in a field of thirteen, while Germany was near the top. Seven nations had ratios in excess of 29 for 1913, and the average ratio for twelve nations (excluding the outlier, India, with a ratio of 8) was 27.

If one focuses on the specific links between bank lending and industrialization, the contrast between the roles of banks in Germany and the United States is greater. In Germany, the universal banks were responsible for providing a large share of industrial finance. The financing of industrial credit involved some four hundred joint-stock banks operating more than one thousand branches nationwide by 1913. Eleven large incorporated banks accounted for more than one-third of the capital and assets of the system. Banks lent directly to firms through very short-term overdraft accounts (with average maturities of less than one month), held and managed stocks and bonds of firms, and acted as investment bankers for firms' securities issues. The importance of universal banking in German industrial finance was especially pronounced after the 1890s' consolidation movement in banking, which Jeidels (1905, pp. 83–107) argues largely reflected the increasingly large-scale financing needs of industry.

Consistent with section 4.2's discussion of the changing role of universal banks over the life cycle of the firm, new projects were often financed directly through short-term bank loans. Later, financing was transformed to long-term securities, placed by the bank that had originally made the loan (Jeidels 1905, pp. 109–22; Riesser 1911, pp. 364–69; Whale 1930, pp. 37–38; Eistert 1970, p. 91). Jeidels (1905) provides a detailed accounting of the involvement of banks over the life cycle of firms. The first stage of the firm-bank relationship saw keen competition among banks in the loan market for overdraft credit accounts (Jeidels 1905, p. 122). Interest costs for overdraft credit were typically set at the interbank lending rate plus 1 percent (Whale 1930, pp. 37–38). In the early stages of the firm life cycle, the bank's main lever of influence over the firm was the threat of revoking the line of credit. Jeidels (p. 126) cites as an example of bank discipline a 1901 letter the Dresdner Bank wrote to one of its customers, threatening cancellation of credit if an upcoming vote by the board of directors went the wrong way.

As the firm-bank relationship matured, equity took the place of overdraft credit and the bank's role in corporate governance changed from threatening the board of directors to becoming part of the board of directors (Jeidels 1905, p. 128). On occasion, when bank positions were challenged by other members of boards of directors, banks resorted to massive purchases of company stock to secure controlling interest (Jeidels 1905, p. 111). Still later in the firm's life cycle, the influence of its principal banker typically waned, and other banks competed for its underwriting business (Jeidels 1905, pp. 128–30).

With respect to the quantity of bank holdings of claims on firms, Table 4.4 reports Eistert's year-end estimates of the amount of direct overdraft financing of industry (a component of overdrafts, or *Kontokorrentkredite*, from which Eistert excludes overdraft lending for securities transactions and bankers acceptances for financing trade). Table 4.4 also reports the amount of "permanent" participations of the banks (typically confined to bank shares in subsidiary financial institutions: Whale 1930, pp. 47–48, 150), banks' other securities holdings (including underwriting inventories), and the amount of bankers' acceptances financing commerce. The table also displays each of these asset categories as a fraction of total bank assets. While banks played an important role as holders of claims, just as important was their role in helping firms graduate (apparently rapidly) to find ultimate sources of funds outside the banking system. Thus, the banks used their special position as "delegated monitors" to "lever" their clients' finances – allowing their clients to reach a

Table 4.4. *Selected assets of the German credit banks, levels and percentage of total assets*

	Industrial credit (millions of marks)	%	Acceptances (millions of marks)	%	"Permanent" participations (millions of marks)	%	Other securities (millions of marks)	%
1888	329.1	12	448.3	16	32.4	1	338.4	12
1893	416.5	12	631.5	18	67.9	2	351.9	10
1898	902.1	14	984.4	15	183.4	3	728.0	11
1903	1,334.2	15	1,301.2	15	236.1	3	956.5	11
1907	2,336.6	18	1,890.7	15	439.4	3	1,289.6	10
1913	2,930.3	18	2,450.6	15	—	—	—	—

Notes: Some asset categories are omitted from this table, including cash assets, collateralized loans, and lending for securities purchases. Industrial credit is defined as *Kontokottenkredite* (overdraft account credit) for industrial purposes. Acceptances are bankers' acceptances used primarily to finance goods in transit. Permanent participations are long-term securities holdings of banks, which are mainly stock held in other (essentially subsidiary) financial institutions. Other securities pertains to all other securities held, which mainly reflects ongoing underwriting activities.

Sources: Industrial credit and acceptances derived from Eistert 1970, p. 92. Data for permanent participations and other securities are from National Monetary Commission 1910, Table 15, except for total assets for 1913. Total assets for 1913 is taken from Deutsche Bundesbank 1976, p. 56.

broad market for external finance by providing direct lending at early stages of projects, and later underwriting equity as a signal of their clients' quality possibly and as a vehicle for sharing in capital gains (as argued in Section 4.2's discussion of time consistency).

Jeidels (1905, p. 106) and Eistert (1970, p. 142) interpret the rising importance of *Kontokorrentkredite* after 1890 as evidence of increasing bank involvement in financing new industrial projects after the 1890s, which they see as significant evidence of the role of banks in priming the pumps of industrial finance during this crucial period of German industrial growth. The bank acted as a monitor of the firm's conduct, a source of discipline over management (through directorates and voting of clients' shares), and a source of advice on financial and business organization.

Specific evidence from industry case studies on the role of German banks in industrial finance is abundant. Jeidels (1905) and Riesser (1911) provide lengthy discussions of the evolution of the major German industries and the roles played by banks. For example, Riesser (1911, pp. 713–21) argues that assistance by informed bank lenders was crucial to the development of the electrical industry. He discusses the coevolution of firms and banks and describes how the role banks played changed with the industrial organization of the industry. Initially, banks promoted widespread entry by a multitude of firms, and funding of firms' needs was accomplished through direct lending, followed later by placements of securities. As the industry developed, consolidation of firms raised the scale of financing needs, which in turn increased the need for interbank cooperation through financing syndicates. Banks reinforced the trend toward industrial concentration by helping to coordinate decision making among firms. The history of the electrical industry illustrates how banks encouraged technological innovativeness at the crucial early stage of industrial development and made efficient large-scale operations feasible. The Germans developed a larger and more interregional electrical utility system than that of Britain or the United States during this period (Hughes 1983). Carlson (1991) argues that the greater fragmentation of the U.S. electrical system reflected financing constraints. On the demand side, utility customers were financed by electrical manufacturers rather than banks. According to Carlson, this hampered the ability of manufacturers to expand and integrate their operations, and led to a less standardized range of products in the United States.

Links between industrial firms and banks were much weaker in the United States. This reflected in large part the small size of incorporated banks relative to the large needs of industrial borrowers. More than twenty-six thousand banks were operating in 1914, and the overwhelming majority of these were not permitted to operate branches, even within their home state. Even the limited operation of universal banking through securities affiliates did not begin in earnest until after World War I. The first three investment affiliates of national banks were organized between 1908 and 1917, and served as models for the growth of affiliates in the 1920s (Peach 1941, pp. 18–20, 61–64).

Much of bank financing of firms occurred without any direct (much less ongoing) relationship between the bank and the firms it financed. Intermediaries' claims on firms primarily took the form of corporate bond holdings placed through syndicates. According to Goldsmith (1958, p. 222), for the period 1901–12, bonds held by all intermediaries accounted for 18 percent of funds supplied by external sources (that is, excluding retained earnings) to nonfinancial firms. Commercial banks accounted for two-thirds of corporate bond holdings by intermediaries in 1912.[16] Based on flow-of-funds accounting, bank loans (for all purposes) accounted for 12 percent of externally supplied funds for 1901–12. Using balance-sheet data of nonfinancial corporations for 1900 and 1912, Goldsmith, Lipsey, and Mendelson (1963, 2: p. 146) calculate that bank loans amounted to roughly 10 percent of firms' debts, and less than 5 percent of firms' assets. Bonds and notes accounted for roughly half of firms' debts, and trade debt made up 15 percent. The use of short-term bank lending to finance industrial operations, as distinct from commerce, cannot be quantified (see Goldsmith 1958, p. 344).

Reliance on bank loans was relatively high for small firms. Large manufacturing firms relied more on bond issues as a means of indirect bank finance (Goldsmith 1958, pp. 217–18) and less on loans from banks as a source of financing, especially prior to the 1940s. Of course, under a unit banking system, large-scale firms operating throughout the country would have had to borrow from many small unit banks simultaneously. Bond market syndications facilitated this transaction by providing a means for banks to share risk and coordinate capital allocations. The commercial paper market (a unique innovation of the American financial system) performed a similar role for short-term borrowing needs of large, high-quality borrowers. From humble beginnings in the 1870s, the commercial paper market reached its pre–World War II peak in 1920 at $1.3 billion, consisting of the debts of over four thousand borrowers (Selden 1963, p. 8).

Dobrovolsky and Bernstein (1960, pp. 141–42) report funding sources for a sample of fourteen large manufacturing firms from 1900 to 1910, based on accounting records of sources of net inflows of funds. For the

---

[16] Goldsmith (1958, p. 335) gives total intermediaries' holdings of bonds. He provides data on commercial banks' bond holdings, decomposed according to type of issuer (pp. 339–40).

period 1900–1910, these firms reported a total financial inflow of $1.2 billion, of which $357 million came from external finance. Of this, only $29 million was in the form of short-term debt. Some bank loans during this period also took the form of long-term debt, but judging from Goldsmith (1958, pp. 335, 339), long-term loans from commercial banks were uncommon around the turn of the century.

While small firms relied more on banks, it does not follow that banks contributed to the financing of industrial capital expansion by small firms any more than they did to that of large firms. Two detailed studies of the sources of capital in manufacturing provide a glimpse of the contribution of banks to industrial expansion in Illinois (Marquardt 1960) and California (Trusk 1960) in the mid- to late nineteenth century. In the case of California, thirty-three of seventy-one manufacturing firms studies over the period 1859–1880 financed their investment entirely from internal sources. The others incorporated, took in partners, and supplemented these sources with earnings of existing partners from other sources, sale of stock or real estate, "eastern capital" (in three cases), and loans from a *private* banker (the same banker in both instances). Apparently, commercial banks had no role in the expansion of manufacturing capital in California prior to 1880.

Illinois's experience was similar, but the role of banks in financing industrial expansion may have been greater. The rapid expansion of manufacturing in Illinois began in the 1860s. From 1860 to 1870, manufacturing production and capital each increased sevenfold, and employment increased sixfold. From 1870 to 1880, manufacturing production doubled. Marquardt (1960) examined the personal and business histories of fifty entrepreneurs. She found that these firms were financed initially from accumulated savings of would-be manufacturing entrepreneurs, or by entrepreneurs taking on a partner with savings. Subsequent funding typically was provided by retained earnings. Occasionally, this was supplemented by the sale of entrepreneurial assets, the expansion of the partnership, or incorporation. In twenty-six out of fifty cases, manufacturing entrepreneurs of relatively mature firms used profits to invest in an interest in a bank, which "marked the beginning of more rapid success for them. They owned in part or had access to, funds, either large or small, which would enable them to grow and to progress." This was especially important in the 1860s because manufacturing was moving rapidly toward mechanization and opportunities for expansion outpaced accumulated profits (p. 507). In short, firms progressed up the pecking order as they matured. Entrepreneurs secured access to external funds by investing in banks, on which they could rely for funds. While Marquardt's study does indicate a role for banks in industrial finance, it says as much about the limits of that role as it does about banks' potential importance. Access to bank funds was extremely limited, and bank stockholders were given preference as bank borrowers. Such a system had worked well to provide the needs of business in New England in the antebellum period (Lamoreaux 1994), but by the 1870s, this system was insufficient. Restrictions on insider lending, combined with the rising scale of manufacturing and the limited size of unit banks, meant that access to a unit bank's deposit base could not keep pace with the needs of bank insiders. Thus, while banks may have played a role in financing industrial expansion in Illinois and elsewhere, the importance of this role was limited to the "adolescent" stage of the firm's life cycle – after the firm had become mature enough to invest in becoming a bank insider, but before the firm had become too large to rely on a unit bank for its funding needs. Even this role of banks in industrial finance is apparent only in the histories of some firms (roughly half of those chosen for case studies by Marquardt).

To summarize, unlike German industrialists, American industrialists could not depend on a single banking relationship to guide them through their growing and changing financial needs over the years. They relied less on banks for credit, especially to finance large-scale projects. At each stage in their financial life cycle, firms had to change their financial relationships as they moved to new financial instruments and new funding sources for their investments. The small size of banks limited bank lending to large-scale firms. Even relatively large banks in major cities considering lending to industrial firms would have foreseen limited future relationships with borrowers, making some lending prohibitively expensive (Mayer 1988). Finally, given the reduced role of intermediaries in direct lending, bank finance of industry was limited mainly to holding securities placed through syndicates. The form of these financial instruments and their costs are subjects to which I now turn.

4.3.4 *Financial instruments and the financial structure of industrial firms*

Section 4.2 highlighted some important disadvantages of long-term debt financing compared to a combination of short-term debt and equity. Relative to short-term debt, long-term debt can be costly because of incentive problems (the firm's incentive to add risk increases with the maturity of debt). Relative to equity, all forms of debt increase the probability of financial distress by raising leverage. Finally, when a firm's debt takes the form of dispersed debt holdings, rather than concentrated lending from intermediaries, the costs of managing financial distress (coordinating workouts) is increased (see Riesser 1911, pp. 365–66, on German banks' roles in managing reorganizations). For all these reasons, long-term debt is a costly form of finance. If, however, firms are constrained to finance themselves through syndication networks rather than through intermediaries, then the transactions costs of rollover of short-term debt can be prohibitive. And equity may not be a feasible alternative to debt, either because the costs of resolving asymmetric information between firms and ultimate sources of funds are large (because the "lemons discount" for equity will be larger than that for debt, as in Myers and Majluf 1984), or because the equity holder is unable to exert control over corporate management (Jensen and Meckling 1976). Baskin (1988) argues that asymmetric information explains the dearth of equity issues historically in the United States. Thus, despite its high costs, long-term debt may be the best means for firms to raise funds. in the absence of large-scale, universal banking. Of course, in light of incentive problems of issuing long-term debt, risky firms may be denied access to this market as well, leaving them to rely on retained earnings alone as a source of finance.[17]

According to this interpretation of long-term debt as a "last resort" in the absence of alternatives – albeit one not available to all firms – one would expect the structure of German firms' balance sheets to rely far less on long-term debt than do American firms. Table 4.5 confirms this prediction. Private domestic corporate bond issues are a much smaller fraction of total securities issues in Germany than in the United States over the pre–World War I period, and represent a relatively small fraction of outstanding corporate claims. Moreover, the German data on bond issues are for gross issues, while the U.S. data are for net issues; thus, the difference reported in Table 4.5 in the relative amount of stock and bond issues understates the true difference. In Germany, firms made a relatively rapid transition from *Kontokorrentkredite* into the equity

---

[17] Indeed, access to bond markets has sometimes been very selective. Calomiris and Hubbard (1995) found that very few firms in their sample of publicly traded firms in the mid-1930s had access to the bond market. Only a quarter of all firms issued bonds, and 10 percent of firms accounted for 90 percent of bond issues. Bond-issuing firms were three time as large as non-bond-issuing firms. Interestingly, while firms with higher measured costs of finance had higher debt ratios, they were less likely to have outstanding debt in the form of bonds. These data support the view that incentive problems of long-term debt may have limited its use. An alternative explanation for the Calomiris-Hubbard sample would argue that access to the bond market was substantially limited by regulatory change in 1935. Prior to the Banking Act of 1935, banks were allowed to sell low-grade bonds to their customers. After 1935, this was prohibited (Haven 1940, p. 7).

Table 4.5. *Corporate finance in Germany and the United States prior to World War I*

Balance-sheet data for nonfinancial corporations

	United States, 1900 (millions of $)	United States, 1912 (millions of $)	Germany, 1900 (millions of marks)	Germany, 1912 (millions of marks)
Equity	19,960	33,108	19,210	31,157
Total liability	15,038	33,246		
Trade debt	3,066	4,355		
Bank loans	1,420	3,780		
Mortgages	778	1,674		
Bonds and notes	7,072	18,096	1,883	3,560

Securities issues data

	U.S. manufacturing and mining		U.S. industrials		German nonfinancial domestic corporations	
	Net bond issues (millions of $)	Net stock issues (millions of $)	Gross bond issues, annual average (millions of $)	Gross bond issues, annual average (millions of $)	Gross bond issues (millions of marks)	Gross stock issues (millions of marks)
1896					177	324
1897					172	381
1898					303	677
1899					329	911
1900	37	128			276	562
1901	557	256			339	276
1902	151	141			263	362
1903	252	119			188	299
1904	74	103			187	398
1905	122	118			339	540
1906	113	165			245	1,251
1907	125	168			272	637
1908	107	136			473	651
1909	139	183			419	682
1910	124	178			221	573
1911	206	203			422	505
1912	50	288			509	984
1913	−10	185			460	811
1900–13	2,047	2,371				
1901–12			110	150		
1896–1913					5,594	10,824

Sources: Balance sheets of U.S. nonfinancial corporations are from Goldsmith, Lipsey, and Mendelson 1963, 2: p. 146. German data on equity and bonds are from Deutsche Bunbesbank 1976, pp. 290, 294. The German data on bonds seem to be face values (which are essentially the same as market values). To calculate the market value of German equity, I combined the book-value estimate (p. 290) with the market-to-book-value index for corporate stocks (p. 294). For example, German equity book value in 1900 was 10,384 million marks and the index was 1.85. Data on securities issues of U.S. manufacturing and mining corporations are from Dobrovolsky and Bernstein 1960, p. 333. Data on securities issues of industrials are from Friend 1967, p. 68. Data on German securities issues are from Eistert 1970, p. 105.

Table 4.6. *Sources of bank financing, Germany and the United States, 1904*

	German Credit Banks (millions of marks)	U.S. National Banks (millions of $)
Net worth (book)	2,873	1,341
Liabilities	6,518	5,364
Deposit accounts	1,897	
Credit accounts	3,301	
Acceptances	1,320	
Currency issued	0	433
Net worth/liabilities	0.44	0.25

Sources: National bank balance-sheet data are derived from state-level data reported in Board of Governors of the Federal Reserve System 1959. National banknotes are from Board of Governors of the Federal Reserve System 1976, p. 408. German data are from National Monetary Commission 1910, Table 15.

market, and relied relatively little on bond finance. In the United States, industrial finance through outside equity was more limited. Indeed, as Carosso (1970, pp. 81–82) points out, for many industrial and retail establishments prior to World War I, outside equity issues were not a possibility. As Doyle (1991) points out in his detailed analysis of sugar-refining and meat-packing industries, equity issues of American firms during this period typically were associated with "strategic" restructuring of the firm's preexisting liabilities, and not with the financing of industrial expansion.

4.3.5 The financial structure of banks

Sources of finance for banks also were very different in Germany and the United States, with German banks relying to a much greater extent on equity rather than deposits as a source of funds. Of course, unlike national banks, the German credit banks did not issue currency, so one might expect them to show larger equity ratios than American banks for this reason. But this does not explain the difference. State-chartered banks in the United States lacked note-issuing authority, but had similar capital ratios to national banks. As Table 4.6 shows, the difference between German banks' and U.S. national banks' capital-to-asset ratios is larger than can be explained by the presence of notes on national bank balance sheets.

The high German capital ratios are especially puzzling when one considers the large size of German banks compared to U.S. banks. Within the United States, larger banks tended to have lower capital ratios than small banks. For example, Calomiris (1993) shows that branching banks in California had half the capital ratios of other U.S. banks. Similarly, adjusting for differences in portfolio risk, large nationwide (nonuniversal) commercial banks in Canada had lower capital ratios than their American counterparts. Calomiris (1993) argues that lower capital ratios for large commercial banks reflected risk reductions brought about by large size. As banks became large, they were able to satisfy depositors' concerns about risk with smaller capital ratios. Banks wanted to conserve on capital because it was a relatively expensive form of finance. The limitation on banks' access to capital is illustrated by the fact that the demand for bank stock was confined mainly to investors located near the bank. A study by the Comptroller of the Currency of stock ownership in national banks in 1897 revealed that the largest out-of-state holdings were for the western and Pacific regions, which had out-of-state holdings of less than 12 percent (Breckenridge 1899, p. 10). Thus a possible explanation of the higher capital ratios of German universal banks could be the higher demand for bank stock by "outsiders."

What would explain higher demand by outsiders for universal banks' stock? First, given the potential for German nonfinancial firms to issue large amounts of equity, "thick-market" externalities may have favored similar financing by banks. Second, if German banks were better able to communicate information about their portfolio risks to their stockholders, then lemons discounts would be mitigated, allowing them to reap the advantages of equity finance. Thus, the efficiency of capital markets in Germany due to universal banking may have helped finance banks, too. Third, the confidence of outsiders in bank stock may have been enhanced by a reputational effect. If outsiders were aware that banks had long-term reputational capital worth preserving, then they should have been less concerned about short-term cheating by banks. Thus, the disciplinary role of demandable debt (stressed by Calomiris and Kahn 1991; Calomiris, Kahn, and Krasa 1991) would be less relevant for German banks. From this perspective, German banks may have been able to finance themselves more through outside equity than American banks because of long-run benefits they could expect to realize through their relationships with firms. These long-run benefits increased the reputational consequences of cheating and helped to support the credibility of bankers.

It may never be possible to distinguish among these explanations for the higher equity ratios of German banks. But this decomposition is rel-

atively unimportant. The important common feature of all these explanations is their dependence on universal banking as a precondition to
permitting banks to rely on outside equity as an important source of
finance.

4.3.6   Investment banking spread as a measure of
financing efficiency

An important dimension of cost savings stressed in Section 4.2's discussion of the benefits of universal banking is the reduction in the cost to
firms of underwriting and distributing securities. The investment banker's
"spread" is defined as the difference between the market value of securities issued and the value received for these issues by the issuing firm.
Data on spreads are useful for three purposes. First, average issue costs
provide an overall comparison of the costs of issuing securities in the
United States and Germany. Second, variation in spreads across securities and firms of different types can be used to gauge cross-country differences in the relative costs of issuing particular kinds of securities. For
example, one would expect equity issues to be especially costly in the
United States relative to Germany because of the greater costs of placing
junior securities in a nonuniversal banking system. Finally, firm-level data
on the factors that raise or lower costs of securities issues offer evidence
on the sources of the costs of issuing bonds and stocks. For example, one
can examine whether bankers' spreads primarily reflect information
costs, physical transactions costs, taxes, or economic rents of the investment banker.

American investment bankers have guarded the details of their financial arrangements carefully, and data on investment bankers' spreads are
notoriously hard to come by. For the United States, detailed data are
known only for a few cases prior to the 1920s, and only after 1936 are
data available for the whole population of securities issuers. For
Germany, I have been able to locate some data on individual spreads for
the pre–World War I period from *Saling 's Borsen Jahrbuch* (the German
equivalent of *Moody's Industrial Manual*). For many firms (roughly half),
Saling's reports details of the underwriting costs of equity issues and/or
the total amount of funds received by firms through equity issues. A
minor problem with the data is that it is not always clear whether
reported numbers include fees other than bankers' commissions. Equity
issues entailed local and national taxes, as well as physical costs (printing, etc.). From examples where the breakdown of such costs is known,
the total costs of taxes and physical expenses seem in the range of 2–3

percent. For example, Harpener Bergbau A. G., a large Dortmund mining company, issued 9 million marks of stock in 1909. The spread was 436,000 marks, or 4.84 percent of the issue. Of this cost, 176,000 marks (40 percent of the total cost) reflected the national government tax on equity issues.[18] Thus, in the absence of the government's securities tax, the bankers' spread would have been 2.9 percent. While reported data on commissions may overstate true commissions (because bankers sometimes paid these fees for firms), and reported data on total costs may understate total costs (because measured costs may not always include federal or local taxes), errors from these sources cannot be large, and data from firms that reported both measures indicate that reported total costs generally included all costs and that reported commissions generally did not include fees other than commissions.

Data on commissions for common stock issues earned by German banks from 1893 to 1913 are provided in Table 4.7. The sample of firms for which data were collected include all reporting firms in the electrical industry (which includes manufacturers of electrical equipment and operating power plants) and firms in the metal manufacturing industry whose names begin with the letters A through K. Both of these industries are important producers of new products, and both are central to the second industrial revolution. The metal manufacturing industry includes many small firms, while the electrical industry is dominated by large firms, so together these two industries can provide some evidence on the role of firm size and issue size in determining bankers' commissions. For both industries, I divide the sample into small and large issues (less than or greater than 1 million marks, which equals $220,000). For metals, I also report data for firms with small total capital in 1913 (less than 2 million marks). The difference between average spreads and average total costs is 1.41 percent for the electrical industry and 1.40 percent for metal manufacturing, which suggests that taxes and physical costs were generally included in total costs and not in commissions. Bankers' commissions averaged 3.67 percent for the electrical industry and 3.90 percent for metal manufacturing. Commissions on small and large issues are essentially the same. Although small metals issues show lower average costs, the difference is not statistically significant for this small sample. Metals firms with low total capital had average commissions of 4.11 percent, compared to 3.90 percent for the industry as a whole. Again, this difference is small and not statistically significant.

---

[18] I thank Richard Tilly for providing this example.

Table 4.7. *Bankers' commissions (spreads) and total issuing costs for German common stock issues, 1893–1913 (%)*

	Mean bank spread	25th percentile bank spread	75th percentile bank spread	Mean total cost	25th percentile total cost	75th percentile total cost
All issues						
Electrical	3.67	2.57	4.55	5.08	3.61	7.00
# firms	13	—	—	12	—	—
# observations	21	—	—	20	—	—
Manufacturing	3.90	2.94	4.35	5.30	2.78	7.60
# firms	19	—	—	15	—	—
# observations	30	—	—	20	—	—
Issues less than 1 million						
Electrical	3.94	3.49	4.26	5.24	4.00	6.72
# firms	4	—	—	3	—	—
# observations	7	—	—	3	—	—
Manufacturing	3.45	2.78	3.86	5.29	3.33	6.92
# firms	10	—	—	10	—	—
# observations	18	—	—	15	—	—
Firms with 1913 capital less than 2 million						
Manufacturing	4.11	3.57	4.80	5.93	3.33	8.80
# firms	3	—	—	5	—	—
# observations	6	—	—	5	—	—

Notes: Percentage of bankers' commissions (spreads) is the difference between the amount paid for an issue by purchasers and the amount paid by the bankers to the issuing firm divided by the total amount paid for the issue. Percentage of total costs is the net funds raised by the firm (net of all expenses, including taxes, printing costs, and commissions) divided by the amount paid for the issue. Data are for firms that reported such information in *Saling's Borsen Jahrbuch* in the electrical industry (electrical equipment producers and power plant operators) and the metal manufacturers industry. The sample includes all reporting firms in the electrical industry and all reporting firms whose names begin with *A* through *K* for the metals manufacturing industry.
Source: *Saling's Borsen Jahrbuch* 1913.

Overall, these data support the view that commissions on common stock were roughly 3–5 percent, and that they did not vary much by industry, firm size, or size of issue.

For the United States, firm-level data on bankers' commissions are not generally available for the pre–World War I period. Indeed, the dearth of equity issues in the United States historically made it difficult for the Securities and Exchange Commission to locate data on common stock spreads prior to 1936. Even with respect to bonds and preferred stock, the SEC's retrospective study begins only in the 1920s. Despite this problem, it is possible to gauge roughly the range of commission charges during the pre–World War I period using data from the later period and a few observations on individual transactions from the pre-World War I period. Data on bankers' spreads for bonds and preferred stocks during the 1920s and common stock spreads for the 1930s reported in Table 4.8 are a reasonable, and possibly a conservative, measure of their pre–World War I values.

There is little evidence of change in preferred stock or bond spreads from the 1920s to the mid-1930s, so there is little reason to believe that spreads were influenced by the Glass-Steagall separation of commercial and investment banking.[19] As argued above, the fundamental restrictions on universal banking were regulations that fragmented the banking system, and these were in place long before Glass-Steagall. Moreover, there is some discussion of spreads for the pre–World War I period that confirms this view. Brandeis (1914, pp. 94–99) discusses bankers' spreads at length in his attack on the money trust. He notes that Morgan's spread exceeded 20 percent for the organization of U.S. Steel, and was 25 percent for underwriting the "Tube Trust." More generally, Brandeis writes: "Nor were monster commissions limited to trust promotions. More recently, bankers' syndicates have, in many instances, received for floating preferred stocks of recapitalized industrial concerns, one-third of all common stock issued, besides a considerable sum in cash. And for the sale of preferred stock of well established manufacturing concerns, cash commissions (or profits) of from $7^{1}/_{2}$ to 10 percent of the cash raised are often exacted. On bonds of high-class industrial concerns, bankers' commissions (or profits) of from 5 to 10 points have been common" (p. 95). These figures are similar to the numbers for the 1920s and mid-1930s reported in Table 4.8.

Interestingly, the spreads for common stock far exceed those for preferred stock, which in turn far exceed those for bonds. This is what one would expect if the spreads largely represent compensation for information costs incurred in arranging the issues. The underwriting (insurance) aspect of the investment bankers' services do not explain the differences in the spreads for different types of securities. In fact, best-effort flotations, on which there is no underwriting risk, show *larger* commissions on average than underwritten flotations. This typically is explained by the fact that best-effort flotations involve riskier firms (Friend 1967, p. 39) and therefore entail greater due diligence and marketing costs.

It is worth emphasizing how large these spreads are. A 20 percent

---

[19] Calomiris and Raff (1995) report data on common stock spreads from the Lehman Brothers deal books and argue, based on these data, that common stock spreads were essentially the same in the 1920s and 1930s.

Table 4.8.   *Bankers' spreads in the United States before World War II*

	1925–29 (% of issue)			1930s (% of issue)		
	Common	Preferred	Bonds	Common	Preferred	Bonds
Issues <$5 million				(1935–38)	(1935–38)	(1935–38)
Total costs	NA	8	6	18	10	5
Compensation	NA	7	5	16	9	4
Other expenses	NA	1	1	2	1	1
# of issues	NA	96	423	241	206	210
All to public, IBs[a]				(1938)	(1938)	(1940)
Total costs				22	12	3
Compensation				20	11	2
Other expenses				2	1	1
# of issues				68	37	76
All to public, IBs[a]				(1938)	(1938)	(1940)
Total cost, underwritten issues				23	4	3
# of issues				16	9	31
Total cost, best efforts[b]				21	14	16
# of issues				52	28	1

[a] All issues of securities to the public transacted through investment bankers.
[b] Best-effort issues are placed by investment bankers without price guarantees.
Sources: Securities and Exchange Commission 1940, 1941.

spread indicates that a firm only receives 80 cents for every dollar of claims it issues. This places a substantial cost on investments, especially by young, unseasoned firms. An investment opportunity must be able to generate enough income to pay interest or dividends to claimants *and* compensate existing shareholders by an amount (in present value) in excess of 20 percent of the project's cost.

There is corroborating evidence that external finance costs placed wedges of this magnitude between the social and private benefits of pursuing investment projects. Calomiris and Hubbard (1995) find that in the mid-1930s roughly a quarter of publicly traded firms in the United States had a cost differential between internally and externally generated funds in excess of 20 percent. They used a firm's dividend-payout reaction to the undistributed profits tax of 1936–37 to measure this shadow price differential. In a study of nineteenth-century profits, Atack and Bateman (1992) find large and widening differences in profit rates between small and large manufacturing firms in the United States of a similar order of magnitude, which suggest barriers to entry and geographic immobility of capital for financing small and medium-sized firms in manufacturing.[20]

The data reported in Tables 4.7 and 4.8 indicate a substantially lower average cost of bringing equities to market in Germany, which helps to explain the relative dearth of equity issues in the United States shown in Table 4.5. German bankers' spreads on equity were less than one-fourth those in the United States. Small German firms were able to issue equity for less than the cost large American corporations paid for issuing bonds. Interestingly, in Germany, spreads did not vary by size as they did in the United States. This is consistent with viewing universal banking networks (which permit internal marketing of new issues) as economizing on adverse-selection costs of marketing stock issues.

One possible explanation for this difference is that German banks earned large anticipated capital gains on underwritings in addition to spreads. While a detailed examination of this proposition must await further research on firm-level data, an analysis of aggregate data suggests capital gains were small. Riesser (1911, p. 466) cites data on income earned from the sum of commissions and capital gains on securities transactions in 1903 published in the *Kölnische Zeitung* (see also Whale 1930, p. 26). A rough measure of capital gains earned by banks on securities holdings can be derived by combining this estimate with Eistert's (1970) estimates of total securities issued to derive a measure of total income from spreads and capital gains as a ratio of total issues. These data are reported in Table 4.9. Using additional data on the composition of securities issues from Eistert (1970, p. 103), and the estimates of bankers' commissions, one can place some bounds on the rate of capital gains. To do so requires an assumption about banks' relative earnings from underwriting government bonds, corporate bonds, and equity. I assume that the banks' earnings from commissions and capital gains on equities are double those for corporate bonds, and that earnings on government bonds are 1 percent. Under these assumptions, the total income earned from commissions plus capital gains on equity issues in 1903 was 8 percent of the amount issued. Given the estimate of 4 percent for equity commissions, this implies a 4 percent capital gain on equity issues. Thus, it seems that one cannot explain the difference between U.S. and

---

[20] Average manufacturing profit rates of firms rose form 18 percent in 1850 to 34 percent in 1880, while profit rates weighted by capital fell from 16 to 15 percent. In the South in 1880, unweighted profit rates were 43 percent, compared to 30 percent in the North. Clearly, for large numbers of small- and medium-sized firms, profit rates did not converge over time within or across regions during this period. Differences of 20 or 30 percent in profit rates across firms were common throughout the period 1850–80.

Table 4.9. *Estimate of German Banks' capital gains rate from securities underwritten in 1903*

Gross profits from commissions and capital gains	55.7 million marks
Total securities placed	1,285.1 million marks
Average spread	0.043
German government bonds placed	343.3 million marks
Bonds placed (excluding German government)	597.1 million marks
Stocks placed	344.7 million marks
Assumed ratio of profit rates from stocks and corporate bonds	2
Assumed profit rate for government bonds	0.01
Implied average profit rate for corporate bonds	0.040
Implied average profit rate for stocks	0.080
Implied capital gain rate for stocks given 4.0% commission	0.040

Sources: Securities placed are from Eistert 1970, p. 103. Gross profits are from *Kölnische Zeitung*, as cited in Riesser 1911, p. 466.

German commissions on equity by appeal to offsetting capital gains by German underwriters.

The U.S.–German underwriting-spread comparison illustrates more than the high cost of capital in the United States. It also indicates that rent extraction is an unlikely explanation of high underwriting costs in the United States. German banking was at least as concentrated and powerful an industry as the purported money trust of the United States. Yet their spreads were quite small. Thus, higher average U.S. spreads likely reflected higher underlying costs of bringing issues to market in the United States. The fact that spreads for small firms and small issues in Germany were the same as for large firms is also significant. In the United States, smaller firms suffered significantly larger spreads, as shown in Table 4.10, and firm size has also proven important in cross-sectional regression analysis of spreads (Mendelson 1967). Thus, the lower cost of equity issues in Germany relative to the United States affected the financing cost of small firms even more than shown by comparisons of average commissions. This lends credence to the view that "time-consistency" advantages and lower information costs (which are most relevant for small, growing firms) are an important part of the explanation for why German commissions were lower.

Additional evidence from time-series and cross-sectional analysis of bankers' spreads in the United States also suggests that spreads were more a function of information cost than of rent. First, the fact that

Table 4.10. *Costs of flotation of primary U.S. common stock issues offered through dealers, post-World War II*

Dates	Size of issue	Number of issues	Average cost as % proceeds
1935–38	Issue <$5 million	241	18
1945–49	Issue <$5 million	208	15
1951–55	Issue <$5 million	178	15
1963–65	Issue <$5 million	369	12
1940	Issue >$5 million	11	12
1945–49	Issue >$5 million	49	8
1951–55	Issue >$5 million	52	6
1963–65	Issue >$5 million	107	7

Sources: Securities and Exchange Commission 1940, 1941, 1970.

spreads were larger for preferred stock than for bonds, and largest for common stock, is consistent with the information-cost interpretation of the spreads, and not with the rent-extraction interpretation. As Miller (1967, p. 157) shows, concentration in American investment banking has always been highest in bond underwriting, yet bonds have always enjoyed the lowest spreads.

Second, as Table 4.10 shows, common stock spreads fell most dramatically from the 1930s to the early 1960s, but this was not associated with increased competition. Miller (1967, p. 163) finds that the only reduction in concentration of investment banking over this period occurred in the bond market, in which spreads fell least. Third, cross-sectional studies of stock and bond spreads (Cohan 1961; Mendelson 1967) find substantial evidence linking variation in spreads to "quality" or information-related variables. For example, bond spreads increase with bond yields. Stock spreads are higher for issues that include "extra inducements," and for issues with lower-quality underwriters, which Miller (1967) and Mendelson (1967, pp. 445, 474) associate with lower-quality firms. The most plausible explanation for the technological change that lowered spreads over time was the increase in bulk sales to institutional investors, which reduced the signaling and marketing costs of appealing to a widely dispersed group of investors (Haven 1940; Mendelson 1967, pp. 413–19). The rise of direct placements after World War II also provided an alternative to syndication. These innovations were a partial substitute for a universal banking system, in which the universal bank would have directly linked issuers and holders.

4.3.7   *Financial returns and access to securities markets*

Arguments about the effects of higher information and control costs in industrial finance in the United States relative to Germany do not have clear empirical implications for expected returns on financial instruments. On the one hand, if universal banking in Germany were superior as a mechanism for limiting *ex ante* lemons discounts on securities, for disciplining firms, and for managing corporate distress in default states, then more high-risk firms would be admitted to securities markets, and more financial claims would be held in the form of riskier junior instruments like stocks. On the other hand, if banks are very good at reducing lemons problems, disciplining firms, and organizing workouts, then to the extent that these risks are *systematic*, overall risk on traded assets could be lower for Germany.[21] Thus, depending on which of these two effects dominates, returns on financial assets could be higher or lower under universal banking.

Comparisons of interest rate and yield "spreads" – returns in excess of the riskless interest-rate benchmark within each country – provide more information than comparisons of nominal returns across countries. There are problems in making inferences from comparisons of returns on financial assets across countries. Imperfect international capital market integration for riskless assets, and different expectations of commodity price movements across countries make direct comparison of nominal yields and returns problematic measures of the banking system's effect on real costs of industrial finance. The spreads between riskless public bonds and private securities returns in both countries

---

[21] According to the capital asset pricing model, the average return on the market portfolio will compensate for systematic (nondiversifiable) risk. If the absence of universal banking increases overall systematic risk for stocks, then it should increase expected stock returns, *ceteris paribus*. Increased systematic risk could result, in theory, from at least three causes. First, under asymmetric information, the stock value of firms subject to borrowing constraints will vary with the shadow cost of external finance, which in turn will increase in times of low cash flow (Myers and Majluf 1984; Gale and Hellwig 1985; Brock and LeBaron 1990). Since firms' cash flows are correlated over the business cycle, this will induce greater correlation in stock returns among firms in an economy without universal banking. Second, expected costs of financial distress also increase firm risk. Again, the probability of financial distress varies systematically for all firms over the business cycle. If universal banking reduces distress costs, then it will decrease systematic risk in the portfolio of stocks. Third, managerial discipline may be more important during certain phases of the business cycle, since managers' incentives to cheat vary with the state of the economy. For example, under limited liability, managers who hold stock in their firm may chose to take on excessive risk in bad times (Jensen and Meckling 1976; Myers 1977; Calomiris and Kahn 1991). As in the other examples, this will induce greater systematic risk for the stock portfolio.

remove elements of difference attributable to the relative supply of savings or expected inflation.

A problem in relating differences in returns spreads to structural differences across countries is the need to infer average ex ante returns on equity from average *ex post* returns. Under the assumption that expected and actual returns were roughly equal on average, ex post returns can serve as a gauge of expected stock returns. The shorter the sample period, the more dubious this assumption becomes. Furthermore, it is not clear whether, under a specie standard, nominal or real stock returns provide a better measure of expected returns. If commodity prices under a specie standard follow a random walk (possibly with long-run mean reversion, as suggested by Klein 1975, Rockoff 1984, and Barsky 1987), nominal averages of returns may provide a superior measure of expected real returns. For this reason, and because of the availability of such data, I report nominal spreads.

Table 4.11 reports data on spreads between government bond yields and private securities returns (bond yields and stock returns) for Germany and the United States in two forms: simple spreads between government bonds and private stocks and bonds, and weighted spreads (using the proportion of stocks and bonds as weights) between private securities and government bonds.

The weighted spread is useful as a measure of the total return on corporate assets (to control for differences in bond or stock spreads resulting from different corporate leverage in the United States and Germany).

These data come from a variety of sources. U.S. stock returns for a market basket of stocks are reported in Snowden (1990, p. 387). Bond yields for U.S. government bonds are from Homer and Sylla (1991, pp. 316, 343). Private bond yields prior to 1900 are the unadjusted railroad bond series from Macaulay (1938). For the period after 1900, by which time other corporate bonds had become important in capital markets, I use Hickman's (1958, p. 81) data on average *ex ante* corporate bond yields for 1900–1909 as the measure of private bond yields.[22] For German portfolio returns, I use Tilly's (1992, p. 103) data on industrial bond yields and returns on industrial stocks. German government bond yields are taken from Homer and Sylla (1991, pp. 260–61, 504).

---

[22] During this period, government bonds had a "circulation privilege," meaning that they could be used as backing for national banknotes issued by national banks. Some researchers have avoided using these bond yields as measures of nominal riskless returns because of a possible liquidity premium making their yields artificially low. Calomiris (1988, p. 726 n. 9) argues against this view on theoretical grounds, and Snowden (1990, p. 388 n. 10) argues against it on empirical grounds.

Table 4.11. *Yields and spreads on financial portfolios, Germany and the United States*

	(1) Government bond yield	(2) Corporate bond yield	(3) Stock return	(4) Private-public bond spread (2) – (1)	(5) Stock spread (3) – (1)	(6) Private portfolio returns	(7) Portfolio spread (6) – (1)
Germany							
1883–1912	3.29	3.65	8.30	0.36	5.01	7.84	4.55
United States							
1880–99	2.68	4.65	5.39	1.97	3.24	5.02	2.52
1900–1913	2.32	5.00	6.80	2.68	4.48	5.90	3.57

Notes: For the United States, equal weights are given to stock and bond holdings in the portfolio, consistent with the evidence in Table 4.5. In comparing realized returns on portfolios with yields, it is assumed that ex post stock returns on average were close to ex ante returns, which cannot be measured.

Sources: Data on stock returns are derived from Snowden 1990, pp. 414–15. U.S. corporate bond yields for 1880–99 are Macaulay's, 1938, unadjusted railroad series, as reported in U.S. Department of Commerce 1975, p. 1,003. Hickman's, 1958, p. 81, data on bond yields for 1900–1909 are used for the later period. U.S. government bond yields are from Homer and Sylla 1991, pp. 316, 343. German bond yields and nominal stock returns are from Tilly 1992, p. 103. German government bond yields are taken from Homer and Sylla 1991, pp. 260–61, 504.

The differences between American and German returns spreads in table 4.11 suggest larger financial portfolio risk associated with German financial assets, which mainly reflects the larger share of equity in German finance, but also the higher returns on equity in Germany. As noted at the outset, such a finding may indicate information-cost advantages that brought higher-risk firms into the market for traded securities under universal banking. The facts that the government-corporate bond yield spread is larger in the United States and that the stock and portfolio spreads are larger in Germany are consistent with German firms' achieving rapid access to equity markets. By themselves, however, the data on spreads do not prove universal banking was advantageous, since an alternative interpretation of high stock returns in Germany is higher economy-wide risk in Germany. One way to sort out whether high financial asset returns reflected well on Germany's financial system is to compare traded portfolio risks and underlying total economic risks in the United States and Germany. If universal banking allowed riskier securities to enter financial markets (the sanguine view of universal banking), then risk differences in traded assets between the two countries should exceed underlying economic risk differences for all assets.

One measure of economy-wide asset risk is the rate of business failure. Using the Black-Scholes model of option pricing, bankruptcy risk is a function of underlying asset risk (sigma) and the ratio of debt to the value of assets. Holding the debt-to-asset ratio constant, a higher risk of bankruptcy indicates a higher asset risk. In fact, debt-to-asset ratios were similar in the two countries overall, despite the higher equity-to-debt ratio in German traded securities. In the United States, debt was 30 percent of total assets in 1990 (Goldsmith 1985, pp. 324–25), while in Germany debt was 32 percent in 1913.[23] Thus failure-rate differences are a good proxy for differences in asset risk between the two economies. Table 4.12 reports data on liabilities of failed businesses in dollars and marks for 1900–1908 (the years for which I was able to locate German data on liabilities of failed businesses), and the ratio of the average annual level of these to national assets in 1912/13. Because Dun and Bradstreet's data on liabilities of U.S. commercial and industrial failures exclude railroads and banks, I have added estimates of those numbers from other sources. This comparison of liabilities of failures relative to national assets gives some sense of the relative magnitude of overall risk in the two economies. The all-inclusive ratio for Germany is slightly

---

[23] The German debt-to-asset ratio is calculated using definitions from Goldsmith's U.S. calculations for Germany (1985, pp. 225, 324–25).

Table 4.12. *Risk of failure in Germany and the United States (liabilities of failures/national assets)*

	Germany (millions of marks)	United States (millions of $)		
		Dun and Bradstreet	Railroads	Banks (assets)
Liabilities of failed businesses				
1900	188	138	0	19
1901	224	113	27	15
1902	392	117	13	8
1903	319	155	0	9
1904	398	144	7	32
1905	499	103	31	21
1906	346	119	15	9
1907	302	197	27	18
1908	311	222	74	208
1901–8	2,979	1,308	194	339 (275 = liabilities)
National assets				
1912			301,500	
1913	639,300			
Average liabilities of failures, 1900–8/national assets, 1912 or 1913				
	0.00052	0.00065		
		0.00055 (omitting bank failures)		

Sources: Dun and Bradstreet's series on liabilities of failed businesses (U.S. Department of Commerce 1975, p. 912) for the United States excludes railroads and banks. Railroad bonds in default (Hickman 1960, p. 250) is a lower bound of omitted railroad liabilities. Bremer (1935, p. 27) reports assets of all failed banks. Calomiris (1993, table 4) reports the liability-to-asset ratio of all U.S. banks in 1904 (0.81), which is assumed to hold for failed banks for 1900–8. German liabilities of all failed firms is reported in *Viertel Jahreshefte zur Statistik des Deutschen Reiches*, sec. 4, various issues. Goldsmith (1985, pp. 226, 301) provides data on national assets for both countries.

lower than that of the United States, and when bank failures are omitted from the U.S. series, the two ratios are identical. This lends support to the view that universal banking lowered the threshold for admission into securities markets, and stock markets in particular. The risk on traded assets in Germany was much higher than in the United States, even though the underlying economy-wide risk was essentially the same in the two economies. This is consistent with the proposition that lower information and control costs under universal banking allowed greater participation of high-risk firms in securities markets.

4.3.8 Summary

Germany and the United States both achieved substantial industrial growth from 1870 to 1913. Comparisons of financial system performance suggest that German industrial growth was helped, and American growth was hindered, by their respective financial systems. Relatively high German ratios of financial assets and physical capital to GNP, and the high proportion of equipment in the German capital stock, are at least partly explained by lower costs of finance for industrial firms. These lower costs of finance are reflected in greater access to equity markets in Germany for risky industrial firms and their bankers, and lower costs of bringing securities to market. The low cost of floating equity issues in Germany, particularly for small firms, is especially revealing. Overall, the statistical comparison of German and American financial systems confirms qualitative historical and theoretical analysis that has linked universal banking to low costs of industrial finance. Unfortunately, much of the analysis that has been undertaken here has been restricted to aggregate comparisons. Comparative industry- and firm-level studies of finance costs are the obvious next step, and an important step before reaching definitive conclusions about the size of the contribution of German superiority in industrial finance to industrial performance.

4.3.9 The inverted histories of German and American industrial finance

Perhaps surprisingly, the United States enjoyed a universal banking system of a sort long before universal banking was established in Germany. As Davis (1957, 1960) and Lamoreaux (1991b) emphasize, New England's antebellum banks were a primary source of funding for New England industrialists. Just as in Germany, the links between industry and banking were very close. The banks were chartered to provide credit to their industrialist founders. In many cases, the officers and directors of the banks were their principal borrowers. New England bank stock was widely held by outsiders, and banks had much higher ratios of equity to assets than banks in other regions. In the mid-1850s, Massachusetts banks' capital and surplus relative to assets was roughly double that of New York and Pennsylvania (Calomiris,

1991, p. 198).[24] As Calomiris and Kahn (1996) show, stock returns were relatively low in New England compared to other regions. New England banks may have been able to attract large numbers of outside stockholders and pay lower returns on equity than other banks because their institutional arrangements mitigated information problems. Each bank's borrower-insiders had incentives to monitor each other, and interbank relationships ensured monitoring among members of the Suffolk system (the New England payments clearing system run by Boston banks) and among commercial banks and savings banks (which financed much of commercial banks' activities).[25]

Lamoreaux (1991b, 1994) documents the demise of this system. By 1900, New England's banks had identical capital ratios to other regions' banks (Calomiris 1991) and had changed toward financing more commercial undertakings and toward lending to bank outsiders. Calomiris (1993) interprets these changes as reflecting the growing mismatch between ever-larger scaled firms, and inherently small unit banks. As firms became larger, small banks found it increasingly difficult to satisfy the investment-financing needs of customers, given the desirability of maintaining a diversified loan portfolio. As Lamoreaux (1991a) shows, many New England banks wanted to respond to the growing scale of firms, and the economies of scope and scale from universal banking, by merging. When banks were able to merge, their profits increased substantially. Ultimately, however, national and state banking laws stood in the way of bank mergers or branching, as unit bankers blocked attempts to liberalize branching laws and prevented attempted mergers.

Over this same period (1850–1900), a German financial system dominated by private bankers transformed into the premier universal banking system of the world. Early examples of success in chartering limited-liability industrial banks elsewhere in Europe (notably the Credit Mobilier) and legal changes in Germany allowing limited-liability banking on a national scale paved the way for financial innovations that spread rapidly after 1870 (Tilly 1966, 1992; Kindleberger 1984). In contrast to the United States, where banking powers were limited compared to the growing

---

[24] In Calomiris 1991, I argued that Boston and Providence banks were mainly responsible for the difference in capital ratios between New England and other states. While it is true that Providence had unusually high capital ratios, even for New England, I overstated the difference between city and country banks in New England. My claim that "the capital of Massachusetts banks falls from 51 percent to 33 percent" (p. 199) when one removes Boston banks from the sample was based on a calculation error. In fact, city and country banks in Massachusetts had nearly identical capital ratios.

[25] It is interesting to note the many similarities to the German system, including the close relationships between banks and firms, and the use of savings institutions as investors in industrial banks. Savings cooperatives (*kreditgenossenschaften*) were large depositors in the German credit banks (Riesser 1911, pp. 198–202).

powers of industrial corporations during the Progressive Era, Germany was relatively liberal in its treatment of banking powers and restrictive of nonfinancial firms (Tilly 1982, p. 653).

4.4   The persistence of inefficient regulation

Thus far I have argued from comparisons of German and American financial systems that differences in banking regulation inhibited the development of an optimal mechanism for corporate finance in the United States. Restrictions on branching and consolidation restricted the size of banks. These became important constraints on the development of universal banking during the late nineteenth century as the size of firms and their borrowing needs expanded. The Clayton Act of 1914 may have further hampered America's ability to develop universal banking, by limiting bankers' influence over client firms through interlocking boards of directors. Thus, universal banking of the German type was never possible in the United States, even before Glass-Steagall restrictions on underwriting by affiliates of commercial banks.[26]

Nevertheless, during the 1920s, the U.S. financial system began to "converge" to a system of larger banks operating branches and performing combinations of commercial banking, investment banking, and trust activities like German universal banks. As shown in Table 4.13, the progressive trend in the United States in the 1920s is visible in many measures, including bank branching and consolidation, bank financing of industry, the development of long-term lending from banks to industrial enterprises, and the growing proportion of equity finance relative to debt. Consistent with the argument that economies of scope in universal banking are enhanced by large-scale banking, the dramatic increase in bank involvement in securities markets in the 1920s coincided with a dramatic increase in consolidation and branching by banks. Investment banking affiliates of national banks played an important part in these progressive trends. They operated on a larger scale than their investment bank competitors, performed a greater variety of functions, and often charged lower commissions to customers in securities transactions

---

[26] Kroszner and Rajan (1994), in their study of differences between the bond-underwriting activities of investment banks and investment banking affiliates of commercial banks, find little evidence for greater efficiency of affiliates. The experience of the 1920s in the United States indicates little, however, about the advantages of universal banking. Removing Glass-Steagall prohibitions along with repealing the Clayton Act and removing branching restrictions on banks (which would permit U.S. banks to operate true universal banks) would likely have a much larger positive effect. Furthermore, investment banking affiliates in the 1920s were very new enterprises. Given more time and experience, their performance might have improved.

Table 4.13. *Progressive developments in U.S. banking and corporate finance, 1920s*

Banking trends

	# Banks in securities	Bank mergers	# of banks absorbed	Branching banks (branches)	Bank short-term loans to nonfinancial corporations (millions of $)
1910		127	128	292 (548)	
1911		119	119		
1912		128	128		3,902
1913		118	118		
1914		142	143		
1915		154	154	397 (785)	
1916		134	134		
1917		123	123		
1918		119	125		
1919		178	178		
1920		181	183	530 (1,281)	
1921		281	292	547 (1,455)	
1922	277	337	340	610 (1,801)	8,834
1923	314	325	325	671 (2,054)	
1924	372	350	352	706 (2,297)	
1925	413	352	356	720 (2,525)	
1926	464	429	429	744 (2,703)	
1927	493	543	544	740 (2,914)	
1928	561	501	507	775 (3,138)	
1929	591	571	575	764 (3,353)	10,699

Gross sales of corporate securities issues, annual averages (billions of $)

	Stock	Industrial stocks	Corporate bonds	Industrial bonds
1901–12	0.5	0.15	0.9	0.11
1913–22	0.7	0.40	1.3	0.35
1923–27	1.6	0.64	3.6	0.78
1928–29	6.5	2.70	3.4	0.68

Sources: Corporate finance data are from Friend 1967, p. 68. Data on banks operating securities affiliates are from Peach 1941, p. 83. Bank merger data are from Chapman 1934, p. 56. Bank branching data are from Board of Governors of the Federal Reserve System 1976, p. 297. Bank lending to nonfinancial firms is from Goldsmith 1958, p. 339.

(Preston and Finlay 1930a, 1930b). While investment banking affiliates did not lead to universal banking of the German kind (branching restrictions still applied in many states and branching was not allowed across state lines), the relaxation of branching restrictions in the 1920s was associated with a trend toward greater bank involvement in underwriting. Even in nonbranching states like Illinois, concentration of deposit and trust activities in large Chicago banks encouraged bank underwriting (Bureau of Business Research 1928).

In the wake of the Great Depression of the 1930s, however, the United States chose to limit the scope of banking with the restrictive Banking Acts of 1933 and 1935, to discourage bank consolidation through mergers, and to eschew the relaxation of branching laws in favor of deposit insurance as a means to insulate small banks and their depositors from the threat of bank failure and systemic panic. This reversal in direction in the 1930s is hard to understand on efficiency grounds and seems best viewed as the last and most successful in a long series of attacks by populist forces on large-scale banking. It also suggests that, with respect to financial regulation, the United States was singularly incapable of learning from the past.

Explanations for the change in direction that occurred in the wake of the Great Depression have been suggested by Calomiris and White (1994). They argue that politicking by powerful unit bankers (Stigler 1971) does not explain the change in direction in banking regulation. The power of unit bankers was at an all-time low in 1930 due to the many failures of small banks. Furthermore, deposit-insurance legislation won by unit bankers from 1908 to 1920 in eight states was responsible for financial devastation in the states that had passed such legislation (Calomiris 1989, 1990, 1992).

Calomiris and White (1994) argue that despite these facts the credibility of large bankers, and of large banks operating securities affiliates, was undermined by the accusations of the Pecora hearings and by the political campaigning of Steagall and others who managed to portray big banking, and links between securities markets and banks, as the cause of the Great Depression. Furthermore, unprecedented depositor losses galvanized support for deposit insurance. Once the Great Depression legislation was passed, it resuscitated unit banks as a powerful special interest resisting reform or repeal of Great Depression protections.

Since the Great Depression, other factors may have worked against repeal of Depression-era regulations. Endogenous technological changes induced by inefficient regulations may have helped to perpetuate regulations by reducing their costs. For example, technological changes that produced declines in underwriting costs in the United States in the 1960s, notably the increased role of private placements and of securities purchases in bulk by institutional investors, may have lessened the pressure to repeal the separation between commercial and investment banking. Another example is the rise of finance companies and the modern commercial paper market, beginning in the 1960s, and the development of the relatively unregulated bank CD market, which kept Regulation Q restrictions from significantly increasing industrial finance costs. Today, the effects on financing costs from increased capital requirements and other regulatory costs on banking are mitigated by the growth of loan sales markets and asset securitization.

Of course, the past is not always a perfect guide to the future. Perhaps pressure from globalization of finance has lowered the tolerance for poor regulation in the United States. There is much discussion about expanding bank powers to branch and provide a wide array of products, and some limited progress has been made on both fronts. New entrants from abroad have encouraged these trends. From this perspective, recent international coordination in bank regulation (the Basle capital standards) is a particularly interesting development. It may signal the erosion of domestic autonomy in bank regulation and greater international competition, or it may be a harbinger of agreements among governments to limit international competition and protect regulatory autonomy. Time will tell.

References

Atack, Jeremy, and Fred Bateman. 1992. Did the United States Industrialize Too Slowly? Working paper, Vanderbilt University.

Barsky, Robert B. 1987. The Fisher Hypothesis and the Forecastability and Persistence of Inflation. *Journal of Monetary Economics* 19 (January): 3–24.

Baskin, J. 1988. The Development of Corporate Financial Markets in Britain and the United States, 1600–1914: Overcoming Asymmetric Information. *Business History Review* 62: 199–237.

Benston, George J. 1989. *The Separation of Commercial and Investment Banking: The Glass-Steagall Act Revisited and Reconsidered.* Norwell, MA: Kluwer Academic.

Benveniste, Lawrence M., and Paul A. Spindt. 1989. How Investment Bankers Determine the Offer Price and Allocation of New Issues. *Journal of Financial Economics* 24 (October): 343–61.

Berle, Adolph, and Gardiner Means. 1932. *The Modern Corporation and Private Property.* New York: Macmillan.

Board of Governors of the Federal Reserve System. 1959. *All Bank Statistics.* Washington, D.C.: Board of Governors.

1976. *Banking and Monetary Statistics, 1914–1941.* Washington, D.C.: Board of Governors.

Bodenhorn, Howard. 1992. Capital Mobility and Financial Integration in Antebellum America. *Journal of Economic History* 52 (September): 585–610.

Boyd, John H., and Stanley L. Graham. 1986. Risk, Regulation, and Bank Holding Company Expansion into Nonbanking. *Federal Reserve Bank of Minneapolis Quarterly Review* 10 (spring): 2–17.

1988. The Profitability and Risk Effects of Allowing Bank Holding Companies to Merge with Other Financial Firms: A Simulation Study. In *The Financial Services Industry in the Year 2000: Risk and Efficiency,* Proceedings of a conference on bank structure and competition, Chicago: Federal Reserve Bank of Chicago, 476–514.

Boyd, John H., Stanley L. Graham, and R. Shawn Hewitt. 1988. Bank Holding Company Mergers with Nonbank Financial Firms: Their Effects on the Risk of Failure. Federal Reserve Bank of Minneapolis Working Paper no. 417.

Brandeis, Louis D. 1914. *Other People's Money and How the Bankers Use It.* New York: Frederick A. Stokes.

Breckenridge, Roeliff M. 1899. Branch Banking and Discount Rates. *Sound Currency* 6 (January): 1–14.

Bremer, C. D. 1935. *American Bank Failures.* New York: Columbia University Press.

Brewer, Elijah. 1989. Relationship between Bank Holding Company Risk and Nonbank Activity *Journal of Economics and Business* 41: 337–53.

Brewer, Elijah, Diana Fortier, and Christine Pavel. 1988. Bank Risk from Nonbank Activities. *Federal Reserve Bank of Chicago Economic Perspectives* (July–August): 14–26.

Brock, William A., and Blake LeBaron. 1990. Liquidity Constraints in Production-Based Asset-Pricing Models. In *Asymmetric Information, Corporate Finance, and Investment,* ed. R. Glenn Hubbard, 231–56. Chicago: University of Chicago Press.

Brown, David T., Christopher James, and Robert M. Mooradian. 1993. The Information Content of Distressed Restructurings Involving Public and Private Debt Claims. *Journal of Financial Economics* 33 (February): 93–118.

Bureau of Business Research. 1928. Chicago as a Money Market. Bulletin 17, University of Illinois, Urbana.

Butters, J. Keith, and John Lintner. 1945. *Effect of Federal Taxes on Growing Enterprises.* Boston: Harvard University Press.

Cain, Louis P., and Donald G. Paterson. 1981. Factory Biases and Technical Change in Manufacturing: The American System, 1850–1919. *Journal of Economic History* 41 (June): 341–60.

Calomiris, Charles W. 1988. Price and Exchange Rate Determination during the Greenback Suspension. *Oxford Economic Papers* 40 (December): 719–50.

1989. Deposit Insurance: Lessons from the Record. *Federal Reserve Bank of Chicago Economic Perspectives* (May–June): 10–30.

1990. Is Deposit Insurance Necessary? A Historical Perspective. *Journal of Economic History* 50 (June): 283–95.

1991. Comment on "Information Problems and Banks' Specialization in Short-Term Commercial Lending: New England in the Nineteenth Century." In

Inside the Business Enterprise: Historical Perspectives on the Use of Information, ed. Peter Temin, 195–203. Chicago: University of Chicago Press.

1992. Do Vulnerable Economies Need Deposit Insurance? Lessons from U.S. Agriculture in the 1920s. In *If Texas Were Chile: A Primer on Bank Regulation,* ed. Philip L. Brock, 237–349, 450–58. San Francisco: Sequoia Institute.

1993. Regulation, Industrial Structure, and Instability in U.S. Banking: An Historical Perspective. In *Structural Change in Banking,* eds. Michael Klausner and Lawrence J. White, 19–116. Homewood, IL: Business One–Irwin.

Calomiris, Charles W., and Gary Gorton. 1991. The Origins of Banking Panics: Models, Facts, and Bank Regulation. In *Financial Markets and Financial Crises,* ed. R. Glenn Hubbard, 33–68. Chicago: University of Chicago Press.

Calomiris, Charles W., and R. Glenn Hubbard. 1995. Internal Finance and Investment: Evidence from the Undistributed Profits Tax of 1936–1937. *Journal of Business* (October): 443–82.

Calomiris, Charles W., and Charles M. Kahn. 1991. The Role of Demandable Debt in Structuring Optimal Banking Arrangements. *American Economic Review* 81 (June): 497–513.

1996. The Efficiency of Self-Regulated Payments Systems: Learning from the Suffolk System. *Journal of Money, Credit and Banking* 28 (November), Part 2: 766–97.

Calomiris, Charles W., Charles M. Kahn, and Stefan Krasa. 1991. Optimal Contingent Bank Liquidation under Moral Hazard. Federal Reserve Bank of Chicago, Working Paper WP-91-13.

Calomiris, Charles W., and Daniel M. G. Raff. 1995. The Evolution of Market Structure, Information, and Spreads in American Investment Banking. In *Anglo-American Finance: Financial Markets and Institutions in 20th Century North American and the U.K.,* eds. Michael Bordo and Richard Sylla, 103–60. Homewood, IL: Business One–Irwin.

Calomiris, Charles W., and Larry Schweikart. 1991. The Panic of 1857: Origins, Transmission, and Containment. *Journal of Economic History* 51 (December): 807–34.

Calomiris, Charles W., and Eugene N. White. 1994. The Origins of Federal Deposit Insurance. In *The Regulated Economy: A Historical Approach to Political Economy,* eds. Claudia Goldin and Gary Libecap, 145–88. Chicago: University of Chicago Press.

Campbell, Tim, and William Kracaw. 1980. Information Production, Market Signalling, and the Theory of Financial Intermediation. *Journal of Finance 35* (September): 863–81.

Carlson, W. Bernard. 1991. *Innovation as a Social Process: Elihu Thomson and the Rise of General Electric, 1870–1900.* Cambridge: Cambridge University Press.

Carosso, Vincent P. 1970. *Investment Banking in America.* Cambridge: Harvard University Press.

Chandler, Alfred D., Jr. 1977. *The Visible Hand: The Managerial Revolution in Amen-can Business.* Cambridge: Harvard University Press.

Chapman, John M. 1934. *Concentration of Banking: The Changing Structure and Control of Banking in the United States.* New York: Columbia University Press.

Cohan, Avery B. 1961. Cost of Flotation of Long-Term Corporate Debt since 1935. Research Paper 6, School of Business Administration, University of North Carolina.

Creamer, Daniel, and Israel Borenstein. 1960. Capital and Output Trends in Manufacturing and Mining. In *Capital in Manufacturing and Mining: Its Formation and Financing,* eds. Daniel Creamer, Sergei P. Dobrovolsky, and Israel Borenstein, 3–108. Princeton: Princeton University Press.

Davis, Lance E. 1957. Sources of Industrial Finance: The American Textile Industry: A Case Study. *Explorations in Entrepreneurial History* 9: 190–203.

1960. The New England Textile Mills and the Capital Markets: A Study of Industrial Borrowing, 1840–1860. *Journal of Economic History* 20: 1–30.

De Long, J. Bradford. 1991. Did Morgan's Men Add Value? In *Inside the Business Enterprise: Historical Perspectives on the Use of Information,* ed. Peter Temin, 205–36. Chicago: University of Chicago Press.

Deutsche Bundesbank. 1976. *Deutsches Geld- und Bankwesen in Zahlen, 1876–1975.* Frankfurt: Deutsche Bundesbank.

Diamond, Douglas. 1984. Financial Intermediation and Delegated Monitoring. *Review of Economic Studies* 51 (July): 393–414.

1991. Monitoring and Reputation: The Choice between Bank Loans and Directly Placed Debt. *Journal of Political Economy* 99 (August): 689–721.

1992. Bank Loan Maturity and Priority When Borrowers Can Refinance. Working paper, Graduate School of Business, University of Chicago.

Dobrovolsky, Sergei P., and Martin Bernstein. 1960. Long-Term Trends in Capital Financing. In *Capital in Manufacturing and Mining: Its Formation and Financing,* eds. Daniel Creamer, Sergei P. Dobrovolsky, and Israel Borenstein, 109–340. Princeton: Princeton University Press.

Doyle, William M. 1991. The Evolution of Financial Practices and Financial Structures among American Manufacturers, 1875–1905: Case Studies of the Sugar Refining and Meat Packing Industries. Ph.D. diss., University of Tennessee, Knoxville.

Dunlavy, Colleen. 1993. *Politics and Industrialization in Early Railroads in the United States and Prussia.* Princeton: Princeton University Press.

Eistert, Ekkehard. 1970. *Die Beeinflussung des Wirrschaftswachstums in Deutschland von 1883 bis 1913 durch das Bankensystem.* Berlin: Duncker und Humblot.

Fazzari, Steven, R. Glenn Hubbard, and Bruce C. Petersen. 1989. Financing Constraints and Corporate Investment. *Brookings Papers on Economic Activity,* 114–95.

Field, Alexander. 1983. Land Abundance, Interest/Profit Rates, and Nineteenth-Century American and British Technology. *Journal of Economic History* 42 (June): 405-31.

1987. Modern Business Enterprise as a Capital-Saving Innovation. *Journal of Economic History* 46 (June): 473–85.

Friend, Irwin. 1967. Over-All View of Investment Banking and the New Issues
   Market. In *Investment Banking and the New Issues Market,* eds. Irwin Friend,
   James R. Longstreet, Morris Mendelson, Ervin Miller, and Arleigh P. Hess,
   Jr., 1–79. New York: World Publishing Company.
Gale, Douglas, and Martin Hellwig. 1985. Incentive-Compatible Debt Contracts:
   The One-Period Problem. *Review of Economic Studies* 52 (October):
   647–63.
Garber, Peter, and S. Weisbrod. 1991. *The Economics of Money, Liquidity and
   Banking.* New York: D. C. Heath.
Gerschenkron, Alexander. 1962. *Economic Backwardness in Historical Perspec-
   tive: A Book of Essays.* Cambridge: Harvard University Press.
Gilson, Stuart C., Kose John, and Larry H. P. Lang. 1990. Troubled Debt Restructurings. *Journal of Financial Economics* 27: 315–53.
Goldsmith, Raymond W. 1955–56. *A Study of Saving in the United States.* Princeton: Princeton University Press.
   1958. *Financial Intermediaries in the American Economy since 1900.* Princeton:
   Princeton University Press.
   1976. The National Balance Sheet of Germany, 1850-1972. *Konjunkturpolitik*
   22: 153–72.
   1985. *Comparative National Balance Sheets: A Study of Twenty Countries,
   1688–1978.* Chicago: University of Chicago Press.
Goldsmith, Raymond W., Robert E. Lipsey, and Morris Mendelson. 1963. *Studies
   in the National Balance Sheet of the United States.* Princeton: Princeton University Press.
Gorton, Gary. 1985. Clearing Houses and the Origin of Central Banking in the
   U.S. *Journal of Economic History* 45 (June): 277–83.
   1989. Self-Regulating Bank Coalitions. Working paper, University of Pennsylvania, Philadelphia.
Gorton, Gary, and James Kahn. 1992. The Design of Bank Loan Contracts, Col-
   lateral, and Renegotiation. Rochester Center for Economic Research Dis-
   cussion Paper no. 327.
Gorton, Gary, and Donald Mullineaux. 1987. The Joint Production of Confi-
   dence: Endogenous Regulation and Nineteenth-Century Commercial Bank
   Clearinghouses. *Journal of Money Credit, and Banking* 19 (November):
   458–68.
Haven, T. Kenneth. 1940. *investment Banking under the Securities and Exchange
   Commission.* Ann Arbor: University of Michigan Bureau of Business
   Research.
Hickman, W. Braddock. 1958. *Corporate Bond Quality and Investor Experience.*
   Princeton: Princeton University Press.
   1960. *Statistical Measures of Corporate Bond Financing since 1900.* Princeton:
   Princeton University Press.
Hoffmann, Walther G. 1965. *Das Wachstum der Deutschen Wirtschaft seit der
   Mitte des 19. Jahrhunderts.* Berlin: Springer-Verlag.
Homer, Sidney, and Richard Sylla. 1991. *A History of Interest Rates,* 3d ed. New
   Brunswick: Rutgers University Press.

Hoshi, Takeo, Anil Kashyap, and Gary Loveman. 1992. Lessons from the Japanese Main Bank System for Financial Reform in Poland. Working paper, Graduate School of Business, University of Chicago.

Hoshi, Takeo, Anil Kashyap, and David Scharfstein. 1990a. Bank Monitoring and Investment: Evidence from the Changing Structure of Japanese Corporate Banking Relationships. In *Asymmetric Information, Corporate Finance, and Investment,* ed. R. Glenn Hubbard, 105–26. Chicago: University of Chicago Press.

1990b. The Role of Banks in Reducing the Costs of Financial Distress. *Journal of Financial Economics* 27 (September): 67–88.

Huertas, Thomas, and Harold Cleveland. 1987. *Citibank.* Cambridge: Harvard University Press.

Hughes, Thomas P. 1983. *Networks of Power: Electrification in Western Society, 1880–1930.* Baltimore: Johns Hopkins University Press.

James, Christopher. 1987. Some Evidence on the Uniqueness of Bank Loans. *Journal of Financial Economics* 19: 217–35.

James, Christopher, and Peggy Wier. 1988. Are Bank Loans Different? Some Evidence from the Stock Market. *Journal of Applied Corporate Finance.* 1: 46–54.

1990. Borrowing Relationships, Intermediation, and the Cost of Issuing Public Securities. *Journal of Financial Economics* 28: 149–71.

Japan Development Bank. 1994. Policy-Based Finance. World Bank Discussion Paper no. 221.

Jeidels, Otto. 1905. *Das Verhaltnis der deutschen Grossbanken zur industrie, mit besonderer Berucksichtung der Eisenindustrie.* Berlin: Schmollers Forschungen.

Jensen, Michael C., and William H. Meckling. 1976. Theory of the Firm: Managerial Behavior, Agency Costs, and Ownership Structure. *Journal of Financial Economics* 3: 305–60.

Kaufman, George G., and Larry Mote. 1989. Securities Activities of Commercial Banks: The Current Economic and Legal Environment. Working paper, Federal Reserve Bank of Chicago.

1990. Glass-Steagall: Repeal by Regulatory and Judicial Reinterpretation. *Banking Law Journal* (September–October): 388–421.

Kennedy, William, and Rachel Britton. 1985. Portfolioverhalten und wirtschaftliche Entwicklung im spaten 19. Jahrhundert: Em Vergleich zwischen Grosbritannien und Deutschland: Hypothesen und Spekulationen. In *Beitrage zu quantitativen und vergleichenden Unternehmensgeschichte,* ed. Richard H. Tilly. Stuttgart.

Kim, Sun Bae. 1992. Agency Costs and the Firm's Ownership Structure: The Japanese Evidence. Working paper, Board of Governors of the Federal Reserve System.

Kindleberger, Charles P. 1984. *A Financial History of Western Europe.* London: Allen and Unwin.

Klein, Benjamin. 1975. Our New Monetary Standard: The Measurement and Effects of Price Uncertainty. *Economic inquiry* 13 (December): 46: 1–84.

Kroszner, Randall S., and Raghuram G. Rajan. 1994. Is the Glass-Steagall Act Justified? A Study of the U.S. Experience with Universal Banking before 1933. *American Economic Review* 84 (September): 810–32.

Lacker, Jeffrey. 1991. Collateralized Debt as the Optimal Contract. Working paper, Federal Reserve Bank of Richmond.

Lamoreaux, Naomi R. 1991a. Bank Mergers in Late Nineteenth-Century New England: The Contingent Nature of Structural Change. *Journal of Economic History* 51 (September): 537–58.

1991b. Information Problems and Banks' Specialization in Short-Term Commercial Lending: New England in the Nineteenth Century. In *Inside the Business Enterprise: Historical Perspectives on the Use of Information,* ed. Peter Temin, 154–95. Chicago: University of Chicago Press.

1994. *Insider Lending: Banks, Personal Connections, and Economic Development in Industrial New England, 1784–1912.* Cambridge: Cambridge University Press.

Litan, Robert E. 1985. Evaluating and Controlling the Risks of Financial Product Deregulation. *Yale Journal on Regulation* 3 (fall): 1–52.

1987. *What Should Banks Do?* Washington, D.C.: Brookings Institution.

Macaulay, Frederick R. 1938. *Some Theoretical Problems Suggested by the Movements of Interest Rates, Bond Yields, and Stock Prices in the United States Since 1856.* Cambridge: National Bureau of Economic Research.

Mackie-Mason, Jeffrey K. 1990. Do Firms Care Who Provides Their Financing? In *Asymmetric Information, Corporate Finance, and Investment,* ed. R. Glenn Hubbard, 63–104. Chicago: University of Chicago Press.

Marquardt, Mary O. 1960. Sources of Capital of Early Illinois Manufacturers, 1840–1880. Ph.D. diss., University of Illinois, Urbana-Champaign.

Mayer, Cohn. 1988. New Issues in Corporate Finance. *European Economic Review* 32 (June): 1167–89.

Meinster, David R., and Rodney D. Johnson. 1979. Bank Holding Company Diversification and the Risk of Capital Impairment. *Bell Journal of Economics* 10 (autumn): 683–94.

Mendelson, Morris. 1967. Underwriting Compensation. In *Investment Banking and the New Issues Market,* eds. Irwin Friend, James R. Longstreet, Morris Mendelson, Ervin Miller, and Arleigh P. Hess, Jr., 394–479. New York: World Publishing Company.

Miller, Ervin. 1967. Background and Structure of the Industry. In *Investment Banking and the New Issues Market,* eds. Irwin Friend, James R. Longstreet, Moms Mendelson, Ervin Miller, and Arleigh P. Hess, Jr., 80–175. New York: World Publishing Company.

Myers, Stewart C. 1977. Determinants of Corporate Borrowing. *Journal of Financial Economics* 5: 147–75.

1984. The Capital Structure Puzzle. *Journal of Finance* 39: 575–92.

Myers, Stewart C., and Nicholas Majluf. 1984. Corporate Financing and Investment Decisions When Firms Have Information That Investors Do Not Have. *Journal of Financial Economics* 13: 187–221.

National Monetary Commission. 1910. *Statistics for Great Britain, Germany, and France, 1867–1909.* Washington, D.C.: U.S. Government Printing Office.

Neuburger, Hugh, and Houston H. Stokes. 1974. German Banks and German Growth, 1883–1913: An Empirical View. *Journal of Economic History* 34 (September): 710–32.

Peach, W Nelson. 1941. *The Security Affiliates of National Banks.* Baltimore: Johns Hopkins University Press.

Pennacchi, George. 1983. Maturity Structure in a Model of Unregulated Banking. Working paper, University of Illinois, Urbana-Champaign.

Piore, Michael, and Charles F. Sabel. 1984. *The Second Industrial Divide.* New York: Basic Books.

Pozdena, Randall J. 1991. Is Banking Really Prone to Panics? *Federal Reserve Bank of San Francisco Weekly Letter* 9: 1–35, 11 October.

Preston, H. H., and Allan R. Finlay. 1930a. Era Favors Investment Affiliates. *Journal of the American Bankers Association* 22 (June): 1153–54, 1191–92.

    1930b. Investment Affiliates Thrive. *Journal of the American Bankers Association* 22 (May): 1027–28. 1075.

Prowse, Stephen D. 1992. The Structure of Corporate Ownership in Japan. Working paper, Board of Governors of the Federal Reserve System.

Rajan, Raghuram. 1992. Insiders and Outsiders: The Choice between Relationship and Arm's-Length Debt. *Journal of Finance* 47 (September): 1367–1400.

Ramakrishnan, R. T. S., and Anjan Thakor. 1984. The Valuation of Assets under Moral Hazard. *Journal of Finance* 39 (1): 229–38.

Ramirez, Carlos D. 1992. Financial Capitalism in the United States and Germany at the Turn of the Twentieth Century. Working paper, George Mason University.

Riefler, Winfield W. 1930. *Money Rates and Money Markets in the United States.* New York: Harper and Brothers.

Riesser, Jacob. 1911. *The Great German Banks and Their Concentration, in Connection with the Economic Development of Germany* Translation of 3d. ed. Washington, D.C.: U.S. Government Printing Office.

Rockoff, Hugh. 1984. Some Evidence on the Real Price of Gold, Its Cost of Production, and Commodity Prices. In *A Retrospective on the Classical Gold Standard, 1821–1931,* eds. Michael D. Bordo and Anna J. Schwartz, 613–50. Chicago: University of Chicago Press.

Romer, Christina D. 1989. The Prewar Business Cycle Reconsidered: New Estimates of Gross National Product, 1869–1908. *Journal of Political Economy* 97 (February): 1–37.

Schumpeter, Joseph A. 1939. *Business Cycles: A Theoretical, Historical, and Statistical Analysis of the Capitalist Process.* New York: McGraw-Hill.

Securities and Exchange Commission. 1940. Cost of Rotation for Small Issues, 1925–1929 and 1935–1938. Washington, D.C.: Securities and Exchange Commission.

    1941. Statistical Series Release no. 572, June.

    1970. Cost of Rotation of Registered Equity Issues, 1963–1965. Washington, D.C.: Securities and Exchange Commission.

Selden, Richard T. 1963. Trends and Cycles in the Commercial Paper Market. NBER Occasional Paper no. 85. New York: National Bureau of Economic Research.

Sheard, Paul. 1989. The Main Bank System and Corporate Monitoring and Control in Japan. *Journal of Economic Behavior and Organization* 11: 399–422.

Snowden, Kenneth A. 1990. Historical Returns and Security Market Development, 1872–1925. *Explorations in Economic History* 27 (October): 381–420.

Stigler, George J. 1971. The Theory of Economic Regulation. *Bell Journal of Economics and Management Science* 2 (spring): 1–21.

Tilly, Richard H. 1966. *Financial Institutions and Industrialization in the Rhineland, 1815–1870.* Madison: University of Wisconsin Press.

———. 1980. Banken und Industrialisierung in Deutschland: Quantifizierungsversuche. In *Entwicklung und Aufgaben von Versicherungen und Banken in der Industrialisierung,* ed. F. W. Henning, 165–93. Berlin: Duncker und Humblot.

———. 1982. Mergers, External Growth, and Finance in the Development of Large-Scale Enterprise in Germany, 1880-1913. *Journal of Economic History* 42 (September): 629–58.

———. 1984. Zur Finanzierung des Wirtschaftswachstums in Deutschland und Grosbritannien, 1880–1913. In *Die Bedingungen des Wirtschaftswachstums in Vergangenheit und Zukunft,* ed. E. Helmstadter, 263–86. Tubingen.

———. 1986. German Banking, 1850-1914: Development Assistance for the Strong. *Journal of European Economic History* 15: 113–52.

———. 1992. An Overview of the Role of the Large German Banks up to 1914. In *Finance and Financiers in European History, 1880–1960,* ed. Youssef Cassis, 92–112 (Cambridge: Cambridge University Press).

Townsend, Robert. 1979. Optimal Contracts and Competitive Markets with Costly State Verification. *Journal of Economic Theory* 21 (October): 265–93.

Trusk, Robert J. 1960. Sources of Capital of Early California Manufacturers, 1850 to 1880. Ph.D. diss., University of Illinois, Urbana-Champaign.

U.S. Department of Commerce. 1975. *Historical Statistics of the United States: Colonial Times to 1970.* Washington, D.C.: GPO.

Wall, Larry D. 1987. Has Bank Holding Companies' Diversification Affected Their Risk of Failure? *Journal of Economics and Business* 39 (November): 313–26.

Webb, Steven B. 1980. Tariffs, Cartels, Technology, and Growth in the German Steel Industry, 1879–1914. *Journal of Economic History* 40 (June): 309–30.

Whale, P. Barrett. 1930. *Joint Stock Banking in Germany.* London: Macmillan.

White, Eugene N. 1985. The Merger Movement in Banking, 1919–1933. *Journal of Economic History* 45 (June): 285–91.

———. 1986. Before the Glass-Steagall Act: An Analysis of the Investment Banking Activities of National Banks. *Explorations in Economic History* 23 (January): 33–55.

Williamson, Oliver. 1980. Emergence of the Visible Hand. In *Managerial Hierarchies,* eds. Alfred D. Chandler and Herman Daems. Cambridge: Harvard University Press.

Williamson, Stephen D. 1986. Costly Monitoring, Financial Intermediation, and Equilibrium Credit Rationing. *Journal of Monetary Economics* 18 (September): 159–80.

Wright, Gavin. 1990. The Origins of American Industrial Success, 1879–1940. *American Economic Review* 80 (September): 651–68.

## CHAPTER 5

The evolution of market structure, information, and spreads in American investment banking

Charles W. Calomiris and
Daniel M. G. Raff

5.1   Introduction

The fees investment bankers earn for placing primary securities issued by their clients have occupied a central place in the debate over the proper regulation of investment banking since at least the beginning of the twentieth century. In his classic attack on the "money trust," *Other People's Money and How the Bankers Use It,* Louis Brandeis argued that the enormous fees earned by investment bankers – particularly on stock issues – offered conclusive proof of the existence of substantial rent extraction by the "money trust." Brandeis (1914, p. 95) noted that Morgan's gross commission (or "spread") exceeded 20 percent for the organization of U.S. Steel and was 25 percent for underwriting the Tube Trust. More generally, Brandeis (p. 95) wrote:

Nor were monster commissions limited to trust promotions. More recently, bankers' syndicates have, in many instances, received for floating preferred stocks of recapitalized industrial concerns, one-third of all the common stock issued, besides a considerable sum in cash. And for the sale of preferred stock of well established manufacturing concerns, cash commissions (or profits) of from $7^1/_2$ to 10 percent of the cash raised are often exacted. On bonds of high-class industrial concerns, bankers' commissions (or profits) of from 5 to 10 points have been common.

Brandeis considered it self-evident that such commissions could only be produced by an excessive concentration of power in the investment banking industry that gave rise to an effective monopoly over the financial market. This interpretation of investment banking spreads, and of the investment banking industry, underlay the Pujo Committee hearing of 1912–1913 and the Progressive movement's support of the Clayton

The authors thank Charles Bennett, Jack Coffee, Samuel Hayes, Florence Lathrop, Morris Mendelson, Jay Ritter, Carl Schneider, Barry Wigmore, and seminar participants at the University of Illinois, New York University, and Vanderbilt University for advice and comments, and Greg Nuxoll and Joe Mason for excellent research assistance.

Act of 1914, which limited bankers' roles on corporate boards of directors. The same concern over the social costs of excessive concentration of power in large New York City banks encouraged the separation of commercial and investment banking in the Banking Act of 1933 (Calomiris and White, 1994). The concern over the "money trust" that persisted into the 1930s was that commercial banks were using interbank deposits to finance the activities of their investment banking operations. The control over the nation's interbank deposits by a handful of large New York bankers gave the impression that Wall Street had a monopoly over the money market which it employed to secure special power over the origination and marketing of securities. The jaundiced view of Wall Street continued even after the Great Depression reforms, as illustrated by the antitrust suit (U.S. v. Morgan et al.) brought by the U.S. government against the investment banking industry in 1947.

An alternative interpretation of investment bankers' spreads focuses on underwriting risk and frictions in the market for buying securities from investment bankers or their dealers rather than the degree of concentration within the investment banking industry. According to this view, underwriting risk and the information and transaction costs that make it costly to place securities, explain investment bankers' fees.[1] This approach to the costs of placing securities emphasizes the role of investment banking syndicates as mechanisms for credibly communicating information about the characteristics of firms and about the preferences of investors.[2] Hansen (1986, p. 43) summarized this approach to understanding underwriting compensation:

One of the most important roles of the syndicate, then, is to overcome this information gap and provide investors with the assurance that the securities are fairly valued on the basis of management's view of the company's future profitability. When pricing the new shares, syndicate managers repeatedly put their reputation on the line with the purchasing public. To protect their reputation, the syndicate managers investigate and audit the issuing firm's activities; and this process, combined with the sharing of risk by the syndicate, certifies for investors the value of the newly issued shares.

Of course, these two extreme interpretations of bankers' spreads (pure rents v. pure costs) are not the only possibilities. Both factors could be

---

[1] For evidence on the role of stock risk in increasing investment banker spreads, see Eckbo and Masulis (1994). While underwriting risk is clearly an important component of the spread, as we argue below, it cannot explain the dramatic variation in spreads observed across time and across issues.

[2] Theoretical models and related evidence can be found in Beatty and Ritter (1986); Ritter (1987); Booth and Smith (1986); Rock (1986); Easterbrook (1984); Benveniste and Spindt (1989); Ramakrishnan and Thakor (1984); Baron (1979, 1982); Baron and Holmstrom (1980); and Mandelker and Raviv (1977).

important, and there might be interactions between the two explanations. Without some frictions in the markets for placing securities, it would be virtually impossible for investment bankers to extract rents since firms could always choose simply to auction securities directly to buyers. Furthermore, some payments to bankers in excess of marketing costs may be a necessary cost of underwriting as a means to preserve truth-telling incentives of the banker. It is possible to argue that high fees make investment bankers' reputations worth preserving.

This paper reports empirical evidence on U.S. investment banking spreads over the past seventy years. We doubt whether analysis of spread data will ever definitively demonstrate the absence or presence of economic profits. Our empirical objectives in this paper are more modest. We describe differences in spreads across time, issuers, investment banking houses, types of securities, and countries, and consider whether these differences in spreads are best explained by differences in the degree of investment bankers' market power in the various transactions or by differences in the underlying costs of placing securities.

The second section describes the salient findings of the existing empirical literature on the determinants of investment banking compensation. The third section discusses the related empirical literature on equity issuers' choices among methods of placing issues. In the fourth section we provide new evidence from the pre-1933 period on commissions based on the transaction accounts ("deal books") of Lehman Brothers for this period, and we use these and other data from the Pecora Hearings and SEC reports to construct comparable measures of bankers' spreads for the period 1925–1940 for various types and sizes of securities issues and methods of underwriting. The fifth section reviews the important trends in corporate finance that coincided with the dramatic decline of U.S. spreads after the 1930s. The sixth section complements this with new evidence on cross-sectional determinants of common stock spreads for 1950 and 1971 and analyzes changes in those determinants over time. The seventh section concludes.

5.2   Empirical studies of U.S. bankers' spreads on primary securities offerings

Investment banker commissions, or spreads, are defined as the difference between the price paid by buyers and the price received by issuers for securities flotations. They measure a large part of the compensation to the investment banking house but are only one component of the cost to firms of bringing a new issue to market. Spreads are the appropriate measure to focus upon for our purpose – explaining differences in the compensation received by investment bankers – although even for this purpose they are only a partial measure.[3]

The earliest formal studies of U.S. investment banking spreads of which we are aware are those of Cohan (1961) and Mendelson (1967).[4] These studies established the following important facts about spreads in the post-SEC period: Spreads are highest for common stocks, followed by preferred stocks, with the lowest spreads on bonds. Spreads on all securities fall as the amount of issue, or the size of the firm, increases. Size effects are substantially reduced, both for bond and stock issues, when other variables are taken into account. Bond issue spreads rise with

---

[3] Hansen (1986) reviews the various costs to a firm of bringing a securities issue to market. Costs incurred by issuers other than the spread include security underpricing, warrants to underwriters, and overallotment options (on firm commitment underwritings). Any attempt to measure changes over time in the total costs of public issues (as opposed to investment bank compensation) would have to take account of possible changes in the extent of initial underpricing. Tinic (1988) argues that changes in securities regulations after 1933 – which increased the legal liability of underwriters for poor ex post performance of issues – led to greater underpricing of unseasoned securities. He found that one-week excess returns on IPOs averaged 5 percent during the 1923–1930 period, compared to 11 percent during the 1966–1971 period. Tinic also found that these differences were attributable to increased underpricing of the most unseasoned credit risks. A possible problem with Tinic's analysis, however, is the failure to adjust for inflation, which changed the meaning of small issues over the period and which could account for his findings.

Investment bankers do not receive any direct benefits from underpricing since they are required to sell securities at no higher than the offering price. John C. Coffee tells us this was standard practice in the industry prior to its codification in the late 1930s, at least among "reputable" underwriters, although disreputable houses may have attempted to profit from "free riding" prior to regulatory sanctions that prevented it. Hansen (1986) argues that underwriters may benefit from underpricing through reduced underwriting risk and greater investor satisfaction (reputation gains). This argument, however, neglects that investment bankers should care about their reputations with issuers as well as with purchasers.

"Green shoe" (or overallotment) options are part of the investment banker's compensation not measured by the spread. The *ex ante* value of the overallotment option to the banker (not captured by the spread) is equal to the probability weighted value of the commissions he could earn on overallotments (demand for issues at the offering price in excess of the offering amount up to the amount of the overallotment). Overallotment options are regulated by the National Association of Securities Dealers (NASD). Until 1983, allotments were limited by the NASD to 10 percent of the issue; in 1983, this was increased to 15 percent. This seems a minor problem for measuring compensation, since the value of the overallotment option is small relative to the gross spread (Hansen, Fuller, and Janjigian, 1987).

Sometimes marginal and average commissions are not the same. For example, prior to the 1930s, some buyers were given preferential prices (implying smaller spreads on those parts of the transaction). The marginal spread is the highest of the spreads in any transaction, and the appropriate measure of the marginal cost of the marginal cost of issue. Where marginal and average spreads differ in any observations we report below, we employ marginal spreads as our definition of compensation.

[4] Useful tabular analyses of spread data were published irregularly by the Securities and Exchange Commission and by Dewing (1920) and Haven (1940).

the yield of the bond, and both bond and stock issue spreads are lower for "high-quality" firms.[5] Spreads on public offerings of stocks are higher than spreads on rights offerings. Utility stocks have lower spreads, *ceteris paribus*. Stock issues that include "sweeteners" (e.g., warrants), which Mendelson argued serve as a proxy for less-seasoned issuers, have higher spreads, *ceteris paribus*. The absence of a firm price commitment by the underwriter, *ceteris paribus*, was associated with higher spreads on stocks in 1960 and 1961, but this effect was essentially zero in his 1949 sample. This counterintuitive result does not indicate that the underwriter's price insurance has negative value. Mendelson argued that it, like the sweetener variable, serves as an indicator of the quality (seasoning) of the issuer.[6] Investment bankers were less willing to offer price guarantees on unseasoned firms. Stocks with low offering prices (which Mendelson viewed as an indicator of a lack of seasoning) also had higher spreads, *ceteris paribus*.

Mendelson documented that the average change in common stock spreads between 1949 and 1961 is slightly positive, but he argued that this masks two related trends that pushed in opposite directions. Costs were indeed falling. But as the cost of bringing relatively high-spread shares to market fell over time, more of those issuers were attracted to the market. Thus cost reductions do not show up unambiguously in annual averages because the mix of issuers shifts in the direction of higher average spreads. Mendelson compared results of regressions of common stock offering characteristics on the bankers' spread for samples from 1949 and 1961. The average spread for his samples rose from 7.9 percent in 1949 to 11.2 percent in 1961. Mendelson calculated that (using the 1949 coefficients) it would have cost the 1961 sample of issuers 20.3 percent on average to bring their issues to market in 1949. In contrast, if the sample of 1949 issuers had brought their shares to market in 1961 (using the 1961 coefficients) the spreads would have fallen by a trivial 0.4 percent to an average of 7.5 percent.

Mendelson's decompositions indicated that for many issuers (e.g., a large, mature utility company offering stock through a rights offering rather than a sale to the public), spreads did not fall significantly from

---

[5] For example, Haven (1940, pp. 23–39) gives detailed breakdowns of spreads against "ratings." For common stock issues, thirty issues for 1933–1937 rated B++ or B+ had spreads averaging 8.7 percent, while seventy-five issues rated C++ or C+ had spreads averaging 17.5 percent.

[6] See also Ritter (1987) and Sherman (1992) for a discussion of the association between unseasoned firms and best-effort contracting. Sherman points out that an additional contributing factor to the high cost of best efforts is the fact that not all of them are completed. The average cost of "survivors" must be high enough to pay for the underwriters' costs for survivors and nonsurvivors.

1949 to 1961; but for small, unseasoned manufacturing firms, costs of issuing that were prohibitive in 1949 had fallen dramatically by 1961, and this decline in costs of issuing help to explain the increasing propensity of those firms to issue stock.

Mendelson also documented important facts about underwriters for the years 1960 and 1961. As shown in Tables 5.1 and 5.2, the larger the capital of the underwriter and the older the underwriter, the *smaller* the average spread the underwriter charges and the less likely it is that the underwriter will engage in deals that involve negotiable extras (an indicator of a lack of seasoning). Mendelson points out that, in large part, these results reflect the fact that underwriting large issues requires access to large amounts of capital. Large issuers, therefore, tend to be matched with large underwriters, and smaller underwriters do more business with small, unseasoned firms.

Mendelson's econometric work offers substantial support for the view that underwriting compensation is closely related to the economic costs of bringing stock issues to market. Characteristics of issuers that indicate the degree of "seasoning" – which should affect the cost of marketing securities – are among the most important determinants of issuing cost. The characteristics of investment bankers play a secondary role, and here the larger investment banking houses (those most plausibly able to exercise market power) charged *lower* spreads than other bankers, *ceteris paribus*. Otherwise identical issues are much less expensive to place if they are issued to stockholders rather than to the public. This is consistent with an important role for marketing costs in determining spreads.

In a similar vein, Calomiris (1993, 1995) compares investment banking spreads and issuing activity in Germany prior to World War I with those in the United States then and later (shown in Tables 5.3 and 5.4).[7] Germany's universal banks underwrote and placed stock of manufacturing firms through their nationwide branching networks of trust accounts. During this period, the ratio of stock issues to bond issues in Germany was double that of the United States. Spreads averaged under 4 percent on common stock flotations for the period 1893 to 1913 and did not vary importantly by size of issue or size of firm. Germany's smallest manufacturing firms were able to place equity as early as the 1890s at lower cost than large American firms paid for placing stocks in the 1990s. Marketing cost differences, rather than market power differences, seem to account for the higher costs of equity issues in the United States.

[7] The sample of German issuers is drawn from a partial list of the metal manufacturing firms and a complete list of the electrical industry firms for which spread information was available in Saling's Borsen Jahrbuch. This is only a small sample of the actual issues of German common stock, even within those industries.

Table 5.1. *Average spread (percent) on common stock by age and size of principal underwriter, 1960 and 1961*

Age of underwriter (years)	Capital class of underwriter							Not available	All sizes
	$25,000	$25,000 to less than $150,000	$150,000 to less than $1 million	$1 million to less than $5 million	$5 million to less than $10 million	$10 million to less than $25 million	$25 million and over		
1–9	17.6	14.5	13.1	11.2	10.6	15.3	—[a]	16.1	13.6
10–19	—	11.0	12.0	10.8	—	—	6.3	15.8	10.1
20–29	6.7	11.0	12.0	9.5	8.6	5.7	6.3	23.6	9.8
30 and over	—	12.5	10.1	8.8	7.9	7.6	7.2	8.5	8.1
Not available	18.8	—	7.0	—	—	—	—	7.1	11.0
All ages	16.2	13.8	12.4	9.5	8.5	7.5	6.9	15.3	10.2

[a]Dash (—) equals zero or too small to be recorded.
Source: Mendelsohn, 1967, p. 475.

Table 5.2. *Percent of common stock issues with negotiable extras,[a] 1960 and 1961*

Age of underwriter (years)	Capital class of underwriter								All sizes
	$25,000	$25,000 to less than $150,000	$150,000 to less than $1 million	$1 million to less than $5 million	$5 million to less than $10 million	$10 million to less than $25 million	$25 million and over	Not available	
1–9	80	96	85	50	71	—[b]	13	100	85
10–19	—	100	60	33	—	—	—	—	35
20–29	—	25	80	38	—	—	—	100	37
30 and over	—	100	50	19	4	11	10	—	15
Not available	100	—	100	—	—	—	—	—	67
All ages	71	86	77	30	16	10	10	75	41

[a] Negotiable extras are defined as warrants or underpriced stock offerings attached to the common stock issue.
[b] Dash (—) equals zero or too small to be recorded.
Source: Mendelsohn, 1967, p. 477.

Table 5.3. *Bankers' spreads and total issuing costs for German stock issues, 1893–1913 (percent of issue)*

	Mean bank spread[a]	Mean total cost[b]
All Issues		
Electricity	3.67	5.08
No. firms	13	12
No. observations	21	20
Manufacturers	3.9	5.3
No. firms	19	15
No. observations	30	20
Issues less than DM 1 million		
Electricity	3.94	5.24
No. firms	4	3
No. observations	7	3
Manufacturers	3.45	5.29
No. firms	10	10
No. observations	18	15
Firms with 1913 capital less than DM 2 million		
Manufacturers	4.11	5.93
No. firms	3	5
No. observations	6	5

[a] Percent bankers' spreads are defined as the difference between the amount paid for an issue by purchasers and the amount paid by the banker to the issuing firm divided by the total amount paid for the issue.
[b] Total costs include taxes, printing costs, and commissions.
Source: Calomiris, 1995, Table 7.

Germany's underwriting industry was highly concentrated, with a handful of banks accounting for almost all the underwriting activity, in stark contrast to the less concentrated American underwriting market of the 1960s (and earlier).

German bankers were able to keep costs down, however, because the market for securities was largely internal to the banking system. Universal banks placed securities with their customers and, thus, were able to reap economies of scale in marketing. Long-term relationships between universal banks and firms minimized costs associated with monitoring and controlling the use of funds and distributing junior securities

Table 5.4. *Costs of flotation of primary common stock offered through dealers*

Date	Size of issue	Number of issues	Average cost (%)
1935–1938	<$5 million	241	18
1945–1949	<$5 million	208	15
1951–1955	<$5 million	178	15
1963–1965	<$5 million	369	12
1940	>$5 million	11	12
1945–1949	>$5 million	49	8
1951–1955	>$5 million	52	6
1963–1965	>$5 million	107	7

Source: Calomiris, 1995, Table 10.

to investors willing to hold them. This was a two-sided relationship. Banks were able to provide low-cost finance to firms because trust customers were willing to hold junior claims on firms; this willingness reflected confidence by trust customers in bank discipline over firms, which was made possible by concentration of control over stock within the bank (as banks controlled proxies from their trust accounts) and by underwriter/trust managers' incentives to control and evaluate firms' risks properly.

In the United States, in contrast, the large-scale firm of the second industrial revolution received its external finance through the placement of senior securities. As Navin and Sears (1955) note, common stock flotations of industrial enterprises were too difficult to market in the United States. Baskin (1988) and Calomiris (1995) attribute this to insurmountable information problems. Preferred stock became the popular means to raise funds, particularly after the benefits of seniority were proven during the depression of the 1890s. Generally, for the period prior to the 1920s, there was virtually no public issuance of common stock, and typically common stock issues resulted from refinancings of existing firms rather than financings of new projects (Doyle, 1991).

5.3 Issuers' choices of how to place equity securities: underwriting paradoxes

According to a simple model of financing choice which abstracts from cross-sectional differences in firms' information problems or "seasoning," firms would never in equilibrium choose to use a high-cost underwriting method if lower-cost methods were available. The fact that firms sometimes do choose high-cost underwriting methods is sometimes termed the "underwriting paradox." Most of the discussion of investment bankers' spreads on equity issues in the empirical finance literature has focused on explaining "paradoxes" posed by differences in spreads across different types of issuing mechanisms (public offerings with firm price commitments by underwriters, best-effort public offerings, standby rights offerings, rights offerings without any investment bank involvement, and private placements with or without investment bank involvement).[8]

Recent empirical work has shown that most of the various underwriting paradoxes can be resolved by taking into account cross-sectional differences in the information problems that issuers confront in placing their securities and by examining costs of issuance other than the fees paid to investment bankers. In particular, higher fees for some types of underwriting contracts may reward underwriters for greater efforts in communicating issuers' characteristics to buyers, and this may increase the price buyers are willing to pay for issues.

Comparisons of pricing differences across choices of contract, it should be noted from the outset, are potentially subject to selectivity bias. If firms that use high-cost methods differ from firms that use low-cost methods – because of differences in seasoning – then comparisons of average pricing effects across contracting arrangements will be biased against finding a benefit to high-cost underwriting. Firms that expect to suffer the worst price declines from employing low-cost methods will use high-cost methods. This will tend to make it difficult to detect any advantages from high-cost underwriting methods. Comparing high- and low-cost samples of issues could even produce the counter-intuitive result that high-cost methods lead to the worst underpricing.

Smith (1977) compared abnormal returns of a (small) sample of rights offerings with those of a larger sample of public offerings, holding constant systematic risk factors, and found no difference in returns around the offer date. Smith examined other potential benefits of high-cost underwriting and was unable to detect sufficient benefits to stockholders from underwriting services to justify its costs. Instead, Smith argued that

---

[8] There is also the question of why issuers would ever offer equity, since the costs of public offerings of debt are so much lower. Here bankruptcy costs, differences in seasoning, and firms' reactions to changes in the market price of equity may be important. Access to the public bond market tends to be restricted to very large, seasoned firms (Carey, Prowse, Rca, and Udell, 1993). Loughran and Ritter (1995) show that the timing of equity offerings for initial and seasoned issuers coincides with peaks in firms' stock prices.

managers of issuing firms may choose costly underwriting as a means to transfer resources from stockholders to management.

Subsequent work, however, has produced evidence that pricing effects differ across underwriting arrangements (typically prior to the offer date) and provided evidence of important selectivity bias across types of offerings that tend to mask the advantages of high-cost underwriting. Hansen and Pinkerton (1982) found that in direct offers of equity in the 1970s (those without underwriter involvement) issuers had already obtained guarantees of receiving, on average, 90 percent of their desired gross proceeds. This guarantee was typically provided by either a corporate parent or another large stockholder. Over half of these companies obtained a 100 percent guarantee. Clearly, not all firms (for reasons of scale differences alone) would be able to pursue this option.

Hansen (1989) studied differences between underwritten rights offerings (standbys) and underwritten public offerings for 1963 to 1981. By focusing on these two methods, Hansen was able to eliminate the selectivity bias that comes from including preguaranteed non-underwritten rights offerings, although some selectivity bias undoubtedly remains. He found that firms making underwritten rights offerings "paid lower underwriting fees but incurred significantly larger price drops just prior to the offering than did firms making underwritten public offerings." He argued that the price concessions issuers needed to make to sell stock in rights offerings were in excess of the difference in underwriting costs from using public offerings. In other words, firms that used standbys might have benefitted by using public offerings instead, because of the banker's greater role as a source of credible information in marketing the firm's stock in a public offering.

Similar analysis helps to explain the low frequency of use of "shelf registration" (under Rule 415), which was allowed by the Securities and Exchange Commission beginning in 1982. Shelf registration's main supposed advantages are the flexibility it provides firms in choosing the precise timing of their offerings, and the possible increased competition among underwriters, since the firm can register prior to setting the terms of its underwriting contract. Bhagat, Marr, and Thompson (1985) showed that underwriting fees are lower for shelf registrations. Denis (1991) showed that, despite this fact, shelf registration is becoming increasingly less popular, particularly for equity issues. For 1982 and 1983, nearly 25 percent of equity issues were registered under Rule 415; fewer than 2 percent of offerings have been registered under Rule 415 since 1986; and from 1984 to 1988, only three industrial equities were shelf-registered. Denis argued that this reflects a lack of "underwriter certification" under Rule 415. Consistent with this view, Denis found that shelf equity offerings suffered larger negative price effects at the time they were announced. The 0.7–0.8 percent excess decline in price for shelf-registered issues is equal to or slightly higher than the spread cost advantage estimated by Bhagat, Marr, and Thompson (1985).

Ritter (1987) showed that best efforts accounted for one-third of initial public offerings (IPOs) in the United States and that initial underpricing of best-effort IPOs (the percentage difference between the offering price and the first market price) is 48 percent – more than three times the underpricing of firm-commitment IPOs. And, as noted by Mendelson (1967), best efforts tend to be associated with increases in underwriting fees. Why, then, would any firm choose to offer stock through a best effort? Sherman's (1992) answer was that the best-efforts method allows a firm to test waters for its issues and withdraw the offering if the market demand is insufficient. Issuers, therefore, benefit from the information they receive about the value of their firm's stock in the market during the offering process. Since bankers' compensation depends on the success of the offering, the best-effort compensation percentage will be high to compensate the banker for the offerings that are withdrawn from the market. In equilibrium, (*ex post*) good firms will pay for the information produced about (*ex post*) bad firms, although firms do not know their characteristics *ex ante*.

Hansen and Torregrossa (1992) investigated the importance of monitoring for explaining underwriting costs more directly. They found that, in addition to issue size and company risk, other variables that proxy for monitoring costs are significant for explaining cross-sectional variation in common stock spreads. Controlling for risk and issue size, larger firms, firms where managers have large ownership stakes, and greater involvement by large institutional buyers all reduce spreads, which Hansen and Torregrossa interpret as evidence that lower information costs reduce spreads. Presumably, selling issues to large buyers requires less monitoring and marketing effort by underwriters because it is easier to credibly communicate information about issuers to large institutional buyers.

To summarize, the literature on differences in underwriting method generally supports the view that information costs are important determinants of the choice of offering technique for common stock and that differences in information cost help to explain variation in spreads across different issues. The equity underwriting paradox is resolved by evidence that firms of different seasoning do not have identical choice sets (Hansen and Pinkerton, 1982) and by observed pricing advantages of high-spread offering methods (Hansen, 1989; Denis, 1991).

5.4 Underwriting spreads pre- and post-depression

Very little is known about underwriting costs during the decade prior to the separation of commercial and investment banking and the creation of the Securities and Exchange Commission in 1933 and 1934. The Securities and Exchange Commission published some information on bond and preferred stock issues during the period 1925–1929 (SEC, 1941c) but assembled no information on common stock issues prior to 1935. This is an important omission from the history of stock underwriting for two reasons. Stock offerings boomed during the 1920s, and most of the volume of industrial securities issued was in the form of stock; from 1923 to 1929, $3.3 billion in industrial stock was sold compared to $1.5 billion in industrial bonds (Friend, 1967, p. 68).

Evidence about the size of underwriting spreads prior to the separation of commercial and investment banking would also be informative about the relative importance of information costs and concentration in determining those spreads. If the "money trust" were a reality prior to 1933, then one might expect spreads to have fallen somewhat after 1933 in comparison to the 1920s, as Morgan and other banks were divided. On the other hand, if one regards the separation as unnecessary (or possibly even disruptive to the market), then one might expect spreads to rise or remain unchanged after 1933. It would also be interesting to investigate whether the investment bank affiliates of commercial banks (like First Chicago and First Boston) charged lower or higher spreads than their New York investment banking competitors. Comparisons of averages for bond and preferred stock spreads (reported in Table 5.5) show a decrease in bond spreads but no significant change from the late 1920s to 1940 (and possibly an increase in preferred spreads). Given that preferred stock spreads began from a lower level than common, however, it is conceivable that common stock spreads may have fallen during these years.

In Tables 5.6 through 5.8, we report additional data on stock and bond spreads from the pre-1933 period which we gathered from two sources: (1) data on common stock spreads disclosed by Morgan, Kuhn-Loeb, Dillon-Read, and Drexel during the Pecora Hearings (bearing mainly on large common stock flotations) and (2) data on smaller stock and bond flotations which we assembled from the deal books of Lehman Brothers. Together these data provide a few observations over the entire spectrum of common stock issues.

The Lehman Brothers' deal books are an important new source of information for the period 1925–1933 (and afterwards). Lehman Brothers was an important actor in the marketing of equity during this period.

Table 5.5. *Percent spreads on bonds and preferred stocks, by industry, 1925–1929 v. 1935–1938, issues of less than $5 million*

	Bonds		Preferred stock	
	1925–1929	1935–1938	1925–1929	1935–1938
Extractive	6.7	3.6	24.2	11.9
Manufacturing	5.6	4.0	6.7	9.6
Financial	1.9	5.6	—	10.9
Merchandising	4.7	3.3	8.4	6.1
Transportation & Communication	6.2	3.3	6.5	5.9
Utilities	4.9	2.7	6.0	3.4
Others	5.4	4.5	15.1	12.8
Total	5.2	3.4	7.1	8.9

Source: SEC, 1941c, Table 7.

As Carosso (1970, p. 82) notes, Lehman Brothers and Goldman Sachs were the first investment banking houses to experiment with underwriting stock issues of small manufacturing and retail firms. Beginning in 1906 with the historic underwritings of United Cigar Manufacturing and Sears, Roebuck & Co., Goldman Sachs and Lehman Brothers established a long-lasting niche as underwriters to small, growing firms, particularly in retailing.[9] Thus, Lehman Brothers' deal books should contain a sampling of small, unseasoned offerings of equity.

Table 5.6 summarizes the spread information from twenty-five deal books over the period 1925 to 1933. All of the stock transactions predate 1930. We only report information for deals that involved primary flotation of stock or bonds and exclude exchange offers. Table 5.7 compares Lehman's bond and preferred stock spreads with deals of similar size reported by the Securities and Exchange Commission for the pre-1933 period. Taken as a whole, these data indicate no important difference between Lehman Brothers and other underwriters during the pre-1933 period. There are small differences within individual size categories; but, given the small sample size of the Lehman deals, such variation is to be expected.

Table 5.8 provides a comparison, by size of issue, of common stock spreads for the period 1938 to 1940 with the pre-1933 common stock spreads observed from four Lehman Brothers common stock underwritings to the public and nineteen common stock underwritings

[9] During the pre-1933 period, retailers and manufacturers are the dominant type of firm found in the deal books.

Table 5.6. *Percent spreads[a] on issues through Lehman Brothers, by security and issue size ($Millions), 1925–1933*

Security type	Less than $0.5 million	$0.5 million to less than $1 million	$1 million to less than $2 million	$2 million to less than $5 million	More than $5 million
Common only					
Average	23.0	—	14.2	7.8[b]	9.3
Count	1	0	2	2	1
Common + Preferred					
Average	—	—	—	12.9	9.0
Count	0	0	0	6	3
Preferred only					
Average	—	—	13.6	5.2	5.0[c]
Count	0	0	2	1	1
Debt only					
Average	—	—	—	7.2[d]	6.5[e]
Count	0	0	0	4	2

[a] Spreads for deals that involve a mixture of common and preferred are calculated as a ratio of the total amount of the joint issue. All spreads are calculated relative to the offering price of the security. Securities were omitted if they involved exchange offers or if we were unable to discover the spread.

[b] These two issues are each special. One is a rights offer, the other is partly a private placement.

[c] This is the only utility issue in the sample. It is issued with warrants.

[d] One of these issues is a private placement; another is issued with attached warrants.

[e] One of these bond issues included warrants.

reported in the Pecora Hearings. Our sample size is small because we only used information on common stock flotations where gross spreads were clearly defined and where only primary public issues of common stock were involved.[10] Within each size classification the spreads are similar to those in the late 1930s, although the later spreads are slightly higher. The number of observations is again small; but when the data are combined with the comparisons in Table 5.5, a clear overall impression emerges that no important change in average underwriting spreads occurred after 1933. Indeed, if Brandeis's facts about underwriting spreads for the pre-World War I era are accurate, it seems that underwriting costs for bonds and stocks remained roughly unchanged over the first forty years of the twentieth century.

[10] Meaningful information about common stock spreads is hard to disentangle in deals that involved simultaneous or combined offerings of common and preferred issues.

Table 5.7. *Spreads on bonds and preferred stock issues[a] to the public—Lehman Brothers,[b] 1925–1933 v. SEC data for 1925–1929, 1935–1938, by size*

	Less than $1 million	$1 million to less than $2 million	$2 million to less than $5 million	More than $5 million
Lehman Preferred, 1925–1933				
Average	—	13.6	5.2	5.0
Count	0	2	1	1
SEC Preferred, 1925–1929				
Average	7.5	8.0	6.9	—
Count	35	31	30	0
SEC Preferred, 1935–1938 or 1938[c]				
Average	13.0	8.7	6.1	3.8
Count	135	47	24	9
Lehman Bonds, 1925–1933				
Average	—	—	7.2	6.5
Count	0	0	4	2
SEC Bonds, 1925–1929				
Average	5.7	4.9	5.2	—
Count	142	118	163	0
SEC Bonds, 1935–1938 or 1938[c]				
Average	5.0	3.5	3.0	2.2
Count	100	52	58	46

[a] We restricted the sample to issues of preferred stock or bonds alone and to issues that did not involve the placement of shares with special parties.
[b] Lehman Brothers' data are taken from Lehman deal books.
[c] Data for small (i.e., less than $5 million) issues are for 1935–1938, from SEC, 1941c. Data for large ($5 million and larger) are for 1938 only, from SEC, 1941a.

Table 5.8. *Spreads on common stock issues to the public[a] – Lehman Brothers[b] and Pecora hearings data,[c] 1925–1931 v. all issues,[d] 1938–40, by size*

	Less than $1 million	$1 million to less than $5 million	$5 million and more
Lehman, 1925–1929			
Average	23.0	14.2	9.3
Count	1	2	1
Pecora Hearings Sample, 1927–1931			
Average	—	11.7	8.8
Count	0	5	14
SEC, 1938–1940			
Average	20.7	14.8	10.4
Count	37	29	13

[a] In all cases, we restricted the sample to the issues of common stock alone and to issues that did not involve the placement of shares with special parties.
[b] Lehman Brothers' data are taken from Lehman deal books.
[c] Pecora Hearings data are taken from the U.S. Senate, 1933, passim, and mainly comprise deals managed by Dillon-Read and Kuhn-Loeb, which together account for 10 of 19 public common stock issues.
[d] Data from the 1930s are from SEC, 1941b, 1941c.

Comparisons of the pre-1933 period and the period 1938 to 1940 lend no support to the notion that the separation of commercial and investment banking, or the break-up of Morgan, significantly reduced the cost of placing securities. Spreads remained roughly the same, and initial underpricing seems to have increased. Tinic (1988) finds that the increase in underpricing is mainly attributable to the most unseasoned initial public offerings, and he links increased underpricing on those offerings to new liability regulations that placed investment bankers at risk for poor *ex post* performance of initial public offerings of unseasoned firms.[11]

Evidence of a lack of any decline in post-1933 average spreads is reinforced by the growth of private placements that occurred during the late 1930s (discussed below in detail). Private placements channeled smaller firms away from the public equity market, which should have produced

---

[11] Tinic did not control for inflation when comparing underpricing of small issues over time. Inflationary bias may account for his results, since cross-sectionally underpricing is greater for small stocks.

a decline in average spreads because of changes in the composition of firms going public toward more seasoned issues.

Given the constant or rising costs of securities issuance after the 1930s, one might have concluded by 1940 that the high bankers' spreads of the pre-Depression era were not largely a function of pre-Depression concentration within the investment banking industry. The federal government, however, reached a very different conclusion – that more regulation was needed to break the monopoly power of the money trust and (presumably) bring down underwriting fees.

Beginning in the 1930s, the Securities and Exchange Commission experimented with the idea of requiring certain issuing firms to use sealed bids when engaging an underwriter and threatened to withhold permission from registrations with "unreasonable" spreads (Carosso, 1970, pp. 431–57). This idea was the brainchild of three private citizens, two of whom were prominent investment bankers who hoped to use competitive bidding to pry utility and railroad customers loose from their competitors (Carosso, 1970, pp. 431–42). As the rule was formally implemented, after April 1940, it applied mainly to bond issues of large utility companies and, later, railroads. Competitive bidding placed the burden of paperwork at the early stage of some securities offerings in the hands of the issuer rather than the investment banker but otherwise likely had little effect. Securities with the largest spreads were exempted from the regulation. One possible effect, however, was to favor private placements, which were also exempted. Carosso (1970, p. 451) argues that, if anything, competitive bidding served to increase the concentration of investment banking, and its effect on spreads was small and mainly limited to the bond issues of high-quality corporations, whose spreads had averaged between 1 and 3 percent prior to the change in regulation (Carosso, 1970, pp. 451–57).

Opposition to competitive bidding within the investment banking industry was probably more costly than the regulation itself. Such opposition encouraged the perception of monopoly and set the stage for the six-year ordeal of an antitrust case against the industry beginning in 1947 (Carosso, 1970, p. 461). The failure of the government to make its case and the opportunity the case gave the investment banking industry to provide detailed refutation of allegations of monopoly and conspiracy ultimately put to rest the persistent attempts to regulate investment banking syndication. As Carosso (1970, p. 495) points out:

The image of the investment banker that emerged from these disclosures was entirely different from the one that had existed before the trial started. At that time, the generally held view of the role and function of the investment banker was the one made popular by Pujo and Brandeis a generation earlier and reaffirmed by the Pecora and TNEC hearings. It was largely on the basis of their findings, which had become part of the accepted folklore, that the government rested its complaint and hoped to win its case. The trial disproved many of the misconceptions that had grown out of these earlier investigations and shattered the old myth of a Wall Street money monopoly.

The Securities and Exchange Commission's concern over possible excesses of market power by investment bankers did not end with the industry's court victory in 1953. Like the establishment in 1941 of Rule 50 on competitive bidding, Rule 415 (shelf registration) in 1982 was designed to produce a decline in the market power of bankers in their relationship with issuers. While Rule 50 sought to give the issuer greater independence from a particular banker in the early stages of the issue, Rule 415 extended this logic to allow firms to wait until the issue was about to be released to the market to enlist the help of an investment banker – which was supposed to reduce the market power of investment bankers. As discussed above, however, Denis (1991) shows that equity issuers have found little benefit from shelf registration, which belies the notion that the convention of having an investment banker managing a transaction from the beginning is costly to issuers.

5.5 Corporate finance trends and financial innovation after the 1930s

Comparisons across time of the size of spreads can be useful for gauging the relative importance of information/marketing costs and underwriters' market power for explaining variation in spreads. But it is difficult to construct a series over a long time period measuring underwriting costs on comparable transactions (controlling, as one should, for issue size and differences across types of issues) for three reasons. First, data for the period prior to 1936 are hard to come by. Second, as noted above, changes in underwriting costs affected the selection of firms that chose to issue securities. In particular, as the underwriting technology improved, relatively unseasoned issuers were more likely to issue securities; thus, measured declines in spreads tend to understate true improvements in the cost of underwriting. Third, our sources do not consistently report underwriting costs other than the spread (warrants, rights of first refusal, overallotment options). It is possible that the history of gross spreads does not provide an accurate picture of the changes in total underwriting cost.

Table 5.9 measures as best one can the decline in spreads from the pre-World War I period to the 1970s. We report average spreads for bonds, preferred stocks, and common stocks, and for a roughly

Table 5.9. *Percent spreads on primary issues sold to the public through investment banks for cash, 1913–1993*

Date	Bonds	Preferred	Common stock	Common stock, small[a] manufactures	Annual common stock issues, small[a] manufactures
circa 1913[b]	5–10	7.5–10	20–25		
1912–1915[c]	4	8–14	above 20	above 20	
1925–1931			9–23[d]	14–23[e]	
1926–1929 (large)[f]	3.1				
1925–1929 (small)[g]	5.2	7.1			
1935–1938			16.4	17.4[h]	43[h]
1935–1938 (small)[g]	3.4	8.9			
1938	2.6	10.5	20.0	13.2	28
1939	1.9	8.8	16.6	16.5	42
1940	2.1	7.4	15.9	15.9	42
1951, 1953, 1955	0.8	3.3	8.8	11.1	15
1963–1965	na[i]	2.4	7.9	10.9	27
1971–1972	1.5[i]	1.5	8.4[j]	10.1[j]	206
1992–1993	1.5	4.1	6.7	8.7	130

[a] The definition of "small" is adjusted in a rough manner for inflation as follows: For 1935–1940, only firms with issues less than $1 million are included. For 1951–1965, firms with issues less than $2 million are included. For 1971–1972, firms with issues less than $4 million are included. For 1992–1993, firms with issues less than $10 million are included. This roughly parallels the changes in the implicit GNP deflator for nonresidential investment, which has the following values: 1929 = 39.9, 1939 = 38.7, 1951 = 83.1, 1963 = 106, 1972 = 145.7 (Council of Economic Advisers, 1974, p. 252, and 1994, p. 274).
[b] These numbers are from Brandeis, 1914, and no source is given.
[c] These numbers are from Dewing, 1920, p. 150, and are reproduced in Haven, 1940, pp. 31–35. The lower bound of the range for preferred stock commissions is the average for utilities; the upper bound is the average for "local industrials." No common stock data are reported. The range reported here is based on the assumption that common spreads are greater than preferred and Dewing's, 1920, p. 149, statement that "very frequently the gross profit on the preferred stock of an industrial is as high as 20 percent."
[d] The range represents the averages for different size categories of issues. Lower spreads characterize larger issues. The limited sample is drawn from the Lehman Brothers' deal books and from the Pecora Hearings. These data are discussed in detail in the text.
[e] Based on data solely from the Lehman deal books, thus excluding large issues found in the Pecora Hearings data.
[f] Haven, 1940, p. 34, notes that this sample is not representative of bond issues generally, because it tends to include larger issues.
[g] Data are for issues of under $5 million.
[h] These data are for 1936–1938.
[i] For 1963–1965, spreads on convertible bonds averaged 3.7 percent. For 1971–1972, spreads on convertible bonds averaged 3.2 percent, and on other bonds, 1.1 percent.
[j] These data not only include primary offerings to the public but also "mixed" offerings of primary and secondary issues.
Sources: Brandeis, 1914, Dewing, 1920, Haven, 1940, SEC, 1941a, 1941b, 1941c, 1957, 1970, 1974, Securities Data Co., 1994, and Tables 5.6 and 5.7.

consistent category of small manufacturing firms' issues of common stock. We also report the annual volume of public common stock issues by small manufacturing firms, which shows how changes in common stock spreads were associated with substantial changes in the number of unseasoned public stock issues. From roughly 1913 to 1930, there is some indication of a reduction in spreads for common and preferred stocks and bonds. From 1930 to 1940, bond spreads continue to fall, but there is not evidence of any change in common or preferred spreads. From 1940 to the 1950s, improvements in stock spreads for small firms coincided with a decline in the annual number of stock issues by small manufacturing firms. As we will argue, this likely reflected the role of private placements as a substitute for public stock issues for unseasoned firms, rather than a true reduction in the costs of public issues for such firms. In the 1960s and 1970s, however, the cost of public stock issues was low for small manufacturing firms and the volume of such issues was high, indicating a clear reduction in spreads on public issues.

The timing of the declining trend of average spreads on securities issued to the public through underwriters (shown in Table 5.9) reinforces the view that reductions in information and marketing cost, rather than a decline in the market power of underwriters, was the crucial factor producing reductions in spreads over time. From the 1940s to the 1970s, there is no evidence that stock underwriting became more competitive, but there is substantial evidence that the costs of monitoring and marketing were reduced.

Miller (1967) examined the degree of concentration in underwriting bond flotations and stock flotations from the 1930s to the early 1960s. Table 5.10 reports his finding that concentration in stock and bond underwriting did not decline significantly over this period. In common stock underwriting, which shows the largest average spread decline from the 1930s to the 1970s, there is little change in concentration over this period.[12] Furthermore, while bond spreads are much lower than stock spreads throughout this period, bond market concentration is much higher. Miller also examined whether the identity of investment banking houses that most often act as syndicate managers changes over time. As shown in Table 5.11, he found substantial changes in rankings of bankers' shares of syndication management, using three three-year periods (1935–1937, 1947–1949, and 1961–1963). Of the top ten syndicate managers in 1961–1963, only five were in the top ten in 1935–1937, and eight were in the top ten in 1947–1949. Of the top five syndicate managers in

---

[12] It is important to keep in mind that the average decline in spreads for common stocks reported in Table 5.9 likely understates the true decline. As discussed by Mendelson (1967) and below, as costs of high-spread issues fell, more of these firms entered the market.

Table 5.10. *Concentration in underwriting, 1934–1963: cumulative percent of securities flotations managed by or with the participation of a select group of underwriters*

Panel A: Flotations managed

Period	Largest one firm	Largest three firms	Largest five firms	Largest ten firms	Total volume of underwritten flotations ($ billions)
Stock					
1961–1963	10	22	31	46	7.3
1952	13	34	44	61	1.6
1951	14	33	42	62	1.5
1934–1938	9	24	35	51	1.2
Bonds					
1961–1963	17	45	55	74	14.6
1952	18	50	65	82	2.7
1951	29	49	58	76	1.8
1934–1938	28	49	59	76	6.4

Panel B: Participations

Period	Largest[a] one firm	Largest[a] five firms	Largest[a] ten firms	Largest[a] twenty-five firms
All Securities				
1963	4	15	26	48
1952	5	18	30	52
1951	5	19	30	50
1934–1938	8	31	46	71
Stock				
1963[b]	3	15	27	47
1952	4	15	25	45
1951	4	16	27	48
1934–1938	6	20	34	54
Bonds				
1963[b]	4	17	28	50
1952	8	23	35	57
1951	10	24	35	57
1934–1938	9	34	50	75

[a] "Largest" refers to share in type of flotation indicated. Hence, the composition of any given number of "largest" firms may vary for other types of flotations.
[b] Convertible bonds are included with stock.
Source: Miller, 1967, pp. 157, 163.

Table 5.11. *Ranking of leading syndicate members in numbers of issues, various dates*

Firm	1961–1963	1947–1949[a]	1935–1937[a]
Halsey, Stuart & Co.	1	1	9
White, Weld & Co.	2	10	
First Boston Corp.	3	2	1
Kidder, Peabody & Co.	4	7	22
Lehman Brothers	5	3	5
Eastman Dillon, Union Securities & Co.	6	12[b]	
Merrill Lynch, Pierce, Fenner & Smith	6	8	12
Salomon Brothers & Hutzler	6	5	10
Blyth & Co.	9	4	5
Smith, Barney & Co.	10	13	3
The Ohio Company	11		
Paine, Webber, Jackson & Curtis	12	13	19
Dean Witter & Co.	13	19	
Morgan Stanley & Co.	14	11	2
Dillon, Read & Co.	15	16	12
Goldman, Sachs & Co.	15	17	10
Kuhn, Loeb & Co.	17	19	4
Harriman, Ripley & Co.	18	6	7
Dempsey-Tegeler & Co.	19		
Bear, Stearns & Co.	20		
F.I. duPont, A. C. Allyn	21[c]		
Equitable Securities Corp.	22		
Hornblower & Weeks	23		12
Glore, Forgan & Co.	24	21	12
Hayden, Stone & Co.	24		22

[a] Positions are recorded in 1947–1949 and 1935–1937 only for firms falling in the top twenty-five. In comanaged issues, each comanager is credited with one issue.
[b] Union Securities Corp.
[c] Merged in 1963. Data combined for three-year period.
Source: Miller, 1967, p. 161.

1961–1963, only two were in the top five in 1935–1937. Clearly, there was significant opportunity for entry into and exit from the top echelons of investment banking over this period.

The secular decline in underwriting spreads was, however, associated with other trends that indicate improvement in the technology for financing corporations after the 1930s – notably the increasing extent of corporations' reliance on external funding sources as opposed to retained earnings (Table 5.12), the early growth of private placements of securities (Table 5.13), and the growing importance of institutional investors

Table 5.12. *Share of funds of nonfinancial corporations supplied by internal sources, various dates*

Period	Percent	Period	Percent
1901–1912	55	1946–1956[b]	58
1913–1922	60	1958[b]	66
1923–1929	55	1960[b]	69
1930–1933	([a])	1962[b]	61
1934–1939	98	1901–1913	59
1940–1945	80	1913–1939	66
1946–1949	64	1946–1956	64
1946–1956	61		

[a] Total sources were negative.
[b] Department of Commerce estimates. Other data are based on Goldsmith.
Source: Miller, 1967, p. 171.

Table 5.13. *The growth of private placements*

Year	All corporate offerings	Percent private placed	Year	All corporate offerings	Percent private placed
1934	397	23.2	1947	6,577	34.0
1935	2,332	16.6	1948	7,078	43.6
1936	4,572	8.2	1949	6,052	41.3
1937	2,309	14.3	1950	6,362	42.1
1938	2,155	32.1	1951	7,741	44.1
1939	2,164	32.6	1952	9,534	41.5
1940	2,677	28.6	1953	8,898	36.3
1941	2,667	30.5	1954	9,516	36.6
1942	1,062	39.5	1955	10,240	32.2
1943	1,170	31.8	1960	10,154	32.3
1944	3,202	24.6	1965	15,992	51.0
1945	6,011	17.0	1967	24,798	28.1
1946	6,900	27.8	1970	38,944	12.5

Sources: Sec, 1952, p. 3; and Jarrell, 1981, p. 670.

Table 5.14. *Percent ownership structure of corporate equities, by sector,* *1946–1980*

	1946	1950	1955	1960	1965	1970	1975	1980
Households	93	91	89	86	84	79	72	70
Foundations	—	—	5	4	4	3	4	3
Investment Companies	1	2	4	5	5	5	5	3
Insurance Companies								
Life	1	2	1	1	1	2	3	3
Other	2	2	2	2	2	2	2	2
Pension Funds								
Private	0	1	2	4	6	8	10	11
Government	0	0	0	0	0	1	3	4
Foreign	3	2	2	2	2	3	4	4
Other	1	1	1	0	0	1	1	1
Total Market Value[a]	110	143	309	434	714	859	812	1,518

[a] In billions of dollars. Numbers are rounded.
Source: Munnell, 1982, p. 123.

as purchasers of public securities issues (Table 5.14), particularly in the late 1950s and 1960s.

5.5.1 Private placements

Private placements (almost exclusively in the form of debt) grew enormously in importance during the 1940s. From 1934 to 1937, private placements accounted for 12 percent of a small total of corporate offerings. By 1951, private placements accounted for 44 percent of all corporate offerings, 58 percent of all debt issues, and 82 percent of all debt issues of manufacturing firms (SEC, 1952, pp. 3, 5, 6). Private placements as a percentage of securities offerings peaked in the mid-1960s. The resurgence in public offerings of bonds and stocks, beginning in the 1950s, reduced the share of private placements to only 14 percent of total securities issues by 1970 (Jarrell, 1981).

From the beginning, life insurance companies accounted for the overwhelming majority of these purchases – 93 percent in 1947, 83 percent in 1950 – with the remainder held largely by banks – 2.7 percent in 1947, 12.1 percent in 1950 (SEC, 1952, p. 6). For the period 1990–1992, Carey,

Prowse, Rea, and Udell (1993) report that life insurance companies and banks (broadly defined) maintained respective shares of 83 and 11 percent of the private placement market.

The Securities and Exchange Commission (1952) reported that roughly half of private placements of debt were marketed by investment bankers, with spreads ranging from an average of 0.2 percent for large issues to 1.7 percent for small issues, with a median fee of 0.85 percent. Holding size constant, total issue costs for the late 1940s (spreads plus expenses) for private placements of debt were between 25 and 40 percent of the issue costs for public placements of debt, with the greatest savings occurring in the smallest size categories. For equity issues during this period, investment banker spreads were similar to those for bonds. Savings from private placements of equity were larger and also decreased with size; total costs of private placements of equity averaged between 10 and 20 percent of public issuing costs (SEC, 1952, pp. 26–27).

What were the advantages of private placements that allowed them to occur at so low a cost, and why did some firms choose to pay higher fees to place their securities publicly? As the Securities and Exchange Commission (1952, p. 7) remarked:

A number of instances of public utility securities sold by public offering at competitive bidding have been noted where the total cost of money to the issuer over the life of the issue was more favorable than that offered by private placement.

Recent models of the corporate finance "pecking order" are consistent with this observation. "Insider" finance – including bank lending and private placements to other intermediaries – involves costly ongoing monitoring and discipline by intermediaries, while "outsider" finance (public offerings of stocks and bonds) involves very different methods of evaluating and controlling corporate performance. Firms' costs of going to outsiders vary with their "information intensity" (Calomiris and Hubbard, 1990, 1995; Calomiris, 1995) and fall as they become relatively seasoned credit risks (James and Wier, 1990).

Using intermediaries economizes on spreads but involves the payment of higher interest to compensate for a greater concentration of risk (in the intermediaries' portfolios) and for the ongoing costs of monitoring and control (James, 1987). Public markets have the added possible advantage of greater competition in bidding for claims on the firm. But unseasoned credit risks who use outsider sources of funding may pay higher costs of funds than they would using insiders because of outsiders' needs to attach a substantial "lemons discount" to the claims of unseasoned firms to compensate for less information about and control over credit risk (Jensen and Meckling, 1976; Myers and Majluf, 1984).

Until recently, little formal analysis has been done of private placements and their position in the pecking order. A recent monograph by
Carey, Prowse, Rea, and Udell (1993), however, shows that firms that
choose private placements of debt (at least in recent years) tend to be
much more "information-problematic" than bond issuers. Private placement borrowers are "typically medium-sized companies for which information is not widely available or large corporations with complex
financing requirements" (p. 3). Lenders in the private placement market
"produce the information required to assess the credit quality of the
issuers. In addition they intensively monitor the business and financial
operations of the borrowers after loans have been extended" (p. 3).
Covenants in private placement lending are far more detailed than those
for bonds and share many features with bank loan covenants. Borrowers
in the private placement market are much less likely to have been rated
by Standard and Poor's, have higher sales growth rates, and higher ratios
of research and development expenditure to sales than borrowers in the
public market. According to Carey, Prowse, Rea, and Udell (1993), the
borrowers in the private placement market rank somewhere between
bank borrowers and bond borrowers in the financial pecking order.

Because private placement borrowers are "information-problematic,"
the likely alternative for many private placement borrowers would be
bank loans or stock issues, rather than the public bond market. The
public bond market has been a relatively exclusive club. Calomiris (1995)
argued that this reflects two facts: rollover costs of widely distributed
issues favor long-term public debt issues, but long-term debt increases
problems of "asset substitution" – the incentives of borrowers to take on
risk after placing their debt (Jensen and Meckling, 1976). Without the
option to threaten to "call" a borrower's loan (not to roll it over), bond-
holders in the public market would have little recourse against asset
substitution.

There has been little research attempting to explain the burst of
growth in private placements from 1933 to 1950. One possible explanation is higher regulatory cost after 1933. New regulations on public offerings may have encouraged the development of a relatively unregulated
alternative. Carosso (1970) pointed to regulatory costs – including
liability laws, waiting periods, pricing policies, bidding rules, and other
rules on public underwritings – that made public offerings more costly
to underwriters than before. But regulatory costs by themselves cannot
explain the timing in the growth of private placements, which was concentrated in the mid- to late 1940s.

The timing of the rise of private placements in the 1940s is associated
with steady growth in the value of life insurance companies' reserves,
although this does not "explain" the timing of this innovation. Insurance

industry assets grew from 2.5 percent of national assets in 1929 to 4 percent in 1933; and by 1952 they had reached 6 percent (Goldsmith, 1958, p. 319). Demographic factors favoring the growth of life insurance companies (Goldsmith, 1958, pp. 27–29, 43–44) may help to explain the surge during the 1940s. Similarly, significant changes in the method of marketing life insurance policies (including the introduction of group and wholesale insurance) may have encouraged insurance company growth (Stalson, 1942).

Kemmerer (1952) stressed that the rapid growth in life insurance company assets – which grew during the 1940s by nearly a billion dollars a month – encouraged life insurance companies to find new uses for their funds and helped to usher in the age of the private placement. In fact, the proportion of life insurance companies' assets devoted to financing corporations grew even more dramatically than life insurance assets. Business finance comprised 39 percent of life insurance assets in 1933. By 1952 it was 49 percent of assets (Goldsmith, 1958, Table A-8).

The retreat of life insurance companies from agricultural mortgages in the face of widespread default and mortgage moratoria in the 1920s and 1930s (Woodruff, 1937) partly explains the increasing share of business assets in life insurance company portfolios. Farm mortgages fell from 13.9 percent of assets in 1929 to 2.1 percent in 1950. Furthermore, changes in the market for U.S. government bonds – the post-World War II shrinking in outstanding bonds (Studenski and Krooss, 1963, pp. 476–80) – implied that insurance companies would have to invest a smaller proportion of their assets in government securities. Finally, the Treasury-Fed accord, which brought to an end the period of stable long-term interest rates on government bonds, encouraged greater interest in shorter term debts like those available in the private placement market. From 1945 to 1950, the assets of insurance companies increased from $40.5 to $56.5 billion. Over that period, the asset share of U.S. government bonds fell from 48.9 percent of assets to 22.5 percent. Over that same five-year period, business debt other than that of utilities and railroads (a proxy for private placements) rose from 4.6 percent of assets to 16.8 percent. By 1952, U.S. government bonds had fallen to 13.8 percent of assets, and nonrailroad and utility debt had risen to 20.7 percent. Nonfarm mortgages were the other major category of asset growth – increasing from 13 percent of assets in 1945 to 25.1 percent of assets in 1952.[13]

The growth of private placements offered a new and important financing margin for industrial borrowers. Regulations on consolidation and

[13] Data for life insurance portfolios are taken from Best's Life Insurance Reports (1940–1960).

branching that restricted the scale of commercial banks meant that as borrowers became large, they could not rely on local commercial bankers to meet their needs at reasonable cost (Calomiris, 1995). Private placements offered a cost-effective alternative for firms that would have faced high costs of public equity issues and that did not qualify for the long-term debt market. The likely effect of private placements on equity spreads, therefore, was that they reduced the proportion of high-spread issuers that came to the public equity market. This, rather than improvements within the market for public securities, seems to explain best the reduction in average spreads during the 1940s visible in Tables 5.4 and 5.9.

5.5.2   Institutional investors and economies of scale in purchasing securities issues

The 1950s and 1960s witnessed a second set of financial innovations – the new growth of institutional investors (pension funds and mutual funds) – which was associated with the resurgence in public offerings during this period. Like insurance companies, which had spurred the growth in private placements, the new nonbank intermediaries also found ways of avoiding the high costs of public issue. These private placements largely took the form of private equity (venture capital) investments. But unlike the life insurance company-supported private placement revolution of the 1940s, which only affected the mix of equity issuers coming to the public market, the new institutional investors also made block purchases of public equity and thus had a direct impact on spreads by reducing the costs of placing equity issues publicly.

The growth of pension funds' and mutual funds' holdings of equity was particularly dramatic in the late 1950s and 1960s, as shown in Table 5.14. In 1946, investment companies (mutual funds) and private pension funds held 2 percent and 0.8 percent shares, respectively, of corporate equities. By 1970, those shares had risen to 5.3 and 7.8 percent, respectively. By 1980, private pensions held 10.4 percent of corporate equity, while investment companies held 4.6 percent. The growth of equity holdings by pension funds reflected more than the seventeenfold growth in total assets of these intermediaries from 1950 to 1971. As Table 5.15 shows, private pension funds holdings of common stock grew from 12 percent of their total assets in 1951 to 68 percent in 1971.

The causes of the growth of pension funds during this period have been studied by a number of scholars (including Andrews, 1964; Greenough and King, 1976; Ture, 1976; and Munnell, 1982), as has their role in placing equity in primary and secondary markets (SEC, 1971). The

Table 5.15. *Asset shares (percent) of private noninsured pension funds, 1951–1974*

	1951	1961	1971	1974
Cash	4	2	1	4
Government securities	31	6	2	5
Corporate bonds	44	35	21	28
Preferred stock	5	2	2	1
Common stock	12	49	68	56
Own company	na	7	6	na
Other	na	42	62	na
Mortgages	2	4	3	2
Other assets	3	4	4	5

Source: Greenough and King, 1975, p. 139.

principle sources of early growth in pension funds were the wage controls of World War II (which favored the use of nonwage compensation for employees) and the tax exemptions enjoyed by pensions, which became increasingly valuable during the 1960s.

The rise of pensions and mutual funds as large block purchasers of equity in primary and secondary markets had dramatic effects on the structure of those markets – so dramatic that in 1971 the Securities and Exchange Commission published an enormous multivolume study, and Congress held hearings, examining these changes.

In the secondary market, institutional holders gave rise to the "two-tier" market for equity trading. In addition to the traditional small transactions for individual holders, a new market arose in block trades among large money managers, which included pension fund managers or their investment managers, particularly Morgan Guaranty, Bankers Trust, and Citibank, which collectively managed 80 percent of the trust accounts of employee benefit plans (Munnell, 1982, p. 121). The main advantages of this development were improvements in market liquidity, as it became much easier to move large amounts of shares over small periods of time.

In the primary public market, institutional investors changed the way equity issues were sold. By acting as purchasers of large amounts of stock, particularly in unseasoned companies, they reduced the marketing costs normally associated with placing such stock. The Securities and Exchange Commission (1971) found that institutional investors accounted for 24 percent of all purchases of 1,684 initial public offerings of common stock from January 1967 to March 1970. Despite enormous short-term profits that some investors realized from rapid sales of initially underpriced IPOs, most institutional investors bought stocks in the primary market to hold as long-term investments.[14] Seventy percent of institutional IPO purchases remained unsold after twelve weeks. Institutional investors did not discriminate in their purchasing according to the size of the issuer but did tend to deal only with the largest underwriters (SEC, 1971, pp. 2348–56).

Institutional investors were very active in the venture capital market as well. In addition to their $1.4 billion in public IPO purchases during the period 1967–1970, institutional investors purchased $3.5 billion of nonpublicly traded "restricted" securities (venture capital investments in equity or debt with equity features), which mainly benefitted small, young firms.

In trying to explain the reductions in the spreads for small, unseasoned companies during the 1950s identified by Mendelson (1967), Friend (1967) pointed to institutional investors as the main source of improvement in market efficiency. Friend, Blume, and Crockett (1970, p. vii) wrote:

These institutions, which first sparked the cult of common stocks, later attracted public attention to "growth" stocks and created the fashion for instant performance. Innovative and inventive, institutional money managers have ventured into areas where older and more prudent investment men feared to tread, taking positions in the stocks of unseasoned companies, setting up hedge funds, devising new types of securities.

Part IV of the Securities and Exchange Commission's (1971) study focuses on the impact of institutional investors on corporate issuers. It emphasizes that, by selling in block to institutional buyers of primary public common stock offerings, investment bankers could economize on the costs of marketing securities. It was easier for underwriters to credibly communicate the characteristics of issuers to a few block buyers, especially if those block buyers were institutional investors or pension accounts managed by New York banks. Moreover, the concentration of stockholdings of unseasoned firms may have facilitated control over management and thus reduced the potential risk of stock purchases and the need for information about the firm at the time of the offering.

Moreover, the Securities and Exchange Commission (1971) emphasized that the benefits of institutional purchasing for reducing issue costs on public equity exceeded the direct consequences of placing shares in the hands of institutional investors. The participation of institutional buyers in an offering also made it easier to sell the remainder of the offering to individual investors.

Retail members of the syndicate have been known to advise their customers in advance of the offering that institutions have indicated their intent to buy the issue . . . While this knowledge of institutional interest may increase the public's

[14] Those that sold immediately after buying primary issues reaped similar profits to other IPO purchasers (a capital gain averaging 18 percent for the first week after the issue).

appetite for any stock, the effect is greater for small, less established issuers than for large established issuers and still more so for first offerings of such small companies. . . . The possible public impression that institutions with their purported research capabilities and sophistication would not allow themselves to be bilked helps explain individual investors' attitudes toward institutional interest. The result, then, of supposed or revealed institutional interest in an offering is to enhance retail interest as well. (SEC, 1971, p. 2393)

In a sense, the new institutional block buying method of placing public shares was similar to the method used under German universal banking discussed above. The rise of institutional investors reduced the costs of communicating issuers' characteristics to buyers and enhanced control over corporate equity issuers by block investors (including New York banks managing large trust accounts).

5.5.3   Summary

The growth of new intermediaries – insurance companies, mutual funds, and pension funds – substantially improved the efficiency of financial markets and led to reductions in the spreads paid to investment bankers on new securities issues. Private placements of debt and venture capital provided an alternative to a banking system hampered by limitations on branching and consolidation and buffeted by the collapse of the Great Depression, and to a fragmented public issues market in which the costs of entry for unseasoned credit risks was high. The growth of mutual funds and pension funds and the concentration of equity purchases by these investors and their trust account managers in the 1950s and 1960s plausibly explain the reduced costs of public stock issues for relatively unseasoned firms.

5.6   The decline in equity spreads from 1950 to 1971

In the second section above, we reviewed the results of Mendelson's (1967) detailed analysis of the changes in underwriting spreads on common stock from 1949 to 1961. In the fifth section, we linked that decline to changes in the role of institutional purchasers of equity, which helped to reduce the costs of underwriting. While Mendelson's data and analysis are very rich, there are points worth pursuing that are not dealt with in his study. First, his data end in 1961, but the improvement in average spreads and growth in institutional investors' share of the market continued into the 1960s and 1970s; thus it is important to update his findings to take account of these changes. Second, Mendelson devoted little attention to the relationship between spreads and the characteristics of the underwriter. It is possible to address the potential role of market power in influencing spreads by considering the relationship between the underwriter's volume of underwritings and the spread. Third, Mendelson did not examine the division of the gross spread between underwriters and dealers. Clearly, this division is relevant in evaluating whether the spread is largely due to oligopolistic rent extraction by underwriters. For example, if declines in spreads were entirely due to declines in concessions paid by underwriters to dealers it would be hard to argue that declines in spreads reflected change in the market power of underwriters.

Before proceeding, we discuss important differences between the data set we use and that used by Mendelson, which limit the comparability of the two studies.

5.6.1   Data availability

The original sources on which Mendelson's (1967) study was based were registration statements filed with the Securities and Exchange Commission. Mendelson (p. 429) described the sample as "drawn from the population of common stock issues offered for cash in the years in question. The samples include only offerings through the investment banking machinery and only offerings to shareholders or to the general public. Offerings to special groups were not included. The sample contains both offerings distributed on a firm-contract (underwritten) basis or agency (best-efforts) basis. The sample was divided into two strata, the fully registered and the Regulation A (or small) issues." The numbers of observations are not reported; it is not clear how complete the sample is or how the sample was drawn from the population of registered offerings. Unfortunately, the data appear to have been destroyed.

In constructing our own data set, we faced several sets of constraints. First, for purposes of comparability, it seemed wise to pick dates that coincided with Mendelson's if possible. Second, we wanted to pick dates on both ends of the institutional investor boom of the 1950s and 1960s. Third, we wanted to pick dates that occurred at similar points of the business cycle (to abstract from differences in issuers' characteristics possibly related to the stage of the business cycle in which offerings occur). Fourth, we had to choose between the Securities and Exchange Commission filings and *Investment Dealers' Digest* as sources for our study (which differ according to the coverage of issuers and the variables reported). Fifth, we had a limited amount of funds and time to gather data for our study. Sixth, we required sample periods with a sufficient number of observations to perform statistical analysis.

In weighing these considerations we chose the first six months of 1950 and the first six months of 1971 as our two dates for constructing a sample of primary common stock issues, for cash, handled by investment bankers. The choice of 1950 permits some comparison with Mendelson (1967), and 1971 comes at the end of the boom years of institutional investors' growth. Both periods are recovery years from recession, and both witnessed a substantial volume of new stock issues.

The difficulty of collecting data from SEC sources ultimately led us to rely on *Investment Dealers' Digest* in constructing our sample. We considered collecting data from SEC filings, but this must be done one firm at a time, and (it seems) one must already be aware of the identity of the issuer before the SEC can locate the information. Furthermore, the SEC only began microfilming records in 1978, and it is unclear whether registration information prior to this period still exists in its files.

The SEC did publish a list of securities issuers beginning in the first quarter of 1950, though it discontinued this practice a few years later. We collected these data for the first six months of 1950 and compared them to the data published in *Investment Dealers' Digest*. Surprisingly, there was substantial information lacking in both data sets. Of all the issues we found from both sources, roughly a third appeared in both sources, less than a third in only the SEC's list, and more than a third only in *Investment Dealers' Digest*.

Because the items recorded in the two sources are not the same, it is hard to define precisely the characteristics of firms that led to their exclusion in one or the other sample. One interesting fact, however, is that roughly half of the SEC's data set consisted of best efforts, while only three of those transactions also appeared in *Investment Dealers' Digest*. It may be that *Investment Dealers' Digest* (at least in its early years of data reporting, circa 1950) excluded small issuers from its reporting. By 1971, we think this is less likely to be a problem.

While there were some advantages to the data reported by the SEC (which include firm asset size and the distinction between best efforts and firm commitments), for our regression analysis we chose the other data source for four reasons. First, the SEC source was not available after the 1950s. For purposes of comparability it seemed best to use *Investment Dealers' Digest* throughout. Second, the SEC source did not contain any information on the identity of the underwriter. This was a severe limitation, since we wanted to investigate the potential importance of underwriter volume in determining spreads. Third, the SEC data did not contain information on concessions to dealers, while the *Investment Dealers' Digest* did. Fourth, the variables only included in the SEC data – the distinction between best efforts and firm commitments, and asset size categories – did not prove significant in regressions using the SEC data that included those variables as well as the variables we report below.

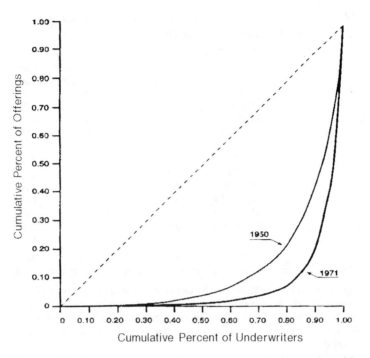

Figure 5.1. Lorenz curves for common stock underwriting, January–June 1950 v. January–June 1971.

To summarize, despite many advantages to using the data reported in *Investment Dealers' Digest* an important qualification of our results for the 1950 sample is that they may underrepresent relatively unseasoned issuers. This may lead us to understate the improvement in spreads that occurred from 1950 to 1971.[15]

5.6.2 Market concentration

Miller's (1967) analysis of trends in concentration within the investment banking industry noted little change in the underwriting shares of large underwriters from the 1930s to 1963. Before proceeding to the analysis of spreads, we update Miller's discussion and consider alternative measures of concentration for our sample of stock issues during the first six months of 1950 and 1971. In Figure 5.1, we plot the Lorenz curves for

[15] *Investment Dealers' Digest* did not report data similar to these for the 1940s. During the 1940s, it did report SEC registrations but gave no information regarding spreads. As noted below, however, for a brief period in 1940, it did report concessions to dealers on a select set of underwritings.

Table 5.16. *Amount and number of common stock issues placed by large[a] underwriters, January–June 1950*

Underwriter rank	Amount issued	Percent of total amount issued	Number of issues	Percent of total number of issues
1	$92,089,702	16.48	12	8.05
2	$34,530,597	6.18	6	4.03
3	$32,349,618	5.79	6	4.03
4	$27,617,238	4.94	3	2.01
5	$26,938,177	4.82	3	2.01
6	$26,612,047	4.76	4	2.68
7	$19,851,254	3.55	2	1.34
8	$17,512,614	3.13	1	0.67
9	$17,063,230	3.05	3	2.01
10	$16,000,000	2.86	2	1.34
11	$15,791,376	2.83	2	1.34
	$326,355,853	58.39	44	29.53

[a] Large underwriters are those that participated in a total dollar amount of issues greater than ten times the median volume of underwriters ($15 million) with at least one percent of the number of issues. The eighth ranked underwriter did, in fact, meet the above stated criteria, although one of its deals was omitted from our sample for lack of additional relevant data.

the stock issues market in 1950 and 1971. If anything, this indicates an *increase* in the concentration of the market during the period of declining spreads. In Tables 5.16 and 5.17 we distinguish "large" from "small" underwriters and examine the shares of big underwriters in the market. We define an underwriter as large if it is involved (either as manager or participant) in a volume of transactions in excess of ten times the median underwriter volume. By this definition, twenty-one underwriters are defined as large in 1971, compared to eleven in 1950. Large underwriters account for 39 percent of the offerings and 70 percent of the volume in 1971, compared to 30 percent of the offerings and 58 percent of the volume in 1950. While there are alternative ways of measuring market concentration – for example, Miller's (1967) measures discussed above – none is clearly preferable, and the various alternative measures seem to lead to the same fundamental conclusion: the decline in equity spreads from 1950 to 1971 cannot be attributed to a decline in the concentration of equity underwriting.

Table 5.17. *Amount and number of common stock issues placed by large[a] underwriters, January–June 1971*

Underwriter rank	Amount issued	Percent of total amount issued	Number of issues	Percent of total number of issues
1	$586,418,697	9.24	24	4.93
2	$562,502,386	8.87	13	2.67
3	$426,465,000	6.72	11	2.26
4	$332,158,869	5.24	7	1.44
5	$307,960,623	4.85	14	2.87
6	$264,040,000	4.16	12	2.46
7	$230,827,250	3.64	9	1.85
8	$224,743,551	3.54	10	2.05
9	$208,810,750	3.29	7	1.44
10	$191,807,063	3.02	8	1.64
11	$174,824,510	2.76	11	2.26
12	$159,218,000	2.51	6	1.23
13	$150,431,066	2.37	5	1.03
14	$116,437,440	1.84	7	1.44
15	$111,587,550	1.76	8	1.64
16	$110,851,108	1.75	5	1.03
17	$75,536,250	1.19	10	2.05
18	$69,648,564	1.10	6	1.23
19	$64,970,811	1.02	6	1.23
20	$63,897,500	1.01	5	1.03
21	$38,534,250	0.61	5	1.03
	$4,471,671,238	70.48	189	38.81

[a] Large underwriters are those that participated in a total dollar amount of issues greater than ten times the median volume of underwriters ($22.5 million) with at least one percent of the number of issues.

5.6.3   Spreads and the characteristics of issues and underwriters

Sortings of our samples by issue size, by industry, by underwriter size, and according to whether the issue is a standby or a public offering are provided in Tables 5.18 through 5.21.[16] Rather than discuss the conditional means reported in these tables, we turn directly to our regression results, which identify the partial correlations apparent in the conditional

[16] The firms in Table 5.18 that are described as "unknown size" of underwriter are firms that are listed in Securities and Exchange Commission (1950) but not in *Investment Dealers' Digest*. These firms were not included in the regression reported in Table 5.22. Tables 5.18 through 5.21 are reported in 1950 dollars, using the GDP deflator for non-residential investment as a deflator (Council of Economic Advisers, 1974, p. 252).

Table 5.18. *Spreads on public offerings and rights offerings of common stock, by size of issue and underwriter,[a] January–June 1950*

	Less than $0.5 million	$0.5 million to less than $2 million	$2 million or more	All
Public Offerings				
All				
Average	0.138	0.086	0.063	0.094
Std deviation	0.063	0.047	0.029	0.057
Count	43	40	49	132
Large Underwriters				
Average	0.067	0.064	0.039	0.050
Std deviation	—	0.022	0.012	0.021
Count	1	7	10	18
Small underwriters				
Average	0.146	0.119	0.086	0.133
Std deviation	0.063	0.054	0.035	0.061
Count	35	15	5	55
Unknown size				
Average	0.109	0.067	0.067	0.072
Std deviation	0.052	0.032	0.028	0.035
Count	7	18	34	59
Rights Offerings				
All				
Average	0.085	0.047	0.038	0.048
Std deviation	0.077	0.029	0.032	0.044
Count	6	8	21	35
Large underwriters				
Average	—	0.034	0.027	0.027
Std deviation	—	0.041	0.018	0.020
Count	0	2	16	18
Small underwriters				
Average	0.085	0.039	0.075	0.069
Std deviation	0.077	0.020	0.041	0.056
Count	6	4	5	15
Unknown size				
Average	—	0.076	—	0.076
Std deviation	—	0.028	—	0.028
Count	0	2	0	2
All Offerings				
Average	0.132	0.080	0.055	0.085
Std deviation	0.066	0.047	0.032	0.058
Count	49	48	70	167

[a] Large underwriters are those that participated in a total dollar amount of issues greater than ten times the median volume of underwriters ($15 million) with at least one percent of the number of issues.

318

Table 5.19. *Spreads on public offerings and rights offerings of common stock, by size of issue and sector, January–June 1950*

	Less than $0.5 million	$0.5 million to less than $2 million	$2 million or more	All
Public offerings				
All				
Average	0.138	0.086	0.063	0.094
Std. deviation	0.063	0.047	0.029	0.057
Count	43	40	49	132
Banking/Financial/ Insurance				
Average	0.100	0.069	0.069	0.074
Std. deviation	0.038	0.032	0.026	0.031
Count	10	19	33	62
Industrial[a]				
Average	0.158	0.118	0.107	0.142
Std. deviation	0.062	0.056	0.016	0.061
Count	30	15	3	48
Utility				
Average	0.066	0.061	0.038	0.048
Std deviation	0.012	0.011	0.019	0.020
Count	3	6	13	22
Rights offerings				
All				
Average	0.085	0.047	0.038	0.048
Std. deviation	0.077	0.029	0.032	0.044
Count	6	8	21	35
Banking/Financial/ Insurance				
Average	0.029	0.022	0.031	0.029
Std. deviation	—	—	0.020	0.015
Count	1	1	3	5
Industrial[a]				
Average	0.0124	0.061	0.056	0.078
Std. deviation	0.099	0.033	0.048	0.065
Count	3	3	4	10
Utility				
Average	0.056	0.043	0.034	0.038
Std. deviation	0.029	0.029	0.029	0.028
Count	2	4	14	20
All offerings				
Average	0.132	0.080	0.055	0.085
Std. deviation	0.066	0.047	0.032	0.058
Count	49	48	70	167

[a] "Industrial" includes all nonfinancial and nonutility firms.

Table 5.20. *Spreads on public offerings and rights offerings of common stock, by size of issue and underwriter, January–June 1950*

	Less than $0.5 million[b]	$0.5 million to less than $2 million[b]	$2 million or more[b]	All[b]
Public offerings				
All				
Average	0.100	0.085	0.060	0.078
Std. deviation	0.016	0.015	0.019	0.024
Count	100	106	155	361
Large underwriters				
Average	0.066	0.070	0.055	0.057
Std. deviation	0.020	0.015	0.017	0.017
Count	4	19	109	132
Small underwriters				
Average	0.101	0.088	0.072	0.091
Std. deviation	0.015	0.013	0.018	0.018
Count	96	87	46	229
Rights offerings				
All				
Average	0.122	0.045	0.039	0.044
Std. deviation	—	0.014	0.023	0.027
Count	1	4	15	20
Large underwriters				
Average	—	0.045	0.033	0.036
Std. deviation	—	0.014	0.015	0.015
Count	0	4	13	17
Small underwriters				
Average	0.122	—	0.075	0.091
Std. deviation	—	—	0.035	0.037
Count	1	0	2	3
All offerings				
Average	0.100	0.084	0.058	0.077
Std. deviation	0.016	0.017	0.020	0.025
Count	101	110	170	381

[a] Large underwriters are those that participated in a total dollar amount of issues greater than ten times the median volume of underwriters ($22.5 million) with at least one percent of the number of issues.
[b] In 1950 dollars.

Table 5.21. *Spreads on public offerings and rights offerings of common stock, by size of issue and sector, January–June 1971*

	Less than $0.5 million[b]	$0.5 million to less than $2 million[b]	$2 million or more[b]	All[b]
Public offerings				
All				
Average	0.100	0.085	0.060	0.078
Std. deviation	0.016	0.015	0.019	0.024
Count	100	106	155	361
Banking/Financial/ Insurance				
Average	0.100	0.085	0.074	0.079
Std. deviation	0.000	0.013	0.014	0.016
Count	5	9	29	43
Industrial[a]				
Average	0.100	0.085	0.061	0.081
Std. deviation	0.017	0.015	0.015	0.023
Count	95	96	109	300
Utility				
Average	—	0.059	0.029	0.031
Std. deviation	—	—	0.009	0.011
Count	0	1	17	18
Rights Offerings				
All				
Average	0.122	0.045	0.039	0.044
Std. deviation	—	0.014	0.023	0.027
Count	1	4	15	20
Banking/Financial/ Insurance				
Average	—	0.046	0.038	0.041
Std. deviation	—	0.023	0.013	0.015
Count	0	2	3	5
Industrial[a]				
Average	0.122	—	0.066	0.080
Std. deviation	—	—	0.030	0.037
Count	1	0	2	4
Utility				
Average	—	0.043	0.030	0.032
Std. deviation	—	0.004	0.016	0.015
Count	0	2	9	11
All offerings				
Average	0.200	0.084	0.058	0.077
Std. deviation	0.016	0.017	0.020	0.025
Count	101	110	170	381

[a] "Industrial" includes all nonfinancial and nonutility firms.
[b] In 1950 dollars.

Table 5.22. *Underwriting spreads (relative to proceeds) for common stock issues – regression results, 1950 and 1971[a]*

	January–June 1950[b]		January–June 1971[c]	
Variable[d]	Coefficient	T-value	Coefficient	T-value
Constant	0.010	0.71	0.038	5.39
Public[e]	0.066	3.64	0.028	3.85
Industrial	0.053	1.78	0.038	2.78
PUBxIND	−0.021	−0.69	−0.040	−2.92
Small underwriter	0.044	4.17	0.032	15.35
Utility	0.015	1.02	−0.003	−0.36
PUBxUtil	−0.048	−2.73	−0.030	−3.33
Issue size[f]	0.0005	0.50	0.00007	0.34
SIZExPUB	−0.0013	−1.38	0.00006	5.40
SIZExIND	−0.004	−1.89	−0.0004	−5.09
SIZExUTIL	−0.0005	−0.49	−0.0002	−1.84
SIZExS.U.	−0.0056	−1.89	−0.0018	−3.26

[a] Corrected for heteroskedacticity.
[b] $R^2 = 0.56$; R^2 adjusted = 0.51
  Observations = 106
  Mean spread = 0.092; std. dev. = 0.067
  Mean issue size = 3.1; std. dev. = 6.0

[c] $R^2 = 0.66$; R^2 adjusted = 0.65
  Observations = 381
  Mean spread = 0.077; std. dev. = 0.025
  Mean issue size = 9.5; std. dev. = 19.2

[d] The omitted sector is financial firms.
[e] The alternative to public offering is underwritten rights offering.
[f] Issue size in millions of dollars.

means. Table 5.22 reports identical regressions for the 1950 and 1971 samples, which describe all spreads in terms of an intercept and a slope coefficient (multiplied by issue size) and which allow both the intercept and the slope coefficient to vary with the type of offering (public v. rights), the broad industry category of the issuer (utility, financial, or "industrial"), and the size category of the underwriter (large or small). These descriptive regressions "explain" a substantial amount of the variation in gross spread percentages. Six principal findings stand out.

First, size of issue is a very useful descriptive statistic, all the more so when one allows the size effect to vary with the fundamental characteristics of the issue. Mendelson (1967) argued that size effects were reduced by the inclusion of other variables in his regressions, but it may be that his finding that size effects are weakened by the inclusion of other variables depends on not allowing size effects to vary by types of issues. Specific comparisons between Mendelson's regressions and ours are difficult, due to differences in regressors.

Second, large underwriters, *ceteris paribus*, charged much smaller commissions than small underwriters. The notion that market power explains cross-sectional variation in commissions, therefore, is hard to defend. The high commissions of small underwriters likely reflect the fact that small underwriters tend to be matched up with relatively unseasoned firms (as discussed above).

Third, industry classification matters. There are a variety of explanations for this finding. We note that public utilities during this period are low-risk operations and that information about their operations is widely available and relatively transparent. Financial corporations may have lower spreads because their common stock is really more comparable to the junior debt of nonfinancial corporations (because the assets of financial corporations consist of debt claims on nonfinancial corporations).

Fourth, rights offerings are much cheaper, which confirms the importance of marketing costs in determining spreads.

Fifth, the signs and significance of the coefficients in the two regressions are similar, but the magnitudes are different. To be specific, factors that tended to produce the largest spreads shrink in magnitude over time.

Sixth, as Mendelson (1967) argued in his analysis of the change in costs from 1950 to 1961, the declining cost of high-spread issues accounts for the average change in spreads from 1950 to 1971. The average decline in spreads for the sample – from 9.2 percent to 7.7 percent – understates the importance of technological improvement (e.g., the rise of institutional investors) during this time. Declines in cost shifted the mix of issuers toward relatively high cost issues. In particular, as the cost of going public declined, many issuers chose public offerings rather than rights offerings. In 1950, 21 percent of underwritten common stock issues were rights offerings; by 1971, only 5 percent were offered as standbys. Presumably, the wider public market's advantage is a higher stock price, if the costs of information are sufficiently low. As shown in Table 5.23, public stock issue spreads fell most from the 1950s to the 1970s, and a small "industrial" issuer's cost of selling shares publicly through a small underwriter fell especially dramatically compared to the costs of other types of issues.

5.6.4   *Alternative interpretations of the measured decline in spreads*

We have argued that the growing importance of institutional investors in the 1960s was associated with significant reductions in investment bankers' compensation, as measured by the gross spread. But there are two alternative explanations for this decline that warrant discussion:

Table 5.23. *Predicted percent spreads for three examples of common stock issues, 1950 and 1971, from Table 5.22 regression results*

	Issue 1	Issue 2	Issue 3
Issue size[a]	$1 million	$10 million	$10 million
Underwriter	Small	Large	Large
Sector	Industrial	Utility	Utility
Offering	Public	Public	Rights
Spreads (%)			
1950	14.2	5.2	2.5
1971	9.2	3.1	3.4

[a] In 1950 dollars.

(1) substitution into forms of compensation other than the gross spread and (2) regulation of investment banker compensation.

With respect to the first point, the spread is only part of the compensation of the investment banker. Other potentially important items include warrants, rights of first refusal on other offerings, and hidden compensation in the form of underwriter charges of expenses or fees kept out of the spread. *Investment Dealers' Digest* does not report compensation other than the gross spread, and thus it is not possible for us to gauge whether increases in other forms of compensation helped to offset reductions in the spread during our period. It is conceivable that changes in underwriter practice between 1950 and 1971 moved some fees out of spreads and into other fee categories, but for two reasons we do not think this possibility could explain our results. First, Mendelson (1967) did have data on warrants and rights of first refusal for the 1950s and 1960s and found that these features were associated with higher spreads, *ceteris paribus*. Thus, it is unlikely that an increased use of these contractual arrangements over time would have been associated with a reduction in spreads. Second, as discussed below, oversight by the National Association of Securities Dealers (NASD) – the self-regulatory agency that began monitoring investment banker compensation in 1968 – would not have encouraged any substitution away from spreads into other costs because the NASD looks at aggregate costs, not just at spreads, when determining the reasonableness of investment bankers' charges. Thus it would be fruitless for an underwriter to attempt to surpass their allowable ceilings by substituting between the spread and some other form of payment.

Another potential source of reduction in spreads from 1950 to 1971 is the regulatory oversight of the NASD. Regulation of underwriter compensation changed dramatically in the late 1960s as the NASD began to place ceilings on allowable total compensation in 1968. In response to pressure from the Securities and Exchange Commission, in 1968 the NASD established an oversight committee (first the Committee on Underwritings, later the Corporate Finance Department) to regulate total underwriter compensation.

In establishing compensation ceilings, the NASD takes into consideration spreads, non-accountable expenses (which accrue only to syndicate managers), consulting fees paid to underwriters, and noncash payments (warrants, rights of first refusal on subsequent issues, etc.). The NASD computes total compensation based on the sum of these components and judges whether the total is "unreasonable." If so, the underwriter must reduce some or all components of compensation to conform to the NASD's guidelines.

We do not think the NASD guidelines can explain our results for two reasons. First, as shown in Table 5.9 and in Mendelson (1967), the reduction in the cost of underwriting equity occurred by the early 1960s, prior to the self-regulation imposed by the NASD in 1968. Second, the NASD guidelines generally would not have imposed binding constraints on the spreads we observed in 1971. The specific NASD ceilings on compensation (which vary explicitly with the size of the issue and the type of underwriting – whether IPO or not and whether a firm commitment or not) remain confidential, but their staff have graciously shared the details of those guidelines with us to enable us to judge whether the NASD guidelines could explain the dramatic decline we observe from 1950 to 1971. Rough estimates, allowing for large costs in addition to spreads, indicate that NASD ceilings likely would have constrained very few of the spreads in our 1971 sample.[17] For both these reasons, we conclude that the NASD acted mainly to constrain "outliers" to act in accordance with typical industry practice, rather than to aggressively reduce standard fees charged by underwriters.

5.6.5   Dealers' concessions

One of the benefits of using data from *Investment Dealers' Digest* is that it provides data on dealers' concessions for most of the transactions described. Dealers' concessions are clearly an expense from the per-

---

[17] Unfortunately, the microfilm records of the NASD decisions regarding spreads for the period prior to 1983 appear to have been destroyed, and thus it is not possible to measure how often the NASD actually constrained spreads prior to 1983.

spective of the underwriters, and thus it is interesting to ask what percentage of gross spread is accounted for by payments to dealers for marketing issues to their clients. Hansen (1986, p. 51) reported that gross spreads divide as follows: 20 percent origination and management fee, 25 percent underwriting fee, and 55 percent selling concession. Clearly, this indicates, almost by definition, that most of the gross spread is related to expenses of organizing and marketing issues. But was this always so? If the decline in spreads from 1940 to 1980 reflected an erosion of bankers' rents, then the proportion of concessions in spreads may have risen over this period.

Data on dealers'concessions generally were not reported during the 1940s (with the exception of an interesting run of information in the 1940 *Investment Dealers' Digest*). We have collected those data from 1940, as well as the data from our 1950 and 1971 samples. We also have a few observations on dealers' concessions for common stock deals from the Lehman deal books.

Data for 71 issues in 1950 and 330 issues in 1971 are summarized in Table 5.24. Overall, the ratio of dealers' concessions to gross spread is large – averaging 59 percent in 1950 and 55 percent in 1971. Clearly, by this measure, the decline in spreads does not seem to reflect a reduction in investment bankers' rents. For public and rights offerings, dealers' concessions do not follow any obvious pattern according to size of issue. In data not reported here, we found that (using SEC data on asset size of issuer) there was a tendency for larger firms' issues to have larger concession shares, which may reflect the greater costs of due diligence and the greater risks posed to the underwriters by relatively unseasoned firms. The ratio of concession to spread was the same for public and rights offerings in 1950.[18]

Data available for 1940 on twenty-five manufacturing firms' dealers' concessions indicate that there likely was little change in concessions relative to spreads from 1940 to 1950. For eleven weeks beginning April 29, 1940, *Investment Dealers' Digest* published a table entitled "Security Offerings Available to Dealers," with the following explanation:

The following is a selected list of securities on which concessions are available to dealers. The source of supply frequently can be ascertained by examination of

---

[18] No concession data were reported for rights offerings in our 1971 sample. For a small sample of rights offerings in 1950, there is a difference in the dealers' concession relative to spread between small and large underwriters. Small underwriters pay larger concessions on rights offerings, and this is true holding constant the size of the issue. We can think of no obvious explanation for the fact that an underwriter size effect would be confined to rights issues only. It would be interesting to see if this fact holds up in larger samples.

Table 5.24. *Concession/spread, by issue size ($ million), in 1950 dollars: January–June 1950 v. January–June 1971*

	Less than $0.5 million	$0.5 million to less than $2 million	$2 million or more
Public offerings, 1950			
Average	0.61	0.55	0.58
Std. deviation	0.13	0.15	0.18
Count	22	18	13
Rights offerings, 1950			
Average	0.70	0.51	0.58
Std. deviation	0.14	0.24	0.22
Count	2	4	12
Public offerings, 1971			
Average	0.53	0.53	0.57
Std. deviation	0.12	0.07	0.08
Count	70	104	153

the advertising columns of this publication. On written request, the source will be supplied by *The Investment Dealers' Digest*.

For this brief interval, it seems, underwriters used *Investment Dealers' Digest* to advertise concessions as well as offering prices. No spread information was reported, and the amounts of the offerings were not given. The locations for potential distribution were limited in the listings in this table. By all appearances, the common stocks listed in these tables were a cross section of American industry, including small companies as well as firms listed on the New York Stock Exchange. The average ratio of the dealers' concession to the offering price on common stock issues of manufacturing firms shown in these tables is 11 percent.[19] According to the Securities and Exchange Commission (1941b, p. A25), the average spread for public issues of manufacturers' common stocks sold through investment banks in 1940 was 17.7 percent. By this estimate, concessions (not including warrants) were 62 percent of the spread in 1940, which is near the average of 59 percent from our 1950 sample.[20]

[19] The variation around the average was small. Fifteen of the twenty-five issues had dealers' concessions of between 9 and 13 percent of the offering price; twenty-one of the issues had concession of between 7 and 15 percent of the offering price. The minimum was 3 percent and the maximum was 20 percent.

[20] Interestingly, our sample of stock issues from Lehman Brothers in the 1920s had much lower ratios of concession to spread – an average of 26 percent for the twelve deals that reported this information. One interpretation of this finding is that in the early years of stock flotations for unseasoned manufacturers and retailers, Lehman's role was larger than may have been typical in other market niches or in later periods.

In summary, while gross spreads on equity issues fell dramatically from 1940 to the present, the share of dealers' concessions in the gross spread remained remarkably constant at roughly 60 percent. The view that improvements in financial technology reduced both the costs of managing issues and placing them with customers is consistent with the constancy of the share of dealers' concessions. The view that the decline in the gross spread primarily reflects reduced rents to syndicate managers is hard to reconcile with the data on concessions.

5.7   Conclusion

The facts about spreads that we describe, based on our work and that of others, can be summarized as follows:

1. Spreads in the United States have always been large relative to spreads for comparable securities issues in Germany as long ago as the 1890s, especially for common stocks.
2. U.S. spreads are especially high for smaller issues, while German spreads varied little by size of issue or by type of security.
3. Spreads in the 1920s were similar to the rates cited by Brandeis for the pre-World War I era and remained roughly unchanged from the 1920s to 1940.
4. Average spreads fell dramatically from 1940 to the 1970s.
5. This decline was greatest for common stocks, which began the period with much larger spreads than preferred stocks or bonds.
6. The decline was greatest for small issues, for "industrials," and for issues marketed to the public (as distinct from rights offerings).
7. Cross-sectional studies of spreads find that spreads vary with price risk faced by the underwriter, but compensation for this underwriting risk does not explain important cross-sectional variation in spreads. Best-effort spreads can be as large as spreads on underwritings with a price guarantee.
8. Proxies for financial maturity of the firm ("seasoning") are important in explaining cross-sectional variation in stock spreads, ceteris paribus.
9. Spreads are often inversely related to underpricing costs, which explains why in equilibrium firms may choose high-spread methods to place securities over low-spread methods.
10. The degree of concentration in the market for investment banking services is not positively associated with spreads across time, across types of securities, or across countries.
11. After controlling for other observable differences in common stock issues, the largest underwriters charged the smallest spreads.

12. Investment bankers pay out a large fraction of their gross spreads in the form of concessions to dealers. The decline in spreads from 1950 to 1971 was not associated with any change in the proportion of spread accounted for by concessions.
13. The decline in spreads witnessed after the 1930s largely reflects institutional changes in securities issuing associated with the new activities of nonbank intermediaries. Private placements of debt and venture capital provided alternatives to public issues, which were especially attractive for unseasoned issuers that faced high public flotation costs. Institutional investors' block purchases of public issues were important in reducing the costs of information and control associated with marketing public issues.

These findings support the view that securities marketing costs, which result largely from intermediaries costs of monitoring, signaling, and enforcing proper behavior by securities issuers, provide most of the explanatory power for observed differences in spreads across time, issuers, underwriters, flotation mechanisms, securities, and countries. Furthermore, regulatory policies toward the financial system that promoted fragmented capital markets in the United States (e.g., restrictions on the scale and scope of banking activities) may have increased the costs of bringing securities to market in the United States (Calomiris, 1993, 1995).

Financial innovations in the post–World War II era helped to compensate for the weaknesses of the banking system by giving rise to a new set of intermediaries. These innovations affected the structure of the market for selling securities through changes in the scale and characteristics of the buyers of new securities issues. Nonbank intermediaries provided alternatives to public securities markets through private placements and venture capital investments. Others (particularly, pension funds, trusts, and mutual funds) mitigated the costs of public issuance by decreasing the fragmentation of the purchasing side of the market, particularly in the case of small firms' issues of common stock.

While the evidence we report points toward marketing costs as the crucial factor in explaining differences in spreads across issuers, securities, investment bankers, time, and countries, that does not mean underwriters' rents have been zero in the investment banking industry. Rather, our findings indicate that a focus on the economics of information, risk, corporate governance, and marketing – rather than the economics of oligopoly – is likely to shed the most light on the forces that led to the large reductions in the costs of underwriting in the United States from 1940 to the present.

References

Andrews, Victor L. (1964). "Noninsured Corporate and State and Local Government Retirement Funds in the Financial Structure." In I. Friend, H. P. Minsky, and V. L. Andrews (eds.), *Private Capital Markets*. Englewood Cliffs, NJ: Prentice Hall.

Baron, David P. (1979). "The Incentive Problem and the Design of Investment Banking Contracts," *Journal of Banking and Finance* 3: 157–75.

(1982). "A Model of the Demand for Investment Banking Advising and Distribution Services for New Issues," *Journal of Finance* 32: 955–76.

Baron, David P., and Bengt Holmstrom. (1980). "The Investment Banking Contract for New Issues under Asymmetric Information: Delegation and the Incentive Problem," *Journal of Finance* 35: 1115–38.

Baskin, Jonathan B. (1988). "The Development of Corporate Financial Markets in Britain and the United States, 1600–1915: Overcoming Asymmetric Information," *Business History Review* 62 (summer): 199–237.

Beatty, Randolph P., and Jay R. Ritter. (1986). "Investment Banking, Reputation, and the Underpricing of Initial Public Offerings," *Journal of Financial Economics* 15: 213–32.

Benveniste, Lawrence M., and Paul A. Spindt. (1989). "How Investment Bankers Determine the Offer Price and Allocation of New Issues," *Journal of Financial Economics* 24: 343–62.

Best's Life Insurance Reports (1940–1960). Institute of Life Insurance.

Bhagat, Sanjai, M. Wayne Marr, and G. Rodney Thompson. (1985). "The Rule 415 Experiment: Equity Markets," *Journal of Finance* (December): 1385–1402.

Booth, James R., and Richard L. Smith, III. (1986). "Capital Raising, Underwriting, and the Certification Hypothesis," *Journal of Financial Economics* 15: 261–81.

Brandeis, Louis D. (1914). *Other People's Money and How the Bankers Use it*. New York: Frederick A. Stokes Co.

Calomiris, Charles W. (1993). "Corporate-Finance Benefits from Universal Banking: Germany and the United States, 1870–1914." NBER Working Paper no. 4408 (July).

(1995). "The Costs of Rejecting Universal Banking: American Finance in the German Mirror, 1870–1914." In N. Lamoreaux and D. Raff (eds.), *The Coordination of Economic Activity Within and Between Firms*. Chicago: National Bureau of Economic Research, University of Chicago.

Calomiris, Charles W., and R. Glenn Hubbard. (1990). "Firm Heterogeneity, Internal Finance, and Credit Rationing," *Economic Journal* 100: (March), 90–104.

(1995). "Internal Finance and Investment: Evidence from the Undistributed Profits Tax of 1936–1937," *Journal of Business* (October): pp. 443–82.

Calomiris, Charles W., and Eugene N. White. (1994), "The Origins of Federal Deposit Insurance." In C. Golden and G. Libecap (eds.), *The Regulated*

Economy: An Historical Approach to Political Economy. Chicago: National Bureau of Economic Research, University of Chicago Press.

Carey, Mark, Stephen Prowse, John Rea, and Gregory Udell. (1993). "The Economics of Private Placements: A New Look," *Financial Markets, Institutions, and Instruments* 2 (3): 1–67.

Carosso, Vincent P. (1970). *Investment Banking in America: A History*. Cambridge: Harvard University Press.

Cohan, Avery B. (1961). "Cost of Flotation of Long-Term Corporate Debt Since 1935." University of North Carolina, School of Business Administration Research Paper no. 6.

Council of Economic Advisers. (1974). Economic Report of the President. Washington, DC: U.S. Government Printing Office.

—— (1994). Economic Report of the President. Washington, DC: U.S. Government Printing Office.

Denis, David J. (1991). "Shelf Registration and the Market for Seasoned Equity Offerings," *Journal of Business* 64 (2): 189–212.

Dewing, Arthur S. (1920). *The Financial Policy of Corporations. Vol. 2: Promotion*. New York: Ronald Press Co.

Doyle, Michael W. (1991). "The Evolution of Financial Practices and Financial Structures Among American Manufacturers, 1875–1905: Case Studies of the Sugar Refining and Meat Packing Industries." Ph.D. diss. University of Tennessee, Knoxville.

Easterbrook, Frank H. (1984). "Two Agency-Cost Explanations of Dividends," *American Economic Review* 74 (June): 650-59.

Eckbo, B. Espen, and Ronald W. Masulis. (1994). "Seasoned Equity Offerings: A Survey." In R. Jarrow, V. Maksimovic, and B. Ziemba (eds.), *North-Holland Handbooks of Management Science and Operations Research: Finance*. Amsterdam: North-Holland.

Friend, Irwin. (1967). "Overall View of Investment Banking and the New Issues Market." In I. Friend (ed.), *Investment Banking and the New Issues Market*. New York: World Publishing Co.

Friend, Irwin, Marshall Blume, and Jean Crockett. (1970). *Mutual Funds and Other Institutional Investors*. New York: McGraw-Hill.

Goldsmith, Raymond W. (1958). *Financial Intermediaries in the American Economy Since 1900*. Princeton: Princeton University Press.

Greenough, William C., and Francis P. King. (1976). *Pension Plans and Public Policy*. New York: Columbia University Press.

Hansen, Robert S. (1986). "Evaluating the Costs of a New Equity Issue," *Midland Corporate Finance Journal* 4 (1) (spring): 42–76.

Hansen, Robert S., Beverly R. Fuller, and Vahan Janjigian. (1987). "The Overallotment Option and Equity Financing Flotation Costs: An Empirical Investigation," *Financial Management* 16 (summer): 24–32.

Hansen, Robert S., and John M. Pinkerton. (1982). "Direct Equity Financing: A Resolution of a Paradox," *Journal of Finance* 37: 651–65.

Hansen, Robert S., and Paul Torregrossa. (1992). "Underwriter Compensation and Corporate Monitoring," *Journal of Finance* 47 (September): 1537–55.

Investment Dealers' Digest. (various issues).

James, Christopher. (1987). "Some Evidence on the Uniqueness of Bank Loans," *Journal of Financial Economics* 19: 217–35.

James, Christopher, and Peggy Wier. (1990). "Borrowing Relationships, Intermediation, and the Cost of Issuing Public Securities," *Journal of Financial Economics* 28: 149–71.

Jarrell, Gregg A. (1981). "The Economic Effects of Federal Regulation of the Market for New Security Issues," *Journal of Law and Economics* 24 (December): 613–75.

Jensen, Michael C., and William H. Meckling. (1976). "Theory of the Firm: Managerial Behavior, Agency Costs and Ownership Structure," *Journal of Financial Economics* 3: 305–60.

Kemmerer, Donald L. (1952), "The Marketing of Securities, 1930-1952," *Journal of Economic History* 12 (fall): 454–68.

Loughran, Tim, and Jay R. Ritter. (1995). "The New Issues Puzzle." *Journal of Finance* 50 (March), pp. 23–52.

Mandelker, Gershon, and Artur Raviv. (1977). "Investment Banking: An Economic Analysis of Optimal Underwriting Contracts," *Journal of Finance* 32: 683–94.

Mendelson, Morris. (1967). "Underwriting Compensation." In I. Friend (ed.), *Investment Banking and the New Issues Market.* New York: World Publishing Co.

Miller, Irvin. (1967). "Background and Structure of the Industry." In I. Friend (ed.), *Investment Banking and the New Issues Market.* New York: World Publishing Co.

Munnell, Alicia H. (1982). *The Economics of Private Pensions.* Washington, DC: The Brooking Institution.

Myers, Stewart C., and Nicholas Majluf. (1984). "Corporate Financing and Investment Decisions When Firms Have Information that Investors Do Not Have," *Journal of Financial Economics* 13: 187–221.

Navin, Thomas R., and Marian V. Seam. (1955). "The Rise of a Market for Industrial Securities, 1887–1902," *Business History Review* 29 (June): 105–38.

Ramakrishnan, Ram T. S., and Anjan V. Thakor. (1984). "Information Reliability and a Theory of Financial Intermediation," *Review of Economic Studies* 51 (July): 415–32.

Ritter, Jay R. (1987). "The Costs of Going Public," *Journal of Financial Economics* 19: 269–81.

Rock, Kevin. (1986). "Why New Issues Are Underpriced," *Journal of Financial Economics* 15: 187–272.

Securities Data Co. (1994). Corporate New Issues Database.

Securities and Exchange Commission (SEC). (1941a). *Cost of Flotation for Registered Securities, 1938–1939.* Washington, DC: SEC.

   (1941b). *Cost of Flotation for Securities Registered Under the Securities Act, 1940.* Statistical Release no. 572. Washington, DC: SEC.

(1941c). *Cost of Flotation for Small Issues, 1925–1929 and 1935–1938*. Washington, DC: SEC.

(1950). *Securities Registered Under the Securities Act of 1933: Cost of Flotation*. Washington, DC: SEC.

(1952). *Privately Placed Securities: Cost of Flotation*. Washington, DC: SEC.

(1957). *Volume and Nature of Corporate Securities Offerings: Supplemental Report to Cost of Flotation of Corporate Securities, 1951–1955*. Section of Economic Research (July). Washington, DC: SEC.

(1970). *Securities Registered Under the Securities Act of 1933: Cost of Flotation, 1963–1965*. Washington, DC: SEC.

(1971). *Institutional Investor Study Report*. House Document no. 92–64, 92d Congress, 1st session. Washington, DC: U.S. Government Printing Office.

(1974). *Securities Registered Under the Securities Act of 1933: Cost of Flotation, 1971–1972*. Washington, DC: SEC.

Sherman, Ann Geunther. (1992). "The Pricing of Best Efforts New Issues," *Journal of Finance* 47 (June): 781–90.

Smith, Clifford W., Jr. (1977). "Alternative Methods for Raising Capital," *Journal of Financial Economics* 5: 273–307.

Stalson, J. O. (1942). *Marketing Life Insurance*. Cambridge: Harvard University Press.

Studenski, Paul, and Herman E. Krooss. (1963). *Financial History of the United States*. New York: McGraw-Hill.

Tinic, Seha M. (1988). "Anatomy of Initial Public Offerings of Common Stock," *Journal of Finance* 43 (September): 789–822.

Ture, Norman B. (1976). *The Future of Private Pension Plans*. Washington, DC: American Enterprise Institute.

U.S. Senate. (1933). *Hearings before the Senate Committee on Banking and Currency: Stock Exchange Practices ("Pecora Hearings")*. 72d Congress, 1st session. Washington, DC: U.S. Government Printing Office.

Woodruff, Archibald M., Jr. (1937). *Farm Mortgage Loans of Life Insurance Companies*. New Haven: Yale University Press.

## CHAPTER 6

Universal banking "American-style"

Charles W. Calomiris

American corporate banking has undergone enormous change over the past two decades. That change reflects a combination of long-run competitive pressures and short-run performance problems that led U.S. banks and their regulators to a new American version of global universal banking. From the perspective of the scale and scope of banks, these changes represent a convergence of U.S. banks to international norms in banking. At the same time, the U.S. version of universal banking entails novel linkages between banks and financial markets in the pursuit of enhancing bank-customer relationships. These new linkages give universal banking a new complexity and richness which banks outside the United States will increasingly imitate.

6.1   Introduction

The last decade has witnessed significant convergence in the practice and regulation of banking across countries, and the United States has done more than its share of changing. Differences remain in structure, powers, and regulation across countries. Nevertheless, banking has become much more uniform internationally, and there is a good chance that current changes being contemplated in Europe, the United States, Japan, and Latin America will reinforce the trend toward convergence.

More important than any single similarity in law, regulation, or practice is the common trend in banking "philosophy." I will argue that global competition in financial services should be credited with producing regulatory, practical, and philosophical convergence, and with making bankers and regulators more willing to learn from each other's experiences.

The United States – uncharacteristically – has been a prime example of this convergence process. The U.S. banking system began the 1980s as a longstanding exception to international norms. It consisted of many geographically isolated banks, with circumscribed activities, where bank relationships with corporate customers were limited by laws and regulations. By the middle of the 1990s, the U.S. banking system had been trans-

334

formed into one that included large, nationwide banks offering a wide array of products in the context of rich, complex bank-client relationships. Many of the key elements of what made the American banking system unique prior to the 1980s – geographical fragmentation, a narrowly defined range of services, and the seniority of bank claims on corporate clients – have now changed permanently.

The two essential dimensions of regulatory change in U.S. banking during the 1980s and 1990s – deregulation of branching and consolidation, and expansion of bank powers – initially were viewed by regulators as largely independent sources of improving U.S. banks' competitive position. Experience shows, however, that they are closely related, and that they have reinforced each other. Large nationwide banks are better able to serve as a platform for universal corporate banking (Calomiris, 1993, 1995; Calomiris and Ramirez, 1996). Small banks have not been as successful in converting new bank powers – especially the abilities to underwrite securities and to invest in equity – into profitable corporate banking strategies.

In this paper, I trace the history of the past two decades of change in U.S. corporate banking, and link it to changes in global competition, macroeconomic circumstances, and regulatory learning. I conclude with an appraisal of prospects for the future.

6.2   The philosophical watershed

6.2.1   The old philosophy (circa 1980)

U.S. banks make senior loans to customers, held on balance sheet, and these loans are financed by a captive market of bank deposits.

6.2.2   The new philosophy

U.S. banks must face global competition by providing a rich array of financial services, and by being willing to hold a variety of claims on their customers (senior debt, junior debt, equity, securitization backup, and swap counter party positions), the scope of which is defined for each bank by the types of customers they wish to serve. Off-balance sheet financing (securitizations, loan sales, underwriting) is preferred in many cases to help expand the customer base the bank can serve with its capital.

Four dimensions of strategic change are most important: (1) cognizance of the need to compete within and across borders for business – with attendant emphasis on customer convenience and bank overhead

Table 6.1. *Sources of on-balance sheet debt finance for U.S. banks*

Bank liabilities	Percentage share of total financing				
	1950	1960	1970	1980	1989
Checkable deposits	69.8	60.0	39.0	26.1	21.0
Small time and savings deposits	26.7	34.9	38.5	37.7	44.8
Large time deposits	0.0	0.5	11.2	19.4	14.5
Other debt	3.5	4.6	11.2	16.8	19.6

Source: Baer and Mote, 1991.

costs in determining bank structure; (2) learning the value of a diverse product base and flexibility in the types of claims banks are willing to hold; (3) focus on using access to markets to lever the bank's capital, rather than seeing markets as competitors to banks; (4) focus on customers as defining the "niches" of products banks will choose to provide.

Much of the progress in U.S. banking has been the child of bank adversity during the 1970s and 1980s. During the 1970s, high inflation and binding interest rate ceilings on bank deposits created strong incentives for depositors to find alternative investments, which set the stage for new forms of intermediation – commercial paper markets, finance companies, and mutual funds – resulting in a sharp contraction in banks' reliance on deposits (Table 6.1). During the 1980s, declines in loan quality crippled many banks and created new opportunities for entry in the wake of bank disappearances or losses of bank capital. The loan losses began in the early 1980s in agricultural and oil-producing regions, but spread to money-center banks after the commercial real estate bust that followed the 1986 tax law changes. By the end of the 1980s many of America's largest banks were suffering unprecedented loan losses, and some were viewed as insolvent on a market value basis (Table 6.2).

Adversity taught banks about new sources of profit and new ways to lever their capital, and also brought new competitive pressure on banks, first from within the United States and later from abroad. As in the 1920s, the distress of small banks during the early 1980s led to greater openness to branching and consolidation in traditionally unit banking states. Between 1979 and 1991, 39 states relaxed their branch banking laws.

As distress spread to large commercial banks, the need for entry and consolidation began to bring large foreign banks into the United States.

Table 6.2. *Problem real estate loans by bank size (third quarter of 1992)*

| | Asset size of bank | | | |
Loan category	Under $100m	$100m–$1b	$1b–$10b	Over $10b
All real estate loans	1.64	2.18	4.05	7.07
Construction	2.76	5.62	12.65	21.96
Commercial	2.10	3.01	5.33	10.84
1–4 Family	1.21	1.23	1.50	1.76

[a] Percentage of loans overdue by more than 90 days, by type of loans.
Source: Boyd and Gertler, 1993.

Table 6.3. *Percentage shares of U.S. nonfarm, nonfinancial, nonmortgage, business debt held*

Year	U.S. bank C & I loans	Foreign bank C & I loans	Finance cos. C & I loans	Bonds, CP, ABS	Government & govt.-sponsored
1983	30	7	10	41	12
1986	26	10	10	47	10
1989	21	12	12	46	8
1991	18	14	12	44	7

Source: Calomiris and Carey, 1994.

Foreign banks increased their share of domestic commercial and industrial loan holdings from 7% in 1983 to 14% by 1991, while U.S. banks saw their share fall from 30% to 18% (Table 6.3).

These influences combined to press U.S. banks to cut their operational and financing costs, and to adopt a *narrower focus on customer niches, a broader focus on types of products and claims, and flexibility in finding ways of satisfying customers' needs.* Throughout this learning process, banks were pushed by new competition (both coming from within and outside the United States), increased scarcity of capital, and threats to their pre-existing protected niches in the deposit and loan markets coming from new markets and types of intermediaries (money market mutual funds, commercial paper, and finance companies). Rather than surrender to the new competition from financial markets, banks found

Table 6.4. *Analysis of sources of U.S. bank income (all insured banks)*

Year	ROE[a]	Net interest margin[b]	Noninterest income/assets
1982	12.10	3.82	0.96
1983	11.24	3.78	1.03
1984	10.60	3.80	1.19
1985	11.32	3.93	1.32
1986	10.23	3.81	1.40
1987	1.29	3.91	1.43
1988	11.61	4.02	1.50
1989	7.33	3.99	1.62
1990	7.29	3.94	1.67
1991	7.71	4.10	1.79
1992	12.66	4.42	1.95
1993	15.34	4.42	2.13
1994	14.64	4.38	2.00
1995	14.71	4.31	2.02
1996	14.60	4.33	2.19

[a] ROE is return on book equity.
[b] Net Interest Margin is interest income less interest expense, divided by total earning assets.
Source: Calomiris and Karceski, 2000.

ways of becoming conduits to those markets for their customers, especially in securitizations and swaps. The result was a remarkable growth in U.S. banks' income from fees (Table 6.4).

Foreign entry into the United States also had a silver lining. The loss of U.S. market share within the United States and abroad promoted the first attempts at deregulation in the areas of consolidation and powers during the late 1980s, as U.S. regulators sought to ensure a continuing future for U.S. banks (Greenspan, 1988, 1990, 1992).

Although banking distress can be credited with the relaxation of state branching laws, more fundamental long-run concerns shaped the Fed's policy both on bank consolidation and on bank powers. The Fed's support for expanding bank scale and scope explicitly reflected concerns that non-bank intermediaries and foreign banks were out-competing American commercial banks, and that relaxation of regulation was necessary to give U.S. banks a fighting chance to survive. Alan Greenspan (1988, 1990, 1992) has repeatedly argued that increased scale and scope in banking is essential to maintaining an internationally competitive U.S.

Table 6.5. *Bank performance in Illinois and North Carolina*

Year	Number of banks		Return on assets (%)		Return on equity (%)	
	IL	NC	IL	NC	IL	NC
1984	1240	63	−0.11	0.97	−1.76	16.47
1985	1233	63	0.63	0.98	9.55	16.82
1986	1218	65	0.71	1.07	10.70	18.22
1987	1209	68	−0.23	0.92	−3.88	15.38
1988	1149	71	0.99	1.06	15.66	16.86
1989	1119	78	0.88	0.97	13.53	15.62
1990	1087	78	0.68	0.85	10.05	13.77
1991	1061	81	0.67	0.74	9.40	10.99
1992	1006	78	0.72	1.03	9.32	15.24

Source: McCoy, Frieder, and Hedges, 1994.

banking sector. For example, in a call for expanding bank powers, Greenspan (1988, pp. 3ff.) argued:

The ability of banks to continue to hold their position by operating on the margins of customer services is limited. Existing constraints, in conjunction with the continued undermining of the bank franchise by the new technology, are likely to limit the future profitability of banking . . . If the aforementioned trends continue banking will contract either relatively or absolutely.

Similarly Greenspan (1990, p. 5) argued:

In an environment of global competition, rapid financial innovation, and technological change, bankers understandably feel that the old portfolio and affiliate rules and the constraints on permissible activities of affiliates are no longer meaningful and likely to result in a shrinking banking system.

Initial deregulation in the areas of consolidation and powers was followed by continuing deregulation, as regulators learned of the advantages (and the absence of costs) produced by relaxing barriers to bank consolidation and new activities. Individual state laws relaxing branching restrictions were followed by regional agreements among states, and culminated in the national branch banking law of 1994. During the 1980s, some bank performance differences related to branching were quite dramatic, and bank consolidation and efficiency gains followed quickly on the heels of regulatory changes (Berger, Kashyap, and Scalise, 1995). As Table 6.5 shows, the performance of banks in branching states (such as

North Carolina) was remarkably stable and profitable compared to that of banks operating in unit banking states (such as Illinois).

The deregulation of bank powers limitations also exhibited important learning effects on the part of regulators. Limited experimentation with relaxing Glass-Steagall limits on underwriting activities by bank holding company-owned underwriting affiliates began in 1987. At the same time, Edge Act banks operating abroad were involved in international underwritings under a much less restricted approach. The domestic underwritings of bank holding company affiliates were limited in size and were accompanied by more than 30 "firewalls" limiting connections among banks, bank affiliates, and underwriting clients, as well as special additional capital requirements for underwriting affiliates. Over time, the Fed raised the quantitative limits on private securities underwritings and lowered all of the special firewalls and capital requirements it had set for these underwriting affiliates. The Fed defended these actions before Congress in March 1997, arguing that experience indicated that these special rules limited bank synergies in universal banking and provided no real benefit. The Fed based its argument largely on a comparison of the domestic (highly regulated) underwriting affiliates (the so-called Section 20 affiliates) and the foreign (little-regulated) Edge Act underwriting affiliates of bank holding companies.

Just as important as regulatory learning, during the 1980s banks learned the value of new product lines, and found that it was possible to lever their capital resources by combining bank "relationship management" and monitoring with market sources of funding and risk management. Many of those important new activities entailed new involvement in the equity markets, and banks came to assume either a direct (ownership or underwriting) stake or an indirect (asset management) stake in these junior instruments.

Venture capital proved to be of extreme value during the capital crunch for several banks (Citicorp, Chemical, First Chicago, and, most of all, Continental). The high profits and diversification potential of venture capital became especially clear during the hard times of the 1980s, when loan losses almost destroyed these banks. Calomiris (1997) finds that for several U.S. banks, profits on private equity investments produced more than 20% of their total net earnings during the 1980s, and tended to be uncorrelated or only weakly positively correlated with earnings from elsewhere in the bank, thus producing significant diversification for the holding company. For these banks, the return on equity for private equity holdings was 21% for the 1980s and early 1990s.[1]

---

[1] Data reported in "Banks Putting Renewed Emphasis on Expanding Venture Operations," *Private Equity Analyst* (February 1995); pp. 1, 10–12.

Banks also learned to make the most of their capital resources by only using capital to absorb those risks which their role as intermediary required them to absorb (because of incentive constraints). The increasing use of syndications, loan sales, and securitizations – and the use of derivatives hedging to preserve capital – ushered in a new era of capital budgeting and risk management for U.S. banks in which return on equity was no longer a simple multiple of return on assets, and in which risks were better taken into account and controlled by banks. The new emphasis on quantifying market and credit risk, deciding which risks to absorb and which to lay off, and the new focus on fee income (as opposed to interest income) all are the fruits of bank adversity during the 1980s.

Given that bank adversity lay at the heart of this new innovativeness, it should come as no surprise that one of the leaders in many of these developments was Continental Illinois, which went from an insolvent basket case, rescued by the government in 1984, to a premier wholesale relationship bank of the early 1990s (before it was acquired by the Bank of America at a hefty premium). After its demise and rescue by the government in 1984, Continental shed its retail operations and outsourced its noncore functions to focus on its core competencies in corporate banking. The bank's niche was defined, not as a set of products per se, but rather as a set of employees (and hence a base of knowledge about certain types of customers) – a set of clients it wanted to have. Continental's internal training program emphasized overall profitability of client relationships, the sharing of information within and across "client teams" and "deal teams" within the bank, and the development of special internal accounting to allocate overhead costs and measure client profitability. Continental's strategy was to use new products as a way to lock in a "share of mind" – to move from simple to complex transactional services, and to provide financial and business advisory services as a means to achieve greater reliance on the bank by the client. By acquiring Continental and moving its headquarters of corporate banking to Chicago, Bank of America expressed its confidence in that approach.

The new emphasis on the economics of relationships, as opposed to productivity or profitability measured at the level of the product or service, is not unique to Continental. Chase's motto, "the right relationship is everything," bespeaks the same approach. Harris Bank's "Vision 2002" is also based on a relationship-focused strategy, both in determining the combination of services, and the location of its branches (Calomiris and Karceski, 1994, pp. 55–59; 1995, pp. 14–26). Similarly, BancOne's framework for profitability accounting places an emphasis on tracking overhead expenditure and evaluating the value of product lines in light of overall client relationships (McCoy, Frieder, and Hedges,

1994). McCoy and his co-authors devote an entire chapter of their book to relationship banking ("The New Search for Growth: Relationship Banking"). In explaining the value of relationships, they explicitly point to the importance of quasi-rents resulting from search and switch costs, though they use a different language (p. 18):

Capturing a greater share of existing customers' wallets through relationships has the potential of raising profitability significantly and locking in a bank's customer base. That is, if customers maintain several products and significant balances with a given bank, they will be less likely to switch to a competitor.

Bankers have come to believe that there are strong economies of scope in combining products within a single intermediary. These economies of scope do not take the form of physical production economies, but rather economies that arise in the context of relationship management. For example, there are marketing and sales cost economies from "cross-selling" – a lending relationship provides an opportunity to discuss additional products with a client. There are also information and monitoring cost economies of scope in relationships. A bank providing a loan or credit enhancement already tracks a firm's performance, and perhaps is enforcing a set of covenants or holding a collateral interest in the firm. It is consequently easier to evaluate and bear the counter-party risk of a swap with that customer, or easier to evaluate the customer's potential for a private or public equity offering.

Because these client economies of scope provide a competitive advantage on any single transactional dimension to intermediaries that already provide other transactional or advisory services to clients, and because such economies also imply costs of searching and switching on the part of clients, client economies of scope offer banks the opportunity to reap quasi-rents from their relationships. As Rajan (1992) points out, however, such an *ex-post* competitive advantage need not translate into *ex-ante* economic profit. The competition for new relationships may guarantee that rents will be dissipated by front-loaded concessions to customers (so-called "loss leaders"). Indeed, underpricing loans as a means to attract customers into a relationship (sometimes referred to as "tying") has become a common practice. Bankers are trained not to judge profitability on the basis of individual transactions, but rather by evaluating the overall resources the bank devotes to a client (consisting predominantly of man-hours and funds) and the overall fees and interest paid by the client.

It is hard to find American bankers opposed to the new relationship banking strategy. The most prominent example of a contrarian was Bankers Trust, which long espoused a "transactional" vision of banking and which argued that relationship banking had been undermined by competition. That vision (which was supplanted by one of relationship banking at Bankers Trust) reflected a confusion between the old monopoly "rents" of the old world of non-competitive banking and the new "quasi-rents" of the new world of universal banking. That confusion led Bankers Trust to discount the value of a client-based strategy and to see its business as a sequence of independent transactions. The enormous losses Bankers Trust suffered in 1994 and 1995 from its trading operations and its Latin American holdings suggest the risks a commercial bank faces when it ignores relationship banking. In contrast to Bankers Trust, Citibank's and Bank of Boston's successful strategies in Latin America were to establish large branching networks in several countries, and to pursue profitable consumer and small business relationships.

The importance of customer relationships and the quasi-rents they create has been widely documented in recent academic work. Over the past decade there has been an outpouring of empirical research documenting the special role of banks as information collectors and enforcers of contracts under asymmetric information (James, 1987; James and Wier, 1988; Hoshi, Kashyap, and Scharfstein, 1990a, 1990b, 1991; Booth, 1992; Slovin, Sushka, and Polonchek, 1993; Best and Zhang, 1993; Petersen and Rajan, 1994; Billet, Flannery, and Garfinkel, 1995; Kashyap and Stein, 1995; and Calomiris and Wilson, 1998).

Focusing on customer relationships also proves important in understanding the way new entry occurs into lending markets, and differences in the profitability of new and existing lenders. Calomiris and Carey (1994) point out that foreign bank entry into the U.S. corporate lending market during the 1980s reflected a cost-of-funds advantage on the part of foreign banks during the U.S. bank capital crunch. But foreign bank entrants suffered an information-cost disadvantage, which is visible in the form and pricing of foreign bank entry. Foreign banks were able to significantly underprice U.S. banks only in the high-quality segment of the market. For high-risk customers (where information costs are more important) foreign bank pricing was similar to that of domestic banks. Compared to domestic banks, foreign banks were much more likely to lend in the low-risk segment of the market, and were much more likely to lend as passive members of syndicates or via the purchase of loans originated by domestic banks. The relationship-cost advantage of domestic banks is also visible in loan performance differences. Nolle (1994) finds that foreign-owned banks in the United States had much lower returns on assets in the 1990s, and that this difference reflects both higher overhead costs and higher loan-loss rates for foreign banks.

In their case analyses of nine bank mergers, Calomiris and Karceski (2000) provide evidence that this new approach to client-based universal banking is central to understanding the merger wave of the 1990s in U.S. banking and its potential efficiency gains. A bank's mix of products and services, and its locational strategy, are set primarily by reference to the client base it is targeting rather than according to the technological costs or synergies associated with particular sets of products or services. Thus mergers and acquisitions must be seen in the context of client-based universal banking strategies.

6.3   American universal banking remains American

As U.S. banks have become larger, and increasingly have pursued new market-oriented activities – including underwriting, swap intermediation, securitization, venture capital finance, and asset management – their stakes in corporate clients have changed from almost exclusively senior debt claims to a mix of senior debt, junior debt, and equity claims. Commensurately, their control over firms has been transformed from arms-length control – where banks are reliant on contractual covenants and collateral to bend clients to their will – to more direct control via their influence over firms as stockholders or as the agents of stockholders. In these senses, they have become much more like their banking colleagues in Europe and Japan.

Like continental universal bankers, American banks are now able to enjoy better control over their clients in some cases, and are able to reap economies of scope in information and control that come from long-term relationships and multiple products and services. U.S. bank holding companies can now provide cradle-to-grave financing. Over a firm's life cycle, they can provide early-stage lending, private equity financing to help transform firms from private to public, underwriting for initial and subsequent equity offerings, and continuing control over firms via asset management.

At the same time, American universal banks have brought their history with them, and remain different from universal banks in other countries. Some of that history implies continuing limitations on what American universal banks can do. For example, limitations on acting as a broker and a dealer for the same security sale remain an important impediment in bank asset management for corporate pensions. Despite enormous progress in permitting banks to overcome broker-dealer limitations via the construction of "Chinese walls" that separate brokers and dealers working on the same transaction within the bank, ERISA (the Employee Retirement Income Security Act) laws still prevent asset managers within the bank holding company from purchasing unregistered foreign securities, or from purchasing in the primary market securities in which another affiliate of the bank is acting as lead underwriter.

On the positive side, however, one could argue that American banks are building a new, and perhaps better, form of universal banking – enjoying new technological economies of scope from combining traditional banking functions (gathering information about clients and controlling their behavior) with new opportunities to access the resources of American capital markets. Now freed from many limitations, American banks are finding ways to bring America's comparative advantage in capital markets into their banks. The limitations imposed on American financial development, which forced U.S. banks to limit their size and scope unnaturally for over 100 years fostered the development of active, technologically dynamic securities markets. Now that U.S. banks have been permitted to do more, they are finding that American financial markets offer an especially rich array of products and services for them to offer their clients. Security market depth in primary markets and liquidity in secondary markets offer U.S. banks underwriting, venture capital, securitization, derivatives, and asset management opportunities not enjoyed by banks in other countries.

6.4   Unfinished business

Glass-Steagall limitations on private securities underwriting were a binding constraint for the largest American universal banks until those limits were eliminated in the 1999 Act. Previously, banks had to limit earnings from private securities offerings of Section 20 affiliates to 25% of the underwriting affiliate's revenue.

Yet it is possible to overstate the progress of universal banking in the United States. In several areas where Congressional action is required to permit additional progress, Congress has expressed little interest in removing barriers.

Permitting the ownership of banks by non-bank firms remains a hotly contested issue. Proposals to reform CEBA (the Competitive Equality in Banking Act) laws to permit expanded activities by non-bank-owned banks have stalled. Congressional concerns over the concentration of power and possible conflicts of interest will not permit the chartering of non-bank-owned corporate banks. Even in the retail banking area, despite the obvious potential gains in technological improvement from allowing high-tech computing and telecommunications firms to enter consumer banking, there is little chance for immediate progress. Once high-tech non-banks (say, Microsoft or AT&T) enter banking – perhaps initially outside the United States – it is possible that U.S. legislators will react by allowing them to do so in the United States, to preserve the competitiveness of America's banking system.

The asset management barriers imposed by ERISA seem another obvious area for relaxation. Pension funds managed by banks will increasingly suffer limitations on portfolio earnings and diversification as equity markets become global, and as U.S. banks take a larger share of global underwriting. Emerging market securities offer unique portfolio opportunities to American investors, and banks often specialize in particular countries or industries whose risks may be unique. By limiting the purchase of non-U.S.-registered securities, or those whose underwriting is managed by a bank affiliate, ERISA may force corporate pension clients to seek asset management services outside large U.S. bank holding companies.

Safety net reform remains one of the key determinants of future progress in eliminating these and other barriers to universal banking. Many critics of further reform, including Congressmen, Senators, and even Chairman Greenspan, point to potential abuse of deposit insurance protection as a concern when considering further regulatory relaxation. Bankers have been led to conclude that deposit insurance reform is the quid pro quo for further deregulation. The Bankers' Roundtable (a private association of America's largest banks) – perceiving that further relaxation of regulation will only follow the credible elimination of any potential taxpayer subsidization of bank risk-taking – proposed a bold plan in May 1997 for introducing market discipline into government deposit insurance.[2] Large U.S. banks now are so convinced of the advantages of universal banking that they are doing their best to eliminate the "too-big-to-fail" doctrine. Despite some weaknesses, that plan provides cause to hope that American universal banks will continue down the path of expanded powers and modernization.

6.5   Conclusion

During the 1980s and early 1990s, America's banks did more than their share of "converging" as they came to learn the advantages of richer corporate banking relationships that have long characterized other

---

[2] See Bankers Roundtable, 1997.

countries. Now, it is the turn of other banking systems to learn from American banks. I believe foreign banks will imitate many of the recent innovations in American banking, and thus I see a new era of American-style universal banking dominating the financial services industry internationally over the next decade. Three observations underlie that prediction.

First, global competition in banking is here to stay because it is driven by new information and transaction technologies that regulators will not be able to tame. Already, competition is causing a reorganization of corporate lending. A fledgling bank loan sales market has just begun to operate in Europe. In explaining the rise of this market, bankers point to increasing pressures to conserve scarce bank capital and boost returns on equity.[3] There may be some setbacks on the road to global banking deregulation, particularly in Europe where the short-run politics of European integration may favor some protection for existing inefficient European banks. Nevertheless, protectionism will likely disappear once it becomes clear that it undermines the global market share of the protected countries' banks.

Second, global competition outside of banks will encourage American-style changes within many countries' banking systems. Financial systems throughout the world are already seeing a new era of the securitization of risk (including Europe, Japan, Latin America, and developing countries in Asia). Their banks, like America's, will see increasing incentives to become conduits to financial markets rather than competitors with those markets. I predict that ten years from now, as banks and markets become more and more intertwined, very few academics will find it useful to divide the world into "bank-based" and "market-based" financial systems (a distinction which I think is of little use even today).

Third, the strategy of relationship banking (which underlies the American style of corporate banking) permits banks to operate more profitably. That economic logic will become inescapable in the new global environment where competition and securitization increasingly force banks to bend toward efficiency enhancement. Thus banks will be pushed more and more to pursue economies of scope. Those economies of scope reflect a combination of physical cost economies of distribution and clearing, informational cost economies of managing default risk (a risk common to lending, managing customers' payment flows, and providing over-the-counter derivatives services), and relationship economies of marketing products.

---

[3] Reported in "Europe's Banks Boost Plans for U.S.-Style Loans Market," *Financial Times* (July 28, 1997), p. 16.

References

Baer, H. L., and L. Mote (1992). *The United States Financial System*, Working paper, Federal Reserve Bank of Chicago.

Bankers Roundtable (1997). *Deposit Insurance Reform: Partnering for Financial Services Modernization*. Washington, D.C.: The Bankers' Roundtable.

Berger, A. N., A. Kashyap, and J. M. Scalise (1995). "The Transformation of the U.S. Banking Industry: What a Long, Strange Trip It's Been," *Brookings Papers on Economic Activity*, 2: 55–218.

Best, R., and H. Zhang (1993). "Alternative Information Sources and the Information Content of Bank Loans," *Journal of Finance* 48(4): 1507–1522.

Billet, M. T., M. J. Flannery, and J. A. Garfinkel (1995). "The Effect of Lender Identity on a Borrowing Firm's Equity Return," *Journal of Finance* 50(2): 699–718.

Booth, J. R. (1992). "Contract Costs, Bank Loans, and the Cross-Monitoring Hypothesis," *Journal of Financial Economics* 31(1): 25–41.

Boyd, J. H., and M. Gertler (1993). "U.S. Commercial Banking: Trends, Cycles, and Policy," pp. 319–368. In *NBER Macroeconomics Annual 1993*, eds. O. J. Blanchard and S. Fischer. Cambridge, MA: The MIT Press.

Calomiris, C. W. (1993). "Regulation, Industrial Structure, and Instability in U.S. Banking: An Historical Perspective," pp. 19–115. In *Structural Change in Banking*, eds. M. Klausner and L. I. White. Homewood, IL: Business One-Irwin.

   (1995). "The Costs of Rejecting Universal Banking: American Finance in the German Mirror, 1870–1914," pp. 257–315. In *Coordination and Information: Historical Perspectives on the Organization of Enterprise*, eds. N. R. Lamoreaux and D. Raff. Chicago: University of Chicago Press.

   (2000). "The Contribution of Venture Capital to American Banks' Profits," Working paper, Graduate School of Business. New York: Columbia University.

Calomiris, C. W., and M. S. Carey (1994). "Loan Market Competition Between Foreign and U.S. Banks: Some Facts About Loans and Borrowers," pp. 331–351. In *Proceedings of the 30th Annual Conference on Bank Structure and Competition*. Chicago: Federal Reserve Bank of Chicago.

Calomiris, C. W., and J. Karceski (1994). *Competing Bank Strategies in Chicago: An Illinois MBA Project Report*. Urbana-Champaign: The Office for Banking Research of the University of Illinois.

   (1995). *The Bank Merger Wave of the 90s: Nine Case Studies*. Urbana-Champaign: The Office for Banking Research of the University of Illinois.

   (1997). "Is the Bank Merger Wave of the 90s Efficient? Lessons From Nine Case Studies." In *Mergers and Productivity*, ed. S. Kaplan. Chicago: University of Chicago Press.

Calomiris, C. W., and C. D. Ramirez (1996). "The Role of Financial Relationships in the History of American Corporate Finance," *Journal of Applied Corporate Finance* 9: 52–73.

Calomiris C. W., and B. Wilson (1998). "Bank Capital and Portfolio Management: The 1930s Capital Crunch and Scramble to Shed Risk," NBER Working paper No. 6649 (July).

Greenspan, A. (1988). "An Overview of Financial Restructuring," pp. 1–9. In *Proceedings of the 24th Annual Conference on Bank Structure and Competition*. Chicago: Federal Reserve Bank of Chicago.

(1990). "Subsidies and Powers in Commercial Banking," pp. 1–8. In *Proceedings of the 26th Annual Conference on Bank Structure and Competition*. Chicago: Federal Reserve Bank of Chicago.

(1992). "Putting FDICIA in Perspective," pp. 1–7. In *Proceedings of the 28th Annual Conference on Bank Structure and Competition*. Chicago: Federal Reserve Bank of Chicago.

Hoshi, T., A. Kashyap, and D. Scharfstein (1990a). "The Role of Banks in Reducing the Costs of Financial Distress in Japan," *Journal of Financial Economics*, 27(1): 67–88.

(1990b). "Bank Monitoring and Investment: Evidence From the Changing Structure of Japanese Corporate Banking Relationships," pp. 105–126. In *Asymmetric Information, Corporate Finance, and Investment*, ed. R. G. Hubbard. Chicago: University of Chicago Press.

(1991). "Corporate Structure, Liquidity, and Investment: Evidence From Japanese Industrial Groups," *Quarterly Journal of Economics* 106(1): 33–60.

James, C. (1987). "Some Evidence on the Uniqueness of Bank Loans," *Journal of Financial Economics*, 19(2): 217–235.

James, C., and P. Wier (1988). "Are Bank Loans Different? Evidence From the Stock Market," *Journal of Applied Corporate Finance* 1: 46–54.

Kashyap, A., and J. C. Stein (1995). "The Impact of Monetary Policy on Bank Balance Sheets," *Carnegie Rochester Conference Series on Public Policy* 42(0): 151–195.

McCoy, J. B., L. Frieder, and R. Hedges (1994). *Bottom Line Banking. Meeting the Challenges for Survival and Success*. Chicago: Probus.

Nolle, D. E. (1994). "Are Foreign Banks Out-Competing U.S. Banks in the U.S. Market?" Working paper. Washington, DC: Office of the Comptroller of the Currency.

Petersen, M. A., and R. G. Rajan (1994). "The Benefits of Lending Relationships: Evidence From Small Business Data," *Journal of Finance* 49(1): 3–37.

Rajan, R. G. (1992). "Insiders and Outsiders: The Choice Between Informed and Arms-Length Debt," *Journal of Finance* 47(4): 1367–1400.

Slovin, M. B., M. E. Sushka, and J. A. Polonchek (1993). "The Value of Bank Durability: Borrowers as Stakeholders," *Journal of Finance* 48(1): 247–266.

General Index

American Bankers Association, 193
asset substitution effect, 219

bank debt: conversion to cash, 96–8; exchanging debt for equity, 223–5; liabilities and illiquidity, 114–19; short- and long-term, 219–20, 246–9 *See also* clearing houses
bankers acceptances, 36
Bankers' Roundtable reform proposals, xxix
bank failures: Australia, 19–22; during banking panics, 4, 141–51; Canadian, 102; circumstances causing, 6, 120–1; in context of branch banking, 101; during Great Depression, xxii, 186–93; of national banks during panics (1873–1907), 141–6; in 1839 panic, 8; in United States, 22–8, 102
bank loans: as financing instruments, 218–20; role in banking panic theory, 116–19; seasonal demand (1870–1909), 137–40
bank runs: defined, 97; 1930s period, 4
bank holding companies: Citicorp-Travelers merger, xv; deregulation of, xi; nonbank affiliates of, xvi; OTC transactions, xvi; regulation of, xvi
Banking Act (1933), 199; branch banking under, 57; factors limiting reform of, xxxi; Pecora hearings resulting in, xv, 195–7, 269, 293; regulatory legacy, xviii; repeal of (1999), xi, xxv; restrictions of, 227, 269, 345; revival of unit banks under, xxiii; separation of investment and commercial banking, 230, 281
Banking Act (1935), 76, 199, 248n17, 269
banking panics, 3–4; association with business cycles, 98; asymmetric information explanation, 95, 107, 111–21, 141–51, 157–9; bank failures during, 4, 141–51; bank liquidations and deposit losses during, 141–51; Canada,

101; Canadian banks in United States during, 154–5; Chicago (1932), xxin13; conditions for ending, 151; currency convertibility (1873, 1893, 1907), 153; defined, 96–8; effect of asymmetric information on probability of, 5–6; England, 101; failed banks (1893), 100; during Great Depression, 100, 153; influence of institutional structure, 101–3; nineteenth century British, 101–2; occurrences of, 96–7; panic (1837), 44–5; panic (1839), 8; panic (1857), 8–9, 25; panic (1907), 147–51, 168; panics (1814, 1861), 99; panics (1890, 1893), 149–51; pre-panic circumstances, 121–41; quasi-panic (1896), 147–51; random withdrawal explanation of, 95, 107–11, 117–21, 141–51, 153, 157; regulatory response to, 93; related to sequential service, 108–10, 112–15 *See also* bank failures; bank runs
banking system: Australia, 19–22; bank failures in Canada (1868–1889), 24; Canada, 14–19; concentration in, 225–7; England, 12–14; as factor in bank instability, 3; Scotland, 11–12 *See also* unit banks
banking system, Canada, 102
banking system, Germany: (1870–1914), 235–67; financing of corporate investment, 54–5; influence on industrial firms, 232–4; nineteenth-century, 266; role in financial system, 235–67; sources of financing for, 250–2 *See also* universal banking, Germany
banking system, United States: (1870–1914), 235–67; bank chartering, 43–6, 59; changes in, 335–44; coalitions to minimize cost, 220n5; collapse (1930s), 4; Comptroller of the Currency as regulator of, xi, xv–xvii, 10, 47, 56, 145, 151; consolidation and branching (1900–1910), 52–4; convergence in,

350

Index of Names

Aharony, Joseph, 6
Allen, W. H., 127, 129, 137, 155–6
Alston, Lee, 72
Andrew, A. Piatt, 111n16, 119, 122, 125–6
Andrews, Victor, 309
Apilado, Vincent, xxivn16
Asquith, Paul, 5, 54
Atack, Jeremy, 241, 256–7

Baer, Herbert, 2
Bagehot, Walter, 13–14
Baron, David, 281n2
Barrett, W. Brian, 28
Barsky, Robert, 134, 261
Barth, James, 78
Baskin, J., 248, 289
Bateman, Fred, 241, 256–7
Baums, Theodore, xxiiin15
Beatty, Randolph, 281n2
Benston, George, xiin2, 76, 196, 230
Benveniste, Lawrence, 50, 216–17, 281n2
Berger, Allen, xin1, 339
Berle, Adolph, 232n13, 234
Berman, Daniel, 172n4, 173n5
Bernanke, Ben, 4, 19, 62, 102
Bernstein, Martin, 245–6
Best, R., 343
Bhagat, Sanjai, 291–2
Bhattacharya, Sudipto, 110–11, 113–14
Billet, M. T., 343
Binder, John, 28
Blume, Marshall, 310
Bodenhorn, Howard, 28, 37, 44, 240–1
Bogue, Allan, 23, 150
Booth, James, 281n2, 343
Bordo, Michael, 11, 14, 19, 100–2, 166n1
Borenstein, Israel, 240n15
Boyd, John, 5, 77, 112n18, 116, 227
Bradford, Frederick, 63
Brandeis, Louis D., 54, 232, 255, 280
Breckenridge, Roeliff M., 9, 15–18, 31, 34–5, 240, 251
Bresnahan, Timothy F., 78

Brewer, Elijah, xxivn16, 227; 77–8
Britton, Rachel, 228–9
Brock, Leslie, 43
Brock, William, 260n21
Brown, Anthony, 28
Brown, David T., 5, 79, 218, 223
Bryan, Alfred C., 60
Bryant, John, 107n12
Bullock, Charles, 43
Burns, Helen, 186–9, 197, 199
Butters, J. Keith, 54, 217, 232n13
Byrnes, Joseph, 192

Cain, Louis, 238
Calomiris, Charles, xiin2, xxn11, xxin124,
    xxiiin14, xxvn17, xxvin18, xxviiin20,
    xxixn22, 6–9, 16–17, 21–3, 25–8, 31, 34,
    38–9, 43–4, 46, 52, 54–5, 59, 61–2, 67, 69,
    72, 77, 103–5, 112n18, 113–18, 122–3,
    132, 134, 140, 158n33, 165, 166nn1, 2,
    167–9, 153, 171, 212, 217, 220nn4, 5, 225,
    234, 248n17, 251, 255n19, 256, 260n21,
    261n22, 265–6, 269, 285, 288–9, 305–6,
    308, 335, 341, 343, 344
Campbell, Tim, 5, 112n18, 217
Cannon, James, 9, 106
Capie, Forrest, 11, 13
Carey, Mark, 290n8, 303–4, 306, 393
Carlson, W. Bernard, 244
Carosso, Vincent P., 49–50, 227, 230–1, 233,
    297–8, 250, 306
Cartinhour, Gaines T., 47, 52, 59
Champ, Bruce, 16–17
Chandler, Alfred, 48, 225, 238
Chapman, John M., 24, 35, 38, 47, 52, 56–9
Chari, V. V., 17, 110–11, 113, 114n22,
    118n25, 120, 126, 157
Cleveland, Harold, 233
Coffee, John C., 283n3
Cohan, Avery, 259, 283
Cone, Kenneth, 108–9
Creamer, Daniel, 240n15
Crockett, Jean, 310

355